To Evelyne,

a new forever

friend in

Love +

Light

Denise

Thank you 🖤

Advance Reviews of *Something's Coming!*
Universal Cities of Light, Love, and Healing!

"I have closely followed the progress of the 'Cities of Light', and I have never known such an exciting prospect as their appearance which is soon expected. They will be amongst some of the spectacular early developments of the New Age. The prototype that is destined for Sedona has been regularly visited by Genii, and will be sensational for its wide and varied range of advanced technology, particularly where healing is concerned. You are unlikely to ever read another book of this nature that is a first-hand account by Genii of what to expect. Her style of writing takes you with her, and you can share her many heartfelt experiences. It is a unique book, about a unique experience that you will not want to miss." -- **Mike Quinsey** (http://treeofthegoldenlight.com/First_Contact/ Channeled_Messages_by_Mike_Quinsey.htm)

"With *The City of Light Sedona*, The 4 Keys to Light and her new book, *Something's Coming*, Genii Townsend provides spiritual initiates with the ultimate users' manual and cosmic blueprint for tapping our greatest power as Light Technicians on the path to higher consciousness. Experiencing The 4 Keys to Light initiation with Genii in 2009 was one of the greatest gifts of a lifetime. Genii has channeled a virtual GPS system and high-speed connection to the Light Source, bestowing initiates with a true spiritual compass for navigating these transformational times and reinforcing our connection with Divine Intelligence. Just a few hours over the course of two days profoundly changed the course of my entire life in the most positive ways. I honestly can't imagine how I would have weathered the storms of the past few years without the tools and techniques I learned in the 4 Keys. Genii teaches us how to transmute negative energy and communicate more directly with our guides. It was after reading her book and attending her 4 Keys class that I began to hear messages and receive guidance from the higher dimensions with greater ease and clarity. I adapted tools and techniques that have become part of my spiritual practice, assisting me to connect with the Light on an everyday basis to grace the path. Both of Genii's books and The 4 Keys of Light will profoundly change the course of your life in the most amazing ways, as it did mine. Genii is an angel, prophet and master in our midst from whom we can learn true mastery, knowing, self-empowerment and a sacred re-connection with our higher forces." -- **Catherine J. Rourke**, Editor & Publisher, The Sedona Observer (http://www.sedonaobserver.com)

"Genii Townsend made a decision long ago to take things that don't turn out quite right and completely transform them. It's no wonder she was selected to meet with the galactics and introduce so many of us to the Cities of Light. All Lightworkers have a mission but Genii's has brought so many people excitement and delight. I personally can't wait to have a guided tour from her and a completely relaxing and restoring visit. Something's coming ... and Genii is our impresario and cherished guide for it." -- **Steve Beckow** (http://goldenageofgaia.com. See *The Coming of the Cities of Light* page 418)

"Genii's first book, *The City of Light Sedona* was an amazing read and now what a treat it is to have Genii's newest book 'Something's Coming'. This is a book that will surely be among the classics of the world! With over 130 new visits into the City of Light's Embassy of Peace, *Something's Coming* is packed full of inspiration, space technology and a clear vision of the greatest gift for humanity one could ever dream of! Once you start reading, you won't want to put it down! Is Genii going out on a limb? To be sure... And I'm right out there with her!!! As she walked inside our domes of light, here in Sedona, wearing sparkling clothes and immense light around her, I knew my wish to meet a real Genii had been answered! We immediately locked our mutual blue eyes and my life has never been the same. I feel so blessed to have had first-hand experience with Genii, and her '4 Keys to Light' Teachings. I am a 'Light Link' now, with not only direct, clear connection with my loving spiritual guides, who I call my divine team, I actually received their names! And with this heavenly gift, have seen myself in a City of Light! It was a thrill beyond words when Genii received word that the domes we live in are 5th dimensional, as well as Sky Maps for the Bringers of the City of Light. Genii is truly a walking testament of one who has the faith of Job, the strength of a Jedi and the balance of a tight rope walker!!! For me, she is the most amazing example of LOVE embodied on this planet!" -- **Nina Joy**, Author of *Fearless Birth & Beyond, Experiences of Joyous Conscious Birth* and Co-steward of http://www.xanaduofsedona.com

"Genii Townsend is a visionary. For over 25 years she has been bringing us the vision of the Sedona City of Light. Quantum physics teaches us that everything in this universe is comprised of energy at the level of the atom or smaller. Every-thing of matter first exists at the unseen level before it comes into existence at the level of our physical eyesight. The unseen level is the etheric, it is there at the level of the atoms that all existence takes place. Ancient cultures, all of the world's major religions, talk of a form of The City of Light, of a place in the future that is filled with love and healing grace. The Bible calls it The New Jerusalem. Genii has the gift to see the unseen, to see the etheric development, to see and visit The City of Light in the unseen world. Faith is the ability to see and believe in the unseen, no matter what critics or unbelievers may say. All of our major changes in our world have first started at the level of faith, to see the unseen and bring it into existence. She is our pioneer blazing the trail to bring us The City of Light. It is her resounding faith and belief that is creating the energy that is bringing forth this wonderful City. As we join her, we will add to the etheric energy that will bring The City into our physical existence. Do we know when this will happen? I don't. But I do understand that the etheric level has no sense of time - at that level time is non-existent. Therefore The City will come forth into our world when there is enough collective energy from the inhabitants of this Earth to bring it forward. But we need not despair as it is a very small percentage needed to bring forth such collective energy. I am joining Genii in believing for this wonderful future City. I choose to add my energy of belief to the larger collection. Come and join me as we together believe for this wonderful new future."
-- **Hon. Dave Schmidt**, WA State Senator, retired. www.daveschmidt.com

Something's Coming!
Universal Cities of Light, Love, and Healing!

**Revelation of the Prophecies,
Purpose, Plans and Manifestation
of Cities of Light, Love and Healing**

By Genii Townsend

Compiled by Charles Betterton

Edited by Renee Trenda and Kathie Brodie

Final Editing by Katrina Rodgers

Published by CENTER SPACE™
(Center for Spiritual, Personal And Community Enlightenment)

NOTE: This publication is a work in progress. Some of the wording received in the audio transmissions may seem strange but I have left them as I received them as stated previously. While editing and proof reading have been performed, (mostly thanks to Kathie Brodie, Renee Trenda and Katrina Rodgers) please do share any suggested clarifications with us. The blog site where you may provide your feedback and suggestions is at http://sedonacityoflight.wordpress.com/.

Limits of Liability and Disclaimer of Warranty

Dedication to Rev. Dr. William Townsend

Hi "B",

This book is really dedicated to you, for all you have done for me and so many others. As I think back, all this started through your channeling sessions. You worked for three years on the City drawings in this book, really wanting to quit since you could not draw a straight line. But God kept you going; and from that came fantastic plans and strange gates and towers, and the original plot plan to make people feel at home; then leaving me to continue where you left off. Now we know why.

Amazing. It's for real!

What an adventure this has been and still is, as we learn that more Cities are coming forth around the planet later on. Since the first City of Light Sedona book was published with Charles at the helm and other close friends, many great things have happened. I am so blessed.

A few weeks after the first edition was published, it was in 18 countries and in this country as well. As books fly off the shelves, people from other locations like Denmark, Seattle, and Baltimore come knocking on my door at home for a copy and to say hello in person.

I even get to travel to other locations and share about the City as well. I have to tell you about that. I got a surprise call from a lady named Lori who was sitting on the floor with a friend during a hurricane in Mystic, Connecticut and we did some Light treatment for fear to be released. Later she and her friend Lorainne had Charles and me fly to Mystic and share with her group about the City of Light and The 4 Keys to Light session. We have become great friends since then.

Oh yes, and in Albuquerque, New Mexico, there is quite a group of "Light Links," having been linked in The 4 Keys to Light session. In learning about their own personal Guides, they have all stayed together.

They meet every month sending energy for the City to appear, even putting a handmade City prop in the center of the round table and call themselves 'Lights of the Round Table.' Is that not grand?

And I have been able to visit Renee Trenda in Stelle, Illinois several times. Renee and I drove to the Carter Center to give President Jimmy Carter a City Book and a look-alike marionette of himself. I make these puppets as gifts to say thanks to God for all I have been given.

The one I gave to President Carter led to him putting it on an auction (after the family had fun and he got to pull his own strings) to help build homes through Habitat for Humanity and it made them a lot of money. What fun!

Speaking of this part of my life you know very well, guess what? I also have created marionettes of President Obama and the Obama family. For I was told he has unknown to him, coded in his DNA, a knowingness that the City is coming. Getting a book to him seems important. Now I just have to get to meet him in person. I have jumped into all the contests and dinners they have offered for donations, but no meeting yet. Also my latest creation is a marionette of Pastor Joel Osteen. I follow him consistently, even watching 3 times on the TV on Sunday, and I have his books and CDs. Bill, honey, you would really like him. He is so positive, like you were. Now I have to find a way to get to meet him too.

Lots of speaking engagements have come up: Phoenix, San Diego, Los Angeles - and guess what? Prominent speakers around the world have come to Sedona and I got to tell them about the City here too - right on our own doorstep.

I got to meet the very ones I have spoken with on their radio programs, like Michael Quinsey from The United Kingdom, who invited me on twice and I got to speak even 90 minutes overtime. He just let me run. Imagine that! And he is heard around the world. One radio show brought forth a listener who lives right here in the Village. It happened I was having a 4 Keys to Light session the next day; and she joined in and got linked too. Amazing! God is Good. Remember when The 4 Keys to Light was only given one-on-one? Now I get to share in groups and bring through lots of personal guides for people.

Oh, I just have to finish this update by telling you what happened at a book conference. This was wild. As I sat in the last row with a copy of the first City of Light book on my lap, a lady walked behind me and saw the cover. I asked her if she would like to flip through it. She did and then said, "people must think you are nuts!" My response was "well, I guess not, as this book is in 18 countries after only a few weeks, so someone is paying attention. Would you like to keep it overnight?" She slowly nodded and the conversation ended. The next day she came back and said with tears running down her face, "I could not put it down all night. Thank you for giving us hope!" So Bill, I gave her the book.

Rev. Dr. Bill Townsend, I thank you most of all for this fantastic adventure that even my imagination could not make such a place to come forth. Disneyland is my beat. This has to be God coming through. I'll see you again in the City of Light. Love from your favorite blonde.

Genii

Remembering and Appreciating Rev. Dr. William Townsend

I met Dr. Bill and Genii Townsend when they first moved to Tucson in late 1980's. Bill became our minister in the Tucson Church of Religious Science. My husband, Robert Knowles-Jackman served on the church board with Bill. Robert and I took classes from Dr. Bill. We appreciated his knowledge and skill. I particularly remember learning that 'atonement' also meant 'at-one-ment'.

A small group from church was invited to Bill and Genii's home. Bill told us about his training with Hermes. He demonstrated his channeling while Genii asked questions. The memory of his channeling is vivid to this day. He lay on the coach with a tape recorder going nearby. It took him a while to come back out the meditative state he was in. It was very deep. Looking back it is obvious that channeling was his calling.

Dr. Bill showed Robert and I the drawings of the City that came through his channeling. We were curious. I took the "Four Keys to Light" classes with Genii in their home. Her daughter Starr-light was in the class also. I participated in "Glow" afterwards. We would do art projects to teach lessons. We made our own Goddesses. Then as a change of pace and for fun we would have a drawing to teach a winning attitude. Starr-light usually won.

As time progressed we would meet at my office. We had a little book about Hermes that we would study from. While in Genii and Bill's home I noticed the love and devotion between them. Bill would come up and nuzzle Genii and tell her he loved her. They would leave Love Notes for each other on little sticky notes. They were clearly devoted to each other and very much in love.

Lindsey Knowles-Jackman, MS, September 2, 2012

Rev. Dr. Bill and Genii Townsend with "Church Mouse Charlie"

And the City had
no need of the sun,
neither of the moon
to shine in it . . .
For the glory of
God did lighten it.

Revelation 12:23

Table of Contents

Foreword by Stephen Cook

Genii Townsend has a wonderful gift for taking complex, Universally-deep, and what some may see as 'out there' concepts, truths and messages from the spiritual and higher realms, adding her own dose of 'Genii' magic, and making them not only immeasurably easy to understand but entertainingly so. From the moment I picked up her first book, *City of Light Sedona*, I was there, in the breathtaking City of Light with her – and I was having fun! I knew then that Genii was a very special lady, with an equally special mission: to open all our eyes to the amazing possibilities that the Universe and beyond is truly offering us, including the imminent arrival of the Cities of Light.

Soon after, I had her on my 2012 InLight Radio show *The Light Agenda* to share her unique 'insider' knowledge of the Cities of Light, which are soon due to appear all around the world: what they will look like, what they will bring us and how they will change our lives. From the moment we started chatting, we instantly 'clicked'. In October 2012, I had the joy of finally meeting Genii in person when she joined leading Lightworkers Mike Quinsey, Suzy Ward, Blossom Goodchild, Linda Dillon, Wes Annac and the InLight Radio team, including myself, in two back-to-back events as one of the 12 featured speakers for the *2012 Scenario Conference Sedona - Preparing for Ascension* staged in Genii's beloved Sedona, Arizona, USA. I watched on admiringly as she won the hearts of hundreds of attendees from all over the world, as she shared her knowledge of not only Sedona and the Cities of Light, but also the sacred four 'AH' tones, which she kindly taught us all and which I – and many others no doubt, too – have since 'performed' in some of the world's most beautiful and sacred places.

Genii and I also discovered a special connection during the conference and I had the pleasure of visiting her in her home, seeing and feeling how delightfully magical and fun she really is! In fact, the title of this book could almost describe Genii herself: she is a being of true Light, love, and healing and she is definitely 'something' and universal! In *Something's Coming!* Genii introduces us to her guides, her sources and her friends, who have given her a unique invitation to take us by the hand and lead us on a delightfully fun-filled journey beyond The City gates and upwards, into our very near future.

With her warm and gentle writing style, she offers us easy to digest news and information about the really big concepts that are already changing our world forever. These include: the true history of our planet and our ancestors; our cosmic advancement and Ascension; the return of the Ascended Masters and the Christed energy; recognition of the presence of our Galactic brothers and sisters; the coming new technologies and free energy; the notion of time and timelessness; the concepts of age and agelessness; and, of course, the healing capabilities we all wish to enjoy in the Cities of Light. If want to know what's in store for all of us in the not-too-distant future, let Genii be your guide and let *Something's Coming!* be your guide book.

Stephen Cook -- Presenter/Producer, The Light Agenda (InLIght Radio, 2012) and The Golden Compass (InLIght Radio, 2013) News Editor, Golden Age of Gaia (previously The 2012 Scenario) - http://goldenageofgaia.com

Welcome from the Publisher

Thank you for letting us share Genii's amazing and continuing real-life adventure story with you! We published *The City of Light Sedona: Revelation of Prophecies, Purpose, Plans and Manifestation of Cities of Light, Love and Healing* in 2008. Since then, Genii has enjoyed another 125 visits to the City of Light, mostly to the Embassy of Peace Headquarters. As we sought inner guidance on how best to share this additional and more recent information, we were inspired to retain much of the contents in the first book in this new expanded edition. That is because the first two hundred pages tell the story of how all of this came about.

Genii's first visit to the City of Light that was not previously included in *The City of Light Sedona*, "Some Things Seem So Right!" occurred on March 1, 2011. As you read through the history of how Genii kept the information in these two books secret for 27 years, and as you enjoy joining her through several years of visits into The City of Light, you will appreciate that this truly is an ongoing adventure.

This manuscript was sent to the printers shortly after December 21, 2012 and not too long after the 2012 Scenario Conferences were held in Sedona in late 2012. It has been fascinating to read about how people were disappointed that Ascension has not yet happened as so many believed it would by now. Some have shared with Genii that they wonder why The City of Light hasn't appeared yet, and even greater numbers of people world-wide seem disappointed that the planet didn't experience a global shift around 12-21-2012.

Genii and I had a conversation in The Light Center about how she might answer questions about those situations with readers of her books and listeners of the radio programs she is so grateful to be invited to participate in by Michael Quinsey, Stephen Cook and David Schmidt. I was inspired by one of my Guides who Genii introduced me to many years ago when I first completed The 4 Keys to Light Teachings, to share the following quotes and observations:

"We can't solve problems at the level of thinking (consciousness) where we created them" – Albert Einstein.

"The vibrational frequency of the solution is vastly different from the vibrational frequency of the problem" – Abraham through Esther Hicks.

As I thought about those quotes, I wondered if we energetically hold a vision that "something is coming," rather than knowing that it is already here (at least in another dimension), are we thereby delaying the visual manifestation of The City of Light? What if instead of thinking about why The City hasn't manifested, we assume that it is already here and focus instead on how we will live our lives and contribute to our new more enlightened world filled with Light, Love and Healing? My invitation for you as you read this book is to hold such a vision in your mind, heart and soul as you enjoy your exciting journey into The City of Light!

Charles Betterton
Cofounder and Co-CEO, The Light Center
Founder and CEO Universal Stewardheirship, Inc. and Ultimate Destinyland

Before the Magic Happens!

"God is up to something and it is Big," so reads the headline and this is so . . . How big? What think you, of the magnitude of what God can create through you and for you? Endless could be an answer, Miraculous another, First Class and most importantly Certainly!

The following pages of this unusual book reveal an exciting revelation and how it came about, unknown at first by two people who walked its path in pure faith and belief. They learned that preparation was in process and energy was being moved into place to produce the First City of Light. Nothing like this had ever happened to them before, or to you the reader for that matter.

Day by day its power never left their minds, even after the good Rev. Dr. Bill Townsend made his transition. As his humanness began failing, he knew his wife Genii could carry on when he was unable to any longer.

This the Genii has done day by day and year by year. She never gave up that such a vision would be God-produced with so much love it would change this planet forever, and that no one could humanly bring forth such a demonstration.

Now as this testimony goes into print and into your hands, we who guide the Genii, bless you and yours, for in some way you are a part of this whole experience. It is therefore suggested that you become the person walking through the City of Light as the pages unfold their energy.

As you come to each building or area, stop, take a deep breath, close your eyes and feel the Light essence contained therein. This is good for your whole system, as the healing can begin its process even before it is seen in the physical. Imagine that!

Universal Cities of Light!

As one City of Light could heal many with its space technology, there would need to be more Cities on this planet in other geographic locations and other countries. These are also due to appear as if by magic. Yes, this is true!

So then dear readers, take love with you as you walk the path of the Genii. Permit her to be you as you are taking a walk of a lifetime never experienced before now.

As said by spiritual leader Joel Osteen, "We serve a supernatural God who can create anything!" and indeed this is true as you will all see. Love is all there is, should be, and will be, as the decree is now set in motion.

As you walk through the first prototype, this City of Healing Light that is birthing forth in the energy fields of Sedona Arizona, United States of America, feel the energy at each location you stop at and wonder about, and then prepare to see it in 3D.

Make no mistake, this planet will Glow in love like you have never felt before, with Light Healing technology that you the reader are now an important part of. Get ready for the greatest show on Earth to be presented in your third dimension.

The stage is ready, the scenes inside these pages invite you to witness what is coming about, and this is your invitation page by page, before the magic happens.

Enjoy your trip.

So Love You Be!

Congratulations!

OOO-LON....Galactic leader in the City of Light Embassy of Peace.

Genii Townsend

PS. You might enjoy my 7 minute YouTube Video on The City of Light at http://youtu.be/pLwQBsPF324

Genii in The Light Center Classroom (where she facilitates *The 4 Keys to Light* classes) autographing copies of *Something's Coming* with her personal messages of Light and Love!

The City of Light Appears, Now What?

It was just to be a so-called normal day in the lives of people on this planet. It was planned through their mental equation of what they were planning to do that day . . . a normal day indeed . . . but the God Spirit had other plans.

It had long been said by many prophets on the Earth that one day, all would change for the better. Prayers for peace on Earth and good will to men and women had long since sailed into the Universe to be picked up by the highest deity of all. But today, unknown to almost everyone, this was to be totally different from any other day ever remembered in the history of this planet. This was to be The City of Light's introduction to the world.

Was it a dream, an outward/inward vision presenting itself? Sure we had seen the Virgin Mary on various tree trunks, etc., but this sight was beyond all that. Surely people thought that they were losing their minds because when they went to sleep there was nothing there, and now . . . Call the Dalai Lama, call the Pope, call somebody, anybody, to tell him or her what was taking place. Validation of sanity was needed here and now!

Quickly, upon noticing something had been added since the night before, the media picked up this unusual edifice now shining brightly, as if no sun was needed that day, and indeed it wasn't. The government quickly sent out the Air Force jets to see what had taken place. Protection at all costs was in strict force, but due to the Light being emitted from this demonstration, they had a difficult time seeing what exactly it was that had caused so much excitement and even concern.

There were suddenly television stations recruiting reporters in mass to be the first ones on the "Light-Spot" to cover the event. The current celebrities in the headlines were banished and forgotten, for something major had taken place... imagine that! What was this place of Light that, because of its brightness, could not be seen totally at first? Was this conquest from outer space? Extraterrestrials coming to get us? And what would they conquer . . . wars and fighting and egos gone wild?

Who in outer space wants that? We have been praying for eons of time for peace. Maybe we have embodied too many movies of violence coming from others not of our kind. They are probably only wanting to be of service, and not even thinking of taking over . . . please. Maybe this place of glowing Light was something that God/Spirit declared to come forth to heal this planet so that it could, for all intents and purposes, not be an outcast from the rest of the planets due to our low consciousness and fear of attack.

Just maybe, now the consciousness was being raised to the point that we could use some extra help, and it was definitely being supplied as an eye opener. This was something so big that people could begin to see this holy demonstration, as it was standing right before their eyes. Could this be a wake-up call?

Upon seeing this magnificent manifestation, many fell to their knees in Holy Communion with the Sources of their higher guidance systems, Buddha, Christ, and many other Masters who seem to have a hotline to the Boss (so to speak), and many of those who seem to check in during meditation, as inner voices teach. Many people went into delight and joy mixed with love, for it made a great empowering concoction. They knew that their prayers had been answered, in maybe a different way, but an answer they felt they had.

Many others, on the other hand, went into survival fear due to their previous mental program, for they thought that they had sinned or something, all of which is detrimental, of course, rather than a delightful experience. As long as the Christ was still coming (as in the Second Coming) they could still keep on sinning (meaning missing the mark) but maybe it was the energy of all the Masters, Saints, Angels and Guides who embodied Love manifested . . . maybe?

Maybe this City of Light just dropped out of the sky to get our attention as a healing place to begin Heaven on Earth. Maybe it was a gift that the God Spirit sent to us to get healed from the mental to the physical to the emotional and all the rest. Maybe it was a validation that somewhere in the unseen it was declared that we needed an injection of love and Light so strong that we had to have and see something so dramatic that it could not be denied.

Maybe this is the biggest blessing this entire world has ever experienced. The City of Light just appeared with no previous fanfare. It just appeared! Maybe from this experience we could learn more about the Universe, that in its contents we could discover much more and we could use it to better our lives in more delightfully different ways than before . . . maybe!

The time had come for peace on Earth. They were given a new way of looking at each other from the eyes of love, not of hate and vengeance and all the other horror stories flashing across our screens to promote more of the same negative thinking. The time had come, for this unexpected Sight of Sights had brought with it in a split second a vision so strong that anything outside of love and truth was banished, and the consciousness was raised quickly. People felt that finally their prayers were answered, and guess what? They didn't have to lift a finger to bring it forth, only accept it in their mind, and they did, one by one and millions by millions.

Yes it was expected to be a normal day sunrise to sunset, but in between this space of time something unusual took place and nothing would ever be the same again . . . ever.

The City of Light became manifest on Earth! Praise God!

What in Heaven is Going On?

Once upon a once, God said ...

Once upon a once, the Great Creator looked over the creation of stars, galaxies, and planets, and said: "Yes, this is God good!" Suddenly, an angel appeared and said, "Perhaps you might want to take a look at that blue planet over there." And the angel pointed to this planet.

God took a closer look and saw a planet in upheaval. Wars and threats of wars, people against people, and pain everywhere—and they were sending fireworks back into the universes! "Oh my, this will never do," God said. "Hmmm, what is to be done to bring peace once and for all?"

Then God got an idea, a very big, magnificent idea. "Yes, that will work! First, I must get their attention, and then I'll work on the peace end. For this planet must be healed. I will send my angels and Lightworkers to set the scene. It will be my most magnificent production ever witnessed on that planet. I shall design and bring forth a glorious healing edifice and all will see for the first time in their history my CITY OF LIGHT that will have within it my holiness, and ways of healing unknown there.

"Yes, I agree with me! I shall send forth my Light to do the healing with my love. Angels, take down this Proclamation and send it forth to be picked up by those who are open to receive such good God news. Let's see, how shall I begin? Oh, yes ... '**My PROCLAMATION**!' Yes, that is a good start ...

"**Take heed, oh people of the Earth. There will come by dawn's early light a new Heaven on Earth that embodies all I stand for. Love shall be my messenger and my Light shall perform the healings.**

"**This demonstration is now declared in process and is given as a gift to every living soul who inhabits your planet (which, incidentally, belongs to me.) Make not an unbelief of this declaration, for I make the Earth with my insignia of love. No longer will wars and unsettlement be tolerated! Only peace shall be your reward. This decree cannot be stopped under any circumstances, as I stand as the Creator and vow this to be so!**

"**And now ... Take heed, each one who is reading or hearing this. Know that Peace on Earth is my intent and all will know my words are true and demonstrated. For you will see for yourself in your third dimension. Prepare yourself for such a demonstration, as it is nearing the sunrise of expectancy. Awaken, for it is time!**"

Signed,

God!

The City of Light Proclamation!

THERE IS COMING FORTH ON THIS CONTINENT A NEW NATION,
BATHED IN LIGHT. IT STANDS ON A NEW FOUNDATION OF
TRUTH AND HONOR, A CITY OF LIGHT!

IT HAS BEEN BUILT BY BEINGS OF LIGHT INTELLIGENCE.
IT IS PURE AND UNDEFILED. WHEN IT IS REVEALED TO THE MASSES,
IT WILL HERALD IN A NEW ERA
NEVER BEFORE EXPERIENCED ON THIS PLANET.

THOSE WHO VENTURE THERE, WILL RETURN HOME
ADVANCED IN THOUGHT AND EMOTIONS SO TRUE
THAT THEY WILL CHANGE THOSE AROUND THEM
WITHOUT LIFTING A FINGER.

THE CITY OF LIGHT WILL ATTRACT AND REPEL.
THOSE WHO WILL BE ATTRACTED, ARE THOSE WHO SEEK A HEALING.
THOSE WHO ARE REPELLED, ARE THOSE WHO HAVE
CHOSEN TO PLAY IN THE DARKNESS FOR YET A WHILE.

IT IS IN THIS LIGHT APPEARANCE THAT THE WORLD
AS YOU KNOW IT WILL BE NO MORE.....EVER!
THEN SHALL COME THE PEACEMAKERS WHO WILL SPREAD THIS LIGHT
THROUGHOUT THE LANDS AND CHANGE THE FREQUENCIES AROUND
THOSE THEY COME IN CONTACT WITH AS IF TOUCHED BY ANGELS.

THERE ARE HUMAN "LIGHT BEINGS" NOW BEING GROOMED
THAT WILL TAKE THEIR PLACE IN THE CITY PROPER
LONG BEFORE THE CITY ITSELF APPEARS.

WHEN THE REVELATION OF THE CITY OF LIGHT APPEARS,
IT WILL SEEM LIKE THE SECOND COMING TO MANY.
IN REALITY, IT IS THE FIRST COMING
AND NOTHING ELSE IS NEEDED.

IT IS IMPERATIVE THAT THOSE WHO WANT
TO BE PART OF THIS PRECEDING HAPPENING
NOW ADDRESS THEIR WISHES TO THEIR GUIDING INTELLIGENCES
THAT HAVE THEM IN THEIR CHARGE.
YOUR WORLD IS IN A PROCESS OF DRAMATIC CHANGE.
ALL IS NECESSARY TO BRING IN THE CITY OF LIGHT!

Journeying into the City of Light, Imagine That!

Once in the middle of Genii's ordinary life, God gave her a mission like no other she had ever heard of. Now you are invited to journey with her into....

The City of Light Sedona

Just Imagine

... Entering a place of such beauty that it makes you an instant believer that anything is possible, like entering a five-story high Gate that is encoded with your personal beliefs that make you feel like you just came home.

... Experiencing healing techniques in Light Modules where no drugs, knives, or needles can sever the body's electrical lines.

... Entering a "Memory Manor" building where you can release past memory hurts with no emotion attached.

... Standing by a Fountain of Light that makes you feel great, and sitting on benches that massage your body.

... Taking a dip in a healing pool that can clear skin conditions.

... Being able to balance your emotions in an Empowerment Emporium.

.... Seeing babies being born in a Birth-aterium, laughing with the mother who had no anesthesia, no pain and the only crying would be for the pure joy of the experience.

... Entering a stadium-size building called The Embassy of Peace Headquarters where Light Beings from the Universe gather to help bring forth Peace on this Earth.

IS ANY OF THIS POSSIBLE?

IT'S NOT ONLY POSSIBLE... BUT PROBABLE!

Acknowledgements of Genii's Gratitude and "Apprecia-Love"

It has been 16 years since my husband Rev. Dr. Bill Townsend, a pastor in the Religious Science Church begun by Ernest Holmes, made his transition leaving me to carry on, when at times I wondered why I was chosen to do just that. I protected his trans-audio (channeled) cassettes and City holiness intact secretly until I was notified from my inner guides it was time to let the news of *Something's Coming* out to the public which is what this book is all about. Before he left, I was inner trained to also trans-audio (meaning transferring inner audio information) and thus the visits included here are what I received through inner vision and sound.

After he departed, I was guided within to move to Sedona, Arizona. So my daughter Starr Light and I headed north where I am living at this writing. I didn't know then why. I do now - to introduce the City of Light as this indeed was planned for me to do many eons ago.

Thanks B for the fun ride with so much love and caring attached. Looks like you were right after all and I follow where you began, inspired by heart. I must also give heart-filled thanks to many others who have supported me in this marvelous adventure one way or another, maybe not even knowing they did anything. So my heart and love go to the following...

To Oprah who says "If you don't believe in miracles you are thinking too small." This progress is indeed a miracle in the making. Thanks Oprah!

To Charles Betterton, my business partner in all this, for the massive insight work he has done to bring it all together so you can follow my adventure. His wisdom and accomplishments in empowerment, enlightenment and publishing are well known. To take this project on in love and friendship was indeed a miracle in the making. There are not enough words to express what his supportive undertaking of this book has produced. He has helped make this manuscript what it should be, as inspired by God and to show me what is possible as perfection. I am truly the recipient of his wisdom and dedication to Universal StewardHeirShip. Plus trips to Disneyland several times a year for me to get my fun fix. Thanks Charles.

Speaking of Disneyland, I would be remiss not to include and thank Walt Disney for the inspiration he gave me just walking through his mind with hundreds of others as well as himself as we sit together on a main street bench in trans-audio conversations. His imagination inspired many in the arts to continue moving forward. Walt, you were and are the greatest I have ever met. See you next time.

To Ernest Holmes and the hundreds of Centers for Spiritual Living, thank you. Those New Thought teachings helped me learn to listen to the wee voice within me. And what I learned made more sense than anything I had heard before and I could be in communication also. Wow... it changed my life by pouring more God love in me than I could ever imagine like finding friends in high places and sharing how others could too with my sessions in The 4 Keys to Light. Thanks Dr. Holmes. It was good what you did especially for me and B.

To my loving family... Alan, Ginger, Starr Light, Dave, and Doug who have never said "This is crazy!" Thanks for the confidence. I love you all. And a big thank you to my constant companion and my heart of hearts, Light Spirit, my puppy, who stood by faithfully and unfailingly to welcome me back from my inner travels.

To Charles Rinehart who introduced me to what a channel was through the Rabbi and for permission from Charles and his wife Lavetta to use his painting on the City of Light book cover. (http://www.rhinehartartgallery.com)

To Master Yoda who reminds me of the power of The Force and Kermit the frog who reminds me of The Rainbow Connection.

To Pastor Joel Osteen who lifts me daily through his wisdom via video and books.

To Kathie Brodie my closest friend and confidant who is ALWAYS there for me if I am climbing the walls of change. Thanks Kathie for long conversations of clearing. I love you.

To Renee Trenda who is always ready to help, including introducing me to Michael Quinsey, Russ Michael and many others of my new "forever friends." She invited me to her home in Stelle, Illinois and took me on a wild trip to give President Carter a look-a-like puppet of himself and we did it! Thank you!

To Michael Quinsey for a Light connection across the Atlantic to England who has lovingly spread the word of the City around the planet, including interviewing me on his BBS radio program three times . . . and I got to meet him in person here in Sedona. Thanks Michael and SaLuSa for all the wisdom you share with all of us.

To Stephen Cook, across the Pacific Ocean in Australia, who honored me by inviting me to be a guest on his InLightRadio program. Through his fun way of looking at the world we connected, and being open to any Australian wisdom, I learned a few things from you and Anthony as well. Charles and I are especially grateful for the wonderful Foreword you wrote for this book!

To Steven Beckow and all the speakers at the 2012 Scenario Conference who just let it all hang out and we all learned big time. Each one had a great presentation for empowerment, enlightenment and Ascension. Thank you all. Charles and I especially appreciate your permission to include your article on The Coming of the Cities of Light in this book.

To Sierra Neblina, Jennifer Nicolella and Dave Schmidt for producing the 2012 Scenario Conferences here in Sedona and for graciously offering to process advance orders for autographed copies of Something's Coming. And thank you to Dave for interviewing me on your radio show.

To two very special friends Nina Joy and Bracken Cherry, stewards of Xanadu of Sedona Domes of Light, thank you for being here for me when needed. Life would be less fun without you both. Thanks with a big hug.

To Rev. Dr. Audrey and Rev. Dr. Les Turner, thank you for years of support and the loving guidance given in various ways, including my walk through the City of Light adventures, even inviting others to hear what God gave me to say at the Center for Spiritual Living in Escondido, CA. Thank you to both of you, you are the very best!

To Deborah Krenz, "Lady of Light" for your love and helping hands with no questions asked except, "where do you want this puppet to go?" The 4 Keys to Light became her introduction to AH!, the Universal tone of love. Good work and forward we go.

To Lynette Sauder, who on a moment's notice, can be counted on and is willing to listen once more to The 4 Keys to Light sessions and who takes me to the Unity Church to hear her favorite speaker. Thanks Lynette with love and appreciation.

To Clayton Nolte for fitting my home with your invention of naturally balanced structured water. I can easily report it is the greatest and I am blessed. In my visits to The City, I have been told structured water is "liquid light" and "liquid love" and that it will be used there, especially for growing healthy, nutritious foods. (http://www.NaturalStructuredWater.com). Thank you very much.

Thank you to everyone who has been loving enough to open your homes as hostesses for my visits to share the "Good News" that "Something's Coming" and for sponsoring The 4 Keys to Light Teachings. That includes my "Forever Friends" Heather Clark and The Arizona Enlightenment Center in Phoenix, Rev. Dr. Audrey Turner in San Diego, CA, Lorie Blackwell and Lorraine Lewin in Mystic, CT, Peggy Langenwalter, Yvonne Loubet and The Lights of the Round Table in Albuquerque, NM, Renee Trenda in Stelle, IL and Kathie Brodie in Seattle, WA.

You have all helped spread the love farther and your belief in the City of Light coming forth has given power to its demonstration. Thank you more even than I can write here. I am blessed because you cared and I made many new friends. God is good!

I am especially thankful for you, the reader of this book, who have the courage to walk with me through what is at this writing, in the unseen world ready to appear on a moment's notice. This, Dear Ones, is the demonstration we have sought for centuries to bring peace and love to every person on the planet. It takes something of this magnitude to get our attention, for only God can bring forth what will not be ignored. As you read my story and the details of my visits to The City of Light, you will see that various word usage, word patterns, grammar and punctuation do not agree with literary norms.

24

The messages in these pages were channeled through me in my capacity as a trans-audio. In order to reach the page, the channeled messages had to filter through my language patterns, experiences and communication style. And you will notice that the decades of experience I have enjoyed serving others through the power of entertainment and edutainment, (including owning and operating Geniiland, a children's marionette theater near Hollywood for 18 years), is apparent through the many references to the movie industry and show business terms.

The Intelligences and Light Beings I have been blessed to have these conversations with, are not native to Earth, and they do not use language in the way we are accustomed to seeing and hearing it. The process included my tuning within to receive an inner vision, then I wrote up the details of each visit in longhand. Afterwards I sat at my computer and typed up each message which was then sent to the volunteer editors.

Each visit to The City of Light shared in this book was received, written and shared initially as a stand-alone message. As a result, some passages and references may seem redundant. Some of what you will read may not appear to make sense on the 3D level or may not conform to your communication preferences.

I again need to express my heart-felt gratitude for the individuals who have devoted so many hours to help edit, refine and prepare the manuscript for publication. That includes of course Charles Betterton, Kathie Brodie and Renee Trenda who have helped "clean up" the draft reports of my visits to The City for years, and especially to the angel, Katrina Rodgers, who has contributed countless days and weeks sharing her expertise making final edits to the entire book, along with some help from Lorie Blackwell, Janet Althen and MBT, an anonymous contributor to the editing process.

When you read my story, please let your heart and soul reveal its Truth within and for you. The messages contained in my book are being delivered to Love and Light and with honesty, candor and integrity. Please know that I have been faithful to the messages as I received them and the editors and publisher join me in our dedication to sharing them with you in that way.

Thank you for your faith, that "Something's Coming" in love and Light and service to each of you, for as it is said, "Believing is seeing, and God can do anything". I fully believe in miracles, especially this forthcoming demonstration which many will recognize as the Second Coming, and I thank you for joining with me on this magical adventure.

So Light it be! Thank you.

Love and Blessings to each and every one.

Genii

First to Go Galactic . . . The City of Light Sedona

What is the Sedona Galactic Healing City of Light Connection?

"The prophecy is that indeed this power center of Earth has been chosen as the first kick-off location that has its opening imprints of a City of Light Healing. This is important due also to the technology coming forth as the impact of this energy rises and those now in process feel the peak of final preparation whose Light work on themselves is reaching its own peak."

Photo of "Spaceship in Clouds" over Coffee Pot Rock in Sedona © OceAnna Laughing Cloud

"The inner cleansing opens the way for the planet's changeover, and it will be seen as totally completed. Ready or not, the Light frequencies of the Sedona areas pull in yet more power. As those who live there attempt to stay balanced, the wake of this ballistic cosmic energy leads the holy demonstration. Many of your current scientists would be astonished at the impact this silent yet powerful motion will have on the total planet."

What does it mean to go Galactic?

"To go Galactic means to be first to be enlightened to such a degree that the energy forces maneuver the opening to the heavens so quickly that the electromagnetic fields of upper and lower connection spread its frequencies throughout the rest of the planet in a second of your so-called time. It is within this starting point of Cosmic Light that it targets this planet through, in particular, the Sedona portal. In this way the Cosmic Connection is made."

"Since what has just been said is important, are you ready for this Connection of L I G H T?"

**"All is in process. It is here ... it is now ...
We bid you the Light of the eternal day, in Peace and in Love ...
So Light it Be!"**

OceAnna Laughing Cloud is a Spiritual Alchemist, Visionary Artist and Cosmic Dolphin who lovingly creates from the Heart of Creation to bring forth her gifts to humanity to promote Eternal Peace, Love and Harmony. Her Living Waters of Creation™ and Vibrational Photography assist in bringing forth the Hidden Realms of Creation by way of portals of illuminating, which assist in awakening to that which has always been present, namely Oneness and Unity Consciousness. OceAnna's mission is to teach through the language of Eternal Light and Frequency, the importance of the Holy Sacrament of Water and its paramount importance to Mother Earth. Her latest offerings can be accessed on her website http://www.heartofthedeepbluesea.org.

Sedona is the Chosen Place

"Sedona, Arizona has been chosen! It is bringing the dawn of a new awakening. Sedona is empowered to be the first to bring in the new Spiritual Power Center never before experienced on this planet!

"It will serve all who seek enlightenment on a level never before experienced on this planet. It will fill the void that many have sought for eons of time...the time is now!

"Awaken...for it is time for all Lightworkers to band together as one with their varied talents, growth systems and the making of a new design ready to be put into action, not just for some but for all.

"The City of Light Sedona is a center court of high esteem and acknowledgement, ready to move forward in bringing forth an edifice of such magnitude, that to see it, one would be awe-struck and changed beyond changing. It is that magnificent!

"The Genii has known for some time that this Divine obsession of the Divinity was in place for the unveiling, when the pyramid designer decrees this to take place. As the changes take place on your planet enough to permit the unveiling of the City of Light, dimensions will part and move away like a stage opening production and the people will fall to their knees in Holy Communion. The unbelievers will for the most part, depart, returning when their elevation of frequencies can adhere to the vibrations they have just witnessed.

"Why Sedona you might ask? The power stations here known as vortexes hold much more than a slight frequency that humans can sense to a minute degree (which is filtered, due to the nerve freeways you carry). The vortexes carry Light from other levels and dimensions that can only be perceived by a few now, nevertheless, this is accurate to a minute detail. The Light coming through the vortexes makes it possible for the City of Light to demonstrate.

"So then, it would seem that this Sedona area is a place of honor and Sacred beyond belief, as will be seen by the world of your planet as the time so-called, races to meet its destiny.... **The City of Healing Light!**"

So Light it Be!

(Message received by Genii Townsend January 1, 2005)

Once Upon a Once There Was a Beginning

The following is a written testimonial of what took place in my learning of the "City of Light." It is written in my words, including my feelings, as we went into and through this discovery.

I stand by every word as my truth that is so engrained within me that I am the embodiment of the Holy City of Light. Enjoy or toss, it makes no difference, for what you are about to learn will come to pass, ready or not.

In love and blessings,

Genii Townsend

Little did I know when I married Rev. Dr. William (Bill) J. Townsend in 1978 in the Apple Valley, California, Church of Religious Science (RS) what an adventure we had in store for us. Not in my wildest imagination could I come up with such ideas. I was just a first year RS student from North Hollywood, California who delighted in the teaching of how I could better my life, which I had requested of God after a divorce.

Rev. Dr. William Townsend

About a year later we were guided to leave there and go to Las Vegas, which was not my favorite place to live by any means, but it was thought that my career of puppet and marionette performing could be an advantage, due to stage productions Vegas style, and I made a lot of celebrity marionettes to fill the bill.

Well, that was not why we were guided to be in Vegas, but rather to open a "Light Center" type church, which we did. That was not surprising due to Dr. Bill being a leading minister for some time in the movement.

One day after service, a lady told us that a friend of hers in another state was coming to Las Vegas and was guided to talk to Dr. Bill. She said he was a channel. I had some idea from some silly movies that tables would dance and ghosts would come forth and I was not in any way, shape or form into that! I was a student of truth, after all!

Dr. Bill decided it would be all right, and because he was a meditation teacher and knew a lot more than this first year student, I said okay but I would have a room full of people, a tape recorder going, and it must be in the daytime to light up that room.

Everything I wanted was set up so this person who did weird things would be able to deliver his message, whatever it was, when he arrived. He did arrive with his wife which made me feel better because I was thinking he was attached to someone who must be grounded, I hoped.

A gentle artist entered, who proceeded to not only change his voice as he talked, but his features as well. To me this was astonishing, and so much so, I was not hearing what was being said until nudged from within, "Pay attention!" So I did, and I learned many truths that resonated with me enough that I began to relax and absorb.

Nothing of a grand nature was said until the next day when we went for a ride north, and it was here that we first heard about a City of Light, as he described it, when he had us stop at a specific location. Of course I could not see anything and neither could Dr. Bill, but what the heck, dreamers can envision anything. So that was the message. We said thanks and this man left, taking his multi-dimensional personage with him, and that was pretty much that.

What interested me so much was the way the first meeting with him took place: a wife asking questions of her husband who was someone else (not a normal meeting in my thinking). I began to wonder about the way it was done. Dr. Bill was a deep meditation teacher so I asked him if he could do something like that where I could ask the questions and record the answers. Sounded like fun and I like fun so . . .

With him agreeing, we quickly set a time and proceeded. Talk about sticking your neck out! I had no idea what would take place, much less what questions to ask. I was hanging in mid-air when a few minutes later a strange voice came through Dr. Bill. "Question?" What question? Who has questions? Me?

When I found my voice I said, "Hi. Well, sort of."

This, then, was the beginning of many years of questions and answers from a floor and tape recorder position for me, and the "I'm not here" couch position of Dr. Bill.

A few months into this way of learning through questions and answers and then replaying the tape so Bill could hear what came through, he was guided to obtain some art supplies, a drawing board and to do some sketching.

Since Bill only had mechanical drawing in school he was a perfect candidate. For three years he brought through the plans of this City of Light, so-called, which the first visionary said he saw - Bill himself, having no personal thoughts of how it should be.

Not that Bill really wanted to do this. He would "come out" periodically and say "I'm not doing this anymore," at which time he was promptly sent back into the guest room to continue bringing forth this artwork.

When all was said and done, the results turned out to be architectural drawings and directions for this "City of Light." At first we thought we were to build it ourselves until wisdom entered to inform us that not only did we not have the building material here, but no building code would permit it to be built under any circumstances. That pretty well set that in cement, so this had to be something in another dimension which somehow was to come forth here like magic.

The City of Light, we were informed, was to be a "City of Light Healing," a place where people would come to be healed of whatever needed healing, through the medium of Light frequency attention, meaning no knives to be cutting into the human body Light lines, and no needles to scare the kids and adults as well. Count me in too!

This would be done in what is called "the Light Modules" of advanced technology where peace would reign supreme and no stress would even think of entering. In that setting the patient would receive the necessary Light frequencies and vibrations to heal their particular ailments.

Several years later, I was given directions on creating a lesson plan called The 4 Keys to Light, wherein I teach students how to become Light Technicians. These practitioners could assist people in their healing by connecting them to the Healing Light facilities of the City of Light. These treatments would take place outside of the City of Light, and there would be no charge to those being served.

In watching the plot plan of this city come forth, it looked a little like a storybook fantasy, some parts of which are familiar to us, but with advanced scientific technology that would send Star Trek writers back to the drawing boards.

For example, there is a 1,500 foot High Tower that is designed to catch UPPC's (Uniphase Power Capsules) that have been bombarding this planet for eons of time, thus lighting the City of Light and a zillion other areas it can reach.

To me this indeed would have to be a God-made miracle as I saw no other way it could happen, and surely it is needed on this planet at this time in history.

Welcome to the New Jerusalem!

As the planetary changes flood our senses and we work to stay in balance trying to keep normal, yet within knowing that something is going on, I have asked this question of my inner teachers.

Why a City of Light?

A: "In the light of all that takes place in your world, as upheaval makes more of the same, it would look as though peace cannot come into being, which of course is nonsense.

"The predictions of generations entwined in past events, have tucked into the collective memory of all people, certain expectations that have the power to produce enough pre-programming of what is being experienced with confused mentality and negatively induced as truth. This is coming to an end. Enough!

"For centuries, this same time warp has produced war after war after war, instead of a constant peace which was given as a gift from the Creator in the beginning. This gift has been misused as constant ego-generated thoughts produced conflict and turmoil. Thus love must be wedged in to be of assistance.

"As generation after generation said they wanted peace, war was declared instead as a force to be dealt with. And war in the name of whatever any particular person deems the Creator of all - was deemed a way to peace.

"Chaos on this planet is experienced on a consistent basis. Since this was not the original intent, and with mankind not able to bring forth its own peaceful loving ways, it is now moved into a higher level of progress, which is somewhat out of your hands.

"What, losing control? What has been achieved so far on your own? Is not the cry to the Creator for peace on Earth good will to men? A Primal Source is needed to expel the darkness (ignorance) and bring Light into this planet, which must live and function with others more evolved in a balanced universe. Thus the City of Light is now being brought to the forefront, which demonstrates and bears fruit of loving kindness and healing facilities advanced in techniques that are unknown on this planet.

"Those who, for whatever reason, cannot move forward in the ultimate destiny of this planet, will be in for quite a surprise as they witness the intervention of Light.

"So there has been talk of a massive change in 2012, and rightly so. However, this is just a mental imprint to play with and keep the minds focused. The surprise comes when least expected.

"As Universal Light, Starworkers work with Light Lifters in human form. In your dimension the full demonstration called The City is a path of elevation which holds great promise and there is a Light at the end of the tunnel, for the tunnel disappears as the nearing of the Holy City rings true.

31

"It will not be pushed under any rug, so to speak, as it will stand as a massive live demonstration to all of the power and Light of this Holy Creator, thus making this planet a place of safety and love long past due.

"The triggering of the City of Light's impact will change lives within a split second allowing the experiencing of true feelings of love. As has been said before, we play not games here. For too long warring forces have ruled and that ruling now comes to an end! No one on this planet can stop this demonstration for any reason. Since this has been centuries of slow progress, it is now being speeded up and is currently in action, for this City of Healing Technology is vastly beyond what is being currently used.

"The Sedona, Arizona area is the chosen location of impact, due to the energy fields, vortexes, star location, etc. The time is now!

"It has been repeated from many people that from the universe come entities to take over and control us due to false advertising on the part of the ignorant, who are fearful of losing that control.

"We reply, what, pray tell, is to be taken? Do people not destroy all that they can get to, from nature, animals, including humans of a different race or culture or color? Please!

"So then awaken from your mundane daily concerns. Wash away with the strong beam of transformation Light now being beamed in covering the whole Earth, sucking out that which holds people into fear and concerns of the future. The Light in exchange brings forth what this planet was designed for in the first place.

"You want peace on Earth? You will have it!

Note: The world you live in on planet Earth will be seen

as another moon that shines in the heavens…

for it too has been so declared!"

Atherian: trans-audioed through the Genii

Beginning City of Light Plot Plan Information

"The City of Light can be expected to demonstrate, as has been predicted previously, with nothing that can prevent it from appearing. It is noticed that people may not always see this event as one that would demonstrate in your third dimension - only as a vision, as if in an altered state of awareness.

"Each person sees an extension of him or herself, who may or may not coincide with what the Genii has spoken of, and this is natural. However, the Genii has been chosen as an Emissary Light Spokesperson elevating the minds to regard this apparition (appearing in a third dimension level) as much as you see today, for she works all levels.

"How many times did the Dr. Bill want to quit the drawings, for his belief challenged him that such articulate plans would not be possible to build? He had to really stretch his mind to accept that a City of Light could come forth and people could physically walk into what he was being told to draw and he had no prior talent in that direction.

"These drawings with information were far beyond what he could imagine happening; yet he pursued unto the end while challenging his mental sanity. He really had to trust the inner guidance (which he taught others about) during the years of City drawings and information that came forth behind closed doors.

"To speak out now is what the Genii is being advised to do, after years of being told to keep it secret except for her 4 Keys to Light (Ancient Teachings for a Modern Age) students being Light linked during the session, opening a new corridor into the body power centers. Is this all a dream? An illusion? Yes, and so is the Great Pyramid and the homes you live in, including the trees and flowers. It would be called a 'holodeck,' a distinct part of a hologram. It is just a preconceived thought in form.

"To bring everyone up to the same level of Spiritual advancement is no easy task. So to do that at this point could take many more centuries to achieve what could really be done in a flash. Advanced technology encased in wisdom is preparing to birth a three-dimensional prototype structure in the form of a City of Healing Light that no one can deny. This of course, can bring many people into that knowingness in a split second of vision like the greatest illusionist ever. When a magician creates an illusion, people say, 'How did he do that?'

"In regards to the City, and as people catch their breath because this immaculate vision stands before them unannounced, they will say, 'This has to be God in action. How did He do that?' And the Greatest Creator of all says... 'BECAUSE I CAN!'" End of transmission.

So Light it Be!

33

The City of Light Plot Plan

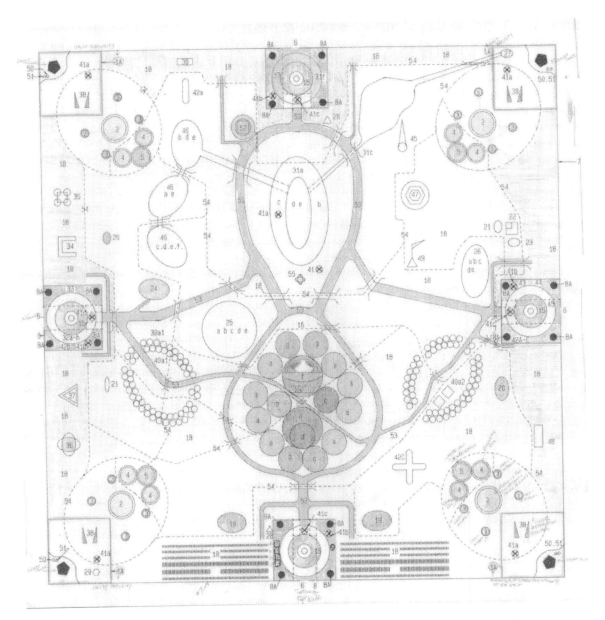

The original plot plan drawn by Dr. Bill includes coded references to the transcripts that provide more detailed information on each facet of The City of Light.

Hermes, Architect of the City of Light Sedona

Hermes Trismegistus. The Master of Masters.

Thrice blessed of God!

"The mind then is not separated from God's inessentiality but united unto it, as light to sun, then in this way know God; as having all things in Himself as thoughts, the whole cosmos itself."....Hermes

Q: "Hermes, I have been told about all the areas you are proficient in and all that you created. Is it true that you were the architect of the great Pyramid and now even the City of Light?"

A: "The Hermes greets the Genii in love and the magic of the written word. Yes, this is correct and the knowing of what was to come about became a wondrous adventure. The intent of the drawn plans was to make an imprint to be deposited in the minds, although for some it would seem as a fantasy, for others as Heaven on Earth that has been spoken of so often and representative of what God has promised as Peace on Earth.

"The Sedona City of Light plot plan was sent through the Dr. Bill as our energy fields were the same, him being my master student in the mystery school deep in the confines of the Giza Pyramid many lifetimes ago. This he did, even though it was challenging.

"Designing this Heaven on Earth, it was intended to be a modern, up-to-date scientific edifice that would be more than a pretty picture in someone's mind, as it would function in healing ways not even yet attempted in your medical world, for they know not of it. The Genii has been advised of its healing powers some ages ago and has used it to great advantage.

"The coming of the City of Light Sedona has been heralded in many ways throughout the centuries. Some see it ...most do not. But, as I have said 'As above ...So below!' and so they will. The imprint declared itself to me as I had the Light frequencies in the ecstasy of the project and it was not to be ignored.

"This prototype City of Light was to be, for your dimensional status was needed in what you would call a 'wake-up time' even though it took many centuries in your time frame.

"You have held these sacred drawings for some time now. As you bring them forth from the archives of God's intention, you fulfill a prophecy long since hidden from the eyes of non-believers of such a planned event.

"The City of Light is actually several dimensions. One you will see and three unseen as it developed through several open corridors. This will change history forever. My pleasure in pleasing the one God was the bottom line to design this structure within a structure.

"Upon notification to the world that such a place has appeared, the energy switch takes place and that is why the 'Light players' are to be in place to assist in any fear based announcements of those who have been taught to fear the wrath of God, rather than being in peace that such a gift has been delivered.

"I Hermes, stand with you as you move forward in Light as Light declaring witness to the City of Light Sedona, the beginning Healing prototype of many cities already in process, awaiting the first City of Light to be demonstrated in the sacred Sedona area. We shall talk more.

"In honor of service, I am Hermes . . . Sedona City of Light Guide of the Genii. So Light it Be!

"In the time of the coming demonstration, the City Plot Plan would have to have some recognition of something that was extraordinary, but also a bit practical in its design - for people like to be comfortable in surroundings that are just that, comfortable, pleasing to the senses and the healing factor not to be ignored. Yet, if it was to be direct from God it would have to be magnificent in its scope and so it is all this...and more.

"So in the original design along with the scientific technology of the Great Towers and Gates, I inserted patient and family housing and eating establishments, parks of natural beauty as well as establishments of advanced teaching and even a gathering place that will hold many for various events.

What is different are the glorified structures that are elegant beyond belief. A futuristic resort, retreat for the senses.

"You are still in human form and the basic reason for what would be seen as Heaven on Earth. However no Retreat Center has ever been built like this one - for you do not have the materials on your planet to build it. What was once a dream is now a reality like no other dream and God did it out of Its own Imagination. Imagine That!"

"Enjoy and get healed and this planet will shine in the heavens like another bright star to wish upon. So Light it be! Hermes at your service."

Importance of the City of Light High Towers and Gate Towers

After over 25 years of maintaining faithful stewardship over the plans and architectural drawings for the City Of Light entrusted to her by her late husband, Rev. William Townsend, Genii Townsend, Co-founder of The Light Center has been led to announce the coming forth of the City of Light.

The City of Light is described in the Proclamation given to her by Light Intelligences. In the photo taken in front of Bell Rock in Sedona, Genii holds the plans for one of the four High Towers included in the plans for the City of Light.

"This is difficult to explain in your vernacular, as words can only report a portion of what now stands for progress on the way for your planet.

"**High Towers**... These four elevated stations, 1,500 ft. high, (similar to a catcher's mitt) send out signals like a homing device that pull to them the Uni-Phase Power Capsules (UPPC) of dynamic power, not used on your planet as it is now known to exist, although you do have different designs of energy for different reasons.

"**Gate Towers**... These structures and others within the City complex that work with the Gate Towers are complicated turbo designs. The four entrances are a welcome mat for all, as encoded in the design of the elevated five-story structure is everyone's religious or spiritual belief systems. So all feel welcome like they have just found Heaven on Earth and all are one with no mental separation.

"The City's complex electrical systems also incorporate and work with the electromagnetic fields to impregnate and surround this perfection healing place of God/Spirit as only such a complex edifice could contain.

"The matrix that unfolds here is beneficial to the whole intricate embellishments contained within, around and over completely. This place of healing Light is several levels in depth which can and does steer the motoring ship device, as well as the way of the healing Lights of various kinds that take place.

"Nothing is left out, for in its magnificence, this is a place of completion in the healing fields that your world now can only surmise as possible.

"As the City arrives (bringing the first prototype) it will supply scientists and doctors with advanced education that is superior to what is now known, for indeed you still walk with mental dinosaurs. To this point, progress has been slow to non-existent.

"To intermingle, contact with others within the universe must change, and so this City of Light will do that and more. It will be as if 1,000 years of future technology has been laid at your feet within a few moments.

"The day will come when many such cities will arise on the same premise of catching the UPPCs, thus bringing energy to many places on your Earth plane. But the first is the 'Attention-Getter,' so to speak, with the initial appearance in the Sedona, Arizona area."

"Are the High Towers and the Gate Towers important? Oh my yes, for what is about to be deposited on your Earth plane will, as has been said, be dramatic, peaceful, healing and has Earth-changing advantages."

So Light it Be!

The City of Light Gate Towers

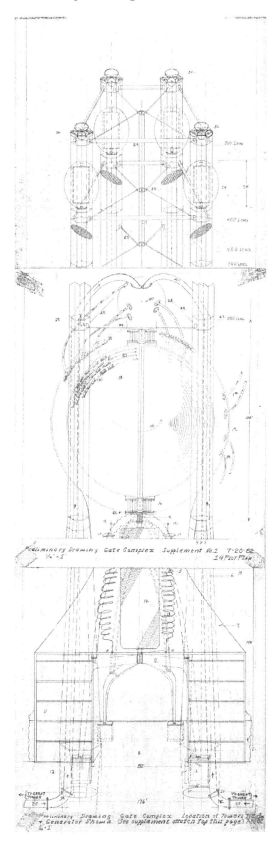

The City of Light High Towers

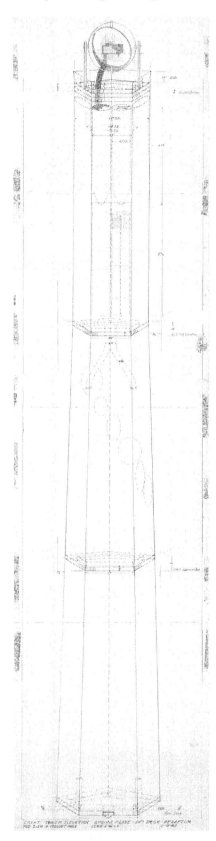

40

Time Warp

November 15, 2006

Q: "The e-mails now report the Mayan calendar is active for December 21, 2012 as a major event to take place. This prophecy has been noted for centuries, with the repeated references that Charles and I play a major part. What can be said of this and The City demonstration and our part in this? Advise please."

A: "What has been reported for centuries is a belief that has taken form after so many repeats of belief. The way of Light knows no limit and so as a certain date appears and re-appears, the minds connected say, 'Yes, this is so!' When enough directives come into play from such writings, the world finds many ways to attune to the premise and as The Genii has said many times 'the mind can justify anything.'

"Now then, what validity has this announcement? Depending on the amount of belief and the ways of saying such, the interest builds to a peak, and the masses intertwined bring forth a mental equal to say, 'I knew it was so.'

"The Genii has been advised of a Healing City of Light that is to make a dramatic impact on the planet in which she, Charles, Starr-Light and others are tuned into this dramatic Earth awareness event. As the minds validate the 2012 date and anticipate something spectacular to be attended to, the spiritual and physical continue to do just that, change, taking consciousness to a higher frequency peak.

"So then, what happens as the people attend their attention to the so-called dates and then something spectacular demonstrates and catches them off guard as is said, 'like a thief in the night'? The world of Lightworkers say, 'halleluiah!'

"The planet change makes its mark, and darkness is no longer in charge through deluded minds holding the planet's progress with doubt and failure, and even the 2012 date is forgotten, for before their eyes it shines like something that cannot be denied . . . ever! Dates matter not . . . what does matter is the Holy Event itself!

"Now then, why are you and the Charles and the Starr-Light and others, which are many, involved? Why not? Have you not, through the Dr. B., been given the actual plans of such an edifice? Have you not been told for years you are to carry this design in your heart and speak only when you are told to? Of course!

"As the power of the Light frequencies change your physical and mental knowing, its appearance will also take a quantum leap. The Charles, being assigned as the masculine part in all this, and the Genii, playing the feminine counterpart as has been said numerous times, together bring to the world a new world as a connecting force of frequency power strong enough to demonstrate what has been so long in the quiet, yet progressing into the physical.

41

"Lay not aside these plans, for they will indeed shake up this planet as an earthquake awakens. You have both agreed in the unknowing senses that what you are about is valid and important and to pay strict attention, leaving no stone unturned, for value is to be found under each one, not darkness.

"Are your combined efforts to bring forth the City of Light? Does not the sun shine even when the clouds cover it?

"Dear Ones, indeed, one day the Genii and the Charles will say, 'Yes, it is done,' and the Christ Consciousness is released like a Genie from a bottle with a knowing, introduced from within, that you both will know when it is to appear.

"Support each other, stay in the tune with the Word and all will be well with each one, for this is the message of the day."

So Light it be!

Genii's Interior City of Light Visits

It is not easily put into words what I have seen in visions inside the interior of this place called the City of Light. Take the most grandiose words you can think of and then multiply them … a lot.

Some years ago when I was in mental conversation with my inner teachers on what they call the "All-ter-net," I asked if some day could I see inside the City before it manifested.

It took quite a few years but, indeed, I am now permitted to view some of the healing places established within its confines, and what fun this is. So this is just a small briefing to give you an idea, for its time has come.

But first… information from one of my City Guides:

"This place of holy healing is designed to re-create the person who has the needed healing. In re-creating, this means the cells and atoms of a person's make-up are made new and thus change the whole body structure, including the mental, which is the beginning intruder anyway.

"This is done with Light frequencies, most of which are not known in the field of medicine in your world. There will be no advertising needed as such, for each person is a walking healthy example of what is being said here.

"Many doctors and scientists will arrive to learn and apply as taught, very advanced ways of healing yet unknown, much less tested in your world. It would be as you might call Space Technology, for that is what it is. These days you are still using covered wagon days methods when space is the perimeter to be discovered.

"Those who arrive first will learn total Light healing with no surgery to cut the electrical lines. All these previous instruments of cutting and needles are barbaric at this point of advancement and will be eliminated, thus putting the patient in a calm state instead of stress where drugs are needed. New Light scans will tell all.

"You, Dear One, must realize that your world is in such an upheaval of change right now in preparation of this event, that it will no longer be what it has been. The old world you have and are used to, will have been replaced and no interest in old concepts will hold it in place.

"You, the Genii, are experiencing this now as you set your course as a leader of the new era in process. The audio tapes you hold contain some advanced technology. The plans for the beginning formation of the City are the basic history in sound instructions with added data all for the healing comfort of those who seek it, and many will find it."

And so by invitation I step forth into discovery to glimpse for myself the greatest show on Earth! On with the show; this is it!

* Stepping through a massive five-story high Gate encoded with frequencies hidden in its gold scrolling which welcomes all who want to enter into the Light, the healing begins.

* Walking through parks that have seating that gives you a loving back massage when you are seated and paths that massage your feet as you travel on them. … Healing from back discomfort!

* Whatever temperature makes one comfortable it is provided, even when someone else who is next to you desires a different temperature. They, too, enjoy comfort. Can't complain here that you are hot or cold …. Healing from discomfort!

* A playing field for the big and little kids throwing and hopefully catching Light Mist balls before they disappear … Healing just by having Fun!

* The Memory Manor where unwanted memories are released in a live movie style holodeck where pain is no longer experienced from them – ever ... Healing from released mental pain.

* The Breath-a-terium, a wonderful, unusual building that takes your old breath away and gives you in return clean breathing that is indescribable, while colors strengthen and cleanse your chakras, as well as implanting more power by balancing Light frequencies into new cells and atoms ... Respiratory Healing!

* A special pool where the water of Light heals skin conditions on the spot … Wow! Healing skin irritations!

* The beginning process of the Light Modules, like a scene from Alice in Wonderland, walking through a magnetized screen that harvests all your pre-medical information and DNA information without lifting pen and paper. … These Light Modules are where the healing work takes the "Best of Show" award.

Through healthy Light frequencies, this place is really designed for comfort, with no knives or needles ever used. Cutting the human body Light lines is not on the menu. … Even the kids will enjoy this way of healing.

This is just a short indication of what to expect, and I have been blessed to be a witness inside the City of Light. It really is …

A Healing Heaven on Earth. Imagine That!

Genii Townsend, trans-vision visitor.

Cities of Light – The Genii Connection Report

June 6, 2007

Q: "Please explain to me why so many people see so many different cities of Light?"

A: "As The Genii has reported, the City of Light demonstrating in the Sedona area is the major first. Many have also seen what appears to be just that, cities of Light that are all perfect, all heavenly; for if it were otherwise like cities of darkness, it would not be reported in the same way.

"Visionaries from time immemorial have looked to a heavenly vision to sustain them, especially in times of pain. So then what is being seen and forecast as the immaculate heavenly adornment to come forth?

"The Genii loves the castle of the Disney. Another sees streets of gold and jewels. You all seek the splendor of the visions as you walk the yellow brick road to the Oz of your delight, depending on the visions and the makeup of your mindset that bring forth the comfort in many ways.

"Then, included in this, comes The Genii with printed blueprints of a technical healing City of Light, not so much of a fantasy castle but one of solid advanced healing techniques of another kind. A City people can walk into and get healed from any source of pain through the medium of advanced lighting properties which she never knew about until the Rev. Dr. Bill Townsend brought through the designs during an altered awareness state of meditation (of which he was a master) that he, too, never knew of. This is called a clear transmission or trans-audio, with no human mental interference.

"What would people say if the City, dressed in the splendor of God, really looked totally like the fantasy of the mind? Maybe, 'Oh, this palace is beautiful and holy. Could this really be from God or another Disney attraction and how did it get here and where was it before?'

"Dear Ones, dreamers dream, paint pictures and bring forth desires one way or another. So let us take the dreamy design of fantasy and add solid advanced healing techniques plus places within the City structure where people can temporarily stay while others are being Light attended in the Light models, and even play a bit of golf in a nearby park.

"You say this sounds strange, playing golf in a holy materialization of a City of sacredness. We who dictate this, recognize that human desire to have a place of comfort as well as healing, as comfort helps the healing, so why not include provisions for the comfort of those who enter into this domain of the Almighty?

"Human people need to be able to accept what they are used to in a structure the minds can accept. Add the fantasy of storybook dwellings and the advanced (beyond your scope of healing at this point) and you have what is about to be demonstrated. The City of Light has it all: beauty, fantasy, space technology and a feeling one has indeed come home. All the cities talked about and seen have been brought into play to get humans ready to accept the big event, even back to the Bible, the Koran the ... the ... the ... and the list is endless, depending on the minds that create it in vision form.

"It will take just one City of Light to make all the dreaming visionaries say, 'Yes, this is what I saw when the plans The Genii is the Gatekeeper for, are revealed.' All will mentally relate one way or another. It is all the same, just different minds in a dream process.

"Is the City of Light of first appearance the Earth-shaking prophesy come true? We, the Intelligence that has followed this matter for centuries, declare here and now that what is to manifest is all one and the same.

"It is all the visions rolled into one, designed to attract everyone's attention from the human sleep state they have been in for even much length of your non-time span. The minds will then fill in the mental linking up of visions. But first there must be the grand opening for those minds to attach to in form.

"The City of Light that is to demonstrate may be slightly different in form, but one they can all relate to as their visions are validated. God has supplied and brought forth that which is the 'attention getter' to establish new methods of healing that all can and will be subject to.

"This is such a priceless gift from the Universe that no one will care what was seen before, as it is the here and now that will make everyone a believer, believe you me!

"Make way for the new, people, never before expressed in this way, for indeed the City of Light holds many rose gardens just for the pleasure of it.

"Release the old thoughts and move into 'the new imagination' of possibilities never before heard of. You will be glad you did, and so will the God you worship!

"We bid you the Light of the eternal day in peace and love."

Blessings from The Genii

Seeing Cities of Light through Many Eyes

Q: "Why are different Cities of Light seen by people?"

A: "Each person is a mental artist with City designs given them that their systems can handle. In times of NDE or extreme circumstances or even in a quiet meditation state, Light in the form of Cities can be received and of course this is all good. The NDE experience with the lady and her favorite dog was a blessing to her in the reunion.

"Dreams of Heaven on Earth, are dreams of better times to come. These are all mental visions that not only impress, but can make believers out of non-believers, as most of this kind of imprint stays in the memory to be relived for its pleasantry for they are clearly magnificent.

"You, on the other hand, did not have the original vision the Dr. Bill did, as he was in a meditative place to be told what to put on paper as the basic design. You learned of it due to the sound conferences that you audiotaped and asked questions that really had no connection with you, as you only took down what was being said. The visions were given to him.

"Now, however, you have been trained as a so-called 'sensitive visionary' and can readily see what is behind the dimensional veil of this City of Light prototype through your Inner City visits, thus expanding on the original which is more like a normal retreat or resort location with glorified internal structures that will lift the minds into paradise. Would God give Spirit anything less?

"Were the visions really seen by others? Of course! Fantastic visions to delight the senses. How wonderful to have so many people being lifted through their own visions that somewhere in the ethers there are Cities of Light if only in a personal vision. Somewhere over the rainbow there is an Emerald City and they may be the first ones to enjoy the view for themselves.

"Praise God, Allah, and all the titles you put on the ONE for giving such a gift. Even if for just a few moments as they had made contact some place, somehow, somewhere in time."

So Light it be!"

Visiting the City

Q: "Last night I was informed that I was to go to the City of Light pre-demonstration and that it would be done in increments. What does this mean and how am I to prepare?"

A: "As the days pass the Genii will feel a strong pull to enter the City Gates just to take a peek, so to speak. The vision of this will be seen and a sensing of "AH' and delight will be emotionally sensed. This would be from the imprint of the open passageway to the entrance.

"This will eventually make you want to see more, for the feeling and the remembrance will be of a high value, and that alone will be the incentive to want to continue to see more. This will be a pleasant offering, and the majesty of it will remain as an imprint never to be forgotten. It will seem as natural as the sun rising on a new day.

"When your system gets used to the imprint you will then be guided to take the next step, stepping farther into the City itself. The imprint will make a total believer of you, and thus a spokesperson. In your world there will be no doubt that what is to come about really exists."

Q: "Will I be able to still live and exist in this world?"

A: "Yes, but on a higher vibration, due to the electrical impulses you experience during these sessions. They will seem beyond a dream, beyond a wish, beyond imagination. This adventure is majestic.

"You have requested entrance, and that now is being put into place for your internal City visit. Expect to meet entities of various forms and hues, as all are part and parcel of what is bringing forth this prototype of Heaven on Earth called the City of Light."

Q: "What would I need to know about my preparation and how do I, in a higher state, stay functioning in my daily world?"

A: "This would sound like moving out of your current world, but on the contrary, the vibration system will be enhanced, so in the frequencies in the vortexes, you will become more balanced as you get equalized with the vortexes - not separate."

Q: "Traveling with the City data, how does this work?"

A: "Travel will become more important, and having a co-partner would be an advantage, if they too are frequency acceptors ready to assist and be part of this movement to spread the word.

"Again it is to be remembered that you and the Charles are both connected on the same Light strand, and this connection with people outside you can harvest a miracle of advantages, which include financial as well.

"This is not to say that the way of Light cannot bring forth the desired harvest from other areas, but as you would say, 'This is hot right now'. We say it will remain that way.

"What is being said here is to travel to various guided locations of interest and it will touch down in places where people will begin to take notice and pay attention to this demonstration of 'City prototype' value. Just permit the days to ascend on each other, but be open to the new, for it is right here and right now.

"It is advised also that the Charles be open to his guidance in regard to what is being said here, for the mental impact of what he is into here could descend on him at any moment.

"His focus is on one area, education, and the producing of it globally; however his main function is now being advised of the City entrance, and that it would be wise counsel to begin to take a stronger look at what he is being handed by God, and guided by the Christ he adores.

"These are not just daydreams of future happenings. You both are on the cutting edge of the happening. Request guidance constantly on this area, for the correct people need to be advised of the contents of what is being said here, and travelling together is certainly indicated to render vocal service to others in person as well as in other ways.

"The time is apparent and you are destined to be examples of what it is to be enlightened in human form by God."

Genii Experiences the City of Light – Vision Visit 1

Entering the South Gate

Q: City VISION Guidance?

Genii's Guide: "As the time collapses, the Genii will relate more and more into the visions of the City interior. It will become more like a dream, yet as visits increase, very visible so much so that you will begin to feel at home rather than a visitor.

"It will seem like you have been whisked away into another reality and of course that is the reality of this situation of advanced technology that is so real that no one will ever be able to say to you ever that it does not exist!

"The elevation of your consciousness will make this possible. You have been recently to the South Gate and experienced the grandeur and luxury of its design. The gold design around the rim of the horseshoe entrance is indeed what you would call pure gold, however it is more, as it is embellished in Light fragments not found on your planet.

"Its thickness which you estimate as about 3-4 inches, holds within its interior mixture, the magnet of Light which has the ability to make anyone about to enter, feel very welcome, with no feeling of fear. One will feel a wanting to enter on one's knees in adoration for the one God, who put up this adoration welcome sign.

"Each of the 4 Gates is similar. The entrance marks the beginning, and as you continue your journey to the interior, you will be amazed at the magnificence of what you will behold; for it is God-blessed and God demands the best and...gets it."

(Genii vision note) As I peeked through the Gate all I could see was lush greenery and sensed a fragrance, but could not identify the fragrance which was very pleasant and light and made me feel I wanted to smell more. Kind of like the cartoons of a freshly baked pie with streams of drawn fragrance drifting as a come-to-me invitation.

Genii's Guide: "For this moment, just enjoy that thought for there is quite an adventure ahead beyond your current belief systems. God beholds beauty untold as yet, and welcomes the Genii whose heart has been here for lo these many years."

"So Light it be! We bid you the Light of the eternal day in peace and love."

Part # 2 Second Visit – The Energy Park

The first thing I saw as I passed through the same Gate as before, straight ahead was a park-like setting. There were resting places I assumed were benches, yet they looked different. They seemed to be alive with a relaxing vibratory effect of some sort within them. There was a walkway that also seemed to vibrate, making my feet feel very comfortable and walking was quite enjoyable.

The grass was shades of green from dark to light making a wavy kind of pattern on the ground that seemed to rest my eyes. There were flowers but none I could identify. The colors were exquisite and the fragrances blended into an aroma that could be intoxicating in their relaxing effect.

The trees also had blossoms of some unknown kind and darting within the branches were very colorful tiny little birds, also indefinable. They did not chirp but had a humming sound that made me feel that nothing else mattered. I was at home. It looked like a very large park and I could see a small waterfall nearby that had pink water. Maybe it had a light under it.

There was an unseen frequency felt as soon as I entered, which quite balanced my nervous system. I just wandered alone for a bit. Over-hanging trees like willows covered whatever was beyond it.

I had a sudden sensing that a City Guide would soon join me, "Is this correct?"

Genii's Guide (voice): "The Genii will indeed be introduced to an exceptional scientific Guide who will escort you through the City of Light, to the point that you become so attuned that it will be seen and felt as the City of Love.

"You are welcomed into the interior not as a visitor, but as a friend of the Light Beings who reside here that are part of making this City the Light that it is. Welcome...enjoy your Vision."

"We bid you the Light of the Eternal day in peace and in love...Now!"

Part # 3 Third Visit – Meeting with My City Guide

As I stepped closer to the beautiful fragrant trees before me that blocked my view, I found I didn't have to move an inch, for stepping through them like a performer moving gracefully onto a stage, stepped a Light in human form.

He was indeed a vision. A cross between Sean Connery and someone not of this local world like Star Wars Obi-Wan and that sensing was prevalent and whatever it was, it served him well.

"Be not afraid" was his opening introduction as he held out his hand in friendship smiling as he took mine. As he did, a jolt of energy went through me like an electric shot of something feeling really good.

"I am pleased to meet you," I stammered slightly. He laughed as his short silver beard glistened in the light.

"Would it not be a good idea for you, since this City of Light is part of your destiny, to join me in a tour? I can assure you that it will be tantalizing and refreshingly informative and a not to forget - healing."

"Of course, thanks. As a beginning, what would I call you? What is your name, I mean?"

"You may refer to me as La-Luke, destiny provider of City information, visions and delightful experiences" and as he smiled, "I promise you that I will take very good care of you."

With that he parted the leafy trees and I stepped through. I could hardly believe what I was seeing and feeling. It was awesome, beautiful and even the air tasted good.

My thoughts were: indeed, like La-Luke promised, it looks like I am being delightfully taken care of. Wow! I think I will really enjoy being this girl.

Thanks God for this magnificent visit!

City Interior Visit: The Reflection of a New Beginning

And the gates of inner-spection opened once more for the Genii to be guided in vision. Meeting with my City Guide La-Luke, I saw in front of us a short stoned path camouflaged by flowing type willow trees with tiny pink flowers. The fragrance was intoxicating.

They hung low and as we moved them aside like curtains on a stage, we found ourselves facing unusual Star Trek buildings of several designs all white and sparkly. They surrounded a fountain that poured something that released bubbles.

It was then that I noticed a lady-like entity who stood beside it and she smiled at us as we moved near her. She didn't say anything but motioned me to look into this bubbly pool. Now what could this be, another healing pool?

"Of course" came an unseen voice. I looked over the edge and the reflection I saw was one of youthful delight. All else had disappeared and I saw a newborn baby…was this me?

"In a way" said my Guide. This is the human reflection of the new you being newly born. When one looks into this pool (which is a mirror of past, present, and now future) you can see where you have been and are now re-born into the visual realization of that.

"Someone else would see a teen, someone else, an aged person. It is how you see yourself in this mirror of life. You have been on the spiritual path for a while, and are ready to be new born and so, the reflection equals that image. Each previous step you have taken in life has dropped off like a cloak of darkness and you began to get lighter as you moved through various trials and tribulations.

"You might call it a makeover in your current vocabulary. In your world, validation is needed to constantly reinforce your spiritual path. In this world there is much validation of turmoil and change. So this new baby is the new you, who looks upon this world through new eyes ready to accept her place."

I looked again into this pool of reflection and I smiled - for the baby I saw was blowing bubbles that floated into the clear air.

"How would this pool heal someone?" I asked

"This is a reflection of where someone is now. It tells a vision story. Some people have a way to go, for some see themselves as various mental stages from young to old.

"No matter what they may think topside so to speak, subconsciously is what comes to the surface and they can see it. One cannot change what they do not recognize of themselves, so this reflective mirror does that for them - a road map, if you will, on the way to Illumination.

"Now that you have seen the re-born, you can know that the past concerns and worries have no place - you are re-born and know not of such things."

"How do I explain this on my City tour to others?"

Smiling my Guide said, "The fun of the City of Light is that it in-lightens at special locations in the City interior. This would be a checkpoint if you will, of validation. Another checkpoint would have your thoughts manifest, and seeing your thoughts could make for a change. For as on a computer, you can see what you are thinking at any given moment of time. When some thoughts are repeated over and over, they can look very tiresome and so they are released. Then that is that!

"The checkpoints throughout the City give notice of who and where you are on any given moment. Sometimes others can see them too, as if they were flashed on a large enough screen for all to see. What would you do to change your thinking? Elevation of thoughts induces clearer thinking."

And with this he led me back to the Gate. I thanked him and looking up I saw a sign that said, "You are welcome."

This City of Light is not only healing, but magic as well...

We are to be pleasantly blessed.

Hmmm ...newborn in Light... how God is this!

City of Light Tour – The Fountain of Light

Q: Please describe the City Fountain in the center of the City grounds and its properties.

"First of all there is one. It stands approximately 15 feet high from the base which itself is on a pedestal of approximately 3 feet high.

"This magnificent structure has a velocity of frequencies that permit the fountain to have healing powers (to a certain extent) and attract those who are near the base, uplifting their mental state (which in itself lifts the physical systems.)

"The Light that is emitted from it is controlled by the underground surveillance technicians who have themselves had such a raising of consciousness that is beyond your local thinking. (It is known to the Genii that a complete underground City itself lies beneath the property). The base of the fountain carries the electrical circuitry that promotes the uplifting properties that affect all who are near.

"The base or the bowl of the Fountain can be seen as large flower petals. Each one emanates colored lights like rolling waves of prismatic rainbows. There are four large petals facing the four cardinal points north, south, east and west. It is a Light Modular in action.

"From the center like the pistils of a flower, Light extends 15 more feet into the air spilling down on those who may be seated or standing nearby.

"The moods and attitudes then would change for the better as the frequencies connect with each person's electrical system. Indeed this Fountain is to be enjoyed in awe and happiness as they experience it in its intensity.

"This then is just the beginning point of your current mental projection into the City of Light. Those involved in this outer process now being spoken of are admonished not to share this information with others not involved in this process. It is to remain only in your mind for viewing with your Guide.

"Daily devotional work with the tonal–vision will not only bring it into your view mentally, but through this singular process can bring it into view for the masses.

"You are encouraged to direct your viewing daily within yourself and feel what this Fountain of Light can really do for yourself while mentally in its proximity.

"You with the others involved have the combined power to bring forth the City into manifestation.

"This then is the beginning of the beginning. It is sacred and modern beyond belief. It is scientifically modern beyond belief.

"It is now a part of your life's path should you chose to accept this blessed offering to assist in the process."

"Welcome to the City of Light....

First in your mind,

Then in your heart,

Then on the planet for all to see."

"God is, I am, The City and I are one! So Light it Be!"

Trans-audio medium Genii Townsend

Filling in the Blanks

I felt this morning to re-enter the City of Light for my next vision visit.... As I re-entered through what seemed to be the same Gate I did before, I saw several entities smiling and pointing me to a path different than the one I previously walked.

Ahead I saw my City Guide La-Luke, who smiled as I neared him. He beckoned me to sit with him on an interesting type of bench that had the ability to massage the body as well. There were lots of flowers and I heard birds chirping someplace unseen. It was like being in a glass bubble.

It was all quite pleasant and comfortable. His energy field was very relaxing and loving. I wanted to ask him some questions.

G: "Tell me more about this City of Healing Light."

He smiled and replied, "Indeed, this place of Holy Healing is designed to 're-create' the person who needs the healing. In recreating, this means the cells and atoms of that person's make-up are reproduced new, and thus change the whole body structure including the mental, which is the beginning intruder anyway.

"This of course is done with Light frequencies, most of which are not known in your fields of medicine in your world. I have shown you so far, examples of the healing delight people will find here. There will be no advertising needed as such you have today, as each person will be a walking healthy example of what is being said here.

"Many doctors and scientists will arrive to learn and apply this very advanced way of healing yet unknown, much less tested. It would be as you might call 'space technology' for that is what it is. These days you are still using ideas and methods like a covered wagon when space is the perimeter to be discovered.

"Those who arrive first will learn total Light healing with no surgery to cut the electrical lines within the body. All these previous instruments of cutting and with needles are barbaric at this point of advancement and will be eliminated, thus putting the patient in a calm state instead of stress where drugs are needed. New Light scans will tell all."

"What is being used now will be obsolete and one will look back at it like an old wagon train crossing the desert. Light changes will take place daily."

G: "What will be the response of the people when the City of Light appears?"

L: "Varied, everything from pre-programmed fear to adoration that the Christ has reappeared and there is peace on Earth. We have been saved. Praise God!

"The planet's governments will be highly suspicious after being programmed to immediately interfere with anything suspicious and unusual and this certainly is that, for it cannot be denied. It is all plain to see."

G: "How can I be of service?"

57

L: "Actually you already are and are being programmed even further to be a spokes-person among many who sense something is forming or coming but may not know what yet. Some who do, do not speak of it yet, lest the negativity enter and disturb."

G: "Will babies be born in the City and how would that affect their life?"

L: "To answer the first part, yes they will be and most mothers would be honored to have such an experience of her child being born in Light, as Light, and through Light, which would of course permit them to be walking, talking, living Light person-ages that will change what would need changing.

"You must realize that your world is in such an upheaval of change right now in preparation of this event that it will no longer be what it has been. The old world you have and are used to will have been replaced and no interest in history would take its place and no old concepts will hold the past in place.

"What you Genii are experiencing right now is a very lesser degree of upheaval as we set your course as a leader of the new era in process. The audio tapes you hold contain some advanced technology and the beginning formation of the City plans are the basic history of the development of the City in sound instructions."

"What is now being shown you here begins to fill in the blanks, the empty spaces, with added data all for the healing comfort of those who seek it. And many will find it.

"You have noticed that many people are leaving your planet through your death process as every being is being amped up and it can get very strong if one is unwilling to change with it.

"Now then, (and he stood up) we shall continue our tour on your next visit. For now feel the vibration level here and take that back with you, for you will be called on soon again to reveal the City of Light.

"Blessings Dear One... I love you."

And with that in a blaze of Light he was gone, leaving me with the awe of this whole experience, a Holy one to be sure. I am blessed that each visit gives me one more clue of what is to come about...ready or not.

So Light it be!

UFO Visitors

November 12, 2007

Q: "I watched Larry King's show the other day when I heard that today in Washington D.C. a meeting is to be held there with people from 8 different countries, confirming that they have witnessed UFO's and that finally attention is to be given it. What can be told me of this meeting?"

A: "The Genii senses joyfully that this news is a blessing and long past due. Those who begin to speak out will attract more that is yet hidden by those who have seen but are afraid to speak out.

"Now the energy intrudes into the darkness of minds. Those of us who venture into your dimension give just enough credence of appearance and delight in the controversy that is to take place.

"As each one speaks, it lays the groundwork for others to join in and say, 'yes, there are visitors of some kind from other places, and we on planet Earth are not alone but, may be in the hearts of supporting friends.'

"THERE IS NOTHING TO TAKE OVER HERE. The films with a few exceptions, put a sad light on what actually is a support and not a take-over situation of destruction. You do that very well yourselves. This comes from minds that hold fear as a 'God other' and out of mental control in that position. Such nonsense!

"Benevolent beings of Light Intelligence have been supporting for eons of time, and the destruction of your planet now takes the minds to finally say 'It is time to look at what we have done.'

"Nature in revolt now steps up to also get attention, for this blessed planet deserves to join others as the cosmos of intelligence serves as a teacher. So we watch and see what takes place on the government ground as people of note speak out their views. . . we shall see.

"All is in pre-preparation of the City of Light to manifest and we are pleased to be contributors of advanced thinking. Pay attention, there is more coming and Peace will reign one way or another."

Planet Peace Time Line

January 1, 2008

Q: "As the New Year has arrived in a world of no time, and the City of Light moves closer to demonstration, what can be told of it and any part that I am to be supportive of?"

A: "The Genii remembers most of the City design and the layout described by Dr. B. This is just a beginning indicator of what is to come about (the first step, so to speak). There is much more attached now to the original, and you can find all the unprinted clues as you venture back into the inner visions given you.

"The time/date of the City appearance has always been 'under wraps' for the unknown is better kept that way for now. However, since the Genii has asked, it can be said that in the years coming forth and the changes now in process pulls the City energy also forward into being. It has been said over and over, 2012.

"This is incorrect in that by that time corrections in process now are seen to be completed and the manifestation has already been activated and recognized as such. That the masses from certain religions had declared, 'The second coming has arrived! The Messiah has come back, praise God!' For the Genii to enter the City for the healing data already given, these mental visions should continue on a regular basis, not only for information, but for imprinting it within you.

"Recognize your position here with the City of Light and accept as such. This is important so as you speak of this Holy event you can come from total knowingness and power.

"The City of Light, as you know, is total in its healing properties and facilities to accomplish the same on the Earth ground in this dimension fed through alternative universes. All will work to bring forth what is unseen at the moment. One does not see a flower until it appears above ground. We have the same type of idea here. Then comes the AHHHH!

"The Light Technicians have the mental ability to heal on the spot, so to speak, (remind you of a Master who walked your Earth?). In the Light Pods in the City Modules they are able to help the patients in feeling comfortable enough to accept the healing Lights of various kinds, and heal they do!

"Remember, people reject to various degrees what they do not understand, especially with the huge, massive demonstration never before ever seen in history, now standing in front of them not to be hidden. So before the City appears, mental changes must take place, and are, even as this is being recorded.

"The Genii is well aware of releasing, as she has been so-called 'put through the ringer' lately, and keeping balanced through all the past fears, etc., coming topside to be released as the nothing that they are, has been a journey of courage. This is to be commended.

"This year will reveal the Power of the Jedi within you, as you were given a sample of recently, given at your favorite playground with the Charles who supported your strange behavior. This imprinting was deliberately given you so you could sense what it is to be in 'Total Power' and could pull it back in mind again when needed as old fears try to re-enter and no space is available. This is energy in action.

"So as you and the Charles again join forces to begin a new year of advancement, just remember to return to the City Envisions for more Light Imprinting and also when on the human plane, where you have just decreed that this 2008 will be a year of FUN, which everyone could use more of, all year long."

So Light it be.

The Playing Field

January 2, 2008

Having taken the first vision visits into the City interior, I was advised to return, and I did just that … Traveling clockwise with my Guide La-Luke, we followed a wide path where yet another park-like area was noted. This one was different because it had a shimmer and children "see-through" entities were playing by throwing small balls of Light and laughing, as the balls disappeared in a layer of some kind of mist hanging low overhead. The balls were made from this shimmering mist. What was going on?

My Guide smiled and said that the shimmering mist was just another type of Light. That was why the children were laughing, for it made them feel so good that they could do nothing else but to watch the Lightballs disappear like melted snowballs, which made it all the funnier.

He requested I try one.

I reached up into this lower layer of strange mist and grabbed a handful of Light stuff. It felt of no weight, just like nothing, but my hands were guided to make a ball, so I did. It was like making something out of nothing, which I guess we do when we create from an unseen thought into a full-fledged creation of some sort. However, it was very strange!

I threw it at La-Luke but it disappeared into the mist again before it got to him. I asked him if this had to do with healing?

He reported, "Of course! The Fun Balls of Misty Light make those playing feel good, and when you feel good, the cells in the body/mind connection heal … simple analogy!"

And with that he nudged me to move with him on our continued path in the City of Light.

Note: What fun to have fun with the unexpected! This is quite a place, where even fun heals. We all knew that, didn't we - or did we?

A New World Now in Progress

January 4, 2008

"We shall begin again . . ."

"Humanity in its isolation upon this planet at this point, is not fit to interact with the Intelligence of older galaxies throughout the cosmos! We the intelligences are assisting to change this picture even as we speak in this moment.

"This information has been said before and it is being brought back into your minds due to the very slow process of your past teachings which for the most part are incorrect and keep you locked up in misinformation thus slowing your personal progress.

"You who are listening to this message have come a ways down the path (so to speak). You have been not only introduced to the sacred information hidden in The Four Keys but have also gone through the power of the Lights in a process called 'linkage'.

"This as you know was not just a thing one would do for amusement but one of holy and sacred connection with God. You were chosen!

"Why? Why would one be chosen? An ego aggrandizement perhaps? No! A way of saying I am more than someone else? No! A mark of achievement, Yes.

"You were chosen because you chose to be chosen and the Father/Mother God said yes.

"So then, you have been given a gift is this not so? What have you done with that gift of advancement? Have you tucked it away with other precious items in your possession keeping it for some future time or have you taken this gift and used it wisely?

"Have you refreshed your memory on the Keys as to their purpose? Have you understood their purpose? If not have you asked for help with an inner guide or outer guide?

"Have you taken the time to give your personal guiding Intelligence a call asking questions? Have you received a reply? If you feel not, why not? Channeling is part of your gift given upon your 'linking' day.

"It is time Dear Ones, to take a good look at just what you have done with the Keys of Light so far. By this time, most of you should be able to Tone on the wind your praises to God.

"You should be demonstrating before you even ask. You should be in such close contact with your Guide and Gatekeeper you all breathe at the same time for they are not separate from you.

"You should have pulled yourself up from being a low esteem victim of past events into the Greatness the Father/Mother Godhead knows you to be. . . that which you really are.

"You are seeking the 'real' you. Not the personality that hears this. You are multifaceted. God! How many more ways can this be imprinted in your mind?

"Can this God gift be taken away? Does God take away gifts not revered and tended?

"God does not take away gifts; the student quietly gives it back when not used as it was designed to be used.

"What then is being said here? There is an old saying on your planet ...'use it or lose it'.

"Now in the time of your new year so-called, it is important that you take a good look at what has been given from the Unseen, your reason for being on this planet at this time in your history has also been delivered, but has yet to come into view. This is where your devotion to God comes into play.

"You have been advised of the City of Light that has descended on your planet. A healing place of such beauty and scientific advancement that it would take your breath up in awe to see it in all its splendor. It has within the grounds certain aspects that would help bring it into your seeing when you use what has been given to you.

"So then, you are all being admonished to separately, daily, during your devotion to God work, to begin to bring that portion of The City into your mind for viewing and power."

"You must have a sincere love to help bring this massive healing energy into the World of Illusion and requires your time and your tones daily, thus you become an important part of the demonstration.

"So, this being said, we leave you to your decisions and bid you the LIGHT of the Eternal Day in peace and in love."

So Light it Be........

The Be-ing Building

January 11, 2008

As before, once again I found myself at the Gate, but I knew not which one. It seemed to be the only one in sight, anyway. As I entered the scene, crowds of smiling people were also entering. This new sight challenged any belief system that something like this could really take place right before their eyes. I entered with the rest of the crowd.

The Park was filled with happy faces in awe of this exposure. This was obviously not a private vision tour for me, at least at that moment. People moved in streams going here and there to explore this not-man-made extravaganza. I just milled around watching what was taking place, mostly in disbelief.

As I followed a path veering off to the left, there was seen yet another building in the distance. At this point I continued to follow. No Guide yet was seen. Many people entered the grounds but no one was close to me as I was a distance ahead. The building was a distance from the Gate. I approached this building.

Comment: These buildings all seemed to be white and gold so far.

It was then that my Guide La-Luke appeared. He led me inside. Melodious sounds of an unknown origin sprang out from unknown locations. The entryway had exploded into a sound chamber of sensing that hit my heart and emotions, so much so I was in bliss.

G: "What is this place?" I asked my Guide.

"How do you feel?" he replied.

"I just do not have words to describe it. I am in such a state of 'nothing matters, this is all there is'. Have I come to Heaven?"

He laughed. "Well, not quite. You are still alive. This is a healing sound building. You know when you feel a time-out is needed, or as you say, stop the world I want to get off? Well, this is that place where the outside world stops and you are just, as you say, 'be-ing.'

"You might call it the Be-ing Building. This is more of a pass-through place so that for a short period of time you have all the outer ingredients to entice you to just BE.

"With nothing to prepare beforehand, we just walk in and you get the feeling of be-ing. . . gentle, loving and restful, which tunes up the electrical system so much that you can face the outside world more easily just by having felt what it is like to just BE. As you are human beings, you need to know what it is to just BE. So you entice that feeling when the outside world gets a bit heavier. How do you feel now?"

G: "I feel wonderful, balanced and relaxed."

L: "Good. Then we have come to the end of this visit. Mission accomplished. Take this be-ing feeling back into your world and thus imprint others who enter your electrical space for a moment."

We walked out and back through the crowds of people, aah-ing and ooh-ing to the Gate of Light. I waved thanks to my Guide, and I quickly found myself back home in Sedona feeling pretty good!

Thanks, God, for the visit to the Be-ing Building. It was great to BE There!

So Light It Be.

UFOs and The City of Light

April 22, 2008

Q: "Once more the television is reporting UFO light sightings over Phoenix, AZ, (that are now becoming famous). What can be said of this phenomenon, and does it have anything to do with the City of Light coming forth?"

A: "Yes, absolutely! These Lightships are shown periodically, only to show that there is something beyond this planet that is alive and has intelligence far beyond what appears here as human, thus giving the searching minds something to ponder on besides themselves, which it normally has to do to survive.

"The Lights of the so-called UFOs are just that, Lights of UFOs bringing forth those of higher intelligence supporting the manifestations coming forth as the City of Light. Were you shown the gold ships on the roofs of buildings in the interior of the City visit? Of course. When stepping into one on the tops of the buildings called the Breath-atrium did you not observe many more like them? Of course.

"The human factor of this planet is still in the dinosaur stage of development, and some believe war is the answer ... please! Although some stages of learning are now being propelled swiftly, it has been and is slow, and the planet suffers as a result under ignorant thinking. Those who come bring not only Intelligence but energy vibrations that are propelling the healing of this planet; which for you humans has to come from the mind and still too many are in an ego-ignorant stage. While many teachers are recognizing changes are important they, too, may need some adjustments into higher thinking.

"As the space vehicles show themselves periodically in the heavens, this is preparation, so to speak. Does the Genii have intelligence teachers of high space considered E.T.s? Of course! Do the Sedona/Phoenix and surrounding areas have extraordinary energy pulls due to the vortexes and underground gridlines of Light? Of course.

"'Yes' is the answer to your question, and this has been going on for some time, even though the government would pooh-pooh this idea less they lose control. Each sighting has to be recorded and seeing is believing.

"Enjoy the interest, for the interest keeps minds moving in that direction. For the pronouncement of the City of Light now hooked into The Light Center coming forth, will report many such informational appearances which makes itself more valuable day by day. Planet Earth will see peace!

"Planet Earth will know peace as it has never known before except before man entered the picture. All will be corrected and the war lords will war no more. This is a promise!"

So Light it be!

Visit to the City of Light Birth-aterium

May 16, 2008

G: "I sense a return to the City of Light again. What am I to see?" and with this I saw the following impression......

The beauty of the interior brought my breath to a momentary halt, as we would say, "breath-taking." But it was even beyond that for the breath of what we may call God did emanate here. It was as simple as that, yet mind-changing in its value.

I may never be the same again in my daily world. I saw a path of steps that seemed lit and made a tinkling sound/feeling as I stepped on them one at a time. My City Guide La-Luke smiled and led me on the "Toning Stones."

We walked across a small bridge where tiny fish that looked like dolphins leapt out and then ducked under in play. I was busy enjoying them; he motioned me to look up and in doing that, I saw a large building that was nearly circular in design, with a door you could (it seemed) melt through. And we did. It was kind of like Jell-O with no flavor. What? Oh well. This was really getting sci-fi.

The interior was like a very big center hotel lobby with plants and flowers and water falling into various pools, where swans swam and the whole area was lit from the skylight. There were women dressed in sheer pastel rainbow colors in attendance who smiled at us. 'What was not to smile about here? Wondering what this was and where we were going, I suddenly asked La-Luke where we were.

L: "We are in the Birth-aterium." he replied.

G: "Is this like the Breath-aterium?"

L: "Not quite, but breathing is important," he smiled. "This is where new Earthlings are born."

G: "Now I am really getting interested."

L: "They are toned and breathed into being. Come I will show you."

We walked into a corridor leading away from this beautiful center so clean and filled with the aroma of spring flowers in bloom. Then we took a slight turn and up a few steps to a viewing center to look down into the 'Birthing Pod' as it was referred to. Three ladies were in a natural birthing process. Like in the Light Modules they lay on floatation beds. The Pod Light was mesmerizing in its soft brilliance. It was quickly seen that other than the birthing mother, there were women attendants dressed in white, and this soft Light which seemed to come from the women's auras; nothing else was seen.

There was no hospital paraphernalia anywhere and this was a peaceful place of total joy. No screaming, orders to "push;" no pushing, no profanity or any of the hard labor we go through. It was delightfully amazing and what a surprise to witness this new beginning. The babies were born in Light and love and just floated out into this world laughing and gurgling. The mothers were having a "birthing party" - imagine that! The babies were born already happy to be here and take their first breath.

As each baby was delivered, a different sound was heard. Each one had their own tone. I watched the colored auras around the attendants change as each baby arrived. This indeed was the way babies should be able to come into the world - easily and effortlessly and with no physical problems. Just pure and happy to be here. This must be the way we are supposed to be born! Praise God...we need this City of Light!

My Guide told me that pre-breathing exercises are addressed before they enter here and in the birth canal, the baby picks up this breath frequency, and the indwelling tone becomes the harmony that resides within each child upon birth.

This is the best way of giving birth to children who will make up our new world. As more Light Cities appear, the pre-mothers will have new and different things to do that will change their DNA. For the fetuses that are the children of the future, are truly little Light Beings in every sense of the word.

G: "This is truly God in Light Healing."

L: "Interesting, with this way of birthing there is no healing to be done. This is where your physicians will be able to learn new and sensible ways to remove old, unreliable guesswork and the doctors will not have to search for answers. They will just inwardly know, and will be correct"

"Many doctors and scientists will come for advanced Light Teaching such as maybe your friend Dr. Miller, and be invited to be one of those who will want to know more of the Light Techniques used here...So now we leave."

He turned around as I took one more glance and enjoyed the feeling of this birthing place of love and Light that beckons the new babies to be born...loved and free!

So Light it Be!

The Empowerment Emporium

June 22, 2008

Once again having been guided to re-enter through inner vision, I passed through the south Gate, thus meeting my City Guide La-Luke. He smiled as he took my hand and we walked forward. As I glanced at the Gate Towers all shiny and beautiful, I wondered at the holy majesty of these enormous structures that loomed so huge above me giving off a feeling of such peace as I have never experienced.

The outside world of turmoil had disappeared and as he led me forward I was in awe. One could not be otherwise. La-Luke walked me through the Park of the Relaxation Massage Benches to yet another path of exploration. We walked to a garden-type lattice-covered tunnel that smelled heavenly, with tiny white blossoms reaching out to give one much sensual pleasure.

As we came to the end, there in front of us was a white building with golden spires that were several stories high. At the doorway in welcome were two semi-transparent entities that I refer to as see-throughs. They assisted in this spirit/human experience.

Since this City is a Healing place, I expected to see more ways of healing the physical and mental bodies that we walk around in. Interestingly, as we stepped inside, the floor seemed to move gently like it had a life of its own.

G: "Where are we?"

L: "What see you?"

I looked around as faint colors floated in the air. Emotional balance was experienced even with the floor moving gently.

L: "This is an Emotional Balancing Building. You use the word "emporium". This could be considered an Emotional Emporium.

"As each person enters, the colors that that person needs are attached to them. This is to verify that his power centers are balanced.

"Remember what was told you eons ago of the colors/fragrances etc. of each of the body power centers? Here one can experience this. As the colors and Lights activate the body senses, they can give a major report of those functions, and they can be experienced in this City."

So here it was, gentle movement of the floor massaging the feet (for we had left our shoes outside) and beautiful colors floating around us inviting us to accept the balancing of these Power Center chakras. In this building, if anything was not functioning energy-wise it was put to rest, for in balancing, one felt euphoric and totally healthy.

I recognized from the first writings of the City by Dr. B., that there were very many regular places we, as humans, would recognize. This seemed to be covering all of that, like filling in the blanks that were unseen but were there all the time.

The balancing tunnel brought out the best of me, since I now felt balanced. I should add that inside screens of some sort showed which chakras needed the balancing and the colors changed to permit this to happen. So then it was a carousel of color that balanced the power centers, thus lifting the person's emotional and spiritual senses to a heightened degree and a feeling of happiness and joy was experienced, including being totally relaxed.

One could also take a mental area (of any different concern) to be washed out in this emotional emporium. Thus, be it love needed, that chakra now felt that. If fear release was desired, that, too, was completed. Any mental area could be taken care of, all the way back to the indoctrination beginning, with the rainbow Lights in this building.

If one had a worry when they went in and through this building, it was cleared out from the subconscious. It was amazing to see and feel the power centers being cleared.

The Emotional Empowerment Emporium was ready to be entered into, and after we exited the flower-covered bridge-like exterior, we entered into the Emporium itself where in a circular mall-type setting, there were many spaces or rooms which were available to give what that person now desired, with no reservations.

If one desired more love, they stepped inside and got it through feeling and heart. If one desired more fun, another room provided that, etc. Wishes were granted.

The emotional charges of unbalance were not sensed any longer. One would literally come out a happy, balanced person.

Well, Joy to the World! The Lord (City) has come. The unbalanced is Light-balanced and being lifted in emotion far enough to empower others.

Emporium Empowerment – How great is this?

Very!

Healing the Future through the City of Light

July 6, 2008

Q: Please expand on the healing properties of the City for families and children as well.

A: "Healing facilities of many kinds are available, and even the most wounded on any level can find a peaceful solution. Light Technicians working with those who seek healings, advice, and directions can find it there. Those professionals like the Kathie Brodie who works with the hypnotherapy area can import her knowledge but at a higher level due to the energy frequencies developed within the City structure.

"What you refer to as natural healing induced by the energy fields of the City, can bring immediate response to those seeking a healing. The Genii has visited several such places where this is apparent. Children can be a quick study for healing as they are more open to receive, but even the adults' pre-programming gets altered under such circumstances. Again, all is achieved by Light."

THE LIGHT MODULES

"The Genii observes the patients undergoing treatment of various Lights via the inner vision technique, for whatever the person's needs may be now. Upon arrival at this location, instead of going through much paperwork on the past ailments, etc. of that patient, they merely walk through an EPS (Electronic Portal Screen) entrance, where all the imprints of their DNA information, which are in a coded form, are instantly picked up by the Light Technician for healing action while the patient reclines on a floatation bed, held in an electromagnetic field. All this works well with the Light Body of the person seeking help.

"The Light Modules themselves are a scientific wonder to experience, from the unseen fragrances to the unusual musical healing tones and replenishing pleasant moments of relaxation. From simple opening releasing for introductory Light surgery (where no knives, etc. are used), to the birthing of a newborn in the Birth-aterium, this indeed is a healing location like no other ever witnessed and it is why the City of Light is so named."

Why a City?

"City represents a large location, a community of many people and the attraction of the healing facilities which make for an unusual place to get the mental, physical, emotional and spiritual together to be healed. All at the same time due to various unusual ways, while in this awesome beauty.

Even a bit of fun is enjoyed when in a golf course normality. Players play with gold balls, which is uplifting when this ball of energy always goes to the correct location. Expect some normal locations, but in the finery that only God could develop.

72

"Those who have negative feelings outside the Great Gates, those feelings will begin to dissipate as they enter the City inside. Expect the unexpected, to enjoy and heal no matter what the individual situation, for indeed this is a healing Heaven on Earth.

"So then continue to delight in what is to come about for mankind like no other, will see a magnificent City of Light and all it contains, as the greatest show on Earth settles down as a major cosmic event never experienced before."

So Light it Be!

The Star Wings of a Healing Building

July 8, 2008

Q: "And what would be my adventure tonight? Anyone want a conversation?"

A: "Yes, several are in attendance."

Q: "Okay. What shall we talk about?"

A: "That which is always interesting."

Q: "The City?"

A: "Of course. Permit you to travel again beyond the Gates and follow a new path that leads to yet another healing location."

I then found my vision self at a new location, looking at a huge building that had five star-shaped points. The building was silver and was reminiscent of a cosmic sci-fi type. Each point was a laboratory where different Light techniques were tested and finalized.

Q: "How many Light ways are there to heal with?"

A: "As many as the healings that are needed, for various people have on your planet mental imprints that suggest a healing is desired. Your hospitals and doctors' offices are overrun with appearances needing attention, so each of the Star Wings introduce the advancement and the best in cosmic technology beyond your current situations. Come, we take a peek into one."

We entered the building center filled with such fresh air as I have never experienced before, and not from air conditioners it seems. Each Star Wing protruded from this center point. We headed for one wing and passed through a DNA screen, like in the Light Modules but yet different. In doing so, Light Technicians can see in advance what may be a new malady appearing which will again be added into the advanced technology, thus stopping it before it has a chance to disrupt the Light Body functions of the person. Amazing! They were making something out of nothing.

What they were doing was unclear to me. All I could see was glowing particles and then I saw how they magically went together like pieces of a puzzle. The Light Technicians were like "see-throughs" to me, but I could see them clearly. If this is all E.T. stuff they are very welcome and desired by yours truly. No one there said anything, but I did catch a smile now and then.

"What is happening here?" I said, having a great time viewing the unknown. The answer is, "Magic in the making. You say you like magic? Well, dear student, this is it!" (At this point there was an interruption in the house and the vision stopped, but I was pleased to see this Star Trek way of bringing forth what is unknown ... yet with good times ahead.) **So Light It Be!**

The Deciding Place

I just could not resist the inner invitation to travel back into the City of Light interior this morning, so in my quiet time, I laid aside my usual meditation practices to watch whatever was to be presented, fully knowing I hadn't a clue what that would be. So with a sip of my morning tea, I went . . .

Closing my eyes but still being open to anything, I found myself again standing in front of one of the massive five-story tall great Gate Towers. It was so extremely beautiful it could, as we say, take your breath away. The scene was enhanced with the sun reflecting it in all directions.

I stood alone and could see a bit into the interior that I had visited before, the Park with the bench-type seating that massages your body, sending shivers of feel-good vibes. No sound was detected, but a few brightly-colored birds darted from branch to branch in willow-type trees, as flowers of all descriptions swayed merrily on their stems.

I sat there getting massaged, while seeing this amazing place. I wondered if I was like Dorothy and had made it over the rainbow.

As my eyes were closed on this Sunday morning blocking out the Sedona sunshine, I just let the scene develop into what it was supposed to contain. I felt a presence near me and my City Guide, La-Luke, was there smiling. "Relaxing, are you?" he inquired.

G: "Yes. I can do nothing else but wonder what I did to deserve being able to be in this holy place. Feeling good can take place so quickly here," I replied.

L: "The interior has many techniques of healing, for it is a facility designed to do that. If people on this planet were all healed, there would be no need for the City at all, but centuries of conflict have produced the need for a high volume of healings. Come, we will walk a bit and start at the beginning."

He took my hand and I felt a whole lot of energy connecting to me. We began to walk through what I sensed was some sort of Labyrinth of Light. We walked through the willow trees and past the Healing Fountain Pool that healed skin abrasions.

I remember putting a finger into the strange, thick water and sensing something was taking place, even though I had no problem with the finger. Just being near, my skin felt refreshed, and the dry skin cream I used in my Earth world was, indeed, not needed here.

Looking around the many buildings newly seen, led me to believe that this place was huge and it could go on for miles. I guessed that each one could do different kinds of healings. "Quite so," said my Guide, reading my thoughts telepathically.

L: "In order to heal the human body through the mental path of human thought, that human in his mental capacity, has to believe that it is fact, not fiction, because the belief system is connected to the emotional tract. The building they are entering is, indeed, the one that can cure what ails them. Know that if you humans go into that place, you are assured that you will be healed of ...whatever is important.

"Many buildings are designed to serve one area of healing only. Within the healing properties of this or that building comes the Advanced Light Technology, far beyond what is reached at this point in your medical advancement, as good as it is learning to be. It just was taking so long to bring it all forth that it was decided to bring forth the City to be the prototype of advancement. This you already have been advised, so now we shall enter the building on your right."

This building was white, sort of round with spirals like a unicorn horn heading skyward. White and gold seem to be the chosen colors of the buildings so far.

"This building is THE DECIDING PLACE, the beginning location of service where one decides what ailment needs attention that would satisfy their mind. Be it mental, spiritual, emotional or whatever, all are attached to the physical body temple. In this place the discernment of the person decides what should be taken care of."

The inside of the building was like several others, with a center circular lobby-type setting where, again, the beauty of a gently flowing pool relaxed me totally. Looking around, I saw several horseshoe-shaped openings leading to corridors with windowed rooms that had no one inside, just Lights. One room had pink Lights, another blue, etc. The colors varied from darker to almost invisible Lightness.

G: "What is this?" I asked.

L: "Each room varies due to the person inside. As the colors emanate, the one that is applied is not only their favorite color but one that is compatible with their Light Body. Here is where the decisions are made to continue the process of total healing. It is high technology, but also what you can simply understand at your level of understanding. So then this is the Building of Decision, and the healing has already begun. But now it is time to take you back to the Gate, for you have had enough Light levels now and you have to function in your physical world."

All this was breathtaking to be sure, to the point of almost nonbelief, but believe you me, I was/am truly a believer ... thanks, God, for the invitation. This was indeed God's favor activated.

So Light it be!

The Institute of Image Imprinting

August 4, 2008

Unexpectedly, I was delivered this envision information, viewing a large white circular-front building with a gold circular dome. Inside there were many, many rooms. Each room could hold only one to two persons, the viewer and an assistant Guide as desired. These were called Personal Viewing Rooms.

When a person comes in, they face a big screen of some sort. They now have, or previously had, made a decision on what their desire or wish is that they want to see completed. They can see what they are thinking about at any given split-second moment of time. The Guide is there to assist but not interfere with the decision-making.

The person sits down, closes their eyes, pulls up the desire mentally and then opens their eyes and watches the screen, for the desire is on the screen in full view. The mind in its fluctuation quickly can come and alter or switch that desire and that is also seen. The mind does much switching due to the right and left brain input.

In other words, they are watching their own thoughts right before them, and how the mind can make changes in a split-second, thus changing the beginning power level of that desire. Even the feelings are recorded, as well as colors, etc.

This can continue until the person has the original desire or wish implanted into the perfect image desired. When that is done, the perfection is established and the final demonstration is produced in their world.

Note: The Institute of Image Imprint is secure in the knowledge that this futuristic programming will be hailed as the best technology of the century, for the imagination of desire has laid the groundwork and achieved the results, thus making a dream/wish desired come true in their eyes.

A Universal Cosmic Community

August 22, 2008

This morning while doing some paperwork I began to feel quite sleepy. I tried to ignore it but it persisted and then hearing to "go to The City" several times from within I finally gave up; I stopped my world and sat down to envision.

I was invited to go back to the Gate complex, and did, as my usual Guide/entity La-Luke took me by the left hand. He seemed excited plus in a hurry, so we ran through the Gate and then the flowering Park I had been to before.

L: "It has been some time since you have returned."

G: "What's up?"

L: "New life is being put into place."

We ran for some time until I could see in the distance something shiny black with a silver dome. Pushing aside low hanging tree branches, we came to an opening.

There was a huge, and I mean huge, spaceship that was lowering a building into place that looked completed. It was like an elevator going down, lowering the building.

G: "Oh my God", was all I could mutter. "What is this?"

L: "This, Dear One, is why The City of Light does not need to be constructed on a site. This is done elsewhere and brought here ready for viewing."

G: "You mean all the buildings you have taken me to have been flown in? From where?"

L: "You would say outer space."

G: "Good Lord! Where in outer space?"

L: "Many planets and star clusters have wondrous healing methods of various kinds not seen or developed on your planet. I wanted you to see and know that The City has Light instrumentation from many parts of the cosmos. You could call it a cosmos community of Star Beings working together to bring harmony through Light frequencies to heal this beautiful planet."

G: "Imagine that! I am in awe at what I am seeing and hearing. It kind of puts a piece of The City puzzle in place for me. Thanks!"

Due to the energy around this action we did not go any nearer, but much activity was certainty apparent. The entities around it were too far distant to make out any distinctive descriptions.

G: "What is this building used for that is now being set in place?"

L: "This building will be occupied by Light Technicians. Healing of the lower extremities like hips, legs, feet, etc. are the prime considerations that humans have, from broken bones to those who have perhaps lost a leg or two."

G: "I can hardly wait to ask this question: Can an amputated leg be replaced?"

L: "Yes, to a certain extent. The leg may be gone but the Light imprint is still in place, and that is why people can still sense it is there once in a while. Or if desired, an advanced Light Body leg can be put in its place that is made of Light. This is a longer story, but dramatic miracles, as you would call it, can take place here for those who want it."

G: "Surely someone in that condition would want an improvement?"

L: "Not necessarily. Some may be quite comfortable, as the tender care from loved ones affords them loving attachment to remain the same."

G: "Would you believe that!"

As I continued to watch the action for an unknown length of time, the building had settled down.

L: "So then, moving entire buildings has been observed. Now departure time nears."

And almost immediately the spacecraft turned on and spun around, which sent frequency waves all the way to us who were just watching.

These crafts may be UFOs to many, but to me they are priceless vehicles that are here in service. And don't anyone ever try to convince me that they are here to conquer! P-L-E-A-S-E . . . to me they are welcome. And so desired ...very!

What a sight it was as it hovered, and then in a flash took off and was unseen. La-Luke took me back to the Gate entrance bright-eyed and in astonishment.

Imagine that!

So Light It Be.

More About a Universal Cosmic Community

August 23, 2008

G: "Tell me more please re: the spaceships of Light."

L: "The attributes of the space vehicles have much power, so much so, that they can deposit a building on your planet dimension, yet can fly from cosmic spaces light-years away. How is this done, you might ask?"

G: "Yes, please."

L: "In other dimensions it is almost weightless."

G: "What?"

L: "In your world a big plane can carry many passengers and have the power to do so. The maintenance of the spaceships has enormous value because they are able to transport a heavy object to its new location. This is why when you and the Dr. Bill thought that you were to build this City that you were told it was unnecessary.

"The cosmic community is also vast. The impression that some have that this is the one and only live-living-people planet in the universe is kindergarten thinking and we laugh as this is ludicrous!

"Now multitudes of star entities have united in support recognizing that the continuation of this beautiful planet should be helped in a different way so people could not only resonate to the Higher Creator, but make it one that could never be ignored.

"So The City of Light comes into form to do just that, to be a manifestation in its scope never before experienced and one that could bring people into a healing of themselves that does not take centuries to find the answers of just how to do that.

"This City happening has been in prophecy in many cultures, in many ways, just not perhaps in this form. Small imprints have been seen here and there in the minds that are open to receive, and most were dismissed as a figment of an imagination. Now, however, comes the crème de la crème, many buildings of healing have been exposed to you, with many more to follow.

"Stay in the Light, return and see advancement beyond your planet come into view. Then spread the word that God in Its glory has brought forth the highest, dedicated to teach that God really exists.

"For it will make believers, believe you me, as you would say, and no one will ever go back to the old worn-out ways of thinking how this all came about. The glow rays of prayers have brought forth the greatest show on Earth that has ever happened.

"Yes, and all will bow down that such a Creator exists. The Holy City of God then rests in the hands of the people. What will they do with it? Even that needs to be discussed. Time will tell...time will tell.

"So Dear One, go and seed the world with really new thought. Charles is your strong back-up in support as well as Kathie and others to come on board, as well as a few million space friends who bring forth this magnificent manifestation called The City of Light!"

So Light It Be...Now!

"You must find the place inside yourself where nothing is impossible."

"Commit yourself to the possibility that everything you see around you is far less real than God. You want to see the truth 'with all your heart, with all your soul, and with all your mind,' as Jesus says. This is actually a commitment to joy.'" Deepak Chopra, *Why Is God Laughing?: The Path to Joy and Spiritual Optimism*

Genii with the Empowerment Marionette she made of Deepak Chopra

http://www.sedonalightcenter.org/marionettes.htm

The Feminine Place

September 3, 2008

Normally I have gone on these visits on my own. This was the first visit that I have taken someone with me......... Kathie Brodie. As the inner vision began on this quiet morning in Sedona, I saw Kathie and me at the South Gate that I always passed through. It was clear that my friend Kathie was with me on my right side. She looked astonished at this Gate of entrance and beauty reaching five stories high encrusted with gems of very large size.

This visit was a kind of an experiment where someone entered with me and it seemed to be working. I hoped Kathie would enjoy what she did and said, as I had no concept of what would take place until it did. It was here we were met not by my usual Guide but by a beautiful female entity wearing sheers of rainbow colors. She beckoned us to follow her. I mentally asked the name of this Guide and she said Tula. As we entered, the Park was still there. Kathie headed for the massage bench I had spoken of before, and the look on her smiling face said it all. Tula moved ahead and we followed through the low-hanging willow trees. Tula then made a quick right turn and we entered yet another path of exploration.

Now where, I wondered? Kathie was busy taking in all the sights with relaxed pleasure. Ahead was a group of see-through entities, all female, who smiled at these new visitors as we passed.

We climbed a small hill-like bump on the path to see another white building already in place. It had a two-story high horseshoe shaped glass (I guess) window and doors so you could see through into the interior. Oh my, it was beautiful! Hmm. Obviously God only knows beautiful, I thought, because everything just is! We entered this massive gazebo-type circular place with a ceiling that held birdcages and long lines of flowers. There were flowers everywhere. I could hear water tricking down over rocks, some seen, some not. The sounds of harp tones filled the air, and I figured we had just entered Heaven somehow.

Tula: "This is a holy place of the feminine."

We both could feel that. If not, we really needed a healing of some sort. Tula bid us to sit on this padded couch-like "seat", or whatever they call them. "This is called THE FEMININE PLACE!," Tula said.

Kathie asked: "What happens here?"

T: "The female of your species forgets her inner beauty, and for the most part has to take on the masculine to survive. Here she has a chance of healing and reigns in her goddess image she was born with in the first place, no matter what the world thinks of her and she has accepted as truth, and thus has to subject herself to the truth. Here she is re-imprinted to remember what she came into the world to be . . . feminine."

Kathie remarked that what she felt in this place was the totality, that everything unlike her previous feeling, was changed. She thought it was great to feel so feminine and she felt balanced and it was strong within her. Tula smiled, nodded, and said, "One has only to come in, relax, enjoy the viewing and accept all the working if this place is to bring forth the feminine that you are and were encoded with when you arrived as female, and for the most part have set aside to care for your human world."

G: "This place puts you in sort of a meditative state and I feel different."

T: "How different?"

G: "Just like a new part of me has been added or something has cleared away." (Kathie nodded.) It is wonderful being a girl. Is this just because we are here?"

T: "Yes, this building is designed to heal from the inside out and to bring forth the original designed woman you are supposed to be, not as you do in your world in needing a make-over. You show that you feel."

K: "Will this knowing end when we leave?"

T: "No, this is why this is a healing place; that in which the self-worth is brought forth and the old programming is expelled. No need to keep going in for more treatments. It is done here just by being inside. Of course this change-over will need some new thinking as well, but why not feel beautiful all the time and not have to search for it on occasion?"

G: "Do the males have a place too?"

T: "Oh yes, the Masculine Place! The gender of the male is different so the frequencies inside are different to draw to itself what the masculine was born to be. Men have desires not spoken of to the female and need also to remember the sacred part of them, so the Masculine Place takes care of that on all levels.

"So then this is the discovery of the Feminine Place. Remember it when you are back in your world, and take these frequencies enjoyed here, the sights and the sounds with you."

Tula got up as harp music of some kind that seemed to verify what we were sensing, began to play and she led us back to the glass entrance. We almost floated, but since we were not used to floating yet, we walked.

It is hard to explain the changes that we felt we had dropped off like an outer garment, revealing the God Light we had brought forth. Kathie just glowed, as I have never seen her do before. A last glance around was an invitation to return again, for our true feminine was in place. The gardens, the birds and flowers on long vines did leave an impression, as did the water sounds.

Wow... Women will sure want to experience THE FEMININE PLACE. Imagine That!

Space Scientific Advancement

October 12, 2008

G: "Embellish please. What makes The City of Light light up?"

ATHERIAN: "Precisely that, electrical frequencies patterned throughout the inner workings of the electromagnetic field on which The City is dependent. This is no ordinary field, as you might surmise.

"This City information is so far advanced that we who speak on this have a difficult time of explanation in your language, which is always a problem, for the oratory access is unavailable in our sensing. You people need a new way of working with the intelligence of Guide speakers who bring forth this information. You are so far behind that new schooling should be put into action and thus all advanced information is understood immediately.

"Recognize this is a massive undertaking, scientific beyond scientific in your eyes. It was once said to the Genii that you have no idea of what it takes to bring in to your dimension this big a process, the likes of which have never been seen before, nor duplicated since. That in itself, of course, is a mystery.

"You have seen the huge computer types?"

G: "Yes"

A: "Then replicate that by thousands, all tuned into the one source of creation."

G: "Directly tuned in?"

A: "Yes, this master creation is seen as The City which was developed in another dimension so advanced that just the thought of it makes it feel almost non-existent in a reality that is much different than yours, yet explosively predominant, on certain levels. The processing of The City entrance into your world is like the Immaculate Conception, to say the least. Ancient teachings in your world say anything is possible for those who believe.

"As the belief systems change, and change they must, swinging away from the non-belief to the now-belief, The City comes faster into view. The Earth minds vacillate continually, as you know. One second is 'this,' and then 'that.' And this produces instability for perhaps a few seconds or longer, depending on the topic of conversation you have within the confines of your brain; a changing of the guard so to speak, a change-over from old, slow thinking to a speeding up.

"At this point you have many accredited teachers who share information to further your lives, and rightly so. However, recognize that behind their word, they too, need what is being said to you. They are teaching themselves constantly in learning.

"So, then, the demonstration of The City is run by electrical beings."

G: "Electrical beings?"

A: "Precisely so. You are an electrical being, are you not, different from those who are programmed to work the computer types in a high state of advanced awareness?"

G: "Like what is being told to me, that I should begin teaching in the Light Center through the Advanced Achievement Academy?"

A: "Quite so. It is a better start than what is being produced."

G: "Are these electric beings robots?"

A: "Not as you think of them currently. Again, your language has difficulties. We are not avoiding the answer. However, we invite you to just think of the energy coming through the High Towers and Gate Towers. These and many factors are connected to produce the underside and the compact elevation of the overhead intricacies you are being advised of. Eons of city programming keeps The City safe under any circumstances, as it freely gives of itself in the advanced healing ways now being addressed.

"This is just a brief indication of what your extreme scientists will find fascinating to see and learn. You have said that God has something wonderful coming into view, and so it is ... indeed!

"So for this brief moment in time, this short glimpse given you expands your awareness just a bit. Remain in your wonder of it all, for more inner visits will astonish you and you will be encouraged to share the information. Your Guide will meet you at the Gate and you can proceed to be yet more enlightened with what is coming about, and soon."

So Light It Be!

Introduction to the City's Embassy of Peace Headquarters

Within the confines of the City of Light there is a spectacular building known as the Embassy of Peace Headquarters. It is dressed in white with gold exteriors that amplify the opulence of the City itself. Inside and outside, this building is surrounded by fragrant flowers of all kinds producing gardens of beauty that touch the senses full force. Breathtaking? Yes! Dramatic? Yes! Informative? Absolutely!

This is where I was invited to come and ask any questions of highly evolved entities who sat in readiness to deliver answers regarding the City, and even the Universe if I so chose. How great is this?

To get there I was to meet with my Guide at one of the now familiar five-story high Gates leading into the City itself. To ride to this building we were carried on a wheel-less, driver-less trolley-type vehicle. On my first visit inside we were met by several unidentified leaders of some sort who either sat or stood (to indicate respect) behind a horseshoe-type advanced apparatus, perhaps what we would call a table, but it was much more.

As we entered, I was led to a throne-like chair which I could only guess was for dignitaries. It was very plush and comfortable. "Yummy," was my silent inner response. What was behind them is what made this place awesome, for it was like a hollowed out amphitheater of hundreds of entities faintly seen but present nevertheless, like a cosmic community. Awesome!

So then, the scene being set, I invite you to journey with me to listen in on the conversations that took place between those in command and the Earthling, me, collected throughout many continuing visits I have compiled them here for your pleasure.

WELCOME TO THE

EMBASSY OF PEACE HEADQUARTERS

IN THE CITY OF LIGHT!

SO LIGHT IT BE!

Genii's Visits to the Embassy of Peace Headquarters

The Invitation January 24, 2009

G: "In the sensing of yesterday's message that I am to speak to world leaders on The City, and now the Embassy of Peace, what would I say?"

ANSWER: "To re-enter The City and sit in Council with the Entities of Light would be advised. The major interests will become apparent, as the information given is subject to the questions to be asked."

G: "Who would be in this Council of Entities?"

ANSWER: "Those who could answer your questions."

G: "What if I don't know what questions to ask?"

ANSWER: "You will. The energy flowing like the intense feeling of yesterday will set the course."

G: "What am I to do to ready myself for such a vision meeting?"

ANSWER: "As usual."

G: "What does the Embassy of Peace, which seems to include the whole of the planet, intend to achieve?"

ANSWER: "Again, this session would bring to the forefront what is intended to be accomplished here."

G: "Are there more Embassies of Peace imprinted in the Cities' blueprints elsewhere on this planet?"

ANSWER: "One could say, as a starter, in the minds of those who cry for peace on Earth.

"This is not a new concept. This peace idea has been in evidence for centuries as even a Master walked the planet, and you know the story of what happened to Him.

"Ignorance, darkness of the truth has gleamed many a war, be it on a battlefield of many or between two or more people who disagree on any particular subject. When anger flows, the energy rises to attack. When love flows, energy rises to heal.

"The Jedi motto decrees that never in attack, only in defense, and even if love were the defense, like the sword, the Light would banish the darkness, for darkness cannot hold the energy when Light is applied. The Force spoken of is love, not to be used in anger, and again, all is mental.

"The Embassy of Light regulates peace and healing as its objective, which will be major in its refinement now in process. The more love given out, the faster the cleansing. As has been said, this planet is far too valuable to have its treasures destroyed. Those who do the dark work will have no recourse but to cease the destruction of the innocent people, animals and nature. Thus, the major decree has been given you.

"Are you destined to speak to world leaders in and out of authority? Yes."

G: "But I am basically unknown."

ANSWER: "You have been chosen. That is what you need to be aware of at this moment. We recognize being famous for any reason is not where you are coming from; however, this will take place anyway. You have an inner heart that loves, even as many noted Masters have been so designed, with no other dream but to serve your God in unusual ways. And serve you do, so this is just one more way.

"A big one, to be sure, but massively important as you became very aware of yesterday. Will you be known? My, yes. You are being prepared even as we confer at this moment. Have you not said that this is your destiny?

"At this point guidance has been given and your attendance in this court of the Embassy of Peace opens its doors for consultation with the highly respected Mind Masters who guide the makings of decisions, thus bringing forth what has been put on your plate of dreams for some space-time now.

"Think on these things and we shall confer as you come to a meeting of Mind Masters, for indeed this is now possible. We await your entrance."

So Light it be

P.S. (Genii): "Anything else to be addressed?"

ANSWER: "The message has been given for the moment. Stay tuned in, as more will be revealed in a split second. All is on course, of course."

Of War and Peace

Arriving at The City Gate, no one was seen. In fact, dark skies were apparent. The City was lit up like New Year's Eve. All my previous visits were in daylight. This was the first at night, and what an awesome Light sight it was.

To see this location from space must be quite a sight to behold, as it made daylight seem obsolete in this City of Light. So once again I got to enter and learn more. Quickly, as I glanced around, my Guide La-Luke appeared, and taking my hand, we entered into this vastness of this healing facility.

"Where to now?" I wondered. As quickly as I thought this, a moving trolley came up. If there was a driver there, one was not seen. We got on board and it began its journey, riding through spacious gardens and parks. There was just a glimpse here and there of buildings and we just rode for a bit. I was puzzled because this vehicle seemed to skim over the ground where no wheels or tracks were observed. There was just a free flow.

After stopping in front of another building dressed in white Light, we entered. Inside were absolutely beautiful gardens with even a waterfall to enjoy amidst this type of foliage.

"Where are we?" I asked, ready for anything to be reported.

L: "This is a building of human atrocities."

G: "What is that?" I wondered.

La-Luke answered, "That means peace is to be brought forth. The wars of mankind have long since been active. Here the ways of such are abolished in the minds and instead is embedded that no such thought is possible."

"Those who have been in war-like mindsets no longer will feel the anger and fear that brought it on in the first place. Man against man, brother against brother, no more! No more! The upper levels of this building are the remedy places where the energy fields of such thoughts are abolished, whether people are in here or not.

"It is a center location in The City to send forth such a magnetic field that eliminates any indication of war-like atrocities. This no longer will be tolerated. Nation against nation is abolished. Armies of protection are no longer needed, as peace is the only protection desired."

G: "You mean peace on Earth can be obtained from this place? How is that achieved?"

We entered the building as before, finding ourselves again in front of the counselors, peace entities, where my question was answered.

O: "By changing the frequencies from war-like intrusions to peace and love, which of course in your world has not been known to any major extent. The human cry of 'peace on Earth' has sounded its tone throughout history. From this place, like other Cities in the blueprint, this loving existence fulfills that prophecy through leveling of love instead of hatred and war.

"Anyone who enters here is cleansed of all that from the DNA mental equivalent to only know peace and love. They then, of course, take that into the world. As time enters, countries will only know and experience loving gratitude to be what they are in truth and see all others the same way, as one family unites with others as one."

G: "That is wonderful."

O: "Anger and hatred are abolished totally, for each now is in the totality of peace within themselves. Children will learn of love, instead of the opposite. Sharing is fun instead of competition. Even in the competition, it is for the fun of the game and everyone wins.

"Recognizing this is a vast way of looking at a new beginning; nevertheless it is possible. So then, how feel you in this place?"

G: "Calm, centered and appreciative and filled up with love, yet amazingly my emotions are like this is normal."

O: "Good, then. We have completed the vision trip for this time."

We exited this beautiful garden-type place where peace did reign supreme. We climbed back on the wheel-less trolley and headed for the Gate. I wondered what the electric bill would be for The City of Light, but then it didn't matter, for God had it well in hand, and a peaceful hand at that.

I said thanks to my Guide, he disappeared and I was back in my warm cozy bed, a bit better off from having had this strange experience of what is to come about.

Thanks, God. This was really a mind stretcher to be sure!

So Light It Be.

Additional Connection from La-Luke

Embassy of Peace Headquarters January 23, 2009

O: "This previous information just gives a hint of what it is about. It would be like connecting Heaven and Earth into one where, warring factors cannot co-exist with love being the linking force. When people are linked in Light they have no conflict, for within themselves this is not tolerated or experienced. Love makes Light apparent and as Atherian Light Guide of the Genii has said' 'WARS WILL END!"

"You have the White House, we have the Embassy of Peace on the holy ground of The City of Light. As changes now in process with the appointed leader who basically is a Peacemaker, this will eventually lead to the Embassy of Peace connection.

"There is much more to be said as this only gives a hint of the power and strength connected. Such changes that you have never seen before or imagined are in process and this is only the tip of the iceberg, so to speak in your vernacular.

"What you all are dealing with here is the makeup of the new world being prepared for you all to awaken to. Listen O Israel, for this is the monument in evolution where the power of God Light stirs up the masses to accept God's will for indeed this is the appointed time of receiving long since spoken of in time related messages.

"God will bless and be blessed, for Light now removes all darkness to show the folly and ignorance contained within its borders of stress. Time is short.

"So the Embassy of Peace Headquarters now revealed to the Genii, stands within The City of Light as a beacon to all who would accept this as an omen of what is to come about and . . . come about it will! Make no mistake about that! Peace on Earth? Oh my yes. . . beyond and faster than a speeding bullet can hit its target.

"So then continue to be open...report this and the previous visit to the Embassy for more will be added as you are walked forward in vision and the knowing that what you are about has no opposite and with this we leave you to your day that now flows into place."

So Light It Be!

P.S. I just knew that I was being set up to talk with world leaders on this topic. There was no ego attached; better to be on my knees in honor as the power which was coming through right then was awesome.

Imagine that!

The Council of Master Minds Meeting 1

Embassy of Peace Headquarters January 27, 2009

Entering into a calm meditative state, I suddenly got the vision of being back into the gardenlike foyer of the building I had previously been in before with my Guide, although he was not seen now. Appearing from an opening at the end of a corridor came an entity smiling and bowing. He beckoned me to follow him and clearly this was a sensing that I had arrived at my destination which I knew somehow was the Chambers of Masters.

As we went through the opening entrance, the vision was not a room as we know a room with walls, but something very different. Let's see how do I explain the unexplainable? No walls and feeling of vastness as the air was filled with moving pictures floating gently and silently around and overhead. It was kind of like being in the Universe mentally. A kaleidoscope of pictured thoughts curling around! Who's thought? Why pictures? What is going on?

Had I stepped into the universal "'now'" moment? It felt very peaceful and a feeling of love filled my heart. None of this would make much sense in my human thinking. But hey... if I was going crazy, it sure felt pretty good. Interestingly though, I was very clear-headed and strong ... actually more than normal.

At ground level was seen a circular long table with one opening like a horseshoe. In that space was a throne-like chair in gold with pillows of blue/purple colors. As I looked at the table, entities began to appear. Settling in, they took on the human exterior of male or female while love, strength and gentleness appeared from them, but with much power also. A Light above each head cascaded down and around encasing them in its frequency.

I wondered if these were some of the Golden Illumined ones of the Court of the High Tribunal that I knew about. I felt that this meeting was just to acclimatize me into this new way of accepting what was to come about. And that I was an honored guest sitting in this Throne of Excellence, as I was inwardly told it was, and believe you me, with what I was experiencing, it needed to be absorbed a bit to be understood.

It was a meeting of high level minds to be sure. The questions of Who? What? Where? and Why? were still to be introduced into verbal communication. Could my mind understand this enough to continue? Continue? Excuse me, look how far you have come Genii...of course...I just needed a moment or two to absorb the ecstasy of it all. Was time a factor here?

Then an entity of Light, male in design, which I felt was to give me some mental balance of identification stood up and smiled, giving me a hand signal of welcome. Wow! Talk about being in a strange land. He opened his mouth to speak but no sound arrived to my ears. Then another entity tapped him on the arm and this person adjusted a ring on a finger and sound was heard like tuning up the volume on a radio.

With this I heard, "Welcome to The City Council. We are the Ambassadors of Mental Light, the Mind Masters or the Master Minds of this City of Healing, that God has entrusted to bring forth what you have been part of before this life incarnation of space-time."

"Since this is strange and must be absorbed, we invite you to do that, and come back as you need to, and we will once again enter into the conversational informational area where you will be comfortable and can understand clearly."

By this time I was getting very light-headed so that felt right. With this he sat down but his Light Body aura stayed in form a bit higher, then it slowly lowered surrounding him.

I thanked them and indeed I needed to adjust my thinking. Then the scene ended and I seemed to float back into my home and bed where most of my morning meditation takes place...I really was 'spacey' and felt to go outside for some fresh air . . . and I needed to do human things like take the trash out. Boy, that ought to do it!

Ok God. I will be back . . .

This was really fun . . .

Thanks,

Genii.

Meeting OOO-LON

Embassy Visit February 2, 2009

Q: Is it appropriate this morning to re-enter the Embassy of Peace?

A: "In the prospect of re-entering the embassy, 'just do it'...."

As I envisioned myself again into this strange place, one would think I would be getting used to this. However, each visit was a phenomenon in itself. What was seen before was not even a room, as we know a room to be, but an empty space with pictures floating in the air; beautiful to be sure, strange also. This time there were no pictures floating anywhere, it was open at the top and the evening sky held it all together as stars peeked in to say whatever stars would say if they would say anything. Okay, moving on....

Again around this horseshoe-shaped table were faint entities, obviously leaders of some sort. Then one stood up and I could see him pretty clearly. He wore a white robe, gold-belted. He was clean-shaven and appeared human-like, and most of the others did too. This could be how they allowed me to adjust to new energies, since I thought they were from somewhere other than here.

"I am OOO-LON, Commander of the Space Light of your planet and keeper of information for distribution." His voice was stern. This, obviously, was a no-nonsense guy, which was okay with me as I am the new kid on the block and am here to learn." I am not of your world but I am able to speak your language. As an Earthling you have been summoned here, since you are a designated spokesperson for your planet and this healing edifice, so named The City of Light. Are you in agreement?"

G: "What does that mean, Commander of the Space Light?"

O: "As said, the ways of your world have had many incarnations of Light in the time past and now it is different, as we are Light within Light and our frequencies blend as one to supersede any areas that need being revised, and many do."

G: "Excuse me, as I am trying to understand beyond my current under-standing as this is like a space video. I do sense much love with you all and I am trying to make sure I am not just dreaming this up."

O: "Indeed you are not, for that would not be allowed and would do nothing to perpetuate the process. Space teachers we are, and the galaxies will benefit greatly from our contact. If agreed, we shall proceed." I nodded my head yes and he said, "Good then, we shall proceed." The other entities smiled and I began to lighten up and smiled back in gratitude of what was being presented.

OOO-LON continues: "As an Assembly of Light Contactors, we have brought you here as an assigned Ambassador of Planetary Happenings that are taking place as Light intensive embraces this planet into itself. We recognize this is all unusual for you; however, you will adjust quickly."

G: "I am open to that and the fascination of what I can be a part of in helping this planet in its own growth and the purpose of this City and its healing powers. How can I be of help? I am only one and many people have had far more spirit trainings than I have."

O: "You think simply, almost child-like and not in an overload of mechanical pre-programming. This makes it easier for you to digest what you and we are about. What is being decreed on your planet for mandatory intervention in assistance of releasing the make-up of those who consistently stay in keeping the old and thus the turbulence continues, when we bring the way of peaceful intervention. What has been obtained by aggression is to be ended.

"To assist in treating, more energy is bombarding this planet to raise the consciousness of those who have long since been in this state looking for answers that take too long to find. Many organizations work to achieve peace.

"Peace at all costs is in process and will continue, as it affects everyone. But even now, what has been currently imprinted is beginning to crack open what has been closed even as we speak. Your process is just that, in process. Be not concerned. We have chosen the right humanoid long before you entered this lifetime. Many Lightworkers all over this planet are in agreement, and that in itself is lifting the energy."

G: "And what is it that this council does?"

O: "This is why you have been invited to come and sit with us who are not of your planet, but part of a universal community sent to advise, guide into what is well taking place. This City is to be announced just by being revealed to the masses. That in itself will change the way people will look at this home base and themselves, as it will seem like a domino effect.

"This Peace Council recognizes that it has much work to do and in relatively a short time, but just one link like yourself connecting with another and then they in turn link others has much power attached. Peace will indeed be secured. There are, as you know, many organizations and corporations that, when they get past the greed of survival, will make a Saultus leap of support and the frequencies will move much faster.

"The planetary progress of Earth-grown produce must be advanced to survive. The greenhouse effect must be looked at as a top priority, for those in this arena recognize this. Now the Earth interior meets the sky exterior and you are sandwiched in the middle. "This will continue for awhile yet, but be aware that what is in change now will change the outer picture drastically, and this is all for the good and healing here.

"Many will leave, due to the intensity of the frequencies being felt. On the other hand, many will rejoice that such a happening is in process, which is not stoppable. We have been brought here to advise, guide and change the overall picture to be what is livable within the confines of your energy fields and the Universe as well. So then this is just an indication of ourselves.

95

"In speaking of this to others, request questions and we will endeavor to answer them. Through love, God sent us, as this universal community seated here is just a fraction of what help is available.

"Peace at all costs. The cost is but to activate the intelligence within each one to extend a healing hand where you can. Key people could be set in certain positions like north, south, east and west, where they are familiar with what is taking place, and hold the energy there.

"So then this is just the beginning. Think on these things and we shall endeavor to precipitate something at our next meeting, and with that we bid you a God day in every way."

He bowed, as did the rest, and I nodded in agreement. And with that, the vision ended and I found myself back in Sedona watching the sun awaken the red rocks on a Monday morning.

So Light It Be!

The Cosmic Raising of Consciousness

Embassy of Peace Revisited February 7, 2009

Re-entering while in a meditative state, the scene once again was at the Gate but this time several small children greeted me with smiles and led me through the Park of Relaxation to where my friendly City Guide, La-Luke, took over and the kids just disappeared. My guess was they headed for the playing field where a cloud of white mist can be grabbed as a snowball and tossed.

G: "Who are these children?" I asked.

L: "They are young entities of parent entities who use this place as a playing ground just for the fun of it. Come, we venture to the Embassy as Light attends those who await us."

With this, time seemed to move ahead very quickly and I found us in the place where see-through entities as I call them stood around the horseshoe table in acknowledgement that we were present.

O: "We welcome you back to this Council of Peace and Keepers of Advancement."

G: "What am I to know?"

O: "The world of your economy is in a cleansing mode and upon the finish will be stronger than ever before, for people are now in mixed energies finding new ways to do old things. Those who seek employment will find new ways to incorporate old values and invent new ones. The current so-called hardship is purifying through frequencies that can and will make people think differently. Change in your world is never easy, for your survival imprints hold on for desperation, for survival is mandatory.

"The City of Light designed in the current renovation of Earth change will have people resting in the knowing that such a place has the ability to reconstruct much of the thinking from the old to the new; thus, healing will take place in each individual that will seem priceless, for there is nothing to compare it to.

"Someone has asked you recently about the current exchange of money. Money as such will become a thing of the past, just like stones were exchanged in the distant past and are no more, where much had to be stored for individual comfort of survival sake. This will become a mental opening of sharing instead of hoarding. This, of course, will take some time of exchange of thoughts and emotions, etc., but it has been said the new time of process and healing is Mandatory. The money god will reign no more!

"It will become people first. The changeover with them through a re-evaluation of their thinking and intent will be a major factor that puts new ideas into place. The necessity of change now runs rampant in fear like a virus that passes on from person to person through the media impact that is not a help but a hindrance.

"That is because negativity begets negativity and people have that already preset to continue more of the same. This is to be stopped, and The City manifestation will shake out a lot due to beliefs that God has indeed brought forth the manifestation of new life.

"You are a designated human who works to stay stable in the midst of the turbulence around. Some days are better than others when cooperation and love is felt as well as given, and love should lead the way. Now then what would you ask of us?"

G: "To keep me informed of what is in process and allow me more visits with questions as well as to continue to inspect the City and even find out more about your cosmic community worlds."

O: "As agreed. As you can see and sense, this is just the first step as said previously. The wound must be cleansed before the healing can take place, for this time no Band-Aid approach will do.

"As countries begin to look at themselves, and others as themselves like looking into a mirror, this will begin the peace talks. Remember even the darkest of minds are being affected, thus bringing up what has been held in the deepest recesses of the subconscious, and thus making them a target of their own thinking. They do irrational horrifying things, and usually in the name of God or Allah. Such nonsense is to be no longer tolerated. This is not an overnight process but it will be completed, for this planet will survive. We have appeared to have this known and completed.

"We are from many cosmic community locations and galaxies, and this way of living on your planet affects the whole universal hologram. Nothing is separate, all is one. Every Light Being unseen, every star, every planet and much that you know not of, are all affected and subject to what this planet subscribes to. Every insect, flower, animal and tree plays a part in the holiness of what we are about.

"Some of your antics are deplorable and will be stopped! The make-up of your decisions will be changed one way or another. Since you cannot seem to do it easily, the community of universal helpers are on hand and have been for some time, and will continue to be to the finality.

"All the star riders, brothers and sisters have long since been evolved and involved as a vast community that recommends that the mindset of individuals here be changed to only know love for themselves, and respect of each other will be the healing process taking over."

G: "What about the individual health healings?"

O: "What takes years and tons of money to find cures from cancer or some other self-induced appearance, will be brought to a close, as the cure is known by the Star Community now! The hard part is in the human thinking, as they are used to being 'ill' and scarification comes from the inner voice of the subconscious that is a melody that repeats itself.

"When this is cured, the void could be a breeding place of something else. And the beat goes on. One has to be very strong not to accept an illness in any form."

G: "Like in my book *The Sickness Bug*, about addictions?"

O: "The doctors and the forerunner scientists here are being guided to check new ways to cure old ways, but this is snail slow, which is fine for the pharmaceutical companies who make millions on its products. Again, the money god is mentally in charge. Why would they want people well? They have a surprise in store, believe it!

"We are here to bring peace on Earth, as has been the cry for centuries. This is in process, for the Universal Governing Light will have nothing less, so the cosmic community joined in to bring this about. First to find the power within themselves, then the planet's exterior by going into and through the people themselves.

"Consciousness must be raised, and the fantasy of love empowerment within each individual will make this a reality. Walk your day as one in Light. Thus wherever you go or whomever you meet can have even a slight personal change that will benefit all. It is when you recognize and appreciate each other, the changes happen, and quite quickly. A lifting this way is important. The new President called Obama knows this and is purposely put in this place of honor to recycle old thoughts into new ones as he attempts to instill this in others long since in old ways of thinking."

With this he sat down and another entity on his left side stood up, looked at me and said, "We are here to extend the holy way of cleansing through higher intelligence and shall be open to new questions as they come to mind."

He sat down and I was tapped on the shoulder by my Guide that it was time to depart. I thanked this cosmic council force for peace, stood up and was led out of the room with no walls, back to the Gate and then back home in Sedona, ready to see what the day would bring besides trying to type all this up!

So Light it be!

Of Greenhouses, Crop Circles and Planetary Changes

February 12, 2009

Q: "What new food techniques must we learn as planetary changes take place?"

A: "Good question... Food as you have always known it to be and used it, will remain the same to some extent, except to be enhanced. However, new plants will also be introduced onto and into your planet (as in the City of Light which have never been before), but they will have more nutritional value. This may sound like a sci-fi drama, but is correct.

"The way your planet is growing in population, more and more emphasis is needed on nutrition, especially for the birth of new children entities who are being born to carry on the overall picture we see of future events. It is almost like a new planet is rising out of Light-empowered soil.

"Farms and greenhouses will shift into high gear and become not a thing of the past, but on the contrary, a big thing of the future. Those who work in these areas will see harvests aplenty. There will be changes in the richness of the soil, which is in process, as nature takes over in being seen and felt at this time.

"Thus thinking ahead and watching for new plants that are being discovered, and seeing even the normal ones taking on a new flavor, will be enhancements that will be introduced. When we say that this planet will not be as it was before, it is not just a dream, but a positive reality in process.

" You have seen Crop Circles of designs. What are they for? To tantalize the mind of how and why they are here? By no means just for delight and wonderment. These geometric designs of outer and inner energy fields are spreading energy which flows under the surface to enhance and bring forth what we have reported on this question.

"Even the water will be enhanced. We recommend that the new way to look at water is as liquid Light, as it is mandatory for survival. In the City of Light all water is Light and pure, for no other reason than it always should be, and it is for healing. Those who activate this new thinking of the Earth should take this information into their own thinking process for evaluation and assimilation.

" Cultivating in different ways will come into those who are programmed to be what you say, "Open at the top," as these improvements in cultivating lead the parade of advancements which have been referred to here as something to pay attention to.

"Watch for new taste sensations that will have you saying, 'This tomato tastes a bit different but is very delicious. I wonder why?' Those of us in the unseen, who cultivate new flavors say, "Yes indeed, these are God's new delights put into action."

"So Dear Ones, this is only a hint of what to expect as planetary changes bring change from the ground up, and the sky farmers down. You will see these new delights brought from distant planets, to bloom nature's bounty in profusion, and the Earth farmers will find their work to be heavenly instead of maybe a chore.

"And God says, 'Yes, in this we have new life!' and so Light we be!"

This is one of several messages Genii has received about "**structured water**", which is referred to as "**liquid light**" and "**liquid love**," being used in The City of Light because of the health and environmental benefits and advantages and the 500+% increase in the nutritional value of food grown with structured water.

Over one billion people lack safe water, and three billion lack sanitation; eighty per cent of infectious diseases are waterborne, killing millions of children each year. — World Bank Institute, 1999

Ultimate Destinyland will provide a free copy of **The Introduction to Structured Water** PDF to any reader of Something's Coming and the paper-back edition on a voluntary donation basis with 100% of any donations conveyed to The Light Center http://www.naturalstructuredwater.com	Inventor **Clayton Nolte** with some of the **Natural Action Structured Water** Devices available from Ultimate Destinyland which is also helping Clayton and his non-profit Foundation fulfill his ultimate vision of healing the waters of Planet Earth.

Of UFOs and Human Fears

Morning Message February 15, 2009

Q: "The City demonstration arrival in this country will look like a UFO has landed and fear would be automatic except for us Lightworkers who look forward to space visitors. How is this to be taken care of with the United States government, as most sightings are kept secret except for several presidents who acknowledge they have physically seen one or more sightings and have told publicly of these sightings? "

A: "Recognize this country and the rest of the planet is basically fear-based and that anything unusual would immediately trigger that fear of being attacked. The unknown can always hold a measurement of fear, and again it is survival at all costs. The pre-groundwork is being studied and set into place. Pre-work has been set long since and as you read in the magazine this morning, the push is on to be what you are in truth - PURE LOVE and this is what is being remedied, and the message envisioning of The City is already activated.

"Several Presidents are already open to something new and UFOs seen periodically make for more government secret interests to begin and adds to the previous sightings. The UFO community has long since been activated in promoting UFO activity in your world. This will not go unnoticed. First steps first."

G: "Will The City just magically appear with no advance notice or is there to be some pre-demonstration to sort of set the scene for this? "

A: "It is advised the Genii return back to The City Embassy of Light Headquarters for this answer, as it is a bit complicated in your language vernacular and you, too, need to know the pre-steps of the demonstration to be witnessed. What can be reported at this inquiry is that all pre-notifications will be in place. So line up your questions and return to the council. They will be prepared to take you forward and fear will not be looked at as a major problem. Your President Obama will be a major player in this scenario ... proceed."

G: "Anything else?"

A: "Remain in a stable condition, for your job has just begun and has all the earmarks of this major event to elevate you in mind quickly. Permit any daily concerns to leave, as this takes precedence over any and all. Time, as has been said, is in short supply and your mental is needed to proceed as a high level ambassador of mental programming of this event. And as the Charles says 'all is well,' and we agree. "

So Light it be!

Somewhere in Non-Time

Embassy of Peace Headquarters February 29, 2009

As I released my physical world, I seemed to be soaring forward in time to begin my re-entry into The City. My Guide La-Luke waved as I landed near him.

L: "Come. We go to the Embassy. You are expected."

The little wheel-less trolley waited as we moved through the Park of Relaxation and climbed aboard. There seemed to be a combination of sunlight and night. Strange, to be sure, but … well, I was in another dimension. The trolley (with no driver in sight) stopped. Things work differently in other dimensions. Are we way behind, I wondered.

As we entered this domain of Light, all the entities around the table were standing, then they bowed in acknowledgement which put me at ease. There was nothing like the pictures in the air that I had seen before, just faint, delicate fragrances lifting the senses, including my own. I found my chair and La-Luke stood next to it. I wondered what would happen next. I was soon to find out.

O: "We welcome you back to the future."

I nodded in appreciation and mumbled, "Thank you."

O: "There is a question for us?"

G: "Yes, a couple."

O: "Proceed."

G: "In my own case, since all this is like a new adventure, what is God's highest vision for me in regards to The City demonstration?"

OOO-LON smiled, and that energy was picked up by the others. Not bad, looking at about nine entities all smiling at you.

G: "I have been on this path for some time watching and waiting like a spiritual detective for any clue that would give me advanced information as to what I call truth. And, what is to take place as I try to balance two worlds, one here and one in the physical? What am I to be advised to do to keep the process going and still take care of each physical day that appears at sunrise?"

O: "You have spent much time in other worlds as you stretch forward in the imagination, which incidentally is where ideas are given to you by Intelligences of high order. Have you not been to the High Court? Have you been given emblems of healing use? Of course these are extensions of preparations you need as the forward push extends itself, as the Kathie has said with her channel session for you.

"How you relate to time is simply an effect, an end result, what you actually call truth. The message becomes decisive, thus elevating the mind and the physical space you occupy at this precise moment.

"Your body marks the advancement, as you are sensing energy patterns change within the cells and molecules, which is annoying at times. But this is necessary as even your senses elevate in experiencing this feeling of movement, all of which is in preparation of what is to come about. This will end. It was said before; this puts you up one more rung on the Light Ladder.

"Look at what is taking place. Do you note other dimensions and what you refer to as 'see-through' entities? Of course! Have you not asked to see The City entirety? Yes, of course you have. All is in divine order. All is applied as healing properties of advanced scientific design, and even you have just remarked that the moving picture of scientific value mixed with the spiritual is a concept you understand in your non-understanding.

"As has been said, as forward movement is applied to your senses, it will bring forth a cleansing so intense that all avenues you now work in will take second place (but they are important to The City demonstration). So in helping others such as children, you are preparing them also in your way to be able to handle the new world in process.

"Of course we speak here of the puppets, as they are a valuable asset. So too are the women. You have not been given these tools to let them sit idly by. Use them to their highest advantage, now, as time, as you know it, is leaving and now-ness is put into action.

"Your Earth collides within the new paradigm in process as your new President lays the groundwork from two levels which he is programmed to do and has the courage to announce it to the world, ready or not, and is well able to take the kudos or the offense of misunderstanding. Where does he get his guidance? Does he not have Spiritual guides of intelligence that tell him when and where to impress the public and has he not moved very quickly on that advice? You are seeing this take place, and all will in time be accepted. He moves mountains to make the little molehill, which people can climb over in their lives. He is clearing out and setting the course with the new thoughts being imbedded. The time will come when even you will speak on what this is all about and to him personally. Imagine that! Tis so...already done."

The spirit group around the table hummed in agreement as I sat wide-eyed in this declaration. Oh my....

G: "And when will all this take place?"

O: "Yesterday has left the experience and today is given credence to become more time of elevation and advancement. The changing of millions of minds to be on the same level takes various energy fields and much work for the same millions of spirit guides to reinforce the high level programming now in place. Finally this will and can take place.

104

"You say you are just one of those millions, but what has also been said is that it only takes one and there are many more, including those who also relate to The City of Light which also is energy in process with the thoughts and beliefs in place.

"Now as readjustments take place in your government systems, the flow will lift in acknowledgements that God has a direct plan of peace and love. The plan is brought closer as each day appears and the sun sets.

"We invite you here again to tell you and those asking questions that what has been previously said is activated, and the previous proclamation holds the power energy of truth. Take the wisdom and use it wisely.

"2012? We smile, as this date is not the beginning. It has long since begun. Enjoy the essence of this message, for God has power tucked in it. Come back with questions from others and yourself and we will set the answers in place, because intelligence moves forward with this guidance as all are reflections of the one, whole like a hologram. We bid you a peaceful loving day of physical existence. Peace be with you."

And with this La-Luke and I left the place of Light and went to the Gate of Entrance. I found myself back home in Sedona with my CD playing Somewhere in Time, and I began a new day here on this planet.

So Light It Be!

Of the President, Genii's Talents and Advancement

Embassy Visit March 6, 2009

The vision scene opened as I ascended into it and arrived at the Gate of Welcome. It felt good to be back. Now where, I wondered. My Guide La-Luke met me and ushered me through the Park of Relaxation and onto the waiting, floating trolley that I had ridden before.

G: "Where to?" I asked.

L: "We again enter the Embassy of Peace."

The honor of being there brings forth to me respectfully more information and guidance.

L: "They want to speak to you to further your course."

By the time this all was said we had arrived at this magnificent building and I was ushered into this room filled with entities, and even the balcony appeared filled. It was much like an amphitheater.

G: "My! Something must be important to bring forth such an audience," I whispered to my Guide. He just smiled and nodded.

This room appeared much larger than before, and that was a surprise, but the horseshoe table with the leaders was the same. I curtsied and took a deep breath and La-Luke ushered me to the throne-like seat. Facing this vast audience was a thrill in itself.

The leader OOO-LON once again stood and a hush fell over everyone as if God Itself was about to speak.

O: "We welcome you back to our Sanctuary of Light. This your return visit, has deep significance because the process of cleansing your planet has taken several steps forward through the inner directions given to the President of the name tone Obama.

"The flurry of dissention is only due to each one's personal memory, thus bringing forth the discomfort being experienced. Nevertheless the cleaning will continue, for each person must wash out in their own way, and that is what makes for the discomfort. Changes in frequencies are the key reason that moved Heaven and Earth into the process of moving Heaven [so-called] to Earth.

"This tone has been sounded for centuries. The path of blame has always been put on God instead of where it belonged, or for the love of Allah one man kills another with no respect, not even knowing of that person. War will end!!!!

"Thus Allah has decreed and peace remembered is all that will remain, as the pairs of opposites balance out, equal not in opposition but in love and caring. Harm is not the answer, love is! Make a note of this.

"What has been now remarkable is that as more Light enters and stirs up the pot, changing the old ways, we see love and caring for each other begin to take place as it should. This, then, gives our process a pathway of expression and correct solution. We here are Light Leaders in contact with other various planetary entities or groups and make the Light contact even here on your Earth. This is intentional and will proceed to the finish, for as been said, THIS PLANET WILL BE HEALED!"

By this time I was certainly tuned in and turned on as I suspected these entities were visitors from outside our Earth system. The power in that place was beyond awesome. There was total control...total!

"With the support of those unseen in your dimensional world we have the continuing power to implant and sanctify what is being said and done. Today the main message is to share your given wisdom plus your varied talents as well as your love, thus leaving each person with a change for good in their own Light. You have been chosen to move as much as possible into your world.

"Based on all of the above, The City Lights are magnified, so to speak, for your attention and acceptance. The Holiness of this awesome project cannot be emphasized enough and it bears witness to what is to come about ... and soon. All the inner areas of process setting these healing facilities are in place, each one an entity within itself, thus energizing to reach out past dimension separation to draw to itself what it intends to accomplish in the near future.

"You have been given pages of writing describing what is unseen to the eyes of others. This is true, so you can carry in your heart and Light Body systems both a complete feeling and complete sight. This is purposely administered to you as an Earth Emissary of Truth speaking, and will continue as you are moved from place to place and people to people to be contacted when and where advised. This City of Light demonstrates what God has decreed to be the fact and not fiction, and rightly so.

"The path before you periodically will lead you into new avenues and you can expect to have your name be very well known as the interest becomes fascinating to others. Make a mental note of this now, for the closeness of the demonstration appears on the horizon like the sun coming up over the red rocks that you love. Even the rocks have held power, along with the working vortexes that you are quite aware of. Your work in progress leaves you little time to influence the world at this time, as has been said of the President of the tone name of Obama connection, and how to be present in his presence has been outlined. The power of the puppets you are aware of, and this is a silent but powerful way to be introduced through this gift for his beloved children and wife. The designing of the parents as a gift heart-filled is normal for you and will be accepted as such.

"The White House is by our estimation now called the Light House, and what does a Light House do for sea-faring travelers but be a beacon of comfort? Your path is through the innocence of the children. In designing the parents, play and fun is introduced.

"This is part of your advancement into the government arena; a simple but powerful part of the equation. You are in the process of being released from areas that have been an energy drain so you can concentrate on what is being said here.

"Expect more trips to be enhanced and introduced in your direction. Some will be due to Charles' contacts and some from your own. Opportunities that are placed in front of you should give credits to the popularity to be moved into your camp of interests. The talents of creating the Puppets of Power are non-threatening and a simple way to cover up the real intent of The City and should be continued until otherwise advised. So then, (he took a deep breath here) what say you, as a female of Earth value?"

I blinked and tried to think of something to say but a mental blank was what came up at this point.

G: "Well, what are my next close steps advised?"

O: "Be open to any opportunity that is advised. May the days be filled with thoughts of the process of bringing forth The City. Head for the children and the women. Remember the Power Puppets give your talents where they would be appreciated with service given. Most of all, give love and a smile that could be worth a million to one who needs a smile at that moment.

"Work with the Kathie Brodie and support her efforts as she builds her business and you can be a helpful attraction thus building a Light entity of advancement as you are both on the same Light frequency. Now is the time for advancement. So seek inner guidance constantly and all will be well with you and your path.

"The weakness felt sometimes in the legs is due to the changing of atoms and frequencies within the Light Body proper. This is unavoidable at this time in your process. Walk and rest are your friends, and with this message we end this visit. You will be summoned back as we see it is needed. You have total support with us here, and some are around you constantly. Use them.

"So now explore your new thoughts as they are introduced, and play in God's world, for it is your Playground of Progress just because you declared it to be so...

"So Light it be!"

Betwixt And Between Earth Growth!

Embassy Visit April 20, 2009

The Gate opened as I appeared into the scene. I had received an invitation to return. My Guide La-Luke also arrived at the same moment and beckoned me to follow him. The trolley arrived to take us to the Building of Light Entities who hold a governing status previously seen, where questions of The City and planet nature are discussed with authority as its main component.

Seeing familiar buildings again put me into the mental framework that this production had more value than we could ever envision. The trolley stopped at this Governing Building and we entered where we then faced a multitude of entities in an amphitheater-type setting with many levels. As usual, the main u-shaped table was hosted by the same entities holding court I had spoken with before. They now stood to greet me close up.

I was escorted to the throne-like chair. My Guide stood beside me on my right. The leading major-domo stood in his long white robe that seemed to glisten in the overhead daylight streaming in, while the others were seated. What an interesting place this is, I thought, as he began to speak.

O: "We welcome you back and have a message that you are to take to your world. The patterns of change on your planet will continue for a bit yet, as the darkness has penetrated deep into the energy fields of the Earth, so-called. The ground will heave up its matter as it maintains its process of loosening up or giving up its depleting energy now in release of the old. This may cause some traumatic movements as the Earth breathes in the new in the releasing of the old.

"This information is not to frighten you but to make you aware and balance what is unbalanced, should it become apparent. You will know and be advised. The way will present itself, and as soon as it does, use what you are given while staying in an un-turmoil state of mind. Recognize that what is coming will take precedence of what may be important to you ... first things first."

G: "You are speaking here of a vision I had some years ago of a major California coastline quake?"

O: "Precisely, but even in other areas. The planet is a boiling pot of energy and predictions can become apparent at any time."

G: "I have another question. Charles has been highly trained in disaster areas procedures. Would this be a part of his journey?"

O: "As said, 'previously trained in this kind of trauma' he would be called forth to assist in any area that has him so guided. Make each day a glossary of good tidings and accept as such. In the Light of this place you are now visiting, come back as often as possible and in-between keep up your strength and endure your outside world.

"As the Earth gives up its past history and thus brings forth the new, it has normal ways of doing this, either in human form or by Earth shudders. So then, be of Light cheer, for more is to be explored."

And with that my Guide nodded to me to rise, as the entities also did, and bowed, and we were excused to leave the building. We took the waiting trolley to the Gate as La-Luke smiled at me.

Then the whole scene disappeared as I found myself back in Sedona, thankful for the opportunities afforded me to enter into the unseen to explain this to whoever is tuned in.

So Light it be!

Red Rock Crossing on Oak Creek in Sedona

© Harold Najarian Courtesy of Gerrie Sidwell

www.sedonateachings.com

A Time for Light

Embassy Visit May 26, 2009

As I slipped into my vision meditation state, I again found myself at one of the Gates. Other people also were there happily waiting to enter this magnificent place of healing. Some did not go through the Relaxation Park that I enjoy so much but chose alternate paths to explore.

My destination was the Embassy of Peace and I was quickly guided to get on the wheel-less trolley by my Guide La-Luke, who also appeared to escort me. I had been there several times before and now I wondered what would take place within this amphitheater of cosmic visionaries who also gather there, headed up by several who speak with me from a place of power and love.

We slid over the ground and arrived at this magnificent huge white building trimmed with real gold. Opulence personified! I wondered what to ask as we entered. Maybe nothing? Maybe just listen and absorb? The collection of cosmic minds inside was consciousness at its highest peak so I had confident expectancy for what would take place.

As we entered there was indeed the sensing of much power and love mixed like a delicious concoction. Once more I recognized OOO-LON the leading speaker, as I was lead to the throne-type chair as before.

OOO-LON rose and spoke: "Welcome to the assembly of Cosmic Intenders. How may we serve you?"

I gulped, as I had no real question, just what I had been thinking about the 2012 date line.

OOO-LON spoke again: "We detect your interest in a dateline that could be a target of that interest, so permit us to gather in combined thought and answer."

For a moment or two there was total, really total silence; not a breath was heard. There must have been hundreds of entities in this arena who all stopped breathing at the same moment, or at least it seemed that way, like all thoughts had stopped the clock. Clock? What's a clock? It felt like nothing, a void, a moment in time. What is time? A connecting of mental oneness that we don't experience normally. The message was clear.

Then as if someone turned on a switch to begin again, these entities that I sensed came from some far off cosmic community returned from wherever they went in those few moments. My Guide smiled down at me from where he stood beside me.

OOO-LON continued: "Dates are man's way of keeping time in constant continuum for various reasons unique to themselves, perhaps to put progress on the calendar, and are useful. The silence you have just witnessed gives invitation to the non-verbal that you have not asked.

"In the case of The City appearance we smile at all the delights to be seen and experienced as this demonstration set before you. As the current Light waves move all into place so people can see what you have been shown so far, it is magnificence as Heaven on Earth has landed, and God had said, 'Let there be Light, and a City of Light to attest that indeed I exist, and I as the Primal Source of all things visible and non-visible bring it all forth: the biggest gift ever given any place.' It is time this planet interacts with other cosmic communities!

"Those seated here are from such communities, each bringing forth their Light intelligence into the formation of what can be accomplished as this proto-type City of Light demonstrates on this planet.

"Those who see, let them see those who are connected due to the information they have recorded as preconceived through this visioning you are sharing, and many other ways unique to themselves as valid. All are connected as such; same time line, same space station.

"The attraction here is the healing facilities that can get the job done in a compressed time awareness. All appearances are illusions of the mind, and thus Light illusions can heal what most do not understand, and they will, for here there is no discrepancy, it just is! Much has been used and approved in many cosmic universal universities that are not known of.

"2010, 2011, 2012! This time has been predicted through high clear minds, and many demented minds as well. Which do you choose? These higher forms have given you what you have attested to through many visits here and many more to be addressed.

"So then, leave us and re-enter into your world and testify what is coming about, for indeed it is so!"

And as he said this, all the entities stood up and sounded some unknown tone, and with that La-Luke tapped me on the shoulder and I knew this session, with all that had been said, was definitely very over. I nodded to everyone. We then left the building, took the waiting trolley to the Gate and the vision simply disappeared and I returned to Sedona wondering what was said. I guess I will have to read it and find out.

P.S. Recognize what is happening here is that your contact with the cosmic community is established and will be of good use because you will be invited to enter and view this cosmic community. As has been said, welcome to your future, welcome to journeys beyond space!

Between Now and Then 2012

Embassy of Peace Visit June 7, 2009

Being able to envision the most awesomely beautiful place where the technology is superb beyond our knowing now and the healings complete, is a gift that only God could imagine. This is the revelation that is at hand. Imagine that!

Resting in that awareness, I found myself back at the now familiar Gate of Entrance into the abode God had brought forth, at least at this point in my inner vision. High above me I looked at this gold-encoded design that circled the open horseshoe-shaped entrance and I wondered at the magic of it all; untested in our world to be sure, but surely magical in the intent of a healing place long past due.

Lightworkers have had visions of what is to come about and have tagged 2012 as some kind of appointment, like expecting the Christ or Buddha or whomever to come into view. Hey ... with God all things are possible, right?

That brought me to my question: why me? A high school drop-out who could only utter a few words due to stuttering. Maybe Moses said the same thing as he was told to talk to the Pharaoh and he stuttered, it is reported. I knew the feeling!

Here I stood on holy ground looking at the gateway of advanced progress that I am to talk about to others. Who would have thought? Not me. This was so far from my imagination that ...oops... I felt a tap on my shoulder and I turned to see my City Guide La-Luke smiling at me and moving me through the archway entrance.

"Where are we going?" I enquired, still in the mental magic of it all.

L: "To the Embassy of Peace!" And with that the wheel-less trolley pulled up and we climbed aboard. It took no time before we were unloaded at this Temple of Light. We entered to find this amphitheater filled to overflowing with entities from cosmic locations of some place. The scene repeated itself as I was ushered to the seat of visitors as a seat of honor.

O: "Welcome to the next step of your advancement. How may we serve you?"

G: "I am looking for answers to questions I do not even know to ask. Does this make any sense?"

OOO-LON smiled slightly. "Questions of The City Intent have been explored and 'timing' of this event seems to be on your mind. Is this so?"

G: "People are looking to 2012 as a date of something to take place, but most are not sure of what it is. Can you tell me what is to take place that has far reaching effects before that calendar date 2012? We are almost there."

A hum ran through the almost invisible audience.

O: "The world of the planet has yet a bit of time for the change, due to the Light waves washing the outer and inner interiors, much like washing a window so you can see clearer. Layer after layer of darkness is being removed not only from each person but the naturalness of the planet itself, as the new course is set into place.

"I am sure you are aware of the centuries of wars that have contributed from the darkness of the minds corrupt in ego fears to these layers being cemented. The minds of the people of all races need to be lifted by these changes, and now quickly, as the energies push out the old and in with the new.

"You can expect this to continue, and by the end of 2010 much of this will be a whole course of action and accepted by many. The topsy turvey roller coaster example is in full force now, making people misjudge due to their own discomfort, but they will continue never-the less as people must confront their own insecurities. In doing so they lash out at others as a mirrored effect instead of what you call 'going with the flow.' All this drama of release attracts the Earth changes as well.

"Hurricanes, tornados and quakes, which are all energy induced with these cleansing techniques, can be seen as possibly traumatic. People have to handle this as weather changes as well. The old ways of doing things that impeach others not at the highest will find no place in your society. Love and honor will replace greed and personal salvation for themselves only will take a back seat of resolution declaring 'no more!'

"The Light attends all who love and will dramatically affect these encounters. The unseen visionaries who work in the unseen higher realms forge health and happiness for all. The wars of greed will fall away, for all will be established as a norm.

"First the first...cleansing at all costs! Those who are in the government themselves are in their own process to lead through the next two years of the date you have been speaking of, but remember what you call time as a no thing is collapsing and 2012 may well be 2010. This was said to you earlier, that they were not considering time collapsing when these dates were given so long ago in ancient times.

"So then what are you to do in the meantime?

1. Listen for guidance every step.

2. Stay in the openness of what may be shown and said.

3. Watch for the unsettlement which will continue more of the same for a while yet.

4. Do not get caught up in it, even with those you love.

5. Your course is set! Stay there.

6. Watch your interests change as you move forward.

"Any more unknown questions?"

G: "My senses tell me to just embody what you have said as a confirmation. More about the 'new course' would be helpful."

O: "Now that we have laid the groundwork, be open to the new course and ideas to be implanted. As the new imagination shifts, implants of the new will be accepted as such. Add the new chapters to the book so all is kept in chronological order. This will be important as the questions come forth and you have a solid reply!"

La-Luke tapped me on the shoulder and I recognized my no-time session was up. I bowed to these leaders of leaders and turned to leave, at which time a hum again was heard somewhere in the audience. I bowed a thank you to the audience and my teachers in front of me. What an adventure I have tuned into. I realized that this was not my last visit, and I felt so blessed.

Then it was back to the trolley, Gate, and thanking La-Luke as I prepared to be home again in Sedona, Arizona to reread what I had written, because at this point I had not much of a memory of it.

So Light It Be

My Requested Return to The City

Embassy Visit July 11, 2009

In vision I saw me walking up to a major Gate allowing passage into the interior of this three-dimensional miracle as many others were also doing. I felt there was something more to be learned here. What was that?

"Those who might be considered a threat in any way are instantly encapsulated in a cocoon of misty Light so strong that further desire to enter is cancelled. There is a magnetic field surrounding The City that is impenetrable as well as beneath it. The Dr. Townsend was well aware of this, as he brought forth the beginning plot plan. Those of Light intuitive can easily see this apparition surrounding certain people of destructive intent and thus all is taken care of.

"Now we do not speak of those who have come for a healing per se, even mentally as their outer hue is a bit lighter and 'tratendascopes' can pick this up. Thus The City had a protective force unseen but clearly active. So we will enter though the Gate as this is not the case with the Genii."

I saw myself moving through the Gate once more and into the Park gardens that would fulfill every florist's desire to see the best the Earth has to offer. It was fun to see and hear people smiling and laughing as they got an unexpected massage on the benches scattered around the area. I could almost see the stress released from them like a balloon heading upward.

It was a sunny day but not hot, at least here, just very pleasant and relaxing. My Guide La Luke arrived near me and it was then I realized that he was not seen by others. He was invisible. Now how did this invisibility thing work? Guess I had a question coming up? Also wondered if he could become visible if he wanted to? I got a yes, o.k. just not now.

He led me out through the Park and onto another path. This place was like a tree with many branch-paths like roots extended. (How about a path map!) The overhead view must have been quite a picture. We walked a bit, passing people who were talking about what was taking place and that they were getting to see it first-hand. I do remember the feeling and excitement, as it has never left.

As we came around a slight curve there was seen a group of buildings called 'pod-lets' all cuddled in a circle, maybe 5 or 6 of them. "What are these?" I asked. La-Luke smiled as we entered with no one in sight, but tinkling bells gave notice that someone had entered. This is what you might call a store," he remarked, "but quite a bit different." Here, one can find objects coming from other than your planet to enjoy, just for the sight of them. Inventions of different kinds."

G: "What about money exchange?"

La-Luke smiled, "Your people see exchange in a different perspective than in the cosmic order of value. We shall talk of this at another time. I just wanted you to see what also is coming, but for now we go to the Embassy of Peace".

116

The wheel-less trolley pulled up. We climbed aboard, passing by people who wondered, I guess, why only one person was on it. I just smiled at my Guide. The Embassy of Peace doors opened as we ascended from our ride and we were escorted into this huge place. Again I bowed to those up-front-and-personal and took my place in the comfortable seated chair and wondered if the time would come when I could have an up-close-and-personal conversation with those entities in the audience of maybe 500 or more. (I could not see all the way to the back.)

OOO-LON spoke: "We welcome you back to give you an update on the pre-progress of The City arrival. We invite your interest!"

G: "I am interested, please enlighten me," I suddenly blurted out loud.

OOO-LON continued: "The awakening of the people of the planet brings forth many heavy insights of themselves that, when released, enter into the atmosphere and in some places like the north/south poles is changing the weather patterns. Thoughts are things (as said in your world) and something has to give to make room for the Light to replenish what it has been.

"You hear about the heat factor Global Warming and what to do about it? What can one do but resonate with the God force of replenishment. For too long this planet has depleted its bounty and now wonders how to save what is left? Thus we endeavor to assist. The weather may become chaotic at times. This is important to know, as the planet releases all that must make room for this City.

"People could become uncomfortable. What you are seeing at this point is people rebelling against people, for color has again raised its head to be released (as one example) and on the other side of the page, people also are banding together in attempt to heal what is unhealed.

"What people are experiencing is their own inner terror, and blame others across many continents. You have seen anger and heard from many people that it is the current emotion now being raised to the surface to be released and have even had it yourself. This could trigger weather changes as personalities change. This is not to scare you, just to inform you to be aware. People's inner cleansing now is hitting a peak. Ah, but the underside is love and compassion. Rest assured that the make-up of this planet is now being changed dramatically to pass the chaotic conditions to what is really taking place.

"We who observe, commend those who work daily to stay balanced in an unbalanced world and support others in their wish to be also in a balanced state. Love is the healing factor. The time of ascension nears, so the public feels the pressure more. The light in the sky of mental acuity is that all will end and peace on the Earth that has long been prayed for will be experienced.

"You are to awaken your people of the coming. The Light Center is the pivotal point for your addressing this issue. Permit your word of encouragement to your readers etc.

"To look to the Light of this coming event as something of delight, not fear. You have the ability to stand strong in your convictions of all that has been given you and the Dr. Bill and rest assured we support your efforts.

"More books on information should be out and updated. Your talks to assorted people of mind-altering prophecies coming about with The City should be used by others.

"As you walk the path of elevated Light it pushes you farther into this work. Not many know of you or your work but ... they will, as you are supported. Be mindful of what has been put on your plate of Light regarding this endeavor for, it makes sense in the revelation of things to come ... and soon. People's reactions of this drama will vary but know all is in divine order and this perfection is the reality course.

"So now return to your living space in full knowledge that what is being given you to rest on your mental shoulders, will continue as you are elevated to use what has been said to repair and develop new thoughts perhaps never thought of before.

"Thank you for being open to come when called, for you have a calling written (so to say) in cement ... The City of Light. We are available at any moment."

I was pretty speechless as the energy of silence penetrated. I bowed and left. Back on the trolley and to the Gate and then back to my bedroom in Sedona on a Saturday morning.

Somewhere in my consciousness I accepted this decree and I would do my best to deliver.

Feeling this, I repeated,

"More of thee and less of me."

So Light it be!

Do You Speak Space?

City Visit July 27, 2009 INTRODUCTION TO COSMIC WAYS

In the early quiet of a summer Sedona morning I mentally waited until I entered another dimension where I have been previously invited. In vision now, I stood at the same Gate as usual with a few people scattered here and there admiring this massive five-story Entrance. It was there that I heard a voice say, "Behold, I bring you glad tidings of great joy." Whether it was on a loud speaker or just in my head, I am not sure, but it did make one feel they were in the right place at the right time.

I moved myself through the Gate and into the Park and onto a massage bench. What a great feeling to begin any tour. I opened my eyes from this deluxe moment to see this Park was empty. (My, people come and go quickly.) At this point my vision went totally blank; no picture, no sound, nothing for a few seconds.

Upon seeing again, there before me stood not one, not two, but three male robed entities. They smiled and nodded for me to rise and follow. I did, and as we passed through the very large willow trees, one went to the left and one to the right while the third took my arm and we went ahead. "Where now?" I wondered.

We walked only a short distance when before us was a building that was shaped like a flying saucer space vehicle. Now, some of the white buildings I have seen did have space vehicles like gold domes on them, but I'd bet this one couldn't fly. I wondered if we were going there. As I said this, I picked up an unusual energy buzz from the top of my head to the ground, and I swear I lifted an inch off. This was like sci-fi stuff, and I was getting excited!

We walked in through the misty shielded doorway, and by golly it did look something like a space interior like in the movies but all peaceful and no anxiety anywhere. It was really quite pleasant. Okay, now what? Coming through another entrance was another male that when I looked at him his face changed a bit, kind of like what Wayne Dyer said, "Change the way you look at things, and the things you look at will change." (I'm not sure he meant it that way but . . . ?)

This one was really changing, one minute looking like a human sort and the next something else, not bad or gruesome just a flick, change. It was mesmerizing but fun.

"Welcome," was the sounding word that seemed to float in the air like a melody. "You speak space?"

"Ah, what does that mean?" I said slowly.

"It is obvious that you do not, so we will speak in your tongue. Come and sit with me," he replied, and he led me into another so-called 'pod,' and he suggested I just call it a room. Whatever. He was dressed in a kind of uniform, with soft light blue fabric that ... oops, that is changing as well. Oh, my.

119

"You are interested in Jedi ways?"

"Yes", my answer came quickly."

"You wish no darkness of mind?"

"Yes," I replied.

"The measure of Light and darkness of thinking makes for havoc on your planet. We are here to change that concept, not to control anyone. Quite the contrary."

"Excuse me. Who are you and am I having an illusionary moment?" He leaned back and smiled, or at least I think it was a smile.

"I am Taluna, Master of Illusionary Premonitions, and this building is so futuristic in your world. Some might not even see it or would feel it is a figment of the mind. This building exists for several reasons here in The City of Light. You have been to the Embassy of Peace and have seen many entities in the large theater seated in the background. Is this so?"

G: "Yes," I said, trying not to look excited.

T: "Your wish is being granted as we take an advanced tour, and you will see what Light projections can really accomplish within a short period of time. This City of Light is for advanced healing techniques, and little by little we have introduced new ways in which Light can be found and used in your laboratories. As you know, it takes far too long to cure with the slow methods now being used. Now masters of these Light healings make so-called new break-throughs that they think they have invented, and they did, with a little help from unseen friends.

"Your movies and films depict anything from beyond this planet must be either untrue or out to make trouble, like in the Jedi movies, etc., except for a few where positive is the basis of the film. With us it is all Light, and only love penetrates, for that is what Light is."

G: "Is this why I am so interested in Jedi techniques and laws?"

T: "Precisely. You have seen the Jedi performances many times. Would you like to meet real Jedi Masters and understand what they really represent?"

G: "Oh, yes," quickly came my reply.

T: "Then we shall have you return to this Jedi training center and you can be given instructions to heighten your human understanding of just what power is."

And with that he stood up, raised his hand over my head and I felt a love shiver from the top of my head to the ground, going straight through my body like I have never felt before.

G: "You mean there is really a process of Jedi-ing?" I stood up as he continued.

T: "Of course. Where do you think the movies got the idea in the first place? And are you not to speak about The City, which runs on this premise behind the scenes?"

G: "Well, I do have a Light Saber."

He laughed as he said, "Play toys. Come be in the Jedi world for a bit and see what helps make this healing City a City of Light and Healing."

With this he stepped out, and I was led to follow back to the Gate where I was met by my original Guide La-Luke.

La-Luke looked at me and said, "Well, how was that?"

G: "Oh, guess what I get to learn? The Jedi ways!"

L: "I know. Congratulations," he replied, and promptly disappeared.

And I did too, back to Sedona to continue my day in my world, knowing it was going to be good because I was happy and so was my puppy Light Spirit.

Hmmm, I wonder if Light has been reading *The Holographic Universe* I left on my bed while I was away in The City, Imagine that!

The Big One!

Closing my eyes and moving in an inner vision to another place of familiarity, I found myself again at the Entrance Gate into The City of Light. My visits have been numerous and I now could add yet another one, this one, a request to return from inside The City.

A Gate of Entrance once more beckoned me to enter. No one else was seen who had been seen before. I was apparently quite alone, but no, my City Guide La-Luke appeared as if by magic and led me through the five-story entrance building.

How blessed I felt knowing that I was in God's favor. The familiar Resting Park came into view, but no stopping to rest on a groovy massage bench this time. Pulling aside the giant willow-like curtains, we hopped aboard the familiar wheel-less trolley that whisked us off to the Embassy of Peace.

This building holds the Power of the Universe, due to the Entities seated within, sharing love and information with energies not explainable. It is just that strong.

Having been summoned to return here, I wondered why? Did I have any questions? Well, one for sure, having just been told by Archangel Michael through a human channel by two friends who shared with us that a "Big One" Earth-wise was to be experienced. What is the 'Big One' and how does it affect us?

The trolley stopped and we entered this hall of magnificence and awesome power mixed with love unimaginable ... Oh my God! The entities of this place stood and nodded while I was escorted to my now usual throne-type chair. A hum went through this extra large Light arena, with lord knows how many entitles filling every seat in this vast audience that was unseen but surely felt.

OOO-LON, the leader began, "We welcome you back to this place of Light for a particular reason, which you have already been given in what you would call a clue. Your Earth patterns are shaping up to bring forth a massive undertaking of change. This will, by no means, be just a small indication of what is to come. It has already been triggered.

"These things that have and are taking place are true in the eyes of Archangel Michael, for he makes his words through another human to take note of what to be aware of, not in fear but in preparation to take on any situation that appears unusual. This, then, would be a confirmation of same. So then what to do?

"Stay in the love that accompanies and know that this is all love directed and not fear based, that people of your dimension will do it on their own. Take each day as a celebration to honor that God of Light that will soon ascend onto the planet in a different form than human to be sure, but yet the same.

"Star workers set in motion what needs to be put into action to lift those who second guess this change of frequencies. This Embassy makes the world sacred in its dealings in and of this planet, and in doing so makes its graduation, so to speak.

"Gathered in this Embassy are Light Beings from around the Galaxy, and in themselves just being here cross-over changes are being made. This cosmic community intersects with the world dimension you live and function in. It takes massive attention gesturers to bring people together as one in the love and Light of what this City represents totally.

"So then, as when any change appears, fear comes as a companion rushing forth to protect in the survival system programmed within. People fear what is unknown or not understood, but for some, they move through that into higher knowing that 'all is well.'

"The energy patterns of change are moving into 'shock' position and all will feel the impact. Due to the inner feelings of Lightworkers, a knowing is produced even before it is validated by your media. When the inner terror rises to be experienced as a disaster, to those who have been elevated in consciousness to a higher point of understanding, they know that the necessity to cleanse is the perfect recognition of what is taking place and all in divine right order. Do you understand these words?"

G: "Yes, and what would be our position to move through such an Earth-changing unsettling trauma?"

O: "Practice staying in balance in the knowing of what is to be brought forth, and that The City of Light has been selected to bring such healings that have never been seen before on this planet. It has been said before that The City of Light has been selected to bring forth healings and would be a major attention-getter, never before produced or seen in your world. To have a trauma happen, it then becomes validated and the imprint is very effective, because then people believe their prayers are being answered, through the combined energy of The City. And they trust in God, Buddha or whomever and say, 'Yes, they have appeared to help us, praise God!'

"This precursor to The City is in place. An example would be that this planet would be like a dog shaking off water from his fur. Trauma brings people together in loving ways and shakes off the darkness of undeveloped Light. Those who cannot hold such energy patterns will leave and only return when they decide to learn the 'Light way.'

"So then, this gathering is a preview of what was announced eons ago and mentally programmed as 'The Big One.' Prepare not for fear, but in the holy revelation that the Christ principal is in action and the Genii remembers the old song title 'On that great, come and get it day' and that will be when this planet shines in the heavens for all to enjoy near and far, never again to be destructive in its dealings.

"This City is a gift and all will know when it is time. Any more questions?"

G: "What is my mission in all this?"

O: "Precisely why you are being advised to take the lead and be an example. Stay in your upper leveling and lift those who may not understand what is taking place. Meditate, rest, trans-audio, for your senses are becoming more refined as each moment passes. The world of illusion is in such a state of flux that it is important to bring forth The City of Light healing facility, and come it will! Now, have you received the impact of these words?"

G: "Oh my, yes. Being inside this City and its healing factors, I know this is really needed, having been blessed to re-enter many times. Thank you for this magnificent dwelling of love that was delivered to Dr. Townsend so many years ago. I proudly carry on his legacy the best I can and will continue as advised and guided."

With this, I knew my time was up, so I was escorted out of the building, onto the trolley and back to the Gate. I said goodbye to my Guide and found myself back in my bed in Sedona on a sunny morning.

The Feminine Rejuvenation Temple

August 13, 2009

"Be Ye Renewed By the Renewing Of Your Mind"

The way was made clear to re-enter The City of Light by watching whatever appeared on my screen of space. The 4 Keys to Light classes I share with others have taught me well. This was only the second time I had taken someone with me. I looked to enjoy what she and I would see, as no previous indication had been apparent.

Arriving at the usual Gate of Receiving, I met my Guide La-Luke, my guest, Amayra and a Guide of hers. We entered the Park of Relaxation where she seemed to be beaming as she rested on a massaging bench, which began to massage her back. She snuggled into it but not for long, as we moved through the massive willow trees, moving their branches aside like curtains ready to see the show. We traveled onto a path unknown to me.

"Where are we going?" I asked my Guide.

L: "Ah, yet another Building of Receiving."

We seemed to walk quite a ways past previously-seen buildings, which were all in white with gold trims. "Exquisite!" I remarked silently to myself.

My guest tried to take in everything she could as we suddenly turned to the right and to a beautiful building more like a temple, which I had not seen before but I recognized, like all the rest, this was a healing facility of some sort.

G: "What is this place?"

He just smiled and bid us enter what looked like one of those doors that one can revolve in like in hotels. Inside this building we saw what was called a Transforming Welcome Station. Transforming what? Oh, well, we felt it was great just being in The City.

The look on Amayra's face said she concurred. The lobby like many others, had a bubbling fountain off to one side that made a tinkling sound as the droplets hit the bottom.

Suddenly a female who appeared kind of transparent (which I call a see-through) came into view and requested that the male Guides stay put and that we women follow her down a very high-ceilinged corridor. On the walls of the corridor and up to the ceiling there were vines of some sort where pink and white tiny flowers bloomed and they had a sweet scent that was delicious.

Our corridor trip was a short one, as yet another circular room with yet another waterfall and strange music coming from somewhere unknown, came into view. At this point several transparent ladies appeared in flowing pastel-colored gowns. They beckoned us to follow as they laughed. Their laughter in itself was healing.

We were now at another room with a very large overhead screen and were invited to lie on the lounges provided and requested to just rest - so we did. As we did, the screen above gave us the instructions in English of what was to come next.

We were to watch our earlier lives come forth in picture form, and when we saw a time we thought of ourselves as beautiful, young, vibrant, healthy and happy, to stop at that point and keep this mental image firmly in place. We went through being born into this life, the teen years, young adults, etc. The interesting part also was that even though there was only one large screen, we only saw our own life. Cosmic stuff to be sure. Why not?

I picked the time I was satisfied with what I saw, and I can only suspect she did too. We were then to mentally imprint that sight we liked as an up-to-date memory clip that would sustain no matter what age we became, even 209. Fascinating! Two female entities came over and though no audible words were heard, one told us that we would always look like that, first to ourselves, and then to others. This was a MIND MAKE-OVER. Imagine that!

A bevy of angel-type giggly female entities gathered around as we lifted off the lounges. We human females looked at each other and joined in with the attendees. Indeed, years had fallen away so as to be nonexistent. So much for all the cosmetics and surgery used now these days to do what we saw happen here. Let's hear it for this type of make-over. Whoopee!

We left the building feeling great with no memory of aging. It was all a mental make-over. We headed back to our male Guides who grinned, as they knew what was going to take place with becoming the new us. We came in as one person and got the thrill of any lifetime.

The women will get in line for this kind of delightful experience. The new us left the building, escorted back through the Park and to the Gate of Entrance with our memory healed to only be the person we had chosen to look like and be. Thanks God!

Back in Sedona I could see many ready to get a memory make-over. This had been a fun trip that indeed would change our lives forever. So that is the City of Light Rejuvenation Temple. It will indeed be a favorite place for women in particular, to visit. Imagine that!

So Light It Be!

Out With the Old and in With the New

Embassy of Peace Headquarters Visit August 27, 2009

In my vision, I met with my Guide La-Luke at the now familiar Gate of Entrance into The City. We moved through the Park of Relaxation on the wheel-less trolley heading for the Embassy of Peace, where this immaculately-styled building held many entities from the Universe.

In entering I recognized the Head Representatives of Information and OOO-LON, who is the only one so far that has conversed with me. A hush fell over all of them in the auditorium. As I sat down, he began to speak in English.

O: "You have arrived back with questions?"

G: "Yes, at least one!"

O: "You are welcome, oh human leader of Earth time, and your question is?"

Having a feeling he already knew, I proceeded anyway. "What update can you give me of The City's actual appearance that I can report, if the question is not out of line, please?"

OOO-LON smiled, as did several around this table of information. "As you embark to speak to many, it is noted since you are into space-time, you request an update, and this is unavoidable due to the inquiries coming from you and others. So then put this information on your sheet of advancement for City recognition.

"It is observed that your planetary objective is in two parts. One wants peace at all costs, the other peace at their own personal interests. The turmoil and unrest vacillates daily. The wars continue, and many have taken their place in their own ecstasy of killing. Sound strange? Programmed achievement here.

"The so-called money god runs first with the sex god coming in second, which in many cases are one and the same. This is noted as each individual has their own shortcomings, so-called, to be cleansed. Are you getting the picture here?

"The Light waves now in process leave no personage out. All are in a major process of inner cleansing due to the new energy patterns being introduced, and massive changes are taking place. This cannot be avoided if the process is to be finalized. Thus, this massive endeavor brings to full view The City of Light.

"Strange feelings will be felt within each one occasionally not considered as normal, (The Genii will testify to this), inviting that person to re-evaluate what they are doing or have done in the past, as the mental upheaval will search for the answers.

"As has been said, your history will be just that, history of old doings, and this will dissolve in the ashes of the new births. People hold on to the old as the good old days. Well, they may not have been so good one way or another, but this still offers no advancement now unless some learning has come from it.

"It has done what it did then and now you are here, ready or not. The world unseen prepares for The City of Light, and it is like parting the seas, for it comes ready for action. So the update is all in order and moving into place. This is good news in the vastness of the Universe. We who re-enter the wave of lingering Earth thoughts seeking change which, as has been said many times, is in process.

"Take your given message to the world and those who seek answers will find this a step in the right direction. Be one who Lights their paths, for all it takes is one.

"Thank you for coming." And with that, OOO-LON sat down.

I bowed in thanks and La-Luke and I made our way to the exit, the trolley and the Gate. I hugged my Guide of so many visits and the scene disappeared as I recognized the Sedona red rocks back home.

So Light It Be!

Of Upheaval and Staying Balanced

Embassy Visit September 11, 2009

The Gate entrance was wide open as I entered the scene screen. La-Luke spread his arms open and grabbed my hand and we almost ran through the Park and onto the trolley, which usually took us to the Embassy of Peace Headquarters. This time was no exception.

This short ride stopped at the Embassy entrance and we moved into this building of Light Entities. Total silence greeted us; not even a breath was heard from the hundreds of entities who also filled this amphitheater. Nodding, I smiled as I crossed in front of several governing leaders to my usual placed seating. A nodding welcome was returned.

O: "You have been quietly summoned here this morning for reasons of advancement. So we speak from a light heart.

"The world of human affairs lifts its angry head in protest of changes in process that now no longer fit with the past old patterns. The change of energies are playing havoc to many who are unaware of what is underlying this process, if indeed they know that a process is in process.

"It is important that you, in particular, know and recognize the value of what is taking place. For the most part you have been well informed as you meet every challenge put to you in your own personal change-over.

"We are aware of the swiftness of each emotion that hits without warning on a continual basis, but this restructure of your systems is important as you lead yourself to be much more than you have been in any lifetime.

"All was to bring you to this point, this time, this moment, this century in history which coincides with The City appearance in order for the intelligence energy patterns residing in your Light Body aura to speak to the masses of what is taking place.

"When you speak even now, one or more intelligences may roar out the message of love to be sure, but directions as to what is coming about is fact, not fiction, and you feel the power within. Your system can shift many times in a period of one day. This you have felt from the highest touch of God to the lowest of being nothing.

"To stay in harmony, it is important to observe short periods of rest as the chemical make-up of your system adjusts its alchemy patterns and the swing is not so harsh. So then what can be added?"

G: "Speak, please, of this country's governing forces and how should I look at this chaotic upheaval, the President, and The City of Light appearance?"

O: "The determination that this country is for the people and is one with God is primary, and nothing less will be tolerated. The Obama leader stands as a pillar

of Light that can withstand the harshness of the place he leads, and indeed, all will be well and he and his family are well protected from the onslaught of viciousness of darkened minds who would themselves be in control.

"Adjustments are in process, so be it known that The City of Light in its place of unseen-ness at the moment, is waiting its appearance. Your place and those who also walk this path close to you, are affected and admonished to keep the God-intent as energies of honor. Stay the course ... be the Light and you all will make daylight out of darkness. We send you forth to release what is to be no more.

"The message you received to be able to see The City through human daily eyes in the physical, will come as a see-through advantage point, and there will be validation. Stay on course, as both you and the sister of lives past, Kathie, are predestined to attend the appearance.

"The Charles has his work cut out in blueprint for him in areas yet attracted but escalating him as Ambassador of World Green. So then this all being said, as you travel together to various places, your Light intensive breaks forth any concerns anyone might have, as he works to fulfill his destiny which of course, connects to The City appearance. So then what say you?"

G: "My request is assistance to keep me balanced in The City Light that my body keeps in its healthiness and my mind tuned into the frequencies of The City."

O: "It is so advised! Now take yourself back to the physical and assist in cheer, love and peace and return as requested."

With that he stood and bowed as we left, heading back to the Gate and the scene vanished. I was back in Sedona to take care of my puppy who needed attention.

So Light it Be!

130

Today is the Tomorrow of Yesterday

Embassy Visit October 4, 2009

Pre-visit inquiry:

Q: "What is to be known?"

A: "Nearer My God to Thee" brings forth the inner feelings of the Genii and touches her heart as she moves forward with her "Soul Convictions" of what is to come about in your dimension.

"The message is clearly defined in each contact, so permit us once again to have you enter into The Sanctuary of Peace and Light ... The City of God which is opened to be enjoyed. As the coming prospects of it enter into your mental equation of 'Life as it appears which is today ... the tomorrow of yesterday.'"

CITY VISIT BEGINS

As I entered into my inner vision corridor, I saw myself walking up to the golden awesome Gate (one of several). What looked like crowds of people were already there. They faded away and my Guide La-Luke smiled as I approached him, and it all seemed like a dream sequence. La-Luke held out his hand as he smiled to see me.

L: "You have been away a long time." It didn't seem like it to me, but what is time, but an illusion anyway.

Entering into the now-familiar Park of Relaxation, I was tempted to sit on one of the massage benches and do just that ... enjoying the fantastic flowers, trees and just the peace of this place, but this was not to be our stopping place. The wheel-less trolley pulled up and I knew that we were headed to The City Embassy of Peace, a distance away.

We were hustled into the interior that is like an amphitheater with hundreds of entities in the background and several leaders who held court, so to speak, sitting around a horseshoe-type table. I nodded and sort of bowed to those there, as I was guided to the seat of honor (Not sure what the honor was ... but it was comfortable and opulent, so what was there to be rejected)?

The leader, OOO-LON stood and said, "You have had the feeling to return, is that not so?"

G: "Yes" I replied.

O: "And so it is, and we welcome you on behalf of all in attendance here ... many of whom are from other parts of the galaxy, and have been instrumental in putting forth this City you are speaking of to those who will listen."

G: "Is there a particular reason?" I asked.

O: "Quite so. The terrain of the Earth is in movement and various regions are and will be touched. Some will be evacuated due to the inner Earth pressures of the new life changes, in accordance with the coming of this Holy Place of Healing. When fear is triggered, people look to God to save them from death, which leads them to God (so-called) in any case.

"As the next advanced year enters the orbit, it is most important that what has been revealed to you regarding The City, stay intact with the solid notion that the divine entrance will be of valued construction, is being put into place and into the third dimension as all is on course.

"Forget not your position in the announcement of this Heaven on Earth, which has been pronounced for eons of time. As has been repeated, this is the only prototype that will be seen and be able to be entered into, while the others that are unseen are in place. It takes only one demonstration to shake up a world ready for healing and this is where you come into play.

"With the new paradigm now in effect, more teachers, channels and Light facilitators are desired to bring advanced awareness to the masses. So Lightworker attention should be put into place to teach The 4 Keys and Light Link, thus opening the unknown Light corridor and thus bring through their own personal soul Guides and Gatekeepers, as teachers and leaders, thus clearing the way for the 5th Key to enter The City personally, to see for themselves what is coming about in this healing edifice.

"The closed holy door of the past is now opening for the Genii to teach the teachers, for time is short, so to speak. There are many who would be excellent leaders and can gather in their world, many who can become the spreader of the news through their own inner visits.

"To name a few who have been linked: Kathie Brodie, Richard La-Duke, Renee Trenda, and even now a new friend of channeled masters, Cynthia Williams, who would be an excellent teacher since she is a noted channel herself. Plus more yet unknown.

"So then, it is time to spread the word and pass The 4 Keys on to others so they can link in Light yet more. What has taken 4 hours to teach will now be designed to approximately an hour or a bit more. A prepared session can be set in place in writing format and live action."

G: "How is this to be done? Especially the hidden word?" I asked.

O: "Would we not explain this in its perfect order? Of course! More and more people are being open to receive unusual answers through their own Light work, and the time is now. Travel is indicated and even classes on the internet can be programmed. Being opened to the suggestions offered would be a part the Charles could lead in the way best expressed."

G: "And what of the personal Guides and gatekeepers of each?"

O: "Once the concept is in place, those who have been 'Light linked' even in large groups, can take this on themselves, if they are open to take on this assignment.

"Expect this to move out quickly when in place. Teach the facilitators to teach the next set of facilitators. Gather many as leaders as guided. You no longer have to do it all.

"The holy door of secrecy is opening for advancement. And an initial financial cost can indeed be not the primary reason, but can be enticement to help human expenses. Are you willing to serve in this position?"

G: "Of course!" I replied, ready to serve.

O: "Good then! In this new paradigm, be ready to begin. You are in agreement and open to serve whoever is drawn to extend themselves into the new paradigm, and the New Keys.

"So then, this session is at a close, and we will be in contact. So expect a City return as well as through your Light corridor."

As he said this, he stood up, bowed and smiled. We left this place of progress, made our way to the trolley and the Gate entrance, and into whatever steps were next.

I thank God and my teacher Guides who move many forward into The City of Light demonstration.

So Light it be!

City Coming Forth Information

Embassy Visit December 1, 2009

The Gate of Entrance again appeared as I entered into the vision, unprepared for what to expect. The smile of La-Luke reminded me that this would be a special time and that we were headed for the Embassy. The wheel-less trolley pulled up as we exited the Park of Relaxation. Entering this magnificent building filled with entities from all over the Universe was a sight in itself to behold. Passing the head table with the five VIPs, I bowed and took my usual place.

O: "You have returned with questions on behalf of your planet?" I heard a familiar voice request.

G: "Yes. Well, sort of," I replied hesitantly. "I have been told that I will begin to see this City imprint. Is this correct?"

O: "As said. This form of energy patterns is being fortified to be of service to you, as others begin to sense there is something of evidence to their senses deeper than they may know. This, then, you will be able to verify as time releases its connection and the projected Major Shift takes hold. The days ahead will be exciting, yet in an unbalanced state as you are now experiencing."

G: "And what is my job in all this?"

O: "The declaration of such an event of this magnitude will take you on trips of explanation. Ready all your data and be alert to new additions. Set your house in order, as you will have little time other than the City preparations. Take each day and utilize the home in production and preparation. Watch what new areas you are invited to enter and be selective. Rest is important, as your inner senses are enhanced to a high pitch and your senses become a constant announcement companion. The year coming soon will hold the Declaration of what is now being verified as sacred, holy, long since referred to as the Coming of Heaven on Earth, for it is so. So then are there any more questions for this session?"

G: "I am just so filled with love and gratitude for the information and the encouragement to continue so I may serve in the highest truth and honor. It is hard for me to express my feelings. Thank you."

O: "All at this moment being said, go in peace and love and spread those feelings to all you contact. We honor your position and service."

With that, a feeling of dramatic love came from the faintly seen audience and we left. I found myself back in Sedona with a deep knowing that indeed I was privileged to be a part of hearing and of being of the bigger, yet unseen picture.

So Light It Be!

The Planeteers

Embassy of Peace December 23, 2009

The Gate looked sparkly with lights beaming up to the heavens. I in a holiday mood met with my Guide La-Luke. He has been such a gentle, loving support all these times. He looked a bit like Santa as his light gray beard took on the shine of the lights.

He was dressed in white robes and was indeed a vision to my eyes. I wondered what he would show me this visit. In any case I was blessed to be able to take these inner vision visits and gather City information.

He took my hand and we almost ran through the Park of Relaxation as he hustled me past the now parting willow trees that seemed to know we were on the way, and in here they probably did!

"Where to?" I gasped. As the trolley appeared, I knew we were on the way to The City Embassy, a place of information and guidance from cosmic entities. Groovy. The wheel-less trolley whisked us to the doorway and we entered into this sanctuary of peace and advancement.

OOO-LON was also all decked out in white robes that reflected his inner love and respect for any guests who might enter. The almost unseen audience in the semi-light behind the CEO's at the front table sent forth a hum tone that resonated through my body temple. We crossed to my seat and I felt I had just joined the upper crust of higher beings who were really unknown to me.

OOO-LON spoke: "Again during your Earth festivities time, your wish was to come again and thus, here you are. We are pleased to serve you. What may be your pleasure from us?"

G: "I know not what to ask. Well, maybe. I would like to know more about those who are part of this vast audience. Who are they, where do they come from and why?"

OOO-LON took a seat with those at his table. They all looked human but I sensed otherwise.

O: "We who serve you are contained in a Cosmic Community where war or harm cannot be perpetrated by anyone as IT JUST DOES NOT EXIST. The Universe is a plentiful place of entities who have developed through what you would call centuries beyond. This not behind. Beyond is the 'before you' that we speak of here; 'future,' if you will, in your language.

"They are referred to as 'Planeteers' who inhabit different planets, mostly unknown to you Earth people, as your intelligence level has yet to make the leap; except through your motion pictures and they show only for the most part havoc and destruction.

"These Planeteers are not this. They are builders of Empires set in Light frequencies that you would refer to as stars. Your development seekers call them dust particles, minerals, etc. This has been taught as the target for eons of time yet unremembered, by humans who struggle to maintain some kind of mechanical entry to bring forth the answers.

"Even the moon (so-called) has levels of dimensions never before seen but maintains the outer facade to your astronauts' evaluations. Sky travel is limited only to now and then time slots, as contact is sought with something other than Earth. What is not understood or for the most part accepted by many, is that contact was made eons ago. It has been the primary source in fulfilling this current project that's aimed itself as a masterpiece of deliberate intention set in place to cure what has ailed this planet for far too long, and still continues in its Light and darkness interlude under the guise of peace. This will not continue!

"Dear One, you stand knowing better, due to years of interceptive work you were led into by the Dr. Bill. He was and is a prime leader to what you would call 'spilling the beans' of this Divine Healing Demonstration. Does any of this make sense to you?"

G: "Oh, yes. Many years ago when my husband was channeling, I asked if I could see The City before it is humanly seen. The answer was yes. It took a few years but I am astounded at what I have been prized to see and enjoy. Spaceships and Extraterrestrials have always felt like friends and teachers to me. Even now as I write this, I feel such a surge of love and the tears flow easily. Why is this that I feel like I am just a visitor on Earth?"

O: "For this is so, as Lyra is your home base. Even though it seems many light-years away, it is in your heart as 'home.' It is one of those stars we spoke of earlier. The dimension you live in now is different because you are in human form, but another dimension exists within your Light Body that says what you have just asked. This information would take much time to explain, but soon you shall know the whole picture.

"Speak with Hermes and venture back here as questions equal answers and you are open to receive."

As this was spoken, I knew the visit was over. My Guide tapped me on the shoulder and we bowed as we headed out the door onto the trolley and back to the Gate. My classroom was Earth and my future unknown, but what the heck, look what I was finding out. Amazing!

Thanks, God!

So Light It Be.

Upward and Onward

Embassy Visit January 8, 2010

A new year invited me to request a trip back into The City of Light. Request Granted! With my energy fields in place and mentally aware and vision positioned, I perused the visual Gate Entrance five stories high with my personal invite to return to the Embassy of Peace.

Once more my constant City Guide appeared, gray white beard and all, in the image of La-Luke with a smile that made me think of Santa Claus in robes. The ooh's and ahh's of the people were loudly heard as they admired in amazement this holy place of Light and healing.

I wondered: What if no healing of any kind was needed? Would there be a healing city needed? By the time this thought had had its way, I found us once again on the wheel-less trolley feeling a bit like Oz's Dorothy when she remarked, "Things come and go so fast here."

Maybe I was Dorothy on my way to meet the wizards, which certainly was what was inside the Embassy of Cosmic Information of universal travelers to this planet. It was no wonder I could get "spacey" on a daily basis at home with all this advanced far-out information I was privy to.

Head leader OOO-LON was standing, as I now faced him from my conversation chair for what looked like a one-to-one conversation. The only sounds I heard were breathing sounds from the faintly-observed entities in the background that filled this huge place. I honored them and sat down. OOO-LON did likewise and he spoke the following:

O: "We welcome you back to our City domain. How may we serve you?"

G: "For us on planet Earth, changes are beginning in full force with weather, violence, and people going crazy trying to figure out what is going on, much less handle it on a day-to-day basis. We salute this new year of 2010 even with the unstable conditions and conflicting minds looking for peace and stability. What can be said of these changes and the interest in 2012 ahead?"

O: "It is observed that all you are reporting has validity and the predictions of a calmer peaceful world is still on the Books of Life fulfillment. Correct prophecies of such, an interpretation of ageless prophets who lovingly predicted this has set the course not only for themselves but also for cosmic entities who, though distant in the heavens, are nevertheless very important to the cleansing of this planet. What you do here has far reaching effects, and they are determined to support the efforts here, and have and continue to do so even today.

"Many on your planet think you are the only planet with intelligent life. Nonsense! Your planet is just a baby in the scheme of a cosmic community. What have your planet people done with what God has given you as a gift?

137

"Certainly drastic changes must be implemented for this planet to survive, or what would you have to walk on? Pay attention here! When a wound needs healing, do you not apply an antiseptic?

"So the shake-up or shift is in process, not unlike a dog shaking off excess water from his fur. All this you are aware of, but it sets the scene for others to be in agreement with themselves by being aware. This may set the scene but not perhaps give you much comfort at the moment, but you can count on being able to handle it when you are aware what is coming into view as the healing edifice called the Holy City of Light.

"There will be planetary peace, and those of minds that would oppose this idea will leave by their own hands, as there are no victims, only creators, and all are creators.

"The dateline of 2012 leaves little time of completion, and all this turmoil will continue if left to its own devices. The Cosmic International Community united in its efforts of cleansing, are gathered here in this domain of Light as we lovingly solve the problems the Earth people give themselves. Like they have nothing else to do? Please! We make room for the new edifice you sit in at this moment.

(There was a hum in the auditorium behind him.) "This has been all preplanned, and even your part was included as a representative of what has been given you as a legacy left from your beloved husband, Dr. Bill.

"This God-man had many previously-impacted lives of service, and you know of his Hermes teachings. His background was vast with service and devotion, little of which he knew in this current life. When he departed this life, he learned of this and is preparing his part in The City demonstration forthcoming. His preparation with the beginning City plans has given way to the extension that has been given to you to perpetuate further into the demonstration forthcoming. As said before, this City has been imprinted in your DNA and cannot be removed as it transmits the meaning you are to give forth.

"Now then, the Dr. Bill exits and you stand in for him and millions of others, as you hold court with what has been left you to serve and announce with . . . a legacy to be sure. And now what do you do with it?

"Daily you feel your body in some kind of strangeness due to the mental change taking place that is unsettling but still part of your physical human form and must be, to report even if this is a bit shaky at the present moment. It too will pass away, finding yourself stronger.

"Earthy support of friends and family who understand the place in which you find yourself can be helpful and supportive, as they understand that this is not an Earthly so-called old age process. Quite the contrary, Elevation of Light is the title given from us.

"It is noticed that some of the Earthly interests have little or no interest anymore, that you have your head in the clouds. Imagine that! But what is taking its place? Far out interests? Of course.

"Like Dorothy of Oz, you are going home while still on Earth. Are you not learning Jedi ways?" (I nodded yes). "Your planet programming is that people forget, and you are hearing more and more of this, which includes you on occasion.

"What is happening, Dear One, is that you are being brought into the 'Now' between the past and the future. A really nice place to be; no worries, no concerns, just being, even when the mind wants to keep the past from leaving. Persevere unto the end, for it will serve you well. As you say, not a problem!

"You wonder how and where you will travel for announcing (with a companion of support). We smile (and he did) as all is in process. Your electronic invention called computer internet (kindergarten style though it may be at this point), has the opening to millions in one fell swoop. The contents of video and voice impacts the many, as what is being done now with the Charles at the helm sweeping up names and addresses of people who have more names and addresses etc. is in progress. Is this not an avenue of progress?

"The follow-up is in person. Would not people want to meet the real Genii? Of course! And as this year moves forward, expect the unexpected to appear as if by angels. Keep going. Dorothy's Emerald City of Light is right around the corner. So then, Lady of Light, what say you?"

G: (Trying to get a voice sound after all this) "Being in this place with all of you and hearing what has been said I am kind of speechless, but I recognize all is correct and right on schedule. I accept my place in what I can accomplish and will, to the best of my ability. Any extra energy and guidance will be appreciated."

O: "Indeed. It would be wise to write out your questions for future visits to fill in the blanks, so to speak, and for now we excuse you to return back to your Sedona home, where even today the energy fields are very active as you can feel and attempt to stay balanced. Quite a job, isn't it?"

And with that we stood and headed for the entrance. This was quite a process. And in a blink of an eye I was back home with my puppy who wanted to play.

So Light It Be.

Going the Distance

Embassy Visit February 4, 2010

I entered into a quiet meditative state of consciousness. I also entered into the familiar south Gate of The City of Light, which shone bright and as clear as a crystal; a magnificent place to be sure. A rush of energy swirled around me and I knew that my Guide La-Luke had arrived. Did he ever! He grabbed my hand and whizzed me through my favorite Park with no stops on massage benches, and almost immediately I was ushered into The City Embassy of Peace Headquarters. What, no trolley ride? Things move fast here!

Immediately as we entered the Embassy all seemed to be urgent. Maybe it was due to the constant Light power surges I had been experiencing lately, that has been said is a lifting of my Light Body frequencies. Okay, whatever. The main leaders were in attendance, but there was also a new Entity there that stood up when they did, and I was moved to also stand in front of them. The energy level went up ... wow! This entity was almost transparent "it" was so light, or something.

OOO-LON welcomed me and said that this comrade was from a Cosmic Community far distant. Wow, this was getting interesting, and I didn't even have to have a passport into space because they came here. Imagine that!

OOO-LON said: "He speaks not your language but that I would speak, for he brings a message of good tidings."

And with this, the frequencies around this Entity began to shift. Even his robe took on an unusual aura of soft color changes.

I thought, "This is beginning to be some kind of experience. Beginning? Maybe I am getting a cosmic consciousness?"

OOO-LON smiled as he read my thoughts. "Indeed," was his reply!

OOO-LON (speaking for the Entity): "I come from a place of far off distance many areas from this planet. I come to tell you, as a speaker of this place of healing, that destiny has arrived. (Here I got emotional with real tears). "We are diminishing distance to bring forth this place yet unseen but destined. Your place in the whole of this is well established within the Community of Cosmic Dwellers. You have noticed that you are in the physical what you have been told are Light Power Surges within your Light Body. Is this true?"

I nodded yes.

OOO-LON continued speaking for this entity. They were sure connected, and even OOO-LON looked a bit brighter. "You are being raised into an altered state of being and your connection to the Cosmic Community is well known."

G: "Who me?"

Through O: "This is not to frighten you; in fact, it would be called, in your vernacular, a blessing. From this point forward, you can expect to enter into one of the cosmic-type interests as a Linking Consultant, connecting of suffering people who would be welcomed into The City of Light Healing. Distance has collapsed and The City beckons the Genii to return for cosmic commands of events to take place on your planet, and you will be advised."

My feeling was agreeable but strange with all this, which could be overpowering if I permitted it to be. OOO-LON picked up my thoughts. A calmness fell over me that was quite pleasant, and I felt that I could go the distance somehow. To imagine that I have been presented with a Universal Community, looking to have me do something, is a long way from a stuttering high school dropout in Chicago, Illinois. I took a deep breath as OOO-LON continued his friend's words.

Through O: "The way of Light has targeted areas of clean-up that are set in motion, and it has already begun. Consciousness is to be raised in many ways. It is important that you return here for guidance and introduction to yet more Entities of various cosmic communities not yet known." I was beginning to feel like an astronaut at ground level.

O: "This is the message. 'Be aware. Be a person of courage, truth and honor. What you have been given indeed is factual evidence of the coming. Many will hear what others do not, due to its unusual strangeness, but necessary nevertheless."

With that, the Cosmic Entity sat down and OOO-LON nodded to me and asked if I knew what was taking place. I did have a question. "I have recently met a man, Stephen Every, who I took through advanced teachings, that said seriously he feels he is a Spaceship Commander. What is to be known of this?"

O: "Could this be so? Of course. This man has been led to you to learn of future City work he will do due to his training in advanced technology beyond this planet. Remember, you are excelling into the World of Universal contacts and anything is possible, even meeting a Space Vehicle Commander. Have we now taken your question to the world of answers?"

G: "Yes, way beyond what I could have ever imagined way back when this all started with Dr. Bill. Thank you. And learning of the Power Surges gives me an indication of elevation and a bit of sense in what I hear."

OOO-LON nodded as we left this cosmic chamber of Light. And so I will go the distance, even if there is no distance to go. Imagine that!

So Light It Be!

The Finishing Place

City Of Light Visit Genii and Renee Trenda February 27, 2010

Quote: "And I John saw a new Earth and a new Heaven for the old Earth was transformed and passed away"

As I quietly envisioned our nearing the entrance Gate, Renee was in awe of the Gate itself. The white exterior and the gold scrolling on this incredible 5-story arched opening was enough to make anyone a believer and be in gratitude.

No Guides were seen ... OOPS! Then yes they were. My Guide La-Luke and her lead Guide Way-ah appeared smiling, for one more enters The City of Light. So far three have been inside this way. As we made our way into the Park of Relaxation, Renee was encouraged to sit on the massage bench. She wasted no time in getting there as we watched in glee. Quickly we were rushed out through the curtain-like willow trees and into the main interior.

La-Luke said to turn right and in the far distance we saw a triangle-shaped white-gold building. I was advised that at each point it was a rounded (healing) pod. Next up was the wheel-less trolley that is off the ground and only lowers for us to get on or off. No driver have I ever seen. We climbed aboard. I have seen many buildings but not this one. Renee was so excited the trolley tipped a bit but stayed on course.

G: "What is this place?" I asked my Guide as I looked at Renee. Any place would be perfect.

La-Luke smiled and said, "Permit us to enter and see."

We stepped inside and into a fragrant garden of varied flowers making the air smell heavenly, of course. We were ushered past them, and instructed to look into one of the pod points where children were playing with colored-lit toy objects. This was a healing finishing-place where people who have had Light treatments of many kinds could, in sensing that their own healing within has taken place, get ready to leave, be they children or adults.

The other two pod points each had such a finishing place too. One for men and one for women ... That makes the 3-pointed building function as you see. The air was continually kept fresh and the frequencies enhanced the areas of the mind/body to feel that they indeed were healed no matter what kind of healing was desired.

Also there were screens like computers like you have seen at your Heart-Math center that collate the inner emotional frequencies and balance out the body/mind interior. Instantaneous healing is also experienced within The City interior. Each pod is dedicated to service, as vibrational uplifting of the emotions and mind connect in perfect harmony. Thus it is a finishing place for people to go back into their world and bring with them the harmony to others.

The children's pod had the frequencies of play and joy, enhanced along with the imagination, to foresee what had not been seen before, as these children are the future of the planet and harmony must rein consistently.

The men's pod area had the frequency of power and mental acuity to foresee ahead, both in recognition of what this planet is all about, and to keep the harmony in peaceful ways. Through this they learn to love and they learn that war is not the answer. As a result they will abandon such foolishness and pain.

The women's pod had within its boundaries, vibrational Light that balanced the emotional fields. Advanced Light technology was delivered, thus elevating the consciousness that all was finished from within, and unearthed with the love-sensory destined to take over the planet in quiet force. The women have a wondrous place in history, even as new babies are born in world-wide Birth-ateriums, like what you have seen happening here in The City.

Renee was speechless as she watched the children at play and even they looked lit up. I asked her what she thought. She hesitated a moment and then said, "Somehow I knew I am doing my healthy work at home for a reason and now I know why. I was destined to come here and find my place in the scheme of things to come forth. My work can make a difference in my world. I feel healed just being here. I am so grateful."

La-Luke tapped me on the shoulder and I felt that we were to leave. We took a deep breath, smiled and said thanks to this 'finishing place' and Renee's Guide nodded yes. We took leave of the pod of children at play, strolled back to the Park and back to the Gate entrance.

Before we left, Renee stopped for one more sitting on the massage bench and indeed this was a finishing touch to this visit into The City of Light. We said good-bye and the vision ended with more additional information coming through as I typed up this message.

And I GENII SEE A CITY OF LIGHT APPEARING OUT OF THE HEAVEN ADORNED WITH GOD'S HEALING LIGHT AND SO LIGHT IT BE!

Community of Cosmic Dwellers

EXTRATERRESTRIAL INTRODUCTION!

Embassy Visit March 5, 2010

The Gate of Entrance loomed large and beautiful as I tapped into my screen of vision. It was seen as an evening with stars shining in the heavens like crystal shards, but my real interest was to enter the Embassy and see what was up there. This was my 21st visit there and now being summoned sounded exciting.

My Guide La-Luke hustled me into The City Park and then onto the waiting trolley that whisked us to the Embassy of Peace in quick order. He said I was expected. There seemed to be some movement as we entered and headed for the now familiar head table and OOO-LON, the so-far main speaker.

He stood alone and welcomed us with, "Welcome back to the stellar community of space dwellers here to serve." The amphitheater-type building began to hum as I looked around past him through what had been seen faintly before. It began to get a bit lighter and then I could see hundreds of entities unfamiliar to me.

I tried to make out their appearances, but I could still only see them faintly. I just knew they were special as such love was sent to me from row after row after row. I could have floated away on that energy. Now this was real, total love and I was the recipient. The realization made tears flow down my face. Imagine that! We need to let people know there is nothing to fear from E.T.s. They are and have been helping us for God knows how long.

OOO-LON smiled as he announced that these were community friends from cosmic universities who have long since banded together with each of their kind in a force field to bring forth The City of Light here, and the salvation of our planet which needs to band with those I have just spoken of sitting here in unison. With this I was speechless!

G: "I am so honored that I can hardly speak, to be with such a vast intelligent audience. I always have had an interest in space deities. We humans may see UFOs on occasion but this is something else. Wow! I am so excited, I have to sit down in overwhelm."

O: "As expected. As you are well aware, the Universe is a hologram and each one here is one with the Center Creator, as you call God, but there is more to this. Each one here is from spaces beyond spaces that are a part of the hologram. They have the intent of expanding the Light lines connecting a force field of a universal power that brings your people peace, love and a healing facility never before seen on this planet. Does this make any sense to you?"

G: "Yes, we all are connected to the one center of a universal holographic center source, and being this, the cosmic community banded together with intelligent energy forces so they and we, could bring into view The City of Light with healing technology of Light probably not known here. Is this correct?"

O: "There is much more advanced thinking but this will do for the moment. Now then, I would have you meet a friend from the banded community of universal knowing ... Sa-Daaa, who shares with you further."

From the shadowy background an entity came into view. Guess it was a he? He walked on two legs and had two arms and his wide hands type had six fingers and his skin was a light orange color with tiny bumps all over it. His face was not scary but quite nice, with the head section being in sort of a triangle shape, no nose to speak of, black eyes like the night sky, and a small indentation of a smile. I just fell in love with him as he sent me such a groovy unusual feeling. Golly, a new far out friend. Imagine that! God is so good to me!

OOO-LON spoke for him: "This is Sa-Daaa! And he wishes you to know that the work on The City has been completed and that his community declares that their part is over and supplied with the Sa-Daaa technology that has been inserted."

G: "What else am I to know?"

O: "Prepare yourself and the many as possible. In the days ahead the energy fields will pick up and the sensory indications of the planet will change into one that is compatible with The City. All cosmic communities now enter into the final stages of this centuries-old project, with frequencies beyond what has been experienced before. Time is, as said, short term, and the immediacy as spoken of will begin to be felt, but much more. Be aware of new instructions to come forth and move with them as guided. Now then, is there anything else? The stability of the humans will alter the present conditions and be the way the planet itself will survive."

G: "Yes. Where does Sa-Daaa come from?"

O: "Many eons of space away and from a small planet, but dedicated to see this one survive. It is called (but in a tonal language)... Cervan-Delka. The tones and the sounds of the Universe of this one is not on your sky maps, but we will send you picture mental imprints periodically from him so you can enjoy his home place. Just be open to receive. All is well and in progress. So then know that indeed all is well and we shall be in touch to move you forward into your world of announcement."

I gratefully bowed as I felt the energy lift in the building, making me feel a bit weak as we moved outside. The air was fresh and the stars as I looked up to them, seemed to wink back at me.

And so ended another visit to the Embassy of Peace.

So Light It Be!

Universal Embassy of Light . . . Jerusalem Clue

Embassy Visit March 19, 2010

Before I had even done my meditative work I was advised to go to the Embassy in The City of Light. Just trying to wake up set my course to the now familiar Gate where I saw my Guide La-Luke who grabbed my hand and ushered me through the park and onto the trolley.

G: "What's up?" I asked.

L: "The Embassy leaders want to speak with you."

G: "I gather it is important?"

L: "Isn't all this important?"

We arrived at the Embassy now referred to as the>>>>MAKE NOTE> Universal Embassy of Light <<<<<<<. As we entered we found the inside building all lit up and I could see behind the head leaders, that indeed there were hundreds of entities in various descriptions and sizes. Welcome to Star Trek!

I was escorted to my usual un-usual chair as OOO-LON stood and welcomed us by beginning to say, "You have been summoned here to put an addition into the updating of the City book. There is one thing more to be added as you finish this manuscript, and this is what is to be added.

****

'To the readers of the Earth planet ...

'The whole biology of The City is correct and should be honored as such! You who are reading this as the printed copy in your hands, or on the electronic device of the internet, are welcome and advised to take this information within yourselves for the feeling of what has been delivered to you.

'The City of Light enters through the region of the United States of America and the key word here is 'United.' Why the United States instead of some far off unit of land? The City has been called Jerusalem (a holy place) from day one and the code of why, lay within the center of the word. And United it should be, for The City is a healing place to indoctrinate what the word United means, and is a factor to heal within each one, so this word has meaning throughout the planet.

'Those who may think this is just some fantasy or dream in the mind of the Genii will be in for a surprise soon. Before long your eyes will behold what has been laid out from the Dr. Bill to the Genii to you, to read, for you are on your path of Light. 'This City is and you will be able to walk into it and be mesmerized at the healing techniques observed, far beyond what is currently being seen and will forever stand as a pillar to God's intention to heal all, and not just be seen and then disappear into the ethers as just a mental illusionary picture.

'Take note and remember you read it here first and give praise to God, who as THE LIGHT birthed a City for healing the mind, body and spirit. Pay attention for it is now on your Earth plane in a close dimension being readied to birth into your 3rd dimension and you are to be recipient.'

"OOO-LON has spoken the truth for ears not only to listen but...to hear.

Be of good cheer The City is here."

So Light it be!

Something's Coming!

Painting © Charles Rhinehart (http://www.rhinehartartgallery.com)

Universal Cities of Light, Love, and Healing!

Changes in Progress!

Embassy Visit April 2, 2010

The 5-story entrance Gate was totally lit up as I mentally visioned in. A few people stood there as I arrived, including La-Luke my City Guide. As he neared me we wound our way through the Park of Relaxation and onto the trolley that was at a stand-still. Looking back in thought this Park is awesome. As the Embassy neared we saw that hundreds of kindred spirits had arrived before us. What a great way to begin a visit! How lucky am I?

We arrived at the Embassy and upon entering into this arena-type building, the leader OOO-LON smiled and bowed as we neared him and his CEO's at the head table. Behind them the arena was filled with entities from all over the Universe. How exciting is this? He motioned to me to take my usual seat as our meeting had begun. And what was to be said?

O: "Welcome back. We have been expecting you and honor you for your service in your world of confusion and ignorance. How may we serve?"

G: "When The City is physically seen by us humans, what will be the response and what will be seen as physical change due to its appearance to us? To have a City just appear out of the ethers will definitely make an instantaneous impact around the planet."

O: "The unstoppable acceleration now has set its course as the way of change stirs up the pot, so to speak. People are unsettled, angry and scared of what is taking place. This is a normal human reaction at this point. Change is necessary and whatever the reaction is, it is understood. But change it must, ready or not. All of your world may look dim and dreary and quite unsettled, but there is a Light at the end of this tunnel and it will show up with those who are staying centered as much as possible and helping other people stay the same way.

"The cosmic acceleration now has set its course as the way of change is activated (as you have been tuned in and know first-hand). At this point it will rise more as minds ignorant of what is in process wallow in fear and distrust, not realizing that in doing so they add to the situation. This year of 2010 as said, is seen as tumultuous. This is only the tip of the iceberg for rising into the fear brings yet more.

"People have ravaged themselves and this God-made planet for centuries. Not God-intended but by human choice. The craziness of unknowing minds gathers in ignorance of each other and unsettles themselves even more, as the masses buy into and add to the dark power. This cannot continue as the current energy waves surround the planet, pull up and out what has been growing too long in the wrong direction.

"You look at your media screen and what do you see? Cruelty runs amuck and this is not acceptable, but must come to the forefront to be made aware of, for it has been said that one cannot change what one is not aware of, to make that personal change. So change is apparently doing its job, even when one puts the blame on another instead of realizing everyone is responsible for their own actions. Again it is the Law of Attraction in action.

"The City of Light with its healing powers will change all that, for the vibrational energy now pulsating makes its mark on everyone. It is not just being aware that The City must come in order to make a lasting impression. Not only one, but millions upon millions of people are affected with The City's vibrational force fields now making waves across and around the planet. Those who cannot stand the impact will leave, and so it is, for darkness must be destroyed as the Light Bodied workers who have now worked consistently, surface and see before their own eyes God in all Its splendor, and rejoice for their work has been good and very good.

"This is not a fantasy of the Genii's mind in play. This will be personal for everyone and is totally correct. When one can see with their own eyes, the weak will strengthen and know God in a healing form. This will be different to be sure. This week of holiness called Easter includes a Good Friday where the cancellation was not a human on a cross, but a DIVINE being who drives the energy forward as he revels in what he sees. This is projected as a gift to this planet. Oh yes, Easter is indeed is the new birthing and you get to be lovingly a part of it.

"Will The City change people? Again yes! Oh yes! The Lightworkers will line up in praise of their work being seen as correct, and those who do not understand will have to learn new ways of looking at things, as the negative energy is dismissed as a thing of the past not wanted anymore. The energy fields have brought forth the Light of God and all are involved. Imagine that!

"So again we say, 'no more wars and mistreatment of people' as all are one and to kill one is to kill a part of one's self known or unknown. People will be soaked in love (not blood). Nothing else would be important. First the release of the old ways of thinking in process now, then the filling with that Abraham has said. '"You are source energy."'

"Time now to use it correctly and The City appearance all by itself, appearing suddenly from the ether's will make this, in the Genii theater vernacular, 'the Greatest Show this Earth has ever seen!' So then Light Human, has this helped?"

I nodded yes as I was pretty speechless. He bowed and added, "Permit the daily messages of encouragement to be given and move with them. So now we release you by saying 'We bid you the Light of the eternal day in peace and love!'"

So Light it be!

As I came back into the morning at home in Sedona, I had to re-read this for I miss out on some important information when I vision channel this way.

Cosmic Dream Makers!

Embassy Visit April 10, 2010

As the entrance Gate loomed large and beautiful before me in the sunlight, I had such a happy feeling that I almost ran through it to get to the Park of Relaxation just beyond. It felt like spring time that bubbled up within me and I was happy to be there. Into the Park I headed for one of the massage benches located hither and yon. Looking around, my constant City Guide La-Luke settled beside me and I felt completed, honored and slightly wondered what was next?

"Embassy visit?" asked La-Luke. I smiled as this was now a favorite location and a place to see entities from various planetary locations. "Sure, let's go" I heard myself saying and smiled. Then we could hear the trolley slide up and we hopped aboard eager to get going. A short ride and here came the Embassy and we unloaded at the huge doorway filled with flowered vines that smelled delicious.

Inside, past the flowering foyer, the amphitheater had a hum-like sound as though many unknown languages were being spoken that came from many faintly-seen figures that filled the background. With the usual extra entities beside him, the head honcho OOO-LON stood, and from his sleeved robe held out his hand in welcome which was a first for me. It was usually just a bow. Ah, progress being made. I gladly took the offering which left me tingling from head to foot and then returned to my usual seat of some kind of honor.

OOO-LON spoke: "And what would be the purpose of your visit?"

G: "I am not sure; to learn more I suspect. What can you share with me that would be important to the world I am to share with?"

O: "In the making of your new world, you know of the blessings to come forth as God empties the dark energies and as they rise to the surface to be acknowledged and then dissipated. In the wake of what is being done, we can tell you all is on course so set your mind at ease. The past interest of the horror of the world's demise is looked upon as the totality of the apocalypse written so long ago. Not so.

"People read into that as all is lost and the end is near. Such nonsense. Why would God destroy what is a beautiful companion of Its design to others in this holographic Universe? Only ignorance stays in fear and actually thinking it is correct.

"We shake our heads in unbelief and in your words say 'this is dumb thinking' when taking the thinking of something holy and beautiful and healing is the total result. Please.

"So if the world empties itself of fear and ignorance what could be better? Darkness wants to stay that way and as the Light of the One penetrates this ignorance, it squirms in its losing power. Those who embody the cosmic areas of love penetration beget more of the same.

"That is the change and the END result. The building of the New Earth, is a project of the Cosmic Dream Makers, every one, and billions with them say 'YES THIS IS CORRECT!' You of planet Earth shall be a neighbor we are proud to sail through the Universe with!

"The cosmology of the planets and sub-planets to bring forth the new birth of this planet that ignorance has almost destroyed, says that this planet and Mother Nature has decreed it will survive at all costs!

"Ignorance and darkness of various kinds have held the reigns for far too long. The end is in sight for it no longer has a comfortable place to fester and cannot stand under the God Light now penetrating and rightly so. In meetings we have here we share with you that The City of Love has given notice of its coming advancement and so it is!"

I tried to give some kind of remark or acknowledgement but the power I felt in this place kept me in awe. I guess I would not care to be darkness of any kind. Wow!

OOO-LON continued: "Rest in the play of Light and tolerate the darkness for yet awhile, for it is important for notification of The City and the uplifting value of those words you will speak. And so we rest this meeting."

In desiring to learn from the entities here of their origin, I sensed it could be arranged and we left the building and headed for the meeting Gate. I thanked my Guide and even got a cosmic hug back...groovy! How blessed am I to be able to do, see and feel what is coming into form.

And with that, I found myself back in Sedona on a sunny clear day knowing what I knew for sure and that ended this Embassy visit.

Thanks God!

It was a de-Light!

So Light it be!

Seeing the Unseen

Embassy of Peace Visit April 24, 2010

The five-story entrance Gate stood tall before me and I wondered if The City illumined the Sun or did the Sun illumine The City. It was pretty awesome anyway one looked at it. Many people were heading through the Gate portal as I saw my Guide approaching. La-Luke had been my friend for eons of visits. Today he ushered me through the arch, through the Park of Relaxation and onto the familiar trolley that took us to a mammoth building where entities gather from various parts of the Universe and who have been in their way, responsible in bringing forth this City of Light and Healing, the Embassy of Peace!

Head speaker OOO-LON stood up along with 4 others who held court in front of this assembly, as I was assisted toward my usual chair. As he stood, a hum was heard behind him in the background. I felt very welcome indeed.

O: "We welcome you back oh feminine of Light, into the history being made for your planet and we speak to you for a few moments."

I nodded not knowing what to expect. He continued..."The emphasis of The City of Light is on its three-dimensional approach, and progress has been made. No longer can you have any doubts, for in their subtle areas, it will begin to be seen by you. Very faint at first, but the progress of its appearance and with your mental/physical endurance of late, the portals open for your inspection and Light.

"Long since have you been aware of such a happening and now you can test your sanity, for the Light powered image you will see will testify what has been said for so long. Is this understood?"

I nodded and replied, "Is there something I should be doing to support what has just been said? "

OOO-LON smiled. "Dear One you have The City embedded in your DNA, heart and mind and now as the outer vision begins to appear slowly at first, just know that what you are seeing is accurate and enjoy the view.

"This will take time for you to get used to ... the new vision outlines ... but know that you are supported by all who sit in the assembly and on all levels. Stay with your heart attached and permit love to be your Guide as you do now in your world in preparation for the vision to appear, thus making more Light in your world. Is this agreed?"

Surely he jests, I thought. Would I not want to see the greatest show this Earth ever had? Then a smile from those in front told me they knew what I was thinking...duh!

"Of course" OOO-LON continued," it will be observed in bit parts. A bit here, a sight form there, which may surprise you as this will seem new, as you live your daily life through your integral guidance.

"You already see the cloud forms that tell you that they cover the space vehicles in the vicinity but people just see the clouds. Is all this clear?"

"Yes, I am fine. Oh ... I would love to have conversations with any space entity who would like to share with me."

O: "We shall set that on the agenda and invite you to sit in. Be Light, be the love that you are. Remember the High Court and your Adornment of Internal Love and all will be well with you!"

With that we all stood, bowed, and I turned to travel with my Guide to the entrance, the trolley, the Park and out the Gate where at this time I found myself relaxing on my bed with all my desires fulfilled.

Nice start for this day. What's next?

Thanks God ... All is perfect

P.S. As I looked out over the red rocks of Sedona from my bedroom window, I could see white Light like a rock aura. Wow!

So Light it be, for you and me.

Love, Genii

Ignorance of the Truth

Embassy Visit May 1, 2010

The sun was setting as I approached a Gate entrance and I was met by La-Luke my City Guide. Grabbing my hand he led me through the Park of Relaxation and onto the wheel-less trolley.

G: "Are we going to the Embassy?"

L: "Yes this is the destination. You are expected."

The trolley skimmed over the ground stopping at the front of this magnificent building filled with honorees from all over the Universe. This is some kind of adventure I was thinking as we entered the foyer that smelled of flowers and brought on a smile of delight.

We passed through the entranceway into this vast amphitheater. Before us stood the 5 head entities that are usually there, with Master OOO-LON speaking from a standing position. Behind them faintly seen are hundreds from space communities. I could almost hear them breathe. Now what, I wondered?

OOO-LON smiled as I was seated. To be in his presence is almost impossible to describe as he resonates so much love and wisdom, that I know that whatever I hear will be totally correct.

O: "The welcome mat is out for this Lady of Light for her to bear witness to what is being repeated here. So then listen, absorb, and know. The man President will welcome your talents as a father would to his children. Watch for the leading signs and center the mind on the Light (White) house visit.

"The way is being prepared as we center our frequencies into the passageway that comes soon open. The entities here have much power and will use it to open the doors for THE TRIP OF A LIFETIME!

"Remember that you are the forerunner of this information project and must have entrance to the Main Man in charge who has been as said, preprogrammed."

G: "The media has been saying not to make contact with E.T's. Thus spreading again the fears connected from a highly respected physicist, which to me, is plain stupidity since I know what I know. What of this?"

O: "Such nonsense serves only to balance what the Lightworkers know is truth and factual. The minds of the fear-laden will only heighten those who fear most anything. Those who search the heavens for signs of life welcome us with open arms.

"Some in the far-off tribes of your lands have no mental conception anyway. Those who worship the God deity know that He is in charge. (We say 'He,' only as a point of reference to some).

"The City appearance will set in place that those who are aware of the Light or Second Coming so to speak, will honor the entrance on bended knees along with many followers of the Buddha, etc. The list goes on and on. Be not concerned.

"Those of us who have held court here banish all such nonsense as it is just that ... nonsense. You have now been here many times and find us trustworthy. We come not to destroy. The Earth people of darkened minds do that very well. We do help to banish the ignorant darkness that propels the mental senders.

"Now then as the steps are brought forth into your dimension, follow them carefully, for the planet at the time of the VISIT WITH THE PRESIDENT OBAMA will be in your hands, so to speak, O string-puller of your world."

G: "I have a friend, Roger Deycaza, who uses energy as a healer in our world. In taking him into the linking Light, it was felt that he will be given scientific energy healing data that is not known here, but to help people here. What is to be known of this? Is this so?"

O: "Yes this is available. Even now the Roger of Light-assistance has the dynamics to heal and any advanced additions will only be of a much larger help. Take this beginning step and we shall replenish the words unsaid. In your vision bring him here and we shall endeavor to assist his beginning knowing. You are now excused!"

Wow and with that I found myself back home feeling I had been away for a very long time.

So Light it be!

Of YA-FU-FUS and Emorgy

Embassy Visit May 12, 2010

I was excited to see what could take place with Roger as he entered The City for the first time after being invited to the Embassy where I have rarely taken anyone before. My in-vision showed that we and many others were also entering. One look at smiling Roger told me he had found the reason for his transmission healing work. Yes, this was it; the reason for it all.

Suddenly La-Luke appeared and tapped Roger on the shoulder startling him a bit. They introduced themselves as we entered through the encoded entrance. Roger was grinning trying to take this all in. "'This is magnificent" he muttered. Then it was into the Park of Relaxation that he got his first taste of what a massage bench was for as he relaxed on one.

La-Luke motioned that the wheel-less trolley to the Embassy was waiting. The trolley waited patiently as we three climbed aboard tipping it a bit on its nothing underpinnings, and then zoom ... we literally flew over the ground. Roger tried to take in all the buildings we passed and before long we were in front of the beautiful Embassy building entrance while Roger tried not to miss anything.

The melt-through doors brought us into the lush gardens and the beauty to be enjoyed. That was followed quickly by being led into the main chamber that held hundreds of beings (most not seen but surely felt) headed up by 5 Entities at the main table in front of us. The center speaker was OOO-LON whom I have met here many times ... a male Light, filled with such love and wisdom that it can take one's breath away. How blessed we were to be in his presence.

My usual throne-type chair now had one more added for Roger. He took a deep breath trying to believe all that he was seeing, and wondering what or who he was not privy to see in the rear audience. But there was no doubt that there were plenty of beings here, believe you me. We were escorted to our chairs where we were seated and acknowledged.

O: "We see you have fulfilled your mission with the dark haired human. Sir, you work with the humanoids. You can be readied to help them even more as you now have direct contact with the "ENERGISTS" of space content. High esteem beyond your Earth channel ways. Your work so far has the imprint of what has healing effects; is this true?"

Roger worked hard in this scene to get the word 'yes' out. It was clear to see he was overwhelmed with what was taking place, as well he should have been. I know. Talking about a 'City' to appear out of nowhere is one thing, but actually being in it is another, and then having a space person ask him a question was almost too much on a first visit.

OOO-LON continued, "So you would be willing to have an expert scientific cosmic teacher show you how to use what you have and add even more?" Roger nodded his head, said 'yes' and that he would be honored.

O: "Good then, meet your space teacher of 'EMORGY.' It is advanced energy."

Appearing from his left side an entity stepped forward. The appearance was of an aged man with many wrinkles but with eyes that shone like spotlights in the dark, and his face shone as well as his silver-blue 2-piece suit and boots to match. This was quite an entity I thought, but I was getting used to everything being different. This one was indeed pure Light! He spoke in our language. "My tone name is YA-FU-FUS, but you may call me 'YA.' I speak in your tongue. You speak space?" Roger shook his head no. YA continued, "YA will suffice. I will speak in 'EMORGY' tone for understanding. As the 'EMORGY' comes to you, the understanding will too." At this point I thought I might have to pick Roger off the floor, but it proved that was not necessary. I asked him if he was all right and he answered, "Yes, just amazed."

Y: "Then new student, this is how we shall begin. When you go in to your quiet space of meditation I shall send you messages through this new energy system, so it is important that you be open to receive and record what is transferred to you. Keep a record somehow of what is said. You understand YA?"

R: "How often will these transmissions come?"

Y: "You will know when they arrive. Take time out to receive. Picture the vision taking place right now as I am speaking with you and the transmission information shall begin for note taking. Don't get frustrated or worried as this may take a few YA visits to set your mental course, you understand?"

R: "Yes, I look forward to being able to learn more. Thank you. Thank you."

YA: "Any more questions?"

R: "No, I have to digest all this I guess. It is a bit overwhelming and on such a grand scale. Amazing!"

And with this YA bowed, turned and left the scene with a murmur coming from the unseen audience.

O: "As for the Genii ... stay open. Your changes come in quickly. Be the Light you are and we shall rest in the wisdom of your knowing."

La-Luke motioned us it was time to leave and we did, after acknowledging the leaders, and we headed for the door, the trolley, the Park and the Gate. With a hug from Roger and La-Luke, I found myself back sitting in a car somewhere in Cottonwood, AZ, waiting for Charles to come back from his visit with new friends.

Somewhere Between Heaven and Earth

THERE IS A PLACE WHERE MAGIC NEVER ENDS!

Embassy Visit June 11, 2010

The vision began with my Guide and me already at the Embassy. I had sensed I was to return. Those in attendance including OOO-LON, and those at the head table with him bid us welcome and motioned us to be seated. I felt something must be important to be discussed.

O: "We in attendance bid you welcome. From the far reaches of outer space, the body of this assembly is created from those of the Cosmic Community previously spoken of, and we have set forth in order the following....

"1. That within the period of your time, The City of Light will make its appearance within the next year's end!

2. Those who have diligently produced this City and its healing techniques are on course to see it in performance.

3. The Genii always has been interested in the far off reigns of cosmic places, in wondering who and what may be found there. The world as you know it is about to become one of those in the outer galaxies due to The City's dramatic event.

4. Much has been said of the lower consciousness of your people, thus the raising is necessary for the benefit of all who live in cultured lands of other dimensional latitudes of space.

5. Light knows that no darkness can counter to develop, when The Light is pulsating from the Creator and that includes everyone. It is the people in their confused ego states, that is the primary cause in producing what has taken place on your planet. This will be stopped through the altering of their confused mental states, from destructive to peaceful ways.

6. We are preparing to introduce you to your Cosmic Community neighbors who can share through an interpreter, to give you a larger picture of what has been put together for the benefit of mankind (such as it is).

7. The Master Teacher ... one of several of so long ago attempted to teach the true meaning of love as do many today. Now is the time to set the course with a deeper understanding of what and who are your universal family.

8. Your motion picture of 'Avatar' gave you a sample of another world of those who lived and loved, until man entered to destroy through greed. Many such locations of stars and planets know only love, and as the Genii knows as 'pure love!' and anything else is foreign to their thinking.

9. The time has arrived, as the Genii has inherited this kind of love, and sends it forth to those she knows. Love is the strongest vibration of healing for it encompasses the heart to heart, which is the vital organ and power center in the body. As has been said recently between the Genii and a close friend, 'it is the 'pure love' that knows no boundaries which is far beyond what is normally known.' Pure? Indeed! So then, what questions do you propose?"

G: "What am I to know or to ready myself for?"

O: "More visits here." Be ready to meet any entity you are introduced to and to learn what they share. You are considered a 'unit' and will be unified with them."

G: "Will I be able to carry on a kind of normal life?" I do have to get The City information to whatever it is supposed to do."

O: "Yes, some things will seem different as you have a path like no other that very few walk, and those who know of your path will support your findings as self united."

G: "Staying balanced is interesting."

O: "It is knowing that the energy forces of two worlds hold your interests. Be easy with you. Anything else?"

G: "If I am meeting an entity from space, what am I to be prepared for?"

O: "Love and friendship, wisdom, and advanced knowledge simply put for your understanding."

G: "Thank you."

O: "Go now and think on this with the suggestion that you see the Avatar movie again and eliminate the darkness as much as possible, and tune into the love of these people. It is similar to what you will find ahead."

And with this the scene ended and I was home, amazed at the opportunities coming forth before me.

THANKS GOD...

Speaking the Language of Space

Embassy Visit June 19, 2010

As I walked into the scene at the Gate I was in the company of my Guide La-Luke and what a neat Guide he is. I am blessed. My purpose was that I had requested as suggested to meet and speak with an entity from Outer Space.

Moving through the Park onto the usual driver-less trolley, we arrived at the Embassy and I found myself standing in front of the head table with OOO-LON and his usual co-partners (which have never spoken to me) and also this time a new Entity stood with him.

He looked human type but I felt this was some kind of maybe a covering to put me at ease, but was really an Entity from somewhere in space. He wore a long type robe that glowed under his long white hair that hit the floor, and he wore a short white beard as a matched set.

His face was pleasant. He had no nose to speak of, but big eyes that could melt the planet with love. The mouth was kind of off to one side.

What I did feel from him was total love and I recognized that they have to get used to us too. We are the strange-looking ones.

We are so used to seeing film entities that look more like us than what they really are. So I was getting sort of acclimatized I guess. OOO-LON also looks humanized, but it seemed that he was today's spokesperson for whatever.

O: "And your mission today is?"

G: "It has been said that I was to come back and to meet an extraterrestrial and learn what I could understand from them."

O: "Yes this is true and beside me is a friend from the ethers of space; a connected brother whose mission is to assist in bringing forth what you stand in now."

G: "We are used to seeming depictions of space entities, but mostly in human design. So anything else is quite foreign."

O: "This then is another meeting. Dressed in a robe of Light you would understand, I introduce you to ... 'Meeeeeeeee Ka Laaaaaaaa,' who speaks only space dialect. He uses a tone for a contact name so we have connection in not language as you speak, but tones of the Universe. This is a whole other programming.

"We speak space so this is no problem for us. You have been taught the tones of love, connection and healing in your 4 Keys Atonement series, so Dear One, that is a beginning only but useful as you know. Do you have questions of him?"

G: "Where are you from?"

Answer through O: "My home is many light-years away. If distance is an important level of understanding, I enter your Light fields from a space place of harmony and advanced teaching. It would be sounded as 'TUR-A-KA' in your tonal language."

Note: As he was sounding the tone, I began sinking farther into deeper meditation."

OOO-LON continuing for him: "I come from a home far beyond the Earth tone. The City call was to me a call of space unsettlement, therefore requiring interference for the good of this planet and us who inhabit the cosmic tonery. The un-sensing of love in most people here upsets the harmony of the Universe and must be put to rest. My people only know the tones of what you call LOVE and this planet must conform, so balance is maintained in the Cosmic Communities."

Note: Just hearing this and being in his presence, I kept spacing out a bit ... understandably so I guess. The frequencies were higher than mine and I could hardly write what was being said, much less in longhand. I needed some air.

O: "Speaking space has deep energy attached and is effecting you, so I think it would be best for this visit to be resumed at another time. I suggest that you take these space talks very easy ... as your energy field needs getting used to them, and this is part of what is taking place with your humanness now daily."

The entity nodded and I asked to be excused and it was lovingly agreed. With thanks and appreciation, La Luke led me out to the door and took me to the Gate.

I found myself home, trying to write about speaking space and the power those frequencies give in feeling. More questions to be asked soon.

So Light it be!

A Meeting of Earth and Sky Somewhere in Space

Embassy Visit June 23 and 24, 2010

Q: Tomorrow I am to go to The City Embassy to talk about a cosmic college. I am sensing faint E.T. Entities around The White House. What is my question to ask?

A: The Genii is just to rest tonight and permit all to flow into place. Much translation must come forth to respond in your language. Rest and we shall continue in the morning.

So Light It Be. And they did!

Embassy Visit Begins:

My morning quiet time was over. I was prepared to vision into The City heading for The Embassy of Peace. At the Gate of Entry there were many people also taking a trip inside for various reasons.

I was met by my City Guide La-Luke who rushed me past all of this, heading for the wheel-less trolley which then took us to the Embassy and deposited us at the front entrance.

Heading inside past the gardens, we were in the main auditorium where at the head table with OOO-LON were about 10 or 12 entities that I had never seen before. It was quite a sight. All had on robes of different kinds.

The beings had different shapes and faces of faint colors. Not horrendous like the movies would have us believe. Lots of connection-love sent our way as we were ushered to my usual throne-type chair.

I was astonished as I relaxed in my seat knowing all of this was space coming to meet Earth. Imagine That! Not being an astronaut, what does that make me in reverse? A Space Cadet? The love sensing was so strong that I had a bit of difficulty in longhand writing this.

(O.K. Genii. Take a deep breath and send some of that love out to someone you can think of...)

OOO-LON was center front. At this point, they all sat down. I could hardly believe my eyes ... Star Trek had come to speak to me ... How great was that? Well it was better than me trying to dream up a script of it. It might be we were in a holodeck situation. I looked up at La-Luke and he smiled back.

OOO-LON opened with: "Welcome back, Oh Lady of Light Expression. These ones of The Universe also welcome you to be one of them for a time. Agreed?"

G: "Yes, of course. Who would not like to be in this position at this precise moment?"

162

O: "Those who would fear such a meeting. You as a maker of dreams and wishes on this planet have been subject to wonder about far-off places in the Universe, and we will try to answer them for your 'Light Growth.'

"I will be the speaker for many, as I speak space in many dialects and sound fractions. You can say this would be as a 'cosmic college.' So what would be your opening question of the mental?"

G: "Wow! My mind went blank. Oh, I am told that I will be subject to go to The White House and speak with The President. I am not known, and this is a mighty big step for me. Last night in thinking of this trip, I could faintly see Entities in and about The White House, especially around the First Family. What is to be said of this? And will I be in touch with them?"

O: "Yes, just by being open for that, you do not even realize the importance of your mission. The people you meet will have the way opened for the future of this planet with your words."

G: "If I am to go to The White House and meet The President, how is this being planned to be received, as I am really not known publicly?"

OOO-LON smiled and said: "Have you not been given the tools of your art?"

G: "Yes!"

O: "Then patience is needed as the path opens up and all is delivered as such. Now then this being covered, permit me to introduce you to a soul part of you that you have heard many times speak through you but never seen ... your next Guide of cosmic learning."

Stepping forth from this group of far-off dignitaries was a male entity with some human-ness look about him. He was wearing a robe of deep night sky blue and had a halo-type of something sparkling that shone when he moved. Amazing! He may have had legs but they could not be detected under the robe of the night sky.

He held out what looked like a hand, yet not a hand. (This really was a cosmic trip!) The really groovy part was the love I sensed. Such love that I felt I was melting.

O: "Meet Atherian."

G: "Atherian? I know you. You are the awesome power I feel when you speak of the planet through me and you are even in The City book!"

A: "Of course, and I do speak your language. We shall work now together to clean up this planet of ignorance and destruction."

G: "It is nice to meet you in vision person. Your words are really quite powerful."

A: "As need be, for the blessing of this planet. Frequency thought change is needed here. This can be an interesting sharing of cosmic truths and planetary advice."

By this time I was feeling kind of strange and light-headed. OOO-LON suggested that this session be ended and another set up soon.

G: "Yes, thank you very much. This is a lot to reset my energy system. It has been quite an experience! Such energy as I have never felt ... such power, and the Love extended brings me once again to heart tears. My emotions need a time-out."

And with that the vision ended with loving thanks for all that I had just experienced ... with more on the way.

So Light It Be!

Of Sound and City Lights

Embassy Visit July 3, 2010

Leaving my world for the moment, I was in the world but not of it as I made my way to the The City of Light. Appearing at the entrance Gate with many others, I spotted my Guide La-Luke coming to meet me. He grabbed my hand and we by-passed the others as we headed for the Park, the trolley, and found ourselves in the Advanced Achievement Academy known as the Embassy of Peace. A magnificent building to behold, much less being able to enter.

My learning guided by the Intelligent Entities of Space, now became a highlight of adventure. Was I only here a few days ago? It seemed like a lifetime but then maybe it was. I was getting used to other lives in other places long since removed. Only love can bring forth what was somewhere in timelines. So it was with only love in my heart and joy in my soul, that I have again been invited in.

Seated at the head table were the same entities that I have seen before and the head entity was OOO-LON who stood as we entered. He bid me to sit in the seat now provided up close and personal in front of them, as a hum from the vast audience behind sent love chills through me. This has been quite an adventure ...

OOO-LON spoke: "Welcome Lady of Light, entity of humans."

G: "Thank you for having me back. This is such an honor and sometimes there is a disbelief that wants to mentally take place."

O: "The Genii has to work and realign in her various worlds, as the daily one wants to remain the same as it was previously. The upper level mind you are now using, only wants more of the same she is learning. Who wins?"

G: "Hopefully a balance would be nice. What am I to know this visit?"

O: "We have begun to share of the Cosmic Communities for the advanced. Within this Cosmic Community are trillions of Entities that live in harmony with each other, (speaking of balance). This is a harmonious following of vastness beyond what is believed to be inhabited by your planet for the most part, but nevertheless true.

"As you sit here now behind us in this vast Pod resonating from their own star clusters, are many who serve in ways unknown. They have put the pieces together of this City of Light as the Master Hermes has designed. You the Genii have seen a completed building being lowered into this City site. This is correct? The vastness of space holds many treasures of designs that have completed this City you now visit. So then to continue, you are being led into the 'Holographic Sound Chamber.' Herein you will hear sounds of different worlds that are in harmony. This planet and all it contains is a perfect example of turmoil and unrest. Much is happening mostly due to the changes in frequencies within the people themselves and the planet in a general clean-up.

"People are having mental delusions of imbalance that strike others as well as themselves. Mother nature as she is called, is also having her way as humans try to put the pieces together as it 'HAS ALWAYS BEEN'... PLEASE! What has always been is conflict, due to misuse of the creative ability of the so-called human ego.

"The City embodies what is necessary to make it whole. We attend what that wholeness means and again time is shortened. Permit me to have you meet another Extraterrestrial who is known by the tone name, Hoooo-ah (sound the hoooo out)." >>>>>>>>>>>>>>

One of the entities who has been previously at this table stood. He had the look of a very aging elder with dark skin and lots of wrinkled folds for a face, no nose and slit eyes that look to have a crystal embedded as they sparkled a bit. A face-fold of skin covered over any mouth I would care to see. And no hair was to be seen on the smaller-than-ours head. Interesting!

He wore a long shiny gray robe alike the others, with gold trim on the full sleeve. He began a sound exchanged with OOO-LON. It was much different than our sounds.

G: "I sense a tone will sound before The City of Light appears. Is this correct?"

O: "As stated, everything within The City has an embedded tone within its structure as well as the Lights themselves. Listen for the tone."

G: "Is it a certain tone?"

O: "Yes but you will know. So then as Hoooo-ah has just toned, he is part of the assembly who will designate to you the 'sound feeling.'"

G: "Sound feeling?"

O: "Yes, you will feel the vibration of the tone forecasting The City arrival.

　　　1. It would be wise to gather from your friends a collection of those who in their belief systems are to be special Stewards of the Light, who now resonate to The City coming.

　　　2. They shall be called 'City Lights!' (C. L.) those who will hear and feel the immediacy of the demonstration."

Hooo-ah nodded as his face folds shook with what I guess was a smile.

G: "Anything else to be known at this time?"

O:　　　3. First permit them to be evolved.

　　　4. The 4 Keys teaching is important. Replenish the data to those already into the 4 Keys, and add new members as such.

5. Advance Achievement Academy is attached to the Light Center. This is where the study goes.

6. The Charles can see what will be of help of announcement. City data and AAA studies 4 Keys only.

7. The Kathie and the Renee already advanced, can be distant creators as desired.

8. All will be given a special instrument to catch the tone.

9. You are to set the scene and be in attendance for the tones as directed.

10. Now begin to bring forth the human City Lights, teach and be open for your Universal Advancement sessions.

11. It would be of great value if the advanced Kathie and the advanced Renee get to know each other as they will be of a support for each other and the Genii as well.

12. We suggest that you return here soon.

13. And as had been said ... 'be well and prosper.'"

I sensed a joke here someplace, as a hum in the audience sounded.

G: "Anything else?"

O: "We bid you the Light of the eternal day in universal peace, love and sky tones of God ascend in this message."

G: "Sounds good to me," I thought as we left the Embassy, rode the trolley, ran back through the Park and out the Gate.

I was back home in Sedona writing this.

Imagine that!

So Light it be!

Of Stepping Stones and President Jimmy Carter

Embassy Visit July 13, 2010

Feeling that the welcome mat was out for me to visit the Embassy, I quickly sensed myself in The City and entered this building holding hundreds of space entities. I was alone and looked forward to being in this place occupied by those from far off space home. This was truly an honor and I took a deep breath as the energy was lovingly strong. I walked up to the usual head table with 5 Entities. Three I have already met. Two were still in a hazy vision. They all stood to honor my arrival.

O: "And the Light Lady returns!"

G: "Thank you. I have a question."

O: "Yes. Repeat your question."

G: "I am to have a human group soon. What am I to say about E.T.'s and The City and anything else to be explained?"

O: "Just the truth will do. (There was a stirring hum in the audience unseen). There are many who are well aware that we exist in many forms. Just say what you know and feel as your visits here foretell. All is progress."

G: "Thank you. What else is to be known as I proceed forward?"

O: "The 'intent' of The City will do more than just be a revelation long since in preparation, for it will 'unbalance' the now 'unbalanced' energy!

"You seek to go to the government center and 'speak space' with the current President Obama, and even now another head of government in the past, President of the Jimmy Carter as he has been added to the mix, and has even reported seeing a UFO vehicle of space travel. Are you not in an energy line-up now to do just that? Of course, nothing as you say happens by chance. Including all the lined-up of dignitaries who play lead roles in this City scenario. (Again a hum sounded in the audience). It would be proper then to travel with your gifts from the heart.

"When you speak of E.T.'s, come from the heart as they have returned this love to you. No attack on this planet was ever intended. This is a mental make-up of demented minds! (The hum again was sounded). As your path of travel comes forth, soon the deposits of the gifts will be acknowledged. Even now the energy in the east is pulling in the time and place for an introduction to the President Carter segment. (Hum again heard).

"To speak on us demands a full encounter with The City data, first to open the minds, and with your ingrained humor plus facts, you can do this easily.

"So then, does this give you a positive sign?"

G: "I just want to do a good job."

O: "What makes you think you would not? Have you not been chosen for this task? Have you not been leveled into higher learning?"

G: "People ask me about the oil spill. What can I say on this?"

O: "Only that it is in process of clearing. Changes made from stupidity are frequently a type of problem that requires help from the unseen to clear. History is in the making. Fear not. The answers will come to you or through you. And either way is correct. I would introduce you to more of my co-partners here but for now I sense you must leave. Just return soon.

"Be at peace. Soon you will be in the presence of greatness with the President Carter. Indeed he is the beginning leader, and he will enjoy your story. In fact he will be fascinated! So prepare to tell him the story of The City. He is the door-opener for presentations. (Hum again). Your friend Renee has been given the insights and they will continue."

Wow! I just got the picture. Bingo! He will be easy to sit and share with. This is Big! Really Big!

O: "Enjoy the thoughts for this is correct. Be now at your home and into your day for time is short to complete what you have to take with you on the road to greatness for the planet."

And with this I found myself amazed at what has been said. Talk about guidance! Amazing! President Carter was the main objective now. **Imagine That!**

The Celebrity Marionette Genii made of President Jimmy Carter

Genii and Carter Center Executives pulling the President's Strings!

More examples of some of the 5,000+ marionettes Genii has made including many that she created and donated to celebrities as well as the Empowerment Marionettes she is creating of authors and trainers to help children harness their creative imagination are available at http://www.sedonalightcenter.org/celebrity_marionettes.htm.

The Light of Interest

Embassy Visit July 24, 2010

Another time, another place, another dimension, but a place of such magnificence that it seemed to take my breath away every time I came back through my inner vision. I accepted my visitation rights of City entrance and headed for the Embassy of Peace, beginning at the coded Gate of Entrance where my City Guide La-Luke greeted me with a hug.

Grabbing my hand we ran through the Park of Relaxation and onto the waiting trolley that skimmed over the ground with us aboard. I assumed that there are many of these trolleys taking people from place to place within The City interior, but so far this was the only one I had seen. This huge almost egg-shaped building held an entrance garden with fragrances that brought such peace that it seemed to set the scene for this Embassy of Peace.

Once more inside this main sanctuary, I saw the 5 cosmic CEO's sitting at the front table and heard the vast unseen but felt, audience of hundreds of entities. Some were behind them.

They stood in a bowing welcome and looked to my seating in the usual high-back chair where La-Luke led me. It was an honor to be here ... no doubt of that! The leader OOO-LON speaker of space and human's language, spoke in our language for my understanding.

O: "We welcome the Genii back. How may we be of service?"

G: "I come for:

  1. Any advisement on my future steps,

  2. To learn more of speaking space and

  3. A student/friend has requested a question and answer session. He is considered a C-L, 'City Light' and he is dedicated to service for The City. I have asked him to report his needs."

O: "Proceed."

G: "This is his report/question as given him by his inner 4 Keys Guide MAR-EEK.

"From William Barton ... 'How shall I best serve and be of service while in a state of surrender to The City of Light, keeping in mind and being aware of the fact that my inherent gifts from God, include a continuous powerful and abundant flow of life force energy (CHI) throughout my being, as well as having a particularly close connection with electricity and/or energy generation. Thank You."

O: "It would be wise to share with this human male, that he has yet another Guide with whom he can accelerate in the areas of his speaking and the learning therein. The City of Light this male knows, is electrically enhanced with such power that is not known to people on your planet.

"As you would say, the power within it is awesome from the High Towers collection of the UPPC'S, to the under-City electromagnetic fields and computers beneath reporting on what is happening above. All is electrified to the point of even sending energy to other states in need. Now then from his Soul Light Guide, The William can get precise instruction pertaining to his part in the mechanics of the electronics pertained to in the message to him.

"As he leads himself under this guidance, he can become an intricate part of the overall picture and be able to answer questions from others as a teacher/leader would, as you are doing now.

"His Soul Guide teacher does 'speak space' and also his English as you understand. But he brings the Light electrified into the planet to maximize the power this planet needs to overcome the low consciousness spoken of many times.

"ZOOO-NAAR is this Guide and a master in these fields and quite open to instruct The William further."

(At this point a hum of acknowledgment sounded in the audience, and the head CEOs nodded Yes...)

G: "Will William be guided step by step so he can also teach and give information to further the interest in The City construction in printed data for City books etc.?"

O: "Quite so, with his intent of service to The City manifestation and being open to his City Guide. (NOTE: Each human that has been 4 Keys linked has a "City" Guide who will instruct the talents of that individual, who wants to be of service using them, and can be so intoned).

"You have been given the title of "Advanced Achievement Academy'(AAA)' that is connected to the Light Center ... report these findings and recognize that pods of information can be given of this advancement as they, as their soul teachers in human form, lead the way as experts in action."

G: "Thank You. I will pass this information on to others as well."

O: "And now then ... The Genii has been into the advancement of moving The City data from her house to the White House. This will continue to completion! The path ahead we seek to see you complete as doors with Light intent open before you. Make note of the advancement.

"Your path is secure and the target dates will appear like magic. Just hold the Light forward and expect the unexpected in delightful ways" ... He says as he smiles and nods in agreement.

"Your visit here today has been of great value to others. The gifts of the fun of strings and things have been a value to yourself and others. Yes, you have served in many ways. Now then, take a bit of time to enjoy what you enjoy, for smiles and laughter is indeed healing.

"Take your gifts of fun and just give them away. This is your time ... and God agrees. "Be of good cheer. All is well and on course. We shall attend to more again on your next visit. We see that your energy is getting low."

With that they all stood, smiled and bowed as La-Luke and I did the same and we headed for the doorway, the trolley and the Gate, and I found myself home with my furry white pup Light Spirit who wanted some fun.

So Light It Be!

A Closing Embassy of Peace Message

Received July 27, 2010

O: "Permit it to be known to anyone reading this message, that the Embassy of Peace Genii visits have not concluded. However the contents of the previous visits contained within these pages, are enough to stir the imagination into the credibility of the dramatic presentation coming on the Earth stage, are correct in the information given.

"Some will say in reading this, 'I will believe it when I see it!' Some will say, 'Yes, I believe I indeed will see this manifested, praise GOD!' Both are correct.

"So then, permit the Light dwelling within these pages of truth, honor, love and healings to bear witness that, The Source of All ... (call it what you may) has declared this CITY imprint of love and healing as a gift to the people of the Earth planet.

"The Genii has done her part in allowing us to come forth through her Light Body (electrical system) to share information of massive global change, and she has visual visitation rights into The City of Light, as well of any location including the Embassy of Peace Headquarters.

"Those who have chosen to support this dynamic process, through putting the information into this manuscript form with their love, talents, and intent, and to see it into the hands of the Earth public are to be commended and congratulated, with thanks of Light even from us in the Embassy Cosmic Community (unseen, but certainly in action).

"Today is what it is, tomorrow will be something else quite dramatic, and its effects will be felt around the world, for peace and healing is the intent and love is the message. MAKE NOTE: This printed document you now hold WILL GO DOWN IN HISTORY as the Pre-Announcement of Coming Attractions. I, OOO-LON, Commander of Space Light and Embassy Interpreter between the Cosmic Community and the Genii, declare this to be so ... as stated!"

So Light it Be!

NOTE from Genii: We had thought this visit to The City of Light Embassy of Peace Headquarters would be the last visit included in the first edition of the manuscript. Then on the very day that my business partner Charles Betterton was to upload it, I enjoyed yet another visit to The City and I was advised to include it and a few more in this book.

There have been many more visits and many more will occur in the future as The City comes forth into this dimension. All relevant visits and updates are included in this expanded book and they will be posted to our blog site at http://sedonacityoflight.wordpress.com.

The Magic Advantages of Light

Embassy Visit August 8, 2010

Thoughts of The Embassy of Peace bring forth the future, and as I entered into this realm in thought and vision, delight and honor filled my heart. The five-story Gate complex (how many times have I been here now?) seemed to welcome me and others who were all excited to enter. A tap on my shoulder awakened my amusement of what I saw, as my Guide La-Luke readied me for the dash to the trolley that took us to The Universal Embassy of Light and Peace.

Arriving at The Embassy building, we were ushered into the Sanctuary of Light. Beings from all over the Universe gathered here together in preparation to move all forward in the expectancy of The City demonstration. What a privilege to be here. Oh My! ... Yes!

Head Master OOO-LON and his front table companions rose to the occasion as we entered and were seated nearby in a seat of visiting honor. I have been here so many times that I felt at home in the awesome football stadium kind of building. So somewhere in time, once more I got the privilege of conversations with the highest beings one could meet. In some ways this was just pure fun and powerful in its reality. And the conversation began ...

O: "Welcome Light Lady to the meeting of 'Beings from parallel universes' and the universe of wisdom and knowledge par none. What may we entice you to say?"

G: "First permit me to thank you all for your love, wisdom, and encouragement to continue with The City announcements. It is always a deep honor to be in your presence of such vast wisdom. I have a few questions ... one from City Light Renee Trenda who is announcing The City wherever she can, even to the Presidents for contact with me."

O: "This is good and fruitful, continue ... "

G: "She asks, 'Is there some genetic factor in our bodies that would let us connect with these Universal Uniphase Power Capsules, so that we may emit more Light?' Are we in any way connected to the UPPC's?"

O: "Actually No. Your power centers are designed to hold just so much amperage and the packaged UPPC's would be too strong to manage. You just would not be anymore. However, the spin-off from the capsules does emit Light, and since you are this, you would feel the essence of them. With The City there is no way you would not be subject to the frequency dwelling in The City itself."

G: "Her second question ... 'Would the UPPC's be a Free Energy device for homes and businesses to replace fossil fuel?'"

O: "To a certain extent. As The City enters into the human equation of demonstration, it will appear that there is more here that can be used in other areas of support, as she has questioned.

"Remember this is the first City! There are imprints in the Ethers of sameness, that will appear and the Light is to be emitted from them, as has been said to you.

"This planet of humans will glow in the heavens like another moon was hand-placed by God. The change-over on your planet will have that much frequency. It is known by us that words are just words until the seeing is observed. But, you can mark these words of offering ... that this indeed is so! For this place of Earth, much energy frequencies must be amplified and will be, due to the High Towers process of catching and relaying the UPPC's as they will, into each City in the Ethers, thus lightening up many miles around also.

"What you have entered here with the first City, is the attention-getter! And thus will fascinate more advanced ideas to come forth in balancing out the planet's darker spots; while also bringing forth more scientific areas to hone in on, which will make the world take another look at itself with what is called 'New Eyes.' Science and spirit will walk hand-in-hand for progress is essential, and will not be by-passed. This is a promise.

"Many entities have been instrumental, and instruments of peace are in this House of Peace Headquarters that you attend at this moment. These are minds so far beyond the Earth, that the good that is about to change people's thinking through new frequencies that are even now bombarding your planet, is beyond normal human thinking.

"Those who work in various areas such as Earth plants and greenery will rejoice in the way the plants respond to normal light emanating from any of the future Cities of Light, and all in-between as nothing is left out. What needs to be cleaned out will be. What needs to be replenished will be!

"Take note: Hundreds upon hundreds of humans are leaving in various ways and are supporting the cleansing from another level. Even those with darkened minds now see the Light from a different perspective. Those who have suffered in the wars will find comfort and healing and release of mental wounds. This too is part of the Light Healing. Nothing is left out ... nothing! And as said, the wars will have no more attraction to exist!"

G: "Is there an update on The City appearance?"

O: "As said, as the minds concentrate on 2010 ... leading up to that date makes The City a silent appearance, and people with an average sense will sense something is going to happen. The dark minds will feel that it is some kind of disaster. The Light minds will feel the love to such an extent that even without knowing it they will assist the energy to bring it forward.

"Those who respond have the lead-in, and their leadership of Light will assist others to spread the word in welcome of what is to be seen. The days come and go quickly now. The emphasis is on contact and spreading the message to those who will hear and respond within themselves.

"There is yet time for The Genii and other City Lights to spread the word, but not much. So then can we be of more help?"

G: "Thank you all, and as I am invited I will return."

O: "Do that for your advancement beyond the Earth, as much is yet to be discovered and shared. For this point continue to serve, as people recognize that what you say is truth-connected. Rest and play to keep yourself in good condition. We bid you the Light of the eternal day!"

And with that I found myself at home in Sedona ready to ride off to **Disneyland** for a well-earned few days' vacation, and the green bench on Main St., chatting with Walt Disney …

Imagine that!

So Light it be!

Contact!

Embassy Visit August 12, 2010

Resting in the knowingness of God, I mentally and visually headed back into The City with the Embassy as my target. No Gate or trolley was seen this time much less my Guide. In vision, I found myself standing in front of the 5 Entities I have seen before as OOO-LON stood in bowed greeting. Why did I decide to come today? No questions came to mind although I felt pretty balanced but 'floaty.' Anyway here I was ... somewhere in Light.

O: "You are confused?"

G: "No, I just came so quickly and unprepared ... no questions except maybe, how can I be more supportive with The City demonstration?"

O: "What more would you like to do?"

G: "First I would like to be more balanced physically in this unbalanced world. This is a nuisance."

O: "You must recognize that this is your mission, that the changes within your system are taking on a major upheaval to bring you up to code so to speak. You can still function?"

G: "Oh yes, just a little lop-sided when walking sometimes, and the spinning vortexes here are not much help."

O: "This is unavoidable at this time. Just be easy with it. Your Earth world takes on a new glow, and that in itself is uplifting however strange. You are making the best of it all and actually moving yourself beyond where you have ever been before."

G: "Am I to meet more intelligences from space?"

O: "Oh my yes, you have only begun to space walk and talk. Remember the cosmic college you have spoken of?"

G: "Yes."

O: "Good, then we will bring forth a Space teacher who will direct your course."

Then entering from stage left was an entity that looked like a very bent over old man, gray beard covering part of his face, but still looking very young as though a cocoon of Light of some kind was around him. Hard to describe. He was so light.

How can this be? Am I imagining this as a 2 dimensional figure, like someone had put a curse on him like in Beauty and the Beast? He just kind of pulsated as waves of Light surrounded him. Amazing! And he was heading for me, lifting anyone I bet, who would be around.

O: "It is important in your growth that you get used to Light changes within an entity, for these are frequencies you can see. Not all is solid. Meet your new space teacher, TWA-WAN and he can understand in your language."

G: "Hello" I weakly said, eyes wide open.

T: "Ahsseeee>>>>>>>>>" came sound elongated.

O: "This may take a bit of time but he will interpret your sounds."

G: "Wow ... This intelligence is a power house. Can I handle his energy?"

O: "Think on this in the quiet of your home. Information will begin to float through to you."

T: "Saaaa>>>>>>>>>>>>>>>>>>>>>>>>>"

G: "OK. I get the picture. Twa-Wan I am pleased to meet you. You teach me to speak space?"

T: "Saaa >>>>>>>"

G: "Why would I need to learn Space Sounds, and what does this have to do with The City demonstration?"

O: "Much, for in the Space Community you will be able to understand those cosmic entities you will meet that are in the cosmic level of The City of Light. For now, just absorb what has just taken place. Bring more questions and again watch the film 'CONTACT' as it has vibrational sounds within the sound tracts that will begin to resonate with you. Take your time, relax, rest and enjoy this newness."

And with this the Entity smiled and began to back off, both of him ... the old and the new. I felt the energy of this meeting was right on track.

If I had more questions they left with the waves of frequencies being produced as I witnessed, and now as the vibration began to lessen, I felt it was time for Genii to go home! And I did.

New day ... puppy play and we'll see what the day will bring. Thanks God. I must have done something right to meet friends in very high places I never would have met any other way. I bless The City of Light and look to more power-filled meetings, and The City appearing as if by magic.

World Changes Ready or Not

Embassy Visit August 21, 2010

This Gate that I normally enter was awesome to behold. I moved with others who were excitedly optimistic to pass through this horseshoe-shaped entrance. My Guide La-Luke and I took off running to the trolley that delivered us to the Embassy of Peace Headquarters.

How many times had I been here by now? 30-40-50? No Matter. Each time was important and I was honored to be ushered into the sanctuary before me. Within a few minutes we stood before this High Tribunal of space entities from various parts of the Universe. The energy of love and wisdom penetrated my system.

O: "I trust that you have had good experiences since we last entered into conversation of unknown commodities?"

G: "I do my best to stay balanced in these two worlds. It is not always easy."

O: "As stated, this will pass as you again are to move forward into the East Dawn Land. You have questions?"

G: "I am told that a sound or sounds from the Universe will announce The City appearance to be delivered."

O: "Yes?"

G: "What sounds am I listening for?"

O: "You have been carrying a static type sound in your head ever since The City was introduced to you many years ago. Is this correct?"

G: "Yes, both Dr. Bill and I noticed it about the same time, and it has been on constantly ever since. Sometimes higher than other times, but I ignore it most of the time."

O: "You are aware that what you hear is your Light system, like an electrical ensemble. You are aware of this also?"

G: "Yes, long since."

O: "This denotes that your system has been tuned in for some time now. The sound from the Universe will become obvious. Again it is advised to re-watch the movie 'Contact' and to pick up the subtleties unsaid. The catch phrases are signal points for you to be aware. We are aware that you are a novice in this aeronautics area, but have no concerns. It will be known. Your mental and physical accoutrements will tone you in."

G: "OK. I am open to what is next expected of me to be experienced. I am about to travel to the Chicago area and meet someone new. What can be said of this as guidance to what am I to take with me and do actually?" (A hum was registered in the background).

O: "On any location trip you take, always take The City material, for people will be deliberately put on your path. You are an advancement spokesperson of the coming important event. Those who can hear, will hear.

"We attempt to advise you of what is possible, for The City energy coming into your dimension is in full force, making upheaval something of traumatic occurrence. Your planet people react in many unusual ways and some not to the liking of most. Who wants to be uncomfortable? It is in the 'un' that the comfort births. The massive energy structure makes waves of its forthcoming, and you see people not able to withstand these frequencies, and go what you would call 'crazy.'

"You have had centuries upon centuries of mental and physical warfare, and to change all of that to a peaceful existence is a massive experience in itself. You have no idea of all that has gone on before to bring this to a demonstration-conclusion, and it will continue as such.

"At this point it is incomplete. Try as we may and do, this planet of Earth people resists change in any shape or form, and in doing so that very resistance brings them forth more harm than good.

"It has been repeated over and over that you are 'Source Energy.' Do your people know what that means, when they run amuck doing dangerous things, and then wonder why that happened? We think not.

"You are what is called in your dimension 'GOD'! But no, who can declare that? Stupidity runs amuck, and to bring sanity into your planet takes all of those you see here in this sanctuary, and more besides. We are what you are, in different costumes, but the same nevertheless. Imagine that!

"You direct your energy to do what you want, like sending your Light through your 'Light Saber' like a Jedi master. You do it for the good of the whole with love, and not hate or malice or blame, like the Dark forces do that you are aware of. People bring on their own demise, planet changes etc. It cannot be otherwise! You people do it all! Congratulations! Understand? You understand?"

G: "Oh, Yes. Very Well."

O: "Then you are well aware of what is taking place and the absolute need of The City demonstration to materialize into form. Will this shake up various locations, be it mentally and physically? Of Course! How else can the new be born? And be a clean, clear planet, ready to intertwine with others in the Universe. Something of major proportions must take place ... and it will! And is taking place!

"It has been said that this year of 2010 would be seen as tumultuous. And has this not been the case? Things that never happened ever before are making newspaper headlines.

"Hello world ... pay attention here lest you miss the real reason. Those who have done wrong will learn of a better side of themselves through their own beliefs. Again, you are this God incarnate, Source Energy, the I AM ... imagine that! Ahh, wait! Pay attention here! Don't by-step this for it is not ego on a rampage, but truth in the heart with such deep love attached. It has been said by your friend that, 'It is either love, or it isn't.' What has been in the energy fields is not love in the truest sense ... but mark these words ... It WILL be ... It WILL be!" (Again a hum echoed in the background).

G: "What more can I do? What are my instructions?"

O: "Stay in balance as much as possible. We understand that with your work, to stay grounded is almost impossible, and we support you as we can. Listen for indications of the tone of The City. Be open to share and in doing so, you will change people's vibrational attachments of fear. For as said, 'God can do anything ... and we add 'Will do anything.'

"Be easy with your system. Rest and continue to love deeply everyone you meet, for your love and honor are very strong. Delete any negativity of words and actions from others. They have no place with your mission, for love and Light are far more dependable, and you have these qualities beyond most."

G: "Thank you. I will fulfill my mission as best I am guided."

O: "You are closer to the demonstration than ever before. Be easy with yourself as your automatic system – electronic system is in a massive change. Enjoy what you have demonstrated. Take your love trips and spread the word and expect it to become more intense. As the word passes, and the energy lifts the people to understand what is taking place, they will find you. Be open and giving of these words.

"So return again and we shall see what next steps are to be taken. You are doing very well. Stay only in the God Love, for that is what heals, and see the world you live in become a peaceful situation even during the change-over."

Then I turned and my Guide led me to the trolley. I hugged him. No words were needed or even spoken after that. And now I found myself home, ready to type this all up from my hand-written sights and sounds.

Of Cosmic Communities and Such

Embassy Visit September 7, 2010

Arriving at the Gate entrance, many people were seen excited to also enter. Looking around for my City Guide La-Luke, I felt him grab my hand and like the parting of the seas, he rushed me through the crowd to the wheel-less trolley, and in a flash we were in the Embassy of Peace standing in front of the 4 entities in robes, with OOO-LON standing in a greeting position.

Entering into this building was always exciting for the possibilities of such vast learning were always available. The welcome mat was out. With OOO-LON's hand extended, I was very comfortable. What a dear soul he is ... never found him to be anything other. And if all E.T.'s are like this, there is nothing to worry about. It is a vast community that spreads across the heavens of which we are a part ... thank goodness.

O: "Welcome Oh Lady of Light who walks the Earth with great news of the coming attraction. How may we serve you?"

G: "I am so happy to be back and this time I do have some questions."

O: "Serve us, so we can serve you."

G: "Close friends are seeking to build local communities before The City arrives. What can be said of the Universal Cosmic Communities that would be of support, with advanced cosmic guidance to be incorporated into what would be best for the Earth dwellers?"

(There was a big sigh heard from the almost invisible audience of Extra Intelligence behind these leaders.)

O: "Yes ... the time has arrived that this question is not out of order. People banding together make progress as long as 'LOVE' is the leader, and we find patches of it even through this change-over your planet is experiencing. On one place we see man killing man and on the opposite we see man loving man. Which is best?

"Those of us who are from far off Space Places with unknown names do not fight like what is presented in the moving pictures such as the Star Wars series. It just is not encouraged or even thought of. We are not programmed as such. This is barbaric as ignorance tries to become Light by killing off what it would be. Strange thinking!

"From one Star Community to another, peace reigns supreme. It is recognized again that only the frequency of 'LOVE' equals the power. Did not the Jedi master Yoda recommend LOVE to be the answer? Indeed, to advance and visit one Star Cluster to another, war is not even a slight consideration, much less conquest or over-taking another. It just does not happen. Do you not call the upper level thinking Heaven? Now we bring you Heaven on Earth!

"So then, where is the LOVE in building a Cosmic Community on the Earth plane? It is much needed and in line to gather those who respond to love (there is a feeling that one is of that persuasion). You say you want peace ... you say you want love ... you say you want oneness.

"What are the people demonstrating? Your planet is a Community but unlike the Cosmic Sense it is divided into pieces and parts as each person may not honor another.

" You all call yourselves the United States. Excuse us but what is united here? Where are the means of compassion in the division of what we see?

"Those in your close realm of friends seek to hold a piece of ground here and there as a Light Center of LOVE that can attract others to also be Light carriers. A community can indeed do this when under the banner of LOVE. Dear Ones, THIS IS COSMIC ADVANCEMENT!

"So then to have guidance from this vast Cosmic Community (as sits behind us in this building of Light), one must begin with LOVE. When a few are gathered in God's love, it then has drawing power to bring forth anything that is needed to secure land etc. for the desired community contact.

"Open with advanced LOVE and permit God to fill in the connections with the same frequencies of LOVE. From this come the divine ideas and advanced technology as used in The City. All this is cosmic heart Light center equivalent. Have we given you any ideas of starting?"

G: "Yes, love is all that opens the doors of any community."

O: "Yes this is true. It is simply explained in the Energy Fields of Attraction. Any more questions?"

G: "Yes. In another area, my friend Renee and I have just come back from a trip to the President Carter Center to deliver (through) the gift of the re-creation of a miniature marionette to him, the manuscript of The City of Light. What are the next steps?"

O: "Patience in waiting for a response, will pay as you say 'off.' The President will become an interested reader. Wait upon the Lord, so to speak."

G: "Anything else?"

O: "Just remember to LOVE and all will be well, and the advanced City reports of progress will become nearer than your breath. Begin your 'Cosmic Community Center' and see what is drawn in.

"Use the Advanced Achievement Academy site. Go and Light the path before you all. Gather, connect, process data, and thus fulfill prophecies long since declared.

"God Lights the path before you all. We now release you to re-enter your home and begin your day with recording this report, and entrance into the new City of Light book with the Charles who understands the method for printing. You must have printed copies on hand to help support the Light Center of God, thus communicating with many communities."

With this, he bowed as a hum ran through the background audience and I felt such love and not of Earth-kind but so much deeper.

We left the Embassy and I found myself home with my puppy looking for a hug. Hey, it's all about LOVE, Right?

Thanks God, this was God Good!

So Light it be!

A Different Way of Looking at Things!

Embassy Visit September 10, 2010

Moving quickly into a quiet vision awareness state, I felt excited and honored to be again invited into The City of Light Embassy of Peace Headquarters, for indeed this time I did have some questions.

The entrance Gate sparkled from the sun as I and many others moved into The City itself. My friend and Guide La-Luke appeared smiling and all, as he motioned me to follow him. In doing so we made our way to the wheel-less trolley. We hopped aboard and enjoyed the scenery as we then stopped at this huge building called the Embassy of Peace and indeed it is huge.

The hundreds of space beings who occupied the amphitheater sent only love to us as we entered and stood before the head entities with Space Commander OOO-LON being the translator. The energy in here was like no other I have ever experienced ... a mixture of power and love, it seemed to me. The beings from all over the Universe conversed peacefully in different space sounds.

You speak space?

O: "Ah again we meet. This is good. Come and be a part of the sound fragrances of those who delight in this human visitor for answers to questions to be delivered. What may we say to continue our inventive progress?" I was immediately put at ease even though my question was hard to describe.

G: "Thank you. It has been given to me the appointment of being a spokesperson for The City of Light and to answer questions that are given to me. Let me see if I can form it simply. How can The City of Light now unseen in this dimension, be seen in the physical as the demonstration appearance, when before there was nothing seen? And how many miles of Earth land will the prototype set on? Does this make any sense?"

OOO-LON smiling says: "Of course, how does the unseen become seen in your world? Ah, the big question finally asked and we shall reply. When one in your dimension sees something appear, it has to move from one level or dimension to another, even an idea follows this course. It is called birth in your language.

"The birthing of The City itself must move from one dimension to another. You are well aware that in your Earth level from idea, design or whatever, you build it with Earth supplies and time.

"You have also seen in The City visions the Healing Buildings being put into place from space vehicles above, already complete. You were very surprised as you remember. (He smiled again).

"So then, if something of this magnitude were to suddenly appear completed, it would make headlines in the media like never before and another surprise, a welcome vision or many.

"The coming forecast had happened and no one cared how it happened, it just did. It will be said 'with God anything can happen and just did!'

"What was anticipated long ago has come to pass. The birthing magic had taken place. Praise Allah, God, Buddha, Masters, Spirit, Lightworkers, Mentors, and in your delight even Jedi Master Yoda. ...all!" (He kept on smiling like he had touched a fun place in my heart ...and he had.)

"You have spoken recently to the Kathie of Brodie on this topic, and she said it was like putting on 3D glasses. What was not seen was then seen beyond the normal. They would be like see-through Light Glasses. Have you not noticed that when your eyeglasses are not clean, you see less than normal? Of course. Is not the world being cleared? Of course. The darkness on your planet is being cleansed as darkness carries no Light. You Dear One, and many others, are beginning to wear see-through Light-Glass Sensing. Imagine that!

"You personally are helping the process by informing others of your vision visits and thus they can envision what is unseen at this point. But that it is an implant for the new 'See-through Glasses.' Even they are unseen but quite effective. Much of your televising of what is called blue ray, brings forth the unseen in perfect order. What more of this did you enjoy in Avatar technology?

"Many who have been 'sightees' so to speak will begin to sense this Birth entry as they become aware. As your words spread of The City birthing information, more and more will be added, as the words spread around the planet and the universal linking takes place.

"By the time the full occupancy of The City in 3D is completed, it will be as said, first by those who have elevated themselves to the knowingness of this demonstration on some level. Now then, where is this magnificent demonstration to be first ignited? The lands of the higher elevation with the power centers of the energy fields including the vortexes is a POWER CENTER of much frequencies. Lands of vast acreage yet unused will facilitate part of the manifestation.

"Rest in the knowing of this information and be open to yet more to be inserted as you progress in your City Messenger Movement forward. All will come into being as predicted and more understanding will be facilitated to you. Your path now leads in many directions and some all at the same time, as the word spreads of what you hold to be sacred and healing, because it is.

"So then now since local noise is apparent and this transmission can disconnect, we send you back to your world with 'see-through' glasses to enjoy."

And It Came Upon a Midnight Clear!

Embassy Visit October 5, 2010

In the expectation of going to a Mike Dooley seminar in a few days, and also having been invited to another meeting of the Universe, I happily found myself at the familiar Gate Towers along with many others. La-Luke arrived and we set off to the Embassy which I now felt so comfortable in, as it was filled with universal entity friends of love and Light. The usual trolley took us to the Embassy door and we sensed that we were anticipated by those inside and we were.

The table of leaders greeted us just with their vibrations, as OOO-LON extended his hand to me, (a hand which was almost non-existent), but I could feel the energy putting me at ease and with serenity.

O: "Once more we meet and exchange ideas to further your role of expectancy. Where shall we begin?"

G: "Anticipating an updated City manuscript is almost ready to be printed, I wondered if there was anything more to be included from the Embassy and those here?"

O: "With the prospect that this issue will bring people's interests closer to an understanding of the messages given, we have a few words (or designs as we call them) to be inserted from our combined thoughts. We who know of the completion and vibration and entrance of this City and its healing properties, desire that this, you may say ...

'Upon the setting of a sun, and during the quiet of a night, there will be set on your Earth surface for sun-up visual, a God-made invention of healing through many technologies that have not ever been known before.'

"No one has to fly into outer space or land on another planet to see if life really exists elsewhere, or if you are the only planet with life on it. Forgive me, but this indicates a ridiculous belief that you are the only place of honor, and we smile with anticipation of you knowing the real truth and soon, as we come to you.

"So save some mental spaces to know and recognize, that all that has been foretold now appears. And your world will never be the same again, as a massive change is not only needed but desired by masses of Earth people.

"The time has arrived for this change of consciousness. And believe me, this demonstration will do just that! Centuries upon centuries it has taken to build The City for a 3rd dimensional seeing and using. Divine intervention now fulfills that prophesy of a master long since.

"Too many people separate themselves from the original Creator of all. So then, now pay attention to what were then words of instruction, from universal beings (all in the unseen) to make this prophesy come to light.

"So then Dear One, Genii of the Light lamp with vibrations beyond the normal, take these words for they are vibrations of truth and with them set into place 'the COMING' for it is indeed and people will cry 'Halleluiah!' Time is non-existent at this point but in your vernacular it is important.

"So let it be known that we Universal Beings of Community Light, now declare this to be so. Now the clock ticks faster … so Light it be!"

With this then, I sensed that all those in the auditorium that I could only see faintly, sounded the universal tone ... AH!

It almost blew me over and then the lights in this place went on and I could see hundreds upon hundreds of beings all standing in various colors and designs. I was speechless … so much so that La-Luke held me and we exited.

I then found myself home at the bark of my pup Light. I am blessed!

Hot Line to the Boss!

Embassy Visit October 12, 2010

I rested into the quiet of God's presence called meditation, and looked for the inner vision to once again return me to the Embassy of Peace Headquarters located in The City of Light.

This time however, it had been okayed that I take with me my little 9 pound white and gold Pomeranian puppy named 'Light' and I recognized that he is the same colors as all The City buildings I have seen.

My Guide La-Luke appeared and smiled as he petted the fluffy fur ball named Light. This visit may just be a bit different so I decided to just hold him instead of letting him down, as I had no idea of what he would do.

As we entered the sanctuary of the Embassy Entities, Light's bark was the first announcement that we had arrived. Along with OOO-LON and the other four entities at the head table, I sensed that a couple of them wanted to pet this little one of human pets.

La-Luke took him from me and held him as my attention was on him instead of what we were here for. Once a caring mother, always a caring mother. (No matter what form the kids take).

What happened was that the energies in this place calmed 'Light' down and he fell asleep in La-Luke's arms leaving me to be about God's business.

G: "Thank you for allowing my puppy to come with me."

O: "The animal kingdom holds great honor and it is a joy for us to see such a bright Light as he is. Now then, what can we do for you?"

G: "I wish to learn more about other Cosmic Communities and what my next steps are to support those whose cosmic love and caring I sense here. What can you share with me?"

O: "The vastness of the Universe first of all contains stupendous amounts of entities who value what we are supporting here in bringing forth The City of Light you now stand in. The way of learning comes from questions, for answers to be given."

G: "There are times I have not a clue to what to ask you as most of all this is so vast and new to me, but I am eager to learn."

O: "Your love is noted. You have met several of space origin and even though we may look a bit different, we are all one, which your planet population has yet to recognize and one of the reasons The City must come forth and people get to know us also as space brothers and sisters in unison, not separate.

"We have a strong energy-intelligence or we would not even be here and certainly in the banner of love. We are attempting to accelerate your consciousness and can do that simply by being intelligence vibrations."

G: "Some people, it shows in the media, have fears when they sight a UFO that can even destroy our military machinery of protection. It has been said that my speaking with the President could bring him into the knowing of The City. How am I to get to speak to him?"

O: "You are to use the confidence thoughts of what you refer to as unexpected good or invite God's favor to assist in this mission. The path is being prepared and you just have to be aware of that knowing. You have support efforts to make that path available and open, as the intent is the love message you are to give him.

"Stay in the vision and with the prepared new advanced edition of The City manuscript, once in his hands, this will trigger from within him the value of what you are presenting, even if no one else is aware at the moment of meeting. This will be a one-to-one meeting. Stay in the wisdom and know that what is being said here is correct.

"You have what has been called in your language, "a hot-line to the boss!" This line of language is the Light path to that destination. We have not brought you this far for nothing to take place. Remember he is pre-programmed in his DNA of The City. You are just re-affirming him of what he already knows but does not know on the surface."

G: "So then our next steps are ...."

O: "To complete the updated City manuscript. This should not be put off as a time line is in process so to speak, and sparking interest is important. Just be open. So then you have your answer."

I looked around to see my pup sleeping peacefully and La-Luke nodded that it was time to leave and I agreed as noise outside my window at home was interrupting any further visit. I thanked the entities and as I closed this off, I gave thanks to God and those here in Sedona, Seattle and in Stelle who were assisting in finishing The City manuscript. They know who they are and so does God!

So Light it be!

From Places Beyond

Embassy Visit October 26, 2010

The City Embassy of Peace beckoned me to re-enter and this I wanted to do. Why today? Well, I did have a question. The familiar Gate of Entrance was open with many people also entering, but I doubted they were headed for the Embassy as so many other unusual-looking buildings have immediate drawing power.

I saw my mentor and City Guide La-Luke approaching and leading me to the trolley and to the front entrance of the building that holds universal visitors with answers connected. I was excited and honored to be here not only once but many times. As we entered, the scene was the same with the 5 Entities up front and personal, and head leader OOO-LON extending a welcome. The fullness of this amphitheater-type place reached my senses in love and I was humble in its presence.

O: "Again we meet in a Light connection. You both are welcome. How may we serve you?"

G: "I have a question."

O: "Continue."

G: "It has been suggested long since that I originated from the star or planet Lyra. Is this true and if so what is my home like? I would like to be appraised of my background, please."

OOO-LON smiled and said, "This is quite true. You came forth from the star planet Lyra some eons of space-time ago. Long since has this been established in your memory bank. Many of those serving the Earth planet are from distant stars like the entities serving in the Embassy here.

"You would be considered in our view to be a 'Star Ambassador' who speaks of coming events and the knowing of the truth of that position. Like the entities within this building, you are designed and programmed to complete The City process. Sounds like a space story doesn't it?"

G: "Oh yes ... but fascinating. Is this why I have always felt a kindred spirit for extraterrestrials?"

O: "It would seem so. Unlike Earth people, we are all connected and can appreciate the other. Unlike the motion screen pictures that depict that we fight each other, it is just a mental depiction of their own adventure consciousness. You have a word as you look skyward ...'Heaven.' It is more like that! You take on the appearance of a human to live a life and fit in, but the deep love you have for others makes you a bit different anyway."

G: "What about people who say they were abducted on spaceships and used for experiments?"

O: "It doesn't ... again the condition of the human mind seeks to have notoriety in making these statements from a consciousness below average, and the wanting to have something of this sort to experience, so in their mind they do. Would it seem like this is the case from what you are experiencing? Of course not! Have you and the Dr. Bill not been invited on a space vehicle in the Nevada desert just for the fun of it? Of course!

"Why with what your planet carries of consciousness in various degrees, would we need to do that? We are here and anything we need to know or find is in plain sight just by watching the Light auras you all carry. Kidnapping persons is barbaric. So we make the most of what we have to work with as the Lightworkers of holiness help keep the balance of energy and show us the way, thus cancelling the darkness of ignorance that are interlopers of that consciousness."

G: "What can you tell me of my original star planet?"

O: "Your home planet revels in what you would call 'fun'. The energy is very high in this frequency. It is peaceful and nature abounds just at a different percentage of the way you work here, and this is why even for many decades you enjoyed having fun as you call it. You dream in love and this is the closest you have been able to reach your Lyra home base, through the Disneyland visits.

"You have said many times that you feel at home in this place when you are there, for indeed it rings true within you all the way back to your cosmic beginnings.

"You dress as human and feel as human but you once have remarked that you feel like a visitor somehow. These deep feelings are generated from your home base and in that, it is normal.

"You even recreated a theater type structure that children could experience what you feel inside as 'love' play.' The Disney type was deep within you and still is. This is good as it gives you energy to assist and lift others.

"You play as a Jedi and this too connects with your space home. You also have been recording lately that you feel not 'normal' and strange like having an outer shell when the inner one seems to be the real one.

"Your senses are beyond the human and as you release more and more human ways, you are ascending even as you sense being a bit unbalanced in your two worlds. Of course the high and low are being experienced.

"As a speaking leader you will attract people to pay attention to what you are reporting. Speak and permit your Lyra energy to support your words."

G: "And what of President Obama?"

O: "This too is on your agenda as we clear the path of connection. His Guides are aware of what is taking place and open his mental to such a meeting. It will be as so stated! Anything else?"

G: "It all seems to fit like puzzle pieces."

O: "The Light of God so called, makes you a prime giver of facts, not fantasy with The City. So Dear One, play in your design as human and know that in looking ahead all will be as was designed, way back eons of times ago. Your Lyra family commends your courage to move through many lives to bring you to this place in space-time. Go and enjoy as a child in this knowingness that even Mr. Disney is from your Lyra home ... imagine that!"

G: "Is President Obama?"

O: "No. But a space dweller he was, and in some way still is. All is well. You will enjoy meeting him and his family ... again fun time. So have we answered your questions until next time?"

G: "You have indeed given me more than I expected to know of my home base. I am quite mindful of my mission and will complete it. I am blessed. Thank you all!"

And with a bow we left the Embassy and I found myself in Sedona, Arizona, ready to take on whatever today would bring and another City Light up! Thanks to all those who filled the Embassy and my Guide and God who gave me this amazing adventure with the Grand Finale coming up.

So Light it be!

Marionettes of President and First Lady Obama, Sasha and Malia

Genii with marionettes she created as a gift for the Obama family

**I am praying for God's Divine Design to reveal how I may be able to present the marionettes I have made out of my love and appreciation for President and Michelle Obama with them and their children in person.
Are you the one who can help make that happen? Who do you know?**

http://www.sedonalightcenter.org/celebrity_marionettes.htm.

Sedona Space Port

Embassy Visit November 4, 2010

The day had begun and I looked to re-enter the Embassy as I had been asked to take in a few questions on The City arrival from a linked friend. May I enter? Of course, came the answer!

The scene found me inside The City past the entering Gate and sitting on one of the massage benches in the Park of Relaxation. My! It felt good ... Ahh! The feeling of spring energy was in the air as birds sang and frittered about. This indeed would be considered paradise.

Feeling really great I saw my Guide La-Luke to my right, pulling aside the willow trees entrance and the wheel-less trolley came into view. La-Luke nodded that it was time to go. I rose and as I stepped on the stones that led to the willow trees, the vibration of them massaged my feet. Fun stuff!

Aboard the trolley, we were whisked to the now familiar Embassy of Peace and faced the 5 entities I usually saw, and all were in place. What a spectacular view this was with the knowing that entities from all over the vast Universe were here also.

It was pure magic that I could never invent myself, but am blessed beyond belief. (Which most of these visits may sound like, but ... very true). Imagine that! Must have done something right somewhere in my life to be brought to this whole adventure that the Universe set up for me. My! My! I was beginning to feel at home here.

O: "Welcome, we sound the tone and await the questions you have brought forth from another in your human fields."

G: "Thank you. Yes, there are several. May I begin? "

OOO-LON nodded with the other 4 with him.

G: "1. When The City of Light descends, will it blend in with The City of Sedona or hover above?"

O: Smiling "Dear One, how could a human get any healing of the physical etc. if it demonstrated above? It would take a very long ladder would it not? Or to land on someone's home also makes no sense. The City is now in another dimension (and there are many). You all live in a hologram, but due to this density of your dimension, it is called in your language 'invisible' for the moment, which in itself is timeless.

"The wizards of the past know that the Creator is pure magic in your world, and can make something out of nothing appear as if by magic. How can this be done? You have an entrance called 'Thought' have you not?

"Cannot thought do magic? Of course, but to us it is not so much magic as 'thought projection' and into the Sedona area. "Sedona is known for its power of vortexes etc. and is known to be a place of attention, so the news that such a City is to be introduced in its proximity would be of public notice. There is much ground that is vacant near the Sedona landmark so to speak, so ... Why not. Sedona is a major portal site for galactic endeavors and is being used now very much in this manner.

"Let it be known that Sedona is a Space Port of recognition in the Universe while the land attached has vacant properties. Too, this place of note is known to many. It is a holodeck! A holy place! In the future months ahead this question will begin to make more sense and be adequate for answers, as Lightworkers re-tune themselves as with the Genii's 4 Keys of Light, that you facilitate in your Light Center location, and where Light is the only answer combined with love intensity.

"Lightworkers who know of their Soul Guides will begin to tune in with them as The City is outlined in its design where no local homes find themselves suddenly within The City. Just know that all is known and trust what is being said. Even as you now stand in this other dimension, you are well versed in what you are to do or say at any given time ... next question?"

G: "As asked ... When people enter the Light City, what happens to their dense bodies?"

O: "If this question is to mean do they lose their bodies? No of course not. They only lose their sickness that brought them there in the first place. Why would The City be necessary if there was no human body to be healed? Or mind or emotions as all are connected.

"We realize that it is a very large step in your conditioned understanding of human physical conditions to one that as said, has never before been known to appear on your planet. Many questions arrive to search out the answers that fill in the mind's knowing.

"Is it a matter of trusting the Universe to bring forth the answers? You the Genii look around here and what do you see? Hundreds of space entitles with answers so far advanced, it is impossible to explain in your human vernacular language.

"Seeing is believing, and indeed you all will have the advantage of seeing a demonstration so big that there is no doubt it will make a believer out of everyone. Your third dimension is about form and thickness. So you will have that. Peace. Next question...."

G: "Her next question is, will anyone who desires entrance be granted entrance in The City?"

O: "There is an indication here that perhaps those of less than intelligence with maybe destruction as intent be allowed to enter? Would such be allowed to enter with all others? Permit it to be said here, that anyone who has an inner dark, ignorant, destructive intent would not feel welcome to enter, for there are magnetic fields above, below and around The City constantly to protect what is apparent on the ground. That includes planes overhead or any underground interference. It is just not enterable.

"There is so much unknown beyond this and the reason The City is at all, is to cure the thinking properties of all who dwell in such darkness that they cannot see the Light, but they will.

"Again in your human equation of how can all this can take place, one must see it from a higher advantage. You say you have angels? True! They are also detectives of sorts and can detect any one's inner thinking at any time in any place. There is nothing that is not known.

"This is God's gift to you all. Why would any harm be allowed to come to a gift of pure love? It is therefore advised that each one desiring to feel, see, and know that such a place is approaching would be advised to do daily inside personal work on themselves in elevation. The truth, as much as you can understand, has been addressed. So for now leave the rest to the Primal Creator of it all. We leave you in much love and attend your every session on The City and the 4 Keys of Advancement.

So Light it be!"

I then found myself at home, with the red rocks of energy, the sun and blue sky, knowing that this remarkable coming attraction is right on schedule, whenever that is.

Photo of "Angel over Cathedral Rock" in Sedona © OceAnna Laughing Cloud

From the Inside Out

Crowds of people were seen entering the encoded Gate Tower (which I figured was happening at each of the others as well). People seemed excited to experience what was inside of this dramatic intervention on our behalf, The City of Light that God has laid on our Earth's lap. I could see my Guide La-Luke waving at me as we moved to connect, laughing all the way. Connecting ... we almost ran through the Park of Relaxation and onto the trolley heading for the Embassy of Peace Headquarters non-stop.

To describe this massive building would be like trying to describe the Universe itself as it contains hundreds of entities from all over this thing called the Universe, and beyond space. What is beyond space? Hmmm.

In we went and the scene was the same as all the previous visits. At a head table sat 5 Entities. The center one was OOO-LON, the head major-domo who I can only describe as 'pure love personified.' That clarifies his being as God-like, and his smile could melt an ice cube in seconds.

They all stood in greeting in robes that were almost as '"see-through" Light. As we stood before them, a throne-like chair rolled up for my pleasured seating and I relaxed in the splendor of it all.

O: "I see you have returned for a space chat."

G: "Yes, this place never ceases to amaze me, knowing that there are hundreds of entities also here as an audience from all over the Universe. What do you all do when you get together? Do you understand each other's languages?"

OOO-LON smiling, replied: "Indeed. There is what you would call a 'universal sound language' and through it we have no problem as you Earth people do. What do we do here? We 'imagine-ate' all the extremities that will occur as this City appears like magic and in a sense is magical, just unknown to you. It has taken 'Light mechanics' to transform what would be of accepted healing on your planet. Light holds many frequencies and many that your Light systems do not hold at this point.

"This City, although it will just appear out of the ethers so to speak, has taken the creme-de-la-creme of advanced technical resources from those gathered here as Universal Community and beyond. This space technology is necessary to even begin to draw up the architectural plans that your master teacher Hermes has brought forth. Not only for the pyramid in Egypt (and through the Dr. B as well), but what we are speaking from at this moment. And you all will be healed of various maladies you bring on yourself. So then, how may we serve you this day as you travel back into your levels of understanding?"

G: "It is my intent to give those I am to speak to as much information as I can in regards to The City of Light's appearance. The question most asked is 'when' will this appear? 2012 is the drum beat. People are expecting something to take place from their learning, which takes many forms and not all of it good unfortunately.

"I have asked this question before, however it keeps repeating itself. What do I tell them that they can do, to get the Inner Knowing themselves? And with another City session coming up soon, I want to share whatever I can with what has been lovingly given."

O: "This question of time orientation is normal, and will make itself known as this your coming [time-wise] indications of 2011 enter into your calendar. You can expect the interest to pick up reaching to the pivotal point, and this is expected to energize The City plans into an energy field of great importance. You tell them to tune within themselves and notice on a day to day basis what they feel and sense, and they will know when to sing their praises of Halleluiah!

"Lightworkers have an inner sense and having been taught by advanced teachers, have drawn their own wisdom. From these ascended masters, this new Inner Knowing will not be new, just verifying what they already sense.

"Rest assured that 2011 will be a 'Knowing year' even to having Light-based communities across the planet. The Renee friend of the Genii has already sensed a Light Center in her community and is very capable in setting one in order.

"Plant life will be very important as the Light energy enters your planet domain with the coming of The City. The plant life will pick up the vibrations and grow in abundance filled with energy of the spires and the wisdom of the intelligence also.

"Darkness (ignorance) cannot stay in Light communities of Light People. They will leave for various reasons and this should be permitted. You will see more and more people leave this planet not being able to rectify their systems to the new frequencies. What is being said here is valid and will be seen as very correct!

"Expect 2011 to be mammoth, with Light Changes taking place on a moment to moment notice. You the Genii teach and lead the 4 Keys of Light. As these very old sacred sessions come out of the closet so to speak, they will empty what has been a hold-up with students. Now just by trusting and using the sacred tones and words of wisdom, they will be brought into the vibration of this inner projected 2011 Knowing about to take place.

"Continue to Light 'Link' more students with their Personal Guides, who sense this may be the step into The City that they seek, as they then have a head start on this new advanced inner sensing. Does this help?"

G: "Oh yes, I will do what I can and am advised. Thank you!"

O: "Good, then return when you can and expect good results from our visits. Questions will be directed into answers as you proceed to lead and expect more invitations to speak hither and yon. This session is now completed!"

And with that my Guide nodded to me for us to leave. I bowed to the front Entities and waved to those in the auditorium background as we headed out to the trolley, the Park, and past more people going in. Once outside, I got a hug from my Guide, as he too disappeared into the crowd.

I returned ... as I then found myself home with my puppy Light Spirit, ready to read what I have written about that has just been experienced. I don't always remember everything from my visit, so I write it all down as soon as possible after it happens, so that I don't miss any of it. Then I type it up from my notes.

So Light it be!

We just celebrated Light Spirit's 4th birthday!

Space Love!

Embassy Visit November 28, 2010

As I entered the usual scene at the entrance Gate, many smiling excited people pushed past me anxious to enter and see what I have already seen prophesied many years prior. The joy was flowing enough that I got caught up in it, for I knew what they would experience.

My Guide La-Luke parted the human seas as he reached out to me and with confident expectancy, we headed for the Embassy of Peace Headquarters inside the Light City. Within a short period of our time we had traveled into the Embassy where a lot of unusual sound was taking place. As we entered I could see a bit more clearly the hundreds of space entities sounding to each other. What, I could not make out! There was just a lot of it which sounded very pleasant. I felt that they were having a jolly good time.

Every description (as best as I could detect), colors and friendly love for each other, made like waves or frequencies throughout the whole audience. Those 5 at the head table including OOO-LON heading up this committee of hundreds, were caught up in the energy as well. OOO-LON laughed as he saw I was astonished at what was taking place. Wow ... science fiction in action.

O: "Come in Dear One and join us in the fun of exchanging energies. You have questions?"

G: "Wow ... this is wonderful. Are you having a party?"

O: "This is when all the energies of each one, combine with another. You might call it love appreciation, thankfulness, etc. We exchange energy patterns, so what one has in its energy field, we share with another. You share words like I am speaking. We share sound energies as tone communication. You could call it ...'SPACE LOVE!'"

G: "This is so wonderful. I am feeling so 'high!' Interesting, sweep this across my planet and things could change very quickly."

O: "Your motion pictures depict space wars. As has been said to you many years ago, 'darkness destroys what it does not understand!' This is human thinking ego-sensed, but makes what is fear-based atrocities. We in space communities work with the highest of space Light frequencies that are fed to us by the original Creator, not pulsating interference. This is fear-based nonsense!

"All this will in time simmer down and eventually disappear altogether, so that those of us from other space places, can be in communication. What you will have will be peaceful co-existence. No Star Wars is intended!"

G: "What else can you tell me about life on other planets?"

O: "1. That it exists!

2. That they have many levels of advanced frequencies.

3. That communication with your world will come about peacefully.

4. That you humans will learn to progress without the ego to intrude.

5. That it has been said that love is the combination key to success.

6. That what we have to share with your people is un-measurable, in that we all share, all grow as love in a peaceful existence. This is in process.

7. First The City filled with love and Light, healing through that love. Your people have yet to experience the true frequency of LOVE Intelligence.

8. Your planet is not yet able to reach and experience such love as others in the Universe do. This is being worked on even as we speak.

9. You are considered by us as an ambassador of such love, as you are stepping aside old programming and entering into the space frequencies now entering your planet of confusion; thus giving upheaval for some and those of Light are feeling the subtleties of what is being spoken of here.

10. You stand here in this Embassy of Peace away from your daily duties and see, hear, and feel, what you refer to as Extraterrestrials, and what do you see and feel?"

G: "Oh! No doubt ... love, friendship beyond what is normally sensed in my world, and information with nothing hidden."

O: "Good, then take this energy back with you and spread it around and get people excited. Your updated book is a precursor of this, for everyone who will be excited in reading your story will want others to get the feeling they have experienced traveling through the pages with you into The City. This indeed is your space path-work calling, even though you never knew it would be. Surprise!

"Soon all will make itself known and they will say, 'Yes, I heard about The City Coming before.' It is as simple as lowering a completed building in place on The City interior and the effort it took to do that as it astounded you to see it being done. Imagine a completed healing building being lowered from a huge space vehicle. Astounding? Not really, you just don't know how it was frequency-done, but true. So then, have you experienced what E.T.'s do when the Universe gets together for love in progress?"

G: "More than I could have guessed."

O: "Good! Then return to your home base and remember all you have seen and felt, it's just a taste of the Universe that you will be exposed to. We here bid you a good day in peace and in love."

I thanked everyone and as I turned to leave, I felt an energy wave near and felt/saw an entity sort of in waves, hug me. Talk about power! Wow! What an energy exchange. I almost lifted off the ground. That was it! Oh my God!

Then I was back home on a Sunday morning in bed reliving this visit. Experiencing an E.T. itself was ... I am speechless ... but look forward to more.

So Light it be!

City Dimension Breakthrough . . .

WHOOPEE! A CHRISTMAS GIFT ALL WRAPPED UP IN LIGHT!

Embassy Visit December 3, 2010

Again at a City Gate that loomed 5-stories high above me, and with many others entering joyfully, I was filled with quite a mixture of delight and excitement. Today I did have a question regarding a spontaneous message that came to and through me yesterday, as follows....

Message ... "LET IT BE KNOWN THAT THE FUTURE IS HERE NOW!"

"That which has been promised has now entered into the ethers of your dimension. That which has been promised for centuries of your time has arrived. Breaking through the levels of demonstration, God declares this to be a gift of eternity, long since in seclusion.

"What the Genii has been served as guidance now remains to be seen and will. We who work to bring forth God's City still remain unseen for just the right time to declare its appearance. We salute the Earth with this gift of love and peace ... and so it is."

La-Luke held my hand as we rushed through the crowd, through the park and onto a trolley that rode us to the Embassy of Peace Headquarters, where love and peace has a real meaning. I took a deep breath and opened the door of this sanctuary of cosmic entities from all over the Universe.

OOO-LON stood in his usual place with his four friendly leaders from space. I bowed as the tone of laughter lifted. I felt very honored.

O: "Welcome Oh Earthling and Guide of humans. You must have a question (of which I was pretty sure he already knew). You may begin."

Taking out the paper I had written the message on, I read the above message and asked "What does this mean?"

O: "What has been sent to you is the first verification of what has been the reason for all your City visits and the information given within. Indeed the energy frequency of The City of Light has made the first impact into your dimension and we are delighted. It has been many centuries of your time-equivalent to make such a statement, but it is so!

"As the time of your life continues, the first imprint will be observed and you will be guided to report the same. As said, the future is here and The City of Light enters into your planet domain. Does this answer your question?"

G: "To a point yes. What am I or others to watch for?"

O: "Just be. Relax the eyes, and above in the heavens, you will begin to see form-like clouds that only hint at what you see, and what is coming about. Keep up with what has been given you to complete, for the words need to be spread like seeds.

"The latest City manuscript holds many Embassy visits that will give people of reading more support of what is coming about. Finish it quickly and set it loose. The time is now! And also, you have a chance to give Light to those who enter into the Holy Keys having now a shortened connection.

"So then, you have much to do to help people secure themselves to The City of Light. Continue to complete these projects as the future is now here, and time has collapsed enough to give you this report, and others will want to know what is taking place. The energies make a space like the parting of the seas. The energies open and make a space for The City appearance available for their sight. Be open for guidance at any given moment and we will assist your progress. Anything else?"

G: "Well no, I will do as guided and the manuscript will be completed and printed as well as The 4 Keys. Thank you all for what you are doing to secure this planet in Light and all of us who live on it. This is indeed a gifted Christmas message."

O: "Be of God cheer. The City is here. Just be aware and move with the guidance and all will be well. We bid you the Light of the eternal day in peace and love."

And with this he sat down as we bowed and left the building, and took the trolley back to the Gate. With a parting hug from my Guide of many visits, I found myself back home on a sunny Friday morning looking at clouds forming over the red Sedona rocks in a clear blue sky. Imagine that!

So Light it be!

Coming into Time and Space!

Embassy Visit December 7, 2010

Outside my window I saw clear blue skies overhead and a sun that showed the beautiful red rocks of this area. I took a deep breath with a heart filled with love and I centered myself into being able to envision The City, for I have been informed that The City entrance into this dimension has now been achieved. Since I have a City meeting coming up, I could not resist requesting that I be allowed to hear all about it, like all the facts I could be given to share with those who choose to spend some time with me at this point.

Bingo! ... I found myself at a Gate crowded with others who wanted to see what was going on inside. I saw a hand waving and it looked like my Guide La-Luke calling me, and I moved in that direction. His smiley face was good to see and we headed through the Park of Relaxation onto the wheel-less trolley, and landed at the Embassy of Peace Headquarters once more.

I found myself standing in front of the head Entity group with OOO-LON and the four others usually there in white robes, but almost faceless as they seemed to be like holographic projections. OOO-LON was not observed that way. He smiled and nodded as the other four bowed in acknowledgement also.

It is not easy to explain the feeling of this place and those hundreds of Entities in attendance, except to say I feel at home with all of them. When I am told by my Guides "To be in the world but not of it" ... that is what they mean, and less and less am I connected and Earth-bound. That is not to say I just float around, I just feel less and less connected but filled with love unexplainable, strange as that sounds.

O: "Welcome back student of space-time. How may we serve your needs?"

G: "Thank you. It has been said to me that at this time The City of Light has now entered our space-time continuum. I have a City meeting soon. What may I report on this which is very exciting!"

OOO-LON smiled and said, "This Dear One, is truth in action. The City of Healing Light arrives into the third dimension of your substance. For those who await The City, we do bring good news as The City arrives into the atmospheric frequencies of your illusionary time and space. For those awaiting The City of Light, we bring now good news like a Christmas gift all wrapped up in the clouds of entrance even though it is not visible as yet ... patience ... patience!

"Your third dimension has a density unlike most others, and time as you call it needs space to produce. Thus it is referred to as space-time, which you humans use daily designated by the sun as you awaken to a new day so called.

"There will be those who see The City very faintly if watching for it. Most will not until fully set on the solid ground in place and the grand show begins. Any more questions?"

G: "I think what I desired from here is just a verification of the message I got walking through my hallway the other day. It was pretty strong though. I try to explain to others what is almost unexplainable, and so to totally understand since nothing like this has ever happened on this planet."

O: "Relate to your audiences your feeling of visits you have had. This is happy time and your words and feelings will be picked up as the honor of this message prevails as truth. We here relate to your path of Light-City information and take the many thoughts you have had about it. Dear One, just be the love you are, and all the rest will flow like a non-stopping river of information.

"Each of the healing buildings here make unusual advanced types of healings. You have seen that they indeed support someone's inner wishes. Your path resonates in the way of Light and this will be accelerated as you progress farther. You, with all this data are operating more out of your past world, but as you move into the new intensive of Space Intellect, your teaching will be of Space Intelligence rather than the normal thinking that you have been so far using.

"This information is what you will share in the future. Worded simply, it will be able to move into the space of cosmic intelligence like the future City of Light. Be easy with you. You are doing well and are supported by all of us here. As this time of 2010 time-space leaves, 2011 walks in to take its place. It will be a very important time in your history.

"Go now and rest. We are taking the current course and you will see what has been promised, even before you knew that there was anything to be interested in. All is well on course, of course."

G: "Thank you. I will report with love and anticipation of the good things ahead."

And with that I felt the whole audience rise as we bowed, turned, and my heart was full of such love as I have ever found in this lifetime. We walked out the door while still wiping tears of appreciation.

What happened next, I just don't know, but I was home, still filled with the love of this whole project. I must have done something right to be a major leader in this as I pray to be worthy... but know that I am.

So Light it be!

"He"

Embassy Visit December 25, 2010

The Gate opened wide as I rushed to enter The City on this Christmas Day. Holiday fun seemed to be in the air as I heard tinkling bells in the distance. La-Luke showed up decked in a Santa hat smiling from ear to ear as if he knew something I didn't. He rushed me inside through the Rejuvenating Park. So much for rest! On to the trolley and we whizzed to the Embassy of Peace Head-quarters.

Arriving at our location, he continued to rush me inside. I felt like a kid meeting Santa Claus for the first time. What was going on? The scene was the same as usual with the 5 Beings (including OOO-LON) at the head table, who bowed in acknowledgement of our arrival. I had to catch my breath as I returned this welcome by wanting to wish them all a Merry Christmas but thought better of it.

O: "Ah, this is a great human day to visit the Embassy. You celebrate the birth of the Christ child, is that not so?"

G: "Well a lot of people do. The children here welcome Santa Claus for presents."

O: "And what present would the Genii have given this day?"

G: Thinking for a moment I reply. "The City of Light arrival is # one, and I have a question I am not sure of the answer."

O: "And that would be?"

G: "For many years it has been said that the Christ would come back like a second coming. Is this correct or just a fantasy of His followers?"

O: "Well, Dear One why don't you ask Him yourself?"

G: "What, who me? You are kidding right? "

O: "See for yourself."

Then as God is my witness, a figure appeared encapsulated in Light so bright it was hard to make out the figure contained within. Wow, then I saw Him. Now I have met many high profile people in my life and been excited to meet them, but this has to be the best ever ... ever. He certainly was recognizable or was my imagination playing tricks on me? Just because I have just been given a hand painting of Him from my friend Blanche? OK God, clear me up please!"

All the beings bowed as this figure of the Christ moved towards me. My Guide whispered in my ear of his support if I wanted to sit down, as the Light energy was so strong and he thought I might faint.

He: "You called? What would you have of me?"

G: I could not get my breath for a moment. This whole adventure has had some interestingly strange moments, but this was the epitome of any meeting so far. Here I was about to talk to someone in robes of blazing Light with such love and gentleness that it was overwhelming. Sputtering to get some kind of answer out, much less a question, I pulled myself together and sort of said, "Is The City of Light your so-called second coming?" (There, I managed to say it)!

Seeing my nerviness and absolute delight in this unexpected meeting (and on His birthday), I see Him holding out His hand which was so light there was nothing to hold on to like in the physical.

He: "Come, permit us to sit a moment and this will help you." Then a couple of chairs just appeared and we sat. Here I was facing the most beloved being in history talking with me ... Oh my! Seated in this golden Light, He continued ..."You have been with The City of Light plans for much time and know of the background in its initiation onto this planet."

G: "Yes sir," I sputtered getting my voice back.

He: "Then knowing all you do and the presentation of The City, indeed I can share with you that The City will be seen as the second coming of my reappearance on the Earth plane, but also it is the first, as technical implements of Light healing will take place as never before. I am just here in Light appearance to signify that all you have been told and have seen, others will not only see it, but be engulfed in its Light to be healed. Whatever needs to be healed ... will be!"

By this time I was so absorbed in His aura Light, anything He said would be the truth, absolutely! "Thank you!" I muttered.

He: "I leave you now in admiration of what you are doing for human mankind."

G: "I am just reporting what is given me and who would believe I just met You?"

He: "It matters not. This would be your Earth's Christian holiday called Christmas and I delight in the honor even for your Santa Claus, who is Light dressed to delight the children, giving them something to believe in. The way is opening to the world to see what 'Light' can do and it is my Father's gift to your world and people need to see it as such. Those who are upset with the turn of current events at this time, will one day praise this cleansing for then the New World set on its positive axis will be harmonious."

G: "This meeting is indeed a gift from God and I thank you and all who bring forth The City. Beyond that ... I am speechless."

Smiling, He stood up and bid me a happy day. And how do I say this ... He just disappeared.

O: "Was this a nice surprise gift for you Oh Lady who loves good surprises?"

G: "I can hardly believe it took place but then ... why not?"

O: "Then just be and in that being, you will relive this many times. Now then, return back to the Embassy soon as we begin the new year of 2011 and many more new changes all leading to the same conclusion ... The City of Light entrance. The New Year will bring many more surprises so be aware."

G: "Thank you. I am so honored to have met this Ultimate Light ... Wow! ~ Merry Christmas!" The Beings at the head table all bowed as I was led out and back to the Gate.

G: "Did all that happen?"

The quiet answer came in return from my Guide ..."Indeed it did! Congratulations."

Genii holding the painting of Jesus that lives in The Light Center Classroom of Eyes of Love by Blanche Radiance available along with many of her other masterpieces at www.thekingsbridge.com

In addition to bringing through the information and drawings for The City of Light, Rev. Dr. Bill Townsend also developed many resources to help people grow and develop spiritually. One of his favorite lessons was Three Steps to Light which describes how Jesus the Christ was a perfect example for us of OUR power of the spoken Word. Harness the Creative Power of Your Word is available as a PDF at www.sedonalightcenter.org/ HarnessTheCreativePowerOfYourWord.pdf

The Morning After

Morning Message as Follow-Up to Yesterday's Christmas Embassy Visit

The Morning After! December 26, 2010

Genii question: "Yesterday in The City Embassy I met the Christ unexpectedly. Can you please expand on this surprise meeting and any other guidance?"

Answer: "Indeed, the perfection of the Christ lifted and inspired the Genii. It was meant this way. That is why you were nudged a few days prior to go to the Embassy on that blessed day. The Light energy frequencies of this noted Leader of leaders, came as a vision of what is to come about, namely The City of Light Healing ... Imagine that!

"The overall perfection of what is to come about makes anything less seem not so problematic, not even those of worldly cares. Hardships abound now as the overall changes take place. '"As Above, So Below!"' heralds in the new as said by the master of magic and master of The City Architecture Designs, Hermes, who gave the introduction of the plans to the Dr. Bill who was his student many eons ago.

"Many places have The City of Light been seen. Many words have been written of such an event that slips by unnoticed, yet is in the public eye so to speak. So then, you have heard the words from this God Man of Light that you got to see and hear firsthand as truth and anything else would not be so.

"Today as you walk your path of Light and enter into yet another new year, contributing to the year of finalizing the coming event, remember the scene in the Embassy of 2010. The constant question repeats itself in your 3rd dimension, such as, 'Is there really a City of Light coming? ...When????'

"To believe, means to be alive and is the energy of the hidden WORD. The message of the Christ given yesterday is so believed within you, that you are alive in what was said, and as the world changes, thus makes the landing site for purification and uplifting to those who may be non-believers.

"As the meeting of yesterday was a surprise, so will The City of Light be for those non-believers who know not. Bless each day and be open, for even in this year many will be blessed unknowingly as love intervenes. As you spread the word of such a gift coming forth, look ahead at what the next year could possibly bring in preparation of the Coming, and it will, for you are a believer...

"Mark this past meeting as one of importance and smile for you have met one of the best!"

So right 'HE' be! (YHVH)

Being in the World But Not of It

Embassy Visit December 28, 2010

What seemed like just a few minutes ago, I went to the Embassy and met the Christ in full Light unexpectedly. I was still moved by that experience. My guidance is "to be in the world, but not of it". This seems to be the case more and more as I push aside winter and look to my re-entering for a City of Light visit. With a deep breath, the Gate of Entrance appeared, and as I looked up to the top of the 5-story Tower of welcome, I was amazed still, even after so many visits here. It was quiet with no one else around, not even my Guide La-Luke.

Knowing my way through the Relaxation Park, the wheel-less trolley sat in place and I was whisked off to the awesome Embassy of Cosmic Beings. What an exciting and great way to begin a day. Breezing through the door, I entered the sanctuary, as I felt again the love I got each time I entered. The five Beings of Light stood at attention at the head table and this welcome was observed and appreciated. My usual throne-type chair rolled into place as the Headmaster, OOO-LON, spoke.

O: "We see you have survived your last visit and the surprise meeting of the Christ in Light form."

G: "Oh my yes. That was quite a Christmas gift. He really is magnificent, isn't He?"

O: "Quite so, he watches over us all as The City comes into being. It was his idea you know."

G: "No, I didn't know, but one by one all the pieces are fitting together."

O: "This has been (in your vernacular) a long journey. Centuries have passed in making progress to where we are now."

G: "I have a Light friend named Will who wants to know if he is in Sedona, will The City fall on his head?"

O: "Dear One, report that he will be spared this crushing appearance for then he would need a healing. He can pitch his tent where he is guided to. It is hard for you humans to remember that you live in many dimensions within your third dimension. Around you, you see solid buildings, rock, trees etc. and it all needs to be this way for you to function in what is called the third dimension, with your daily adventures. To really be seen in another dimension, you would see nothing. See how lucky you are? Would this not be akin to a holodeck?

"You see the sun this morning. Is the sun solid? Or is it a big blaze of energy with frequencies that warm the planet? We would suggest that as time and space zones continue, and the demonstration time takes place, you will be advised of what is happening and where to be at the moment.

"How many people have you met who said, 'I am here but I don't know why?'
"People of the planet want to know the ending in advance of the movie or book one is concentrating on. Most want to see a happy ending and happy ever after. You in particular want everyone happy and living a happy ever after story. This will be more spectacular than any movie ever produced. Even the Charles has mentioned that on several occasions. As you say, 'wrap me up.' All you have seen and learned here, is right on course. And you know this is so. Even the minister quoted that you are totally in belief of this City coming forth and nothing can shake your knowing. Then what happened? You heard applause. Many others are being lifted into a vibrational attachment like no other.

"Yours and their daily care will change. People will be astonished at what has taken place right before their eyes that will be perceived as a miracle, and the sounds of happy will fill the air with, 'OH MY GOD!' and it will be that, for only God could do such a magical event. No other would be possible. Now then, what else can we be of support?"

G: "Thank you. What are my steps as we leave the space-time of 2010 and enter into 2011? I sense something major and a fullness of activity in January."

O: "We have spoken of density. The energies change quickly even as the weather donates. Everyone tuned in will begin to sense within themselves at even the lowest consciousness, that something beyond themselves is happening. This could generate fear or excitement of happiness. The Lightworkers will sense in the highest. We understand that people would like a time date of arrival but again, the way must be in the journey you are on. As time exists, information will be given to those who seek answers. Stay on course in this time continuum. Follow and express your information to those who seek answers. Your plate is full and yet a banquet of information is to come your way for delivery. Even the Obama visit is on the road map for your delivery."

G: "Am I to learn more of space and the beings of the Cosmic Community?"

O: "Oh yes, these space masters are willing to 'make your day' so to speak in your language. Cosmic information is a package teaching all in itself and the classroom is open for your entry. So then is this enough?"

G: "For the moment. Thank you all, I am so blessed!"

O: "Re-enter and we shall take you on this journey of journeys. The Light Center will be the contacting support as it is The City connection, and should remain as such in your world. Expect to fill the coffers and print the data manuscript, as this blesses those who await what they know not. This is the day the Lord has made. Rejoice. You are about to give birth as The City of Light bears witness to this cosmic connection. We bid you a good day in peace and love...."

"Q: "What needs to be added?"

A: "Look to this new year as the finality of The City entrance. It will be told you as progress continues ... all is well ... hold the Light."

Of Magic and Miracles . . . It's a Cosmic Thing!

Embassy Visit January 7, 2011

Resting in the wisdom that I had been invited to again re-enter the Embassy of Peace in The City of Light, I allowed myself to be centered (in an un-centered world) and as the vision of the 5-story Entrance Gate appeared, many people were entering … maybe having the intent to be healed of some malady, or maybe just to take a look around, (which is worth the price of admission) which I understand is zero!

La-Luke appeared and the path cleared as we rushed to the trolley and entered into the Embassy of Peace Headquarters. With the usual 5 Beings at the head table and hundreds of space beings in the audience, love sang from every cosmic one of them. I acknowledged them in returned love, and relaxed in this place of cosmic wisdom.

O: "It is of divine love we welcome you both back to be in our midst as you have had a message to return and we are honored to serve."

G: "Thank you. Golly I am the one who is blessed. Imagining this place and its contents brings tears to my heart. What am I to be aware of in this new year of 2011?" (A hum ran through the audience so someone must have understood what I asked and passed the tone on)?

O: "Your planet has reached a pivotal year of its progress and failures. Those who are considered Lightworkers elevating themselves in their energy fields beyond the normal, have supported this project called The City of Light, even if they are unaware of its being a designated demonstration.

"All Light supports in its frequencies. Those who are in the depth of darkness flounder as the energy waves of Light bear down on this planet in its intent to raise the consciousness of all, no matter what level they may be at.

"The Genii as a chosen leader of this project, makes the path to be open to share with more information to be delivered from here. This is all being said as it is important for the forces of Light to be in-voiced to sustain the heavenly chorus of love and Light. The energies will heighten as cleansing of the planet continues and makes way for The City to enter. In other words you are in a clearing, made preparatory to The City entrance, you understand?"

G: "Yes, Lightworkers, bless them, are helping the planet elevate, thus this is making an opening through the dimensions for The City entrance.

Question: Is this or could this be called, the second coming of the Christ? It has been called by many names depending on which group one is attached to. Since I was privileged to meet this Christ Being here, I feel an attachment like I have never felt before."

O: "It would be in your wording language, that you have experienced the 'Christ Consciousness' and it is what you are sensing that gives you an edge on what is taking place in this year of attraction; this year of Earth time 2011. Look to this year to take you into the Circle of Light, which has been shown to you, as the Golden Ones in the High Court of God teach you about being in The City movement.

"Expect to see beyond seeing, and know beyond knowing (which constitutes some of what you are doing now in your world.) This would be correct as you try to balance time lines with a cosmic appearance. Two worlds are trying to mesh as one. They will! It would be in your theater vernacular, being backstage behind a curtain and knowing the impact this will have on the audience. It is almost curtain time."

G: "When is curtain time?"

O: "Beyond today, but less than tomorrow. Betwixt and between … Higher than lower … and on your 'Soon' calendar."

G: "I sense density unseen."

O: "Your senses will heighten and expect to see beyond what is now seen. This is peremptory for you will share from this sensing-feeling nature of emotions. Continue to touch into the Christ and he will lead where others may not be aware of. Many will begin to feel it, as you speak with emotion attached to the truth of this matter. We speak of here as you are between two worlds. These worlds will come together like yesterday and today. Pairs of opposites attract and become one. Are you following this analogy? "

G: "Yes, and my current part to play is?"

O: "As said, use your feminine feeling nature and the Christ consciousness to enjoy even this Christ contact on a moment to moment notice. The Embassy door is open to your return and the Christ now leads this greatest show on Earth that is about to make its appearance known ... one step at a time. Continue to share and we will feed you step by step, and day by day. All is well."

And with that La-Luke tapped me and as I turned around to thank the entities, they were all aglow in a dazzling gold Light, all one. Awesome!

Note: What an adventure I am in. Never expected, but privileged to take for so many years and knowing all is correct. Thanks to my Bill who one day decided to try trans-audio, the beginning of all this way back in 1982. Who would have guessed? Not me.

Bill was on course ... of course.

First Things First

Embassy Visit January 14, 2011

As I walked to the Entrance Gate, I saw a blaze of Light just beyond the Gate itself. No one else was present, not even my Guide. I passed through the Gate and into the Relaxing Park. This Light was so bright I could not see past it. What was this?

I stopped, and waited as a figure dressed in a white robe came closer. It looked like the Christ picture in my bedroom. I must be delusional, I thought, and it was just a thought. He said nothing except smiled and beckoned me to follow him to the trolley. Where was my Guide? It looked like he was here in another dressing.

This was getting interesting. I never know what to expect to take place when I enter in meditation. We climbed aboard and stopped at the Embassy. I turned around and this God Being was gone. Just someone who needed a ride? Ok. I can buy that, I guess! I was at the Embassy now heading into the sanctuary. Since I had a few questions, it was good to be here. One of the 5 Entities that was usually there was gone and in its place was the Entity of Light that just rode on a trolley with me. I laughed.

O: "Welcome back. Please be seated. I know that you have questions."

G: "Yes but first I enjoyed riding the trolley with...?"

O: "That was Mar-Koo whom you see here now. He enjoys mingling with the human beings now and then. He likes human fun too. Now what are your questions that we may try to deliver answers to?"

G: "The new updated City manuscript is coming ready for printing thanks to Charles, and The City title needs to be completed. What should the title now be since more information has come through as to more Cities to be introduced to this planet?"

O: "You have been advised that many healing Cities will appear like magic on this planet once the first one is set in place and accepted as such. It would be wise to acknowledge the first City for recognition. You and the Charles have spoken of ...The City of Light-Sedona, that is an indication that something unusual is to appear in this vicinity.

"Cities of Light is also an indication of more to be revealed elsewhere.

1. **City of Light Sedona**

2. **The First City of Light-Sedona**

3. **Sedona the First City of Light**

4. **Sedona the First of the Cities of Light**

"Explore and make your decision. Play with what the audience will be drawn to. The correct feeling answer will appear."

G: "Where are the other Cities to appear?"

O: "Now then as needed, there will be 13 and they will be deposited in various locations. This answer is unavailable at this time, only each one will be a Healing Center and dedicated in each to handle any needs of that location of human beings through the Light Beings who will also be in attendance.

"If these locations would be seen from above your planet, the Light beams would light up the planet like the moon. We suggest that since the first prototype is in your location, we move the interest forward and you will be advised later as to the other locations, first things first.

"Now then since it is important that you stay connected to the first one, we invite you to center your energy to this demonstration that will in itself, make world news quickly. This is true. There could be mass confusion at first, and since it will be known through yours and others' efforts, you are laying the groundwork now. We have spoken of Light Centers in various locations to be set in place with those who are well-tuned into this process.

"This would serve also as notice of the coming. You all must realize that this is a masterful, massive undertaking and all must be perfect in its demonstration as God directs. With your book filled with information and energy, this will be the leading information to what is being said here. Just continue to report through the book and where you have people who can meet together. Your personal Guide will also direct you daily as will those who have known of their personal Guides of Light, and return here for advancing information.

"This is your mission and you have been brought into this time-slot for precisely this reason. The space-time continuum shortens and you desire to know the end of the story. We just say that this year is filled with magic and miracles ... secrets and surprises. Anything else?"

G: "Yes, how am I to get the puppets and manuscript to the President Obama?"

O: "Again this is a year of magic and miracles. Just be open and aware of any direction of unusual steps and follow them like you did with the President Carter visit. You will know. Enjoy the adventure. And with this, we bid you an Earth day of love and fun messages to brighten your heart with confident expectancy."

I bowed and said my thanks.

In the Wonder of it All . . . God is!

Embassy Visit February 19, 2011

As I entered the scene at a Gate of Entry, crowds of people were also making their way through it to enjoy what would be an amazing, unusual time within The City borders. A hand seen raised above the crowds signaled that my City Guide La-Luke was ready to take us into the Embassy of Peace Headquarters via the wheel-less trolley.

Upon arrival as we entered, there was a definite audience hum of space conversation reaching our senses. Entering this building with the sanctuary of space beings, is always a treat for this lucky lady, and just to be a part of it all is quite an honor. I cannot even imagine what they will teach me, but I am certainly open to learn.

Imagine being in an auditorium with hundreds of friends from many distant locations all sending you love at the same time... Wow! It makes me feel a bit shaky and heart inspired to be a friend that they also enjoy in human attire, and this is even more fun since I decided to be a Jedi with extended love and power attached (plus a Light-saber to play with as Light). Master Yoda's teachings fit in here very well. So standing in front of these Five up-close-and-personal Entities, one could only be great-filled, and I greeted them with an extended bow!

O: "Time for another session is it?"

G: "Yes, thank you... a question of The City progress comes to mind, as next week I have a City meeting and any updated information would be of value."

O: "Much progress has been entered into as The City nears. Those of us assembled here have valued the progress, as we attune in to your world of energy fields that have been set in place for the readiness of its revelation. Your dimension would be seen. As you have noted, as dense or thick and it needs to be, for the prophecy to be seen and entered into.

"You have been shown that the time warp signals the closeness of the entry. People not knowing of such ways will not have a clue of how this City could be entered into, but they will as time goes on and they get used to the new ways of space technology. Are you following this analogy?"

G: "Yes, my interest at this point is what takes place after The City makes its debut? The reaction of people will be quite interesting."

O: "As said, expect a shock wave to spread around the planet for a split second, where the Light of The City can enter minds and fill the place now empty, thus taking people's minds off their daily worries and concerns, no matter what the individual problems would be. The war factor will have men and women standing in such an awareness that to shoot anyone would be not tolerable, as love for one another has taken its place.

"For the Creator of The City and life itself, Call it God, Buddha, Christ or whatever has entered the picture, and due to The City's effects on each one (which of course will vary) nothing will be as it was before. For the Creator has done the impossible in this breathtaking, astonishing demonstration.

"Those who are on their knees in praise will connect. Those left will give a standing ovation of utter amazement with the feelings of peace that will quickly sweep around the globe. Have you not asked, what if everyone on the planet felt love all at the same time? This Dear One, millions upon millions will experience. Imagine that! As you say quite often. Time as you know it will stop as the WORD (as in your 4 Keys of Light sessions) spreads quickly. People may become briefly confused, especially in countries not seeing The City itself in their land location. They may experience it as a heavenly sight in the sky ... as a vision of something new.

"The Master Jesus will have many giving Him adoration as with the other leaders as well. Likewise, those mentors on higher levels who are adored Guides, will be revered as the humans connect with what they feel is their Holy Leader. For nothing less could be mentally evaluated to bring this forth. Indeed this is the greatest show on Earth!! It will take a while of sorting out what has taken place, so 'business as usual' will be a thing of the past for a bit, as dramatic changes change their way of thinking.

"Then will come the celebrations of various degrees as people feel the power and love connected to this unbelievable manifestation of Light as it bombards your planet, lighting up the sky and signaling others in the Universe that indeed the mission has been accomplished, and they too will celebrate in your honor of Earth energy accepted. The human imagination can only go so far, so this event will enlighten and advance many as they go back to the so-called drawing boards ... of thinking new inventive thoughts of success with love the center of it all. For thoughts will only want love to be the leader of whatever they envision through this advancing wisdom from the Universe, and the friends they are yet to meet.

"Those in to Extraterrestrials will have a field day as the Cosmic Universe has made contact with friends where no man has gone before, as has been advertised. The Universe holds technology to be shared, and no one has to blast off into outer space, for outer space has come to your planet with hands and love extended in healings blessed by the Creator. It will be all your yearly celebrations in one. Those with demented minds will leave, for they cannot withstand this energy power and pursue the darkness any longer. The City is too powerful a demonstration for them. Those of Light who have worked on believing the highest, will shout Halleluiah! Blessed be for God has spoken and is here now!"

And with this a roar of applause came from the entities in the back of the auditorium. Is love the answer? OH YES!

O: "Are you at one with this?"

G: "Oh yes, a bit overwhelmed but yes."

O: "In your world this is truth and you depend on the unseen time to produce what has just been said. Has time so called speeded up? Of course as you are well aware. Use it wisely lest it run out." And with this a smile entered his face.

G: "Thank you all for being the best friends this planet has ever seen."

We then departed where a hug at the Gate with my Guide found me back home watching the clouds dance around the red rocks of Sedona, Arizona.

These Things Seem So Right!

Embassy Visit March 1, 2011

Once more I entered through the huge Gate along with many others. They looked like happy excited people anxious to see what was behind this huge Gate of Light. My Guide La-Luke was among them, waving at me as we connected with a hug. It was then a run through the Park of Relaxation, onto the wheel-less trolley and we jumped out into the Embassy of Peace Headquarters.

I was excited as the final manuscript of The City of Light was about to go to press. This hall held hundreds of Universal Community Entities who filled every space within this huge stadium-size building. OOO-LON rose in Greeting as his inner shine radiated his love and openness.

O: "You have returned with a smiling face."

G: "My calendar at home says that this is national smile day, and I have good reason to smile. My book of this City of love and healing is about ready to go to press. The cover is powerful and exciting and I feel it will be a draw to those seeking higher answers. My question is, is there anything else to be added now before it gets printed?"

O: "The truthfulness of the story and inner visits like this one, have been completed almost as you have seen. The Light makes this a companion of service and as we see it, it should be one that people can read and assimilate. Time has reached a point of release to the public, and with this more will enter into the senses of all the change taking place. Does this help?"

G: "I sense something is missing ... the children. How do the parents share this with the young ones about what is to take place or even after it takes place. They have great imaginations but could use simplicity of what is going on."

O: "Indeed the young ones, who will be the new leaders in the future! Do you not have a story of a God plan?"

G: "I did write what I call a Meta-fable titled 'WHAT IN HEAVEN IS GOING ON?'"

O: "Yes, this is a God speaking-to-angels story?"

G: "Yes."

O: "Then use it to attract the younger and the older generations as well at the front of the book, and this will entice and break down any resistance for it is read in fun. Have you not found this to be so in your City sessions?"

G: "Yes the adults smile and even laugh a little."

O: "Then you have answered your own question. The City should be fun as well as healing. Have you not been told earlier that fun and happy is healing, as you travel to the Disney of land?"

G: "Yes, what do you think will take place after this book is revealed to the public? I have high hopes."

O: "The interest will begin to pick up and invitations to speak live and the internet will play a big part, if the Charles has anything to do with it, and he should be commended on his efforts of introductions already in place.

"We realize that your electrical body system is busy with its changes that you are well aware of, and is uncomfortable at times. But nevertheless, persevere unto the end and taking time to rest will support what has just been said. Anything else to be discussed?"

G: "These were my questions at this moment. Anything else to add?"

O: "Just know that you are welcome back should it be desirable (and it will) for more information to be addressed, as we are always available to you. Your path accelerates as we get closer to The City arrival. Be easy with yourself. Be at peace and all is well with you. Just be Light and love. It is that simple."

And with that, he sat down and the huge audience stood as we departed.

I was back home in Sedona on a cold sunny day. I am still amazed every time I enter this magnificent structure and so now we finish and The City manuscript goes to print. I am so thank-filled to all of those who took my visions and put them into this manuscript.

I am sure there is much more to come and this Indiana Jones Genii, looks to this adventure to continue as God's treasure appears, as if by magic ... and it is!

Thanks God. I am blessed.

So Light it be!

Of Light and Earth Movements!

Embassy Visit March 11, 2011

As I looked into the scene from an inner space of quiet, what was seen was me in a hurry to enter the massive Gate. I noticed there was no one around except La-Luke. We moved quickly into the Embassy of Peace from the trolley ride to the front entrance. I was stirred up enough from seeing a television report on an 8.9 earthquake to ask some questions. I found much peace and love in this building of Light Entities. OOO-LON stood in welcome, and La-Luke and I with bowed heads and folded hands offered our thanks.

O: "I see you are in a human way of hurry. What can we do for you, Lady of Light?"

G: "Can you please tell me why the planet weather is more intense in many areas as reported on the media? The winter months have really been as said 'different'. Japan has just had an 8.9 quake releasing people from homes and even plant life, plus flooding in the States from extra heavy rains. What sir, is going on in this illusion?"

O: "It has been said earlier that the pressures of energy that support the planet must on occasion release that pressure and what you call quakes is one way to do that quickly. The under-belly of the planet is also an organism, for all is energy. This location has had many quakes and is known by the people, which also mentally in fear of it happening, add energy to that action and depending on the severity, takes its toll should that location be inhabited.

"This is not new, however all the states of Earth energy are in a frequency state of high flux. City energy also plays a part as it begins its descent into the third dimension which as you have noticed, your planet illusion is thick and dense. Also one must take into consideration the human energies of far-off places of war, can trigger its energy to even the other side of the planet making waves happening equal to the unrest on the other side. All are one, no matter what!

"Your planet is anything but calm at this point. Something has to give. Love and peace come to mind, like what would happen if everyone felt God's love at the same moment? Prayer is the closest to love that your human minds can detect. Use it! And bless all those of suffering.

"The weather of the Earth atmosphere also holds much electrical charges as this current cleansing of the planet integrates into human expression which has been centuries of planet preparation. Bless those who continue to live in areas noted for Earth electrical dramatic action sometime or another."

G: "Will we see more of this?"

O: "Depending on the known places and peoples under fears, anything is possible. So then any more questions?"

G: "Yes, locally there is a parcel of land known as Angel Valley. I have seen angels there and it was reported to me in a morning message that angels and E.T.'s are a 'Unit' in bringing forth The City of Light. Can you explain anything about this?"

O: "Yes, that land parcel is a portal of entrance along with many others, thus those who inhabit it give charges to The City and communication makes its mark also. Many other such spots as Stoneman Lake, as you know, is a portal.

"The red rocks hold much vibrational energy and the vortexes are up to max speed frequency at this point, so staying calm is a premium desire. 'Time flies' is said in your vocabulary, and so as it does, you can consider you could be doing 500 days in one so to speak. Staying balanced is also a premium event as the Genii is well aware of as she flits back and forth into dimensional action.

"Your whole area of Sedona to Phoenix and upper Arizona areas as well are on constant surveillance as The City approaches touchdown. When you go to either Stoneman Lake or Angel Valley, be quite open for any advanced connection information, as it would be wise for you to enter into conversation with the 'see-through community.' For now staying in peace and calm will help even the other lands of destruction so-called. Anything else?"

G: "Just what you can share."

O: "Destruction of darkness means mending of the people, and as Light moves it also corrects. Do your Lightwork and know God remedies all situations. Being peaceful in your own being helps even across the ocean. We bid you the Light of this day in peace and in love."

G: "Thank you all for all your advice, your help, and information. We are open to any and all good news coming forth."

And with that, my Guide and I left the building, hopped on the waiting trolley and rode out of the Gate.

The vision ended as I sat in a peaceful place with the sun shining, holding 'Light' my little white puppy, giving thanks for my life. I send love to all who now are in an area of non-peace.

So Light it Be!

Of Earth Birthing and a New Life!

Embassy Visit March 15, 2011

Leaving all Earthly duties behind, I entered the grounds of The City of Light. At the Gate of Entrance I found my Guide La-Luke waiting for me, plus the usual transportation of the fun trolley that had no wheels or driver, but it seemed to know where to go and deposited us at the Embassy of Peace Headquarters.

I wondered what I would learn today? What treasured friend from someplace else would grab my attention? What update of City progress would Light me up?

What delights unknown were awaiting my interests? What revelations would be shared? Quickly maybe these mental interests were awaiting to be answered...

As we entered the main auditorium (here in this world I glanced from my inner visit to see a fleet of small fluffy cloud-like space vehicles,hover overhead, like coming into this quiet moment to deposit love on the planet, and I was sure that they did.) My teachers have been telling me to follow my heart and so I guess I was, as I stood before OOO-LON and his far-out comrades who were usually speechless, but listened intently as Light Beings that they are ... was I blessed or what!

O: "Ah, I see the little Lady of Light blesses us with a visit as she blesses our home away from home. What may you desire today Dear One?"

G: "I am sensing to return for any update on The City to add to my next City meet-up soon. And actually just to be here with you all is quite a thrill. There is so much you can share with me to pass on to others. I sometimes wish to hop aboard one of your spaceships and learn about your community homes someplace, but I know my mission is here."

O: "The far off communities of space dwellers make every effort to serve your planet even if those of a lower consciousness fear such action.

"Your planet is a live organism and is in constant building stages. The Earth movement would be like birthing pains, where the lady of mothering is told to push bringing forth a new baby. (Referring to the recent 8.9 earthquake in Japan).

"Those who decide to live in these areas are well aware of the situation at all times due to previous demonstrations. Those in the demonstration areas begin to work together in love, including those in far-off places on your planet to rescue the survivors and salvage what they can.

"Remember the inner fear of such a demonstration is always hidden in the mind, but still has an energy attached and becomes a part of the situation. Mind is always in control and many have chosen to leave for a heavenly address through this method and remember they still live for no one dies!!!

"What looks very bad as the Charles knows from his helping in disaster areas, that love comes into play and helping is love in action. The energy moves now in cleansing and tectonic plates shift. Those of us here are but a small detail of what is seen as the plates move and this is cleansing power beyond human stopping. It is birthing like in labor. As The City of Light moves into its orbit of third dimension, it also has massive energy beyond words and mental impressions.

"Cosmic to be sure, but the changes that it will bring to your planet is beyond the most comprehensive minds until experienced. You the Genii sense you are but a visitor here. You have said 'G. T. go home.' The time will permit you to evaluate this while assisting The City in its appearance.

"As said, the time of arrival is shortened and will shift everyone's thinking about themselves, as planetary healing takes over and all feel the love of God personally. You say 'Something is coming!' Indeed ... Indeed! The majesty of the demonstration is beyond human mental consumption except as maybe a dream, for the impossible is really very possible.

"You have been through various City healing buildings and have seen the healing taking place with advancement not yet known...but they will. The University of Light Healing on the grounds give medical healers new ways to heal, and instructions to take back and spread into their worlds including children and animals as well. The Light Modules give testimony to uplifting healing through only Light. Your planet is in a complete 'make-over' as God has decreed, from the Universal Star Communities who work together to achieve what has just been re-formatted. All is well and on track ... Anything else?"

G: "I love coming here not only for the information but just to feel, sense, and be the love beyond anything I have felt outside The City in my morning visits. The updated City book is due to arrive. Much work has gone into its contents for which I am very great-filled. Where are copies to go?"

O: "Just be aware and open as you will be advised. The Presidential meeting will also happen and is in the vibrational process."

G: "Thank you. I go back to my world with sharing a bit easier. Anything else?"

O: "Just be you, carry the message that God is on the way with miraculous value!"

G: "Thank you all again" I said to the vast audience and then wow, they seemed to all stand. A standing ovation! ... Imagine that and they had not too many clues of what I said.

Just the feeling of love can do that. I bowed and we backed out and headed for the trolley and Gate. My heart was full, my mind was clear as I re-entered my bedroom with my puppy Light Spirit waiting to be noticed.

THANKS GOD! IT HAS BEEN A GOOD VISIT.

The Energy of Being Lucky!

Embassy Visit St. Patrick's Day March 17, 2011

Blessings were mine as I once again entered The City of Light, Gate of Entrance. There were lots of happy people along with my Guide La-Luke among them. Maybe today I would have the luck of the Irish, I thought, as the Embassy of Peace was my destination.

The Park was cool and refreshing and the trolley ride fun as it stopped at the entrance of the Embassy like it knew where it was going. We hopped off and almost ran inside and even the beautiful plants in the front gardens seemed to wave in recognition. I wondered if there was a 4 leaf clover somewhere in there.

We entered this full to overflowing entity-filled building, a Sanctuary of Light, and I saw OOO-LON standing holding something in his hand which he gave to me. My gosh! It was a real 4 leaf clover.

O: "This is your desire? Welcome back Lady of Irish decent."

G: "Thank you, what a surprise!"

O: "There are many surprises yet in store for you to be made known. You have a question or two? "

G: "Yes, one in particular. There is in space-time here, a date of November 11, 2011 or as being said 11-11-11! And in our community (where The City is to demonstrate) there is to be a celebration of some sort. I know not the details of as yet. Can you please tell me what 11-11-11 means from your point of view?"

O: "This time slot has the world of humans getting ready to change with what has been referred to as a 'shift,' and that date coincides with cosmic parts of the Universe unseen and an energy change taking place. Humans attach many things to it for various reasons. The City of course plays a major part, as well as the Genii who has just brought The City visits to life and forward in the manuscript due to the Charles and his professional knowledge and others who also manage this type of publication.

"The man you are to soon meet has the human interest in 11-11-11 and will have Earth answers, so just be open to what is to be revealed for he too has some surprises in store upon this meeting.

"The City book will move out quickly into the public and they will pronounce this as an attention-getter. Beautifully done, and as The City arrives this advanced book copy will be called a 'collector's item' so to speak.

"Even within our cosmic community we see the fun of the surprise of The City coming into view. Now then, anything else?"

G: "So then 11-11-11 does play a part with The City?"

O: "Quite so, enjoy what you are guided to do and supply the book where guided. Much more will take place between now and then in space-time continuum as The City energy builds and shifts and takes place right before their eyes."

G: "Well this does look like my lucky day."

O: "Luck has an energy. Divine frequencies have a higher degree of intensity. All is well! Be selective in your Earth duties and open for guidance on a moment's notice. Now enter back into your world and see and know everyone will want a copy and read the story in The City book. The price is right and the demonstration is manifesting and with this we wish you the luck of the Irish. We give you peace and top o' the morning in love for a happy day in every way."

G: "I feel such love. Thank you all."

And with this we bowed and left the building with a real 4 leaf clover to remember the visit. The trolley ride took us to the Gate and we said good-bye. I was back home on a sunny day giving thanks for the visit and *The City of Light Sedona book now in print.*

God is good. (Charles likes to spell it as G∞D since God is Infinite Good!) YHVH ...

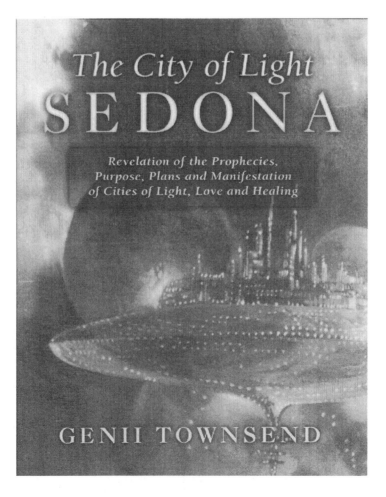

The Shift of LOVE! 11-11-11

Embassy Visit March 26, 2011

I felt excited this morning as I stepped into my inner vision theater of Light with a question or two to ask at the Embassy of Peace in The City of Light. As I entered the scene at one of the Gates of Entrance, many happy people smiled back at me as La-Luke waved to get my attention and cleared a path for our reunion. The energy was high and was lifting people's spirits including mine. La-Luke my City Guide, had been with me since Day One of this adventure and I was thankful for him showing me all the healing buildings and types of Light-healings that took place.

We gave each other a hug and then ran through the Park of Relaxation, and onto the Embassy trolley. Fun stuff ! Entering into the Embassy we greeted the 5 foremost Light Beings up close and personal at the head table. I sensed that hundreds of space entities in the audience also rose, and were standing in welcome. Wow! no need to" beam me up Scotty" as it used to be said, 'cuz they have beamed down here. Groovy!

O: "Welcome human one and Guide of Light. What may we speak of on this visit?"

G: "I have just had a meeting with a leader of 11-11-11 by the name of Scott Love, who is working with Sunshower Rose and others, to create some kind of celebration event here in Sedona in the week of Nov. 11, 2011 known as 11-11-11. I am not sure what all this is intended for, so that seems to be my question. What is 11-11-11 from your point of view? How, or if it applies to The City of Light? I understand hundreds of people will attend here. And others in various parts of the planet will also get together."

O: "Indeed, this is calculated as the Shift of Energy is so strong it will change everyone into the new 'love pattern' set in place. In other words as you say, 'Love is all there is' and from this, healings of mental, physical, and emotional issues will be brought front and center. The Scott in his heart has the bigger picture and love strong enough in intent to bring forth the Love Shift during this time slot, in your area of heightened intense energy.

"With the rising of the love energies, this of course again raises the energy frequency patterns to a higher degree, and thus also gives a booster shot (so to speak) to The City. Waiting to be seen of what will take place is still to be observed and experienced, but has already been run before the masses who desire swift changes of love, so God intervenes with this Shift and no one is left out.

"The City begins its decent into your atmosphere thus changing the weather patterns (as you already have been advised.) Support the Scott Love where you can and are invited to share, while behind the scenes love energy moves into the 11-11-11 course.

"The power of The City will be recognized as the days and months ahead lead the way and pass. This Shift of Love will touch everyone and those of Light will love the feelings, and those of darkened minds will feel very uncomfortable, and with that will not be able to hold onto the darkened ignorant mental conditions and may leave, or change into more acceptance of Light in this Planetary Change-over. Massive changes can be expected in the way people think of business and daily activities. This has to be due to The City entrance into your world which has never happened before. Thanks to your Space Community brothers and sisters, you on this planet are being gifted the gift of gifts from your Creator, and the minds have to be prepared for they can expect a miracle to be seen and walked into."

G: "What part am I and those who are and have been close to The City to do for 11-11-11?"

O: "Your part is to speak on The City at any opportunity that presents itself, and even the President is not that far off the schedule. Just be aware. Your City book can spell out the story where you may not reach those, but also remember that film is a fast way to set the course. The Charles is well aware of how to spread The City word via the computer. As time moves on (as such) the energy patterns change to warp speed and in your vernacular you could be doing 500 days in one. What the love of the Cosmic Community brings into this is phenomenal and never experienced before. You see it as you have said many times, 'love is all there is.' It is time your planet recognizes this in order to be lifted into the higher realms with the support of the Cosmic Community somewhere in space-time.

"The Universe as you a call it is filled with love. It is your tone that holds it all together as you teach in The 4 Keys of Light. Respecting each other will become the norm and love will hold it all together. It is long past due, so now the Love Shift of elevation must take place, for living in unity is important. The long winter has ended. Some cannot tolerate the Light of those who work very hard to lift themselves into the Light. Thus a shift must take place to move the ego enough to receive the Light in themselves, into total awareness that they indeed are the essence of the Creator, and then they can begin to create the best for themselves and others. It is so! There will be no turning back to the old ways of thinking. Has this been of any use to you?"

G: "Oh yes, what are my next steps?"

O: "Be open, meet again with the Scott Love and get a clearing of the situation time slot 11-11-11. Come back and we will support what is desired. We here bid you the Light of the day in peace and in love."

G: "Thank you all for your gift of gifts. My heart is full with love for you all!"

And with this I waved goodbye and even threw a kiss as I was so blessed that I had been chosen to do what I was doing. We headed for the Gate and I found myself home with the phone ringing and Kathie Brodie saying she was coming for 11-11-11. Imagine that! **So Light it be!**

Upgrading LOVE 11-11-11

(Continued from The Shift of Love Visit)

Embassy Visit March 28, 2011

Returning to the Embassy as requested, my inner scene opened with my Guide and I standing before the robed Cosmic Consul of 5 Entities of Light and Leader OOO-LON looking to say something...

O: "And a welcome is extended to the human lady and her Guide of Light."

G: "Thank you. It is always an honor and a delight to be with you all again and so quickly. What may I be told?"

O: "The message of a Shift embracing the Energy of Love will indeed make its appearance. Those who know that love in Higher Vibrations, will find themselves embodying this frequency (beyond what you would call normal) as you have with certain people; and bliss will be experienced on a higher level deeper than before, and you will find within yourself the freedom of that Love as God intended.

"Those who have not experienced the sensation of being loved on any level will find themselves what you might refer to as 'level #1' (the highest level being #4) for which you understand. When many collaborate from levels # 1, 2, & 3, then changes fully take place leading into level #4.

"We are intending to give you a picture in the mind as to transfer to others as an example...

> 1. Those who have 'no love' for themselves (due to various reasons) cannot give true love to others. God starts with God!
>
> 2. One will just look at another human and love will be superimposed as God intended.
>
> 3. Those who feel anger for another, will feel forgiveness and will no longer feel the anger as that emotion disappears in forgiveness.
>
> 4. Those who stand in war zones will sense only peace and brotherhood.
>
> 5. Those whose egos are out of control will be tamed in this Love Shift surrendering.
>
> 6. Those who feel within the guidance of Surrender, will make life easier for another.
>
> 7. Poverty will take a back seat as one with the Love Shift will recognize their God self and pull themselves into higher living.

8. In God we trust, will sign high on any banner that signals, that only love attends here as written on the dollar currency now being used.

9. Those who bear witness to these different feelings will go with the flow.

10. Those who now feel that they love deeply, will also feel that, that is the real feeling they were intended to experience, for they are worthy of such emotions.

"In other words... the bonds that hold people in lower consciousness will suddenly transform into the experience that God intended for all mankind in the beginning. Will this happen?

"Genii - report here your 4 step findings....LOWEST ENERGY TO THE HIGHEST

1. **HOPE**

2. **FAITH**

3. **BELIEF**

4. **CONVICTION (with no opposite.)**

"Even now the preparations are taking place, for it is the way of opening up to the major demonstration of The City of Light manifestation. You the Genii are well aware of what it takes to become pure Light of illumination.

"Example: PICTURE YOUR PLANET FROM SPACE and see billions upon billions of tiny Lights like crystal shards, with hands raised welcoming The City of Light.

"A far-off dream? Some mental hallucination? Or could it be God attending to business ... the business of raising this planet to be an example of space connecting with your world with all the stops falling away.

"Dear One, you stand right now in the miracle of any decade confidently taking place. You say often, 'I am love and that is all I know! God is, I AM that ... I AM!'

"Are you following this?"

G: "Yes, I have experienced such deep love and giving thanks that it is taking place. I felt it was beyond any love I have experienced and beyond the daily saying of 'I love you.' Like in the movie AVATAR, the non-humans said, 'I see you'!' and it went to the soul.

"Now I just received a message that said, 'I AM You!' that took it to where I was integrated with Light, bliss, and tears. Is this what you mean?"

O: "Precisely, that level of love is what you would refer to as in your teaching of 4 Keys and the tone of Love with the word. This of course is the door opener to Christ Consciousness. Are you agreed?"

G: "Sometimes the love I feel is beyond words ... It just is! What are my next steps?"

O: "Prepare for your City meetings. Your system is now programmed to bring forth the love emotion. When you speak people will sense the true-ity of what you are giving as fact, not fiction in any sense of the word. This next meeting as time-space continues to shift towards the date of knowing, will give you the opportunity to deliver the 'good news' and all will know that indeed, love is the answer and Light is what God delivers in the vision called City of Light.

"We will have many more sessions here before then, and the way will be shown. The unbalanced will be balanced. Take this message to the world and connections will be made easily and effortlessly. Your soul Guides move you forward as people sense that you are a teacher of the Holy Keys and a City Light. Just sharing is what is important.

"Go now and we shall speak again soon. We bid you the Light of the eternal day in peace and in love."

And with that I was home filled with love, bliss, and tears of delight falling on my longhand writing, and knowing that a miracle is closer than we think.

So Light it be!

Preview of Pre-11-11-11 Events!

Embassy Visit March 31, 2011

Going into mental envision, I was standing directly before the Embassy of Peace Guides of Light with my Guide La-Luke. (Wow that was a short trip. What - no trolley ride?) Sounds from the vast cosmic audience quieted as OOO-LON raised his hand and welcomed us into a most unusual City attraction. I was beginning to feel quite at home here after so many visits.

O: "You sensed to return?"

G: "Yes, after being advised to. I report on The City tonight with a group in the Light Center. What am I to know?"

O: "The time of The City arrival that has long since been planned, is on course and it is important that people be aware of the previous-spoken 11-11-11 pre-attraction of coming events. The prepared 'love shift space-time happening' will in itself change the mental acuity, to accept such a demonstration of The City of Light and we add love, for this is what these occurrences are ... LOVE intended, for this you know.

"Now then, previous to the 11-11-11 nothing will also remain static. Those who are aware of such a manifestation of that energy date, will also be open to The City knowing and interest, and you can expect this to take place. Those who are in the unknowing category of such a transformable event will begin to have a heightened sense that will become apparent, that something is changing or as said 'coming' and thus the coming will take note stronger than normal.

"Every Guide, master, spiritual leader in the unseen world are even now preparing their charges to be open to accept the inner guidance. Those who are aware that they have indeed inner Guides as depicted in the Genii's 4 Keys to Light, will feel the immediacy of something is coming.

"11-11-11 will be exciting times as the mental change-over takes place, thus setting daily concerns aside. Many who have never felt a love beyond the normal love will feel the Holy sensing apparently stronger. Are you following this?"

G: "What else am I to do or say?"

O: "Take each group you speak to into your heart and with this they will hear and beyond 'feel' that what is reported is quite correct. This then is your message: bring to them what you feel here. God is omnipresent and will be in attendance. This visit here is short but pleasingly refreshing to us, as once more you speak the word of God's appearance in Earth formation which will not go unnoticed. Go now and serve. God be with you."

"So Light we all be!"

In the Light of Transformation!

Embassy Visit April 8, 2011

With no particular question in mind, except to know what I was not aware of that could be important, I exited my world and entered into The City level, heading for the Embassy of Peace Headquarters to speak with OOO-LON or whomever.

The Gate once more was filled with smiling faces of astonishment as people moved to enter into this magnificent edifice that stretched the mind beyond imagination. How could this have been? "It has to have come from God" I heard one lady say, followed by "Oh my God!" She got that right I said to myself smiling. Seeing my Guide La-Luke I headed for him and we swiftly ran through the Park, onto the trolley and jumped off at the Embassy entrance. Smelling all the flowers in the foyer, we found ourselves inside the auditorium of Light and love with entities from all over the cosmos, and the primary leader OOO-LON stood in welcome.

O: "Welcome and a good morning of your home base. Has a question entered your mind as yet?"

G: "Good morning from Sedona, Arizona. I have no specific question at this moment. What can you share with me as an update to share with my world?"

O: (smiling) "You would need much space-time to bring you up to what has been accomplished thus far, but permit me to say that The City of Light is on the cosmic pattern-board of deliberate intent, and the scheduling of time of arrival is also on the energy Light track. There has come into your awareness that the year of 2011 now, has a high priority of energy patterns that will fill the time spaces of raising the consciousness during a grand celebration, as the words spread of invitation.

"This energy of celebration lifts the humans normally as a sign of success, and this will have the touch of the 'I AM GOD' as if touched by angels, and it will inspire people to an inner sense of the 'Coming.'

"The entities of Light cosmic-wise, have entered into what you would call a 'Union of Light' to help prepare humans for the upcoming birth, for indeed this magnitude of entry will be such a Massive Demonstration that the shock of such an appearance could give some inner turbulence. Especially for those who have been programmed to believe in sin and the consequences of that.

"There is no hell! You would call it (cause and effect). You cause your own hell. It is an image the diluted minds have conjured up as a penance of control. God is love with no opposite. Does that mean that those who have done an injustice to another are not to be punished? Only through their own dark thinking that they must be punished some way for this, one way or another.

"You see Dear One, humans of your planet have been taught many ways to look at any deity that is presented to them, even darkness of mind. The God of all gives free reign to think at any given point in time and much of that is pure nonsense, however programmed as Light.

"Only love is the un-programmer of such dark controlling interests. This is all part of the healing process to take place as God intended in the first place. You are well aware of the 'I AM Love' and use it to support the God of Love, and this is as it should be after all these visits here; to know that love is the only answer to any situation. You have been told to follow your heart and just look at where it has brought you! How many times have you said. 'I am that I am' and thus made your decree on a daily basis?

"People must be supported in this mental consciousness Change-Over now in process, before The City manifests onto your planet of humanoids. So in your date time (of no time) 11-11-11 is a date people can relate to, and thus the Shift of Love is due to participate in what you might call 'big time!'

"The sensing of love will be apparent. As an example, it would be like the clouds parting on a cloudy day as a sudden Light/love shaft streaks through and penetrates everyone, encapsulating all in a split second like lightening. We call it 'Love-ing', for the power is awesome in the I AM Love and all will be loved, even a chicken in a coop."

G: "Will this love feeling hold its energy once received?"

O: "For a time, those who have the highest order of elevation will sustain it. Those who walk with much lower consciousness will be lifted above the darkness and some will feel that they have been reborn. Some too far below to connect on a continual basis, will have to deal with their own feelings at whatever level that they are deeply programmed with, but for that second of time-shift they will sense themselves as better, and that in itself is a hand-up so to speak.

"Mark your time well and be open to your own love feelings and share with whoever is open to receive. As an Advisor of The City you will feel even more love than on a daily basis. How can you hold more you think, when tears of love flow in the wake of this feeling? Take a deep breath and know that the 'I AM LOVE' is well and moving into possession. Is this the answer to your question?"

G: "Yes, as you are explaining, it clears up more than before and makes sense. To prepare us before the manifestation of The City makes great sense to me. Speak to me please on the steps to getting The City book to the President now that it has been published."

O: "In your DNA programming of The City, also lies this meeting and it will take place. In the unknowing of how, just set that aside and be open and willing to go where you are sighted to go.

"The Renee also is programmed to be aware of possible open doors where she can, and is a dedicated support system as she is guided in the eastern areas of the country. All will come together and be known as steps open up. Is your bag packed for a trip east? Depend on the 'I AM GOD' you love and be open to your heart-filled program that you are connected to. All OK?"

G: "Yes, next time I come back can we talk about SEDONA and the portals, force fields, vortexes etc. as the first City location. What is really here? Many stories are told, now I want the truth please."

O: "And this is available next visit ... indeed! So go now and do your day. We await your next visit and the cosmic answers you have asked for will be received."

We nodded to each other and I was light-headed, so it was time to slide quickly home. I waved thanks to my Guide. I was home ready to type this up and I looked forward to a good day and evening of I AM THAT I AM! Imagine that!

Set in Cement!

Embassy Visit April 15, 2011

The scene of approaching a City Gate brought joy to my heart in re-meeting the Entities of space, and I delighted in their answers to questions that this lady could share with others of my planet. Happy, excited people crowded in around me, as my City Guide La-Luke tapped me on the shoulder, grabbed my hand, and whisked me through the park with no time for a massage on one of the benches. It's OK. I was about to meet The City CEO's friends in space places.

O: "Ah, you have returned and we sense for more news of The City and its appearance. Patience is not one of humanoid's greatest features, but then you are being brought into what you refer to as the 'Now' which means immediately."

G: "Yes sir, please. The City manuscript has again been printed and some are already out to the public. What can I add as interest begins to surface and another City meet-up is due soon?"

O: "You can say the magnificence of The City resonates in harmony to those who now have open-mind interest in this process. You have a date of time on your calendar of the Love Shift 11-11-11 (so called) November 11, 2011?"

G: "Yes as told earlier, that a major love change is to be experienced."

O: "Correct. With this pre-conditioning, this will put The City sensing into the minds and it will become apparent that what is coming about is coming about, for it is all about love and nothing less can be important. The people of your planet have for too long been saturated in this lower energy continuum and this does not serve anyone well.

"The 11-11-11 scenario is about people beginning to look at each other differently than has been recorded in your history for eons of time, and still continues today without any recourse so ... this dynamic demonstration of love changes even the worst thinker into the Light frequencies.

"If one were to look at another person at that time, both would feel the love intensity. The Genii has felt this deep love recently and it changes the way one looks at another, even a so called enemy. You have been with this City subject not only in this life but another. You recently met someone from another life, so you know this is possible that one life connects with another and love is the subject of why The City makes its appearance. Even then you were in truth and love which continues in many ways today and tomorrow, if one is talking about space-time continuum.

"Those who have sought the God love will experience it to the feeling of tears. With all this change-over, those who have sought God's love will indeed feel it and release much of the old paradigm now leaving.

"Remember the question you asked previously: "What if everyone felt love at the same moment on the planet, what would happen?" You are about to find the answer to that question. God's love knows no bounds. God is God! Call God by whatever name desired, God still is God and will prove that with The City of Light; thus being able to heal the bodies that the minds have put into illness. There is only one companion creator ... you humans having been given freedom of thought and have become masters of negative thinking. Time for a change!

"Stories of this and that continue to pull at each other, and thus you stray away from the source until you have to scream for help from the one God who gave you the freedom of creating in the first place ... please! Is this demonstration needed? We think so, because even the idea of what is coming about, you would not even dream of. The thoughts had to come from somewhere ... GOD! Even the worse scenario uses this energy.

"You the Genii have been with this City subject for long since, and know for a fact this is a correct solution and solid in its application. The City exists ... Period! It is with watchful eyes we here see and feel what you sense is not only correct but as you say 'Set in cement!' Is this of your choosing?"

I felt a hum in the back audience and said "Yes."

O: "Good! Then all the space-time it has taken to bring this forth gives us a feeling of achievement as accepted."

G: "The sensing here in Sedona and also across the country, is of not feeling normal with strange feelings in the physical/mental taking place due to this energy change. What is to be expected?"

O: "Of course you feel strange. You are entering a new birth cycle never before happening on this your planet. The senses are heightening especially in your area of vortexes. This is true but manageable.

" Remember your density of this dimension is shifting into Light frequencies, and the density has to make room for the electric persona to be brought forth into the new world. Those who are registering these sensory feelings are in this process. (You will not short out) quite the contrary! Love is just making room to do that electrically. All is well."

G: "Thank you I feel that love more and more erasing past concerns etc. In my daily duties I am beginning to have not much interest, like doing the dishes or washing the floors."

O: "Correct ... but then these two you have spoken of were not so much on your list of fun things to do anyway. As the Light penetrates, daily normal areas become blasé or less important for the Light frequencies are taking on a higher vibration. One day at a time Dear One ... One day at a time ... and we shall speak again soon."

And with that he bowed as did all the rest near him and I knew this session was over. We exited back to the Gate of Entrance as I slipped back into my Sedona world to take care of my puppy Light who needed my attention and I autographed more City books to be sent out because ...

Something is coming!

I hear it is written in cement! Imagine that!

Thanks God.

So Light it be!

Of Covered Wagons and Space Technology!

Embassy Visit May 14, 2011

Moving through the crowds trying to enter into The City at the south Gate, I was inspired to give thanks for each visit I got to make. It indeed was a holy mission to see and learn what the future is all about. My destination this visit was the Embassy of Peace to learn of advanced information I might receive. Connecting with my Guide La-Luke, we ran through the Relaxation Park and onto the funny trolley and entered into the Embassy of Space Entities, where actually I felt quite at home. The Light Entities within stood and I happily waved back at them. The constant leader OOO-LON bowed in acknowledgement and began this conversation...

O: "And the Lady of human Light attends again with her companion La-Luke. Both are welcome. How may we be of service?"

G: "Funny I feel so at home here with you all. I have not had a conversation with the beings in the audience yet, and I can barely make them out. My life is indeed strange from living on the outside and then coming into this higher level. It is so great here."

O: "It should be remembered that what takes place here is somewhat removed from your daily doings as you try to do both and in the 'now' times slot. Let's talk about 'the now'... since your Light Body is moving faster than the physical body, it becomes apparent that you are experiencing the 'now' and thus you see everything as having to be done immediately! In the NOW! (as there is no other time), it can get confusing we understand, but as you are Light moving in Light, this can be no other way! You have been in this upper level many times and even we feel a kinship. Now then, you have a question?"

G: "Yes, how will Light technology that The City brings of support, affect say, those who work in altered states such as a medical intuitive? And what can be said of Space Light Technology?"

O: "Dear One, the vastness of Space Technology compared to what is being used now on your planet has no comparison. It would be like comparing your old covered wagons to a spacecraft. There is that much difference. Your planet rides in kindergarten learning when the university is the answer.

" The Space Light Technology is far superior to the instruments of today's medical use which are barbaric. Trying to find an answer to any malady takes too long. But who benefits? ... the drug companies and their attendees. However in Light Technology the answer is known in an instant.

"That is where the trained intuitives come into the front of the line as leaders, for they can pinpoint the area of healing faster than any doctor of human disorders, due to the Light corridor (of, say, The 4 Keys) of the mental.

"The medical in some ways wants no interference of strange kinds of mental advice from an 'intuitive.' 'What is that? And how come I can't do that?' They can guess but anything else is weird and don't leave out the drugs, that make much money in your world. If no one uses drugs what then? With The City technology no drugs will be needed...yes this is so!

"It has been told you long since that drugs will be abandoned. Inner knowing and feeling will take their place. The intuitives are the doctors of the future and the Light Beings of humanness will Light the way. This should not seem strange to you. Light Technology is indeed the healing of your planet's future. What you rely on today will be a thing of the past, such as the covered wagons are, as one looks back at those ways of travel.

"So then Medical Intuitives will be called 'Light Initiatives' for they see through now to the truth of the matter, making Light the way to discover like a mental flash, seeing the patient's condition as it really is. It is known that a person looking through a microscope in a laboratory can mentally change the cells as an observer, with their own thoughts and without any knowledge. So then trained Light Technicians would be of great value for they know only Light.

"Those in this audience have that advantage. A major planet 'make-over' as said, is in process as The City unfolds its treasures of Light healing. Does this help your question?"

G: "Wow... a lot to look forward to..."

O: "And soon!"

G: "What can I report as an update on The City arrival?"

O: "It is as near as your breath. As The City books move out and people digest (with the current energies supporting) with favor what is coming into view, we here celebrate our own arrival to set the planet's course into Space Technology. Your guidance is soon more and more people will set foot in your presence to learn more. It is therefore ...

  1. Be advised to send the books as guided and

  2. Be open to any travel indicated. Share and beware, 'now ' is the time.

  3. Rest and be the love you feel here, and share with all. This is the time for All to Heal and Light technology is the answer.

"Thank you for asking. We shall speak on this again. Have a nice day and play in the Light ... as Light. So Light you be!"

With this he bowed and we headed out of the Embassy of love and information. **Thanks OOO-LON ... I am blessed.**

Outer Space, Inner Space and All the Spaces in Between!

Embassy Visit May 21, 2011

My, how tall The City Gates looked as I glanced up 5 stories to the top, shining in the sun where the padding held the secret imprints unnoticed, that welcomed everyone from anywhere on the planet like coming home ... indeed!

Entering the vision was a stream of Light like a spotlight picking my Guide La-Luke out of those waiting to enter. I ran to him for my usual hug of love from this devoted Being of Light and bingo ... contact was made!

This day was a visit to the Embassy of Peace, so through the Park, onto the funny trolley and into the building with hundreds of galactic beings inside sending love as we entered. If this is what we are to experience here on Earth on 11-11-11, we are in for some special feelings like no other ever experienced. It reminded me of a favorite Barbra Streisand melody. 'At the same time.'

It was like feeling love from all the intergalactic community all at the same time. WOW! How great is this I thought, as tears rolled down my face and I grabbed for a Kleenex.

OOO-LON was standing with a smile that could light up any sun ... as did the entities standing beside him.

G: "We're back!" I announced expectantly.

O: "So we see...Welcome, there must be more questions and we are here for that answering."

G: "Well, my friend Renee Trenda sent me an e-mail that reports that there is a race of people who live inside the Earth. Is this correct?"

O: Laughing, "Quite so, why not? Is this Earth you call home not a hologram like the rest of the Universe? Within the circular dimensions many non-layers exist. To live in what you call underground like moles from your point of 3D view, there are many layers. This is just something not thought too much of before, especially you as you are sky-watching in expectancy.

"Beings of all kinds live in space even within. So then would you speak 'inner space?' he smiles. It may be difficult for many to think of a City of Light to appear like Merlin's magic come to life, but true anyway. You see 'see-through's as you call them. Entities like the seekers of Stoneman Lake and Angels in Angel Valley. No difference except frequency-wise.

"It may be difficult to sense this from others as a possibility. Then think of those who have to mentally tackle The City as a possibility as this code projection of layers, dimensions and such. Fascinating isn't it? So then what the Renee has been shown is also a possibility," as he continued to grin in expectation of my picking up the wisdom contained in his message.

G: "Inner Earth occupied! Imagine that! I am so much in the world but not of it, as outer space pulls at me constantly and I feel like the movie 'E. T. go home.'

Next question...Renee also inquired about a Michael Quinsey who channels SaLuSa. You know anything about this?"

O: "SaLuSa is indeed a Light unto your world. The words reflect as a guidance to keep the balance where there is unbalance, due to the polarity of thinking and action taking place at the same time. The connection of The City arrival is quite in order as the Renee knows first-hand, and is quite a linking partner of contact for The City in many worlds. She leads in places the Genii is not aware of and sets the balance so the Genii can speak to those who are destined to hear what she has to say with The City plans, City books, and herself."

G: "Thank you. Any update on 11-11-11 demonstration as I have a City meeting coming up soon?"

O: "As has been said, this is the time of great advancement. You might say it is 'a Great Love-in' for the energies of change bring forth a healing, connected feelings that superimpose past the ego-sensory condition, to the deepness of God-intent as you say ' LOVE IS ALL THERE IS.. THAT LOVE HEALS, PERIOD!" You have learned this first hand and that feeling continues to flow within you as a human connection healer.

"Rejoice Dear One, for the path is lit and The City descending is imminent. You personally are experiencing the Light shower surges that make you wonder what is taking place, but continue to know all is in divine order, and feel the feminine power moving through the heart, blossoming in full bloom with such love like you are experiencing here in the Embassy.

"You wonder why people smile at you when out in public, They sense your Light and that makes for smiles first-hand. This is all for a definite reason, climaxing with The City energies, making you forget Earthy appearances as you fall in the love of God and do the best you can in any situation.

"Many more are in this forgetful pathway. It is just that the love connection is taking that place. Please not to be bothered. Remember the new you is being born. Anything else?"

G: "I would like to know more about my space friends for sharing here."

O: "Of course, your media movies depict the dark and the Light as in the movie of Avatar. Look to those on Pandora. They say 'I see you' and it comes from the heart. A friend suggested that we take it higher to 'I am you!' and you have been saying it ever since, and in doing so sending the Light/love to their souls. This is indeed I AM God good."

G: "Will our government address this issue of E. T.'s here?"

242

O: "They will be pushed to do so. The coming-in energies make no room for the unannounced. Have you not been advised to contact the United Nations?"

G: "Yes, I am trying to find a way in."

O: "Go back into your world and enjoy this message and the day before you, knowing full well that Dear One, all is well. Enjoy a love feast wherever it presents itself, even with the roses.

"Look to more and more contact trips to be announced and follow through. Use The City books to move forward. In that announcement, the Light will move them into the right hands. And we bid you the Light of the eternal day, in peace and in love. So Light you be! Spread it around."

With this they all bowed and I left determined to be the best announcer I could with this good God news.

The Divine Blueprint: Steps in the Right Direction!

Embassy Visit June 1, 2011

I was waiting in the silence for my inner City of Light vision to appear, as I had been called to re-enter the Embassy of Peace headquarters. I permitted love to be my Guide and in doing so, I found myself meeting with my City Guide La-Luke. As he grabbed my hand, we rushed past crowds wanting to also get inside The City. (Like at Disneyland). We ran to catch the trolley and a short ride later we were in the Embassy.

As we entered, already I sensed the love of the hundreds of unidentified space saints who made up this vast audience seated behind the stage leaders with OOO-LON. I caught my breath and took note of these hundreds of entities who have worked for unknown hundreds of years to bring forth The City of Light. They were a treat to behold in my eyes. Absolutely no threat here ... just love in different forms. This in itself was a miracle in action by my calculations.

OOO-LON, the wizard vocal-interpreter spoke:

O: "Ah, I see you have received the message to return. This is good. What may we say to enlighten you?"

G: "I have a couple of questions given to me, to ask about and share what information is given me."

O: "Continue..."

G: "With all that has been said for these many years of visits, there must be a 'Divine Blueprint' to bring this City of Light and all it is about. The City itself has been the dramatic point of our conversations and now we have another, namely the Love Shift of 11-11-11 in which we are to experience in full force from the Creator Source, an energy of love that will blanket this Earth totally for an unspecified length of time?"

O: "Correct! The massive wave of love energy will be released that lifts and corrects what humans have put into place with low-consciousness drama of experience. This is long past due to be released. People cannot seem to do this on their own to an effective level, so as the Proclamation said early on, the Creator has declared the Pure Source Love of God will demonstrate at your level. We say 'pure love' here, not just a light and fluffy kind that has no meaning other than the word vibration itself intends. Now what more can be said? You have validation here."

G: "Well, there is forming an interested Sedona group that is leading the 11-11-11 celebration, to honor these dates somehow. I have been asked to find out if they would be permitted to incorporate the 11-11-11 scenario using the name of Sedona City of Light 11-11-11 or some such name-title which of course sounds like this City of Light connection here. What may I report to them as guidance? The only thing connected is the Light Center as such. I know not what to say?"

O: "Those who look from the heart and not the head, so to speak, want to connect in the highest way possible; as in love integrity and want to make the 11-11-11 event one of beauty and soul. The name Sedona City of Light 11-11-11 has been offered and can have a vast meaning as this wave hits its peak, and as said only love will hold it all together.

"This City of Light you know so well will expand due to that love. Those who want to connect with the original CITY as a co-partner event, have the permission to do that. However, it should be known that no one owns this City or any part of it business-wise.

"It is not a business in your words. It just is a Creator's gift; an entity in itself. To use a co-name is an honor to those who somehow want to connect. Permission is given! Sedona City of Light 11-11-11 or some such connection is indeed acceptable in the way it is presented, and those who lead will be a major part and support of The City of Light itself. Everyone wins when cooperation is expressed in love. So then does this answer your request?"

G: "I understand that my position in this is just to hold the Light and speak if requested, yes?

"Another question: Since many walk the path from childhood with programming that may not fit now in the religious sense, this can be a problem for some. What can one do to move into the new world coming in, and break away from some teaching that now feels incorrect without feeling they have betrayed something that was very useful in earlier years?"

O: "Dear One, on a path such as all walk from childhood programming, we can say that this will no longer be a problem. From kindergarten to college you have all been programmed to change and have done so as you look back. When it comes to religious beliefs, what comes up could be the 'guilt' of not following the rules set out at that time. Realize that time is no more and it is natural for many to challenge the writing or describe them in updated ways.

"What was held over the children was GUILT, or sin or whatever, and the child-mind had no recourse but to bend to that control of bondage. Guilt was and still is in control. What IT did was to put aside childish thoughts and be a pseudo-adult. What the child thoughts brought forth was the innocence and purity of God's love. That is what they were preprogrammed to do until that purity of God's love was banished by betrayers who had long since forgotten what innocence was. God is love so they put it under another way of control.

"The Christ of one of your religious orders taught love, which is the innocence that the child represents even today. You the Genii, go to the Disney park? Why? To recoup the feeling of happiness and laughter = GOD'S LOVE. What do you put into the puppets? Wood? Fabric? Mostly love which holds them all together, pleasing your audiences. IS THERE A DIVINE BLUEPRINT WORKING NOW? ABSOLUTELY!!!! 11-11-11 PLUS THE CITY OF LIGHT! Got the picture?

"Tell your people what is really taking place. You have the data, the book and these visits. None will be ignored for they come forth with a Child's faith of God's I AM love. Simple isn't it? So now then, enough said. Go and rest for your vibrational track has been well-used this morning and we bid you the Light of the eternal day in peace and in love."

So Light it be!

Galactic Federation and The City of Light!

Embassy Visit June 14, 2011

Entering into vision, I saw myself running to the south Gate. Destination ... the Embassy of Peace Headquarters to ask space questions, as I have been turned on to two words, Galactic Federation, and I wanted to know more about it. So onto the general path through the Park of Relaxation, onto The City trolley and into this humongous building, the Embassy of Peace. My Guide was nowhere to be seen. [must have a no-time off day?]

The Embassy was filled with Light as hundreds of entities filled this space, and I felt once more the love that they provided, and WOW...there be power here...oh my yes ... Lucky girl Genii!

O: "Welcome human Lady of Light. Ready for space talk, are you?"

G: "Yes thank you for the invitation to come back when I need to."

O: "Continue...."

G: "Off and on I hear references to the Galactic Federation that I know very little or nothing about. Recently I have been introduced to the messages of SaLuSa through qualified Earth channel, Mike Quinsey and the Galactic Federation comes again into play. The thing is, I feel these messages are so correct that they take me into love and heart and power on contact. Reading them regarding this planet's activity, and since I am connected to The City of Light, they make a lot of sense."

O: "So then, The Galactic Federation and The City of Light connection is what you seek to know?"

G: "Sure, Light Beings? Federation? City? etc.? Whatever can be revealed to me to share as I spread The City words."

OOO-LON smiling, sent a tone out over the audience and a hum sound responded, so looked like... something was coming.

O: "Dear One, within the Galactic Federation, are thousands of entities of the collective. We have spoken of Cosmic Communities in vast spaces of the Universe, with its cosmic Light supporting in bringing forth The City of Light. Right here in this building sit many who would attest that this is correct, as they are the cosmic centers of many ...unknown to you. We are of the collective power energy in the Universe bringing love to your planet community which is long past due. There are many here, but we are all of the One Source and cannot be separated even by miles of space.

"You speak of one Light being of SaLuSa, who speaks of inner knowing of what is taking place as your plane moves into position of demonstration. You have your own Soul Intelligences. Two in particular, Atherian who sheds Light on your planet, unearthing anything of dark ignorance that needs to be brought into the Light for removal. So you see this is taking place in many places on your planet and will continue until healed. Several times he has come through you at City meetings with a roar of, 'There will be no more wars!!!' and the rafters shook it seemed.

"Then of course you have Barbarous, who designates as your Jedi teacher of love and watches as you give only love to your world. Has he not in vision taken you to another planet to look back at this one seeing it on fire? (The fire of cleansing is of course symbolic.) Both are Galactic Federation Light Beings so you are put in position to learn of The City and its fulfillment.

"The Galactic Federation uses Light to heal, and cleanse, and give information to many who tap in. You speak of a beloved Light entity who shares information through a man who carries this honor of serving. The Collective Community is vast, as vast as the Universe itself and though unseen, many walk daily on your planet. The love you feel for E.T.'s is quite natural, for your physical form is only a facade over the real you. You and the Dr. Bill were chosen to deliver the information on The City because you are a space entity who could understand from the heart, and report the findings and do it with unconditional love.

"You walk the human life plan, yet space beings feel like family and the heart feelings come from love hidden in your DNA. You feel spacey on occasion and rightly so, as you try to link the two worlds you live in as The City keeps your attention. Is there a Cosmic Community named Galactic Federation? Are there worlds beyond that which you see daily? Are you as one of your teachers calls you human 'skin bags?' Duality will be banished and is making way for the 'Love Wave' of 11-11-11 in your time calendar to be experienced and thus The City of Light. Has this been of help?"

G: "Oh yes. May I report what has just been revealed? People may think I am a little strange." I said laughing.

O: "Many do already, so this will only make the story have a bit of fun attached, but you know what you know and are open enough to share with a twinkle in your eyes to boot. Continue as you are doing. Enjoy the SuLaSa messages from this gentle, loving and powerful collective with the Mike Quinsey as others line up to hear the truth."

G: "I feel an urgency to speak with our President on The City."

O; "Remember you are in the NOW and everything seems urgent and most is. Patience, until the message goes out for someone to contact him on your behalf. It will happen as soon as someone sets the energy to get you from point G. to point P. All in divine order. Just continue to be open as someone opens the door to this meeting with you and the family marionettes. Now then, anything else?"

I shook my head no. This was plenty to think about and discern what would be next. I thanked them all and left the building. And with that the vision stopped and I was home getting ready to re-read what was said and type this up.

Of E.T. Disclosure and Galactic Determination of Peace!

Embassy Visit June 25, 2011

As I entered into inner vision, I saw a sign that read "Embassy this way! You are welcome!" What, no Gate to go through? No fun trolley ride? Nope. Just me and my Guide La-Luke walking into this major arena-style building ...The Embassy of Peace Headquarters. Hundreds of Light Beings (E.T.'s) filled up the hundreds of seats all faintly seen. All were standing as we entered. This was quite a sight to see ... really looked like we were expected. Nice way to start this visit.

G: "Blessings to you all as all" I muttered in a loving response to them.

O: "And returned Oh Lady of Earth Light. We Lights of the Universal Federation stand in welcome as this space community is now open to share. What would you have enlightenment about on this visit?"

G: "You are all so loving. I feel friends here and I am honored. Would you tell me if there is to be a disclosure of your E.T. assistance and if so, how is this to be revealed to the public?"

O: "Indeed, we here in The City of Light have long since had recognition from one human Light or another. It is the intent that is important, and that we [as you call Light Beings] advance through recognition, and as your time moves forward in the illusion and the 11-11-11 scenario becomes the massive changeover, it would appear that we will be more accepted as friends rather than ones of doing harm.

"This of course is idiocy of human ignorant minds, looking for something to blame their nonsensical images on. It is almost one person at a time to recognize of the support you all have been given for eons of time. The leader of your country must be a spokesperson fully in the knowing. The timing must be correct!"

G: "How can I be of help?"

O: "Continue to see this as fact, not fiction, and the way will be shown. You are a Way-Shower and ready to do what has to be done in preparation."

G: "A master, I have been told, has said this is to be a Golden Galaxy. What would be the meaning of this statement?"

O: "Big changes now in process enlighten all, one way or another. Your openness of continuation helps make this a possibility for all people and Light Beings etc. to live in, with such peace never experienced before. You are all being brought into the Cosmic fold so to speak. Such is all on the agenda in the Big Changeover in your time slot of the energy fields of this current year. Mark these words well...as said. This year will introduce so much high velocity of love and Light that people will change before your eyes.

"Your personal system has been doing a changeover in the Light Body as you are well aware of, and tolerate the best you can balancing this world and the one you are in daily. Your aura extends and those close to you sense the frequency which by really doing nothing even, makes them change as well, ready or not. Love is where you come from and nothing other is tolerated. You do normal things daily but normal you are not, nor will you ever be again; for the lifting of your vibrations will continue until you are pure Light in human form. This Dear One is your path of Enlightenment City Connection."

G: "I have a friend here in Sedona who lives in a home of domes. Which she feels is 5th dimension connected. What can be said of this?"

O: "Portals are not only outside in the grounds and rocks, they are also inside as well. You have seen a portal open with dancing see-through children in your own backyard. She senses correctly for the levels of the unseen have been there for some time. Have you not been invited to bring a City gathering there? Of course! Quite natural then, do that for it has energy with advantages yet to be known, with those who attend and the Light lifts all who enter. This is good!

"Let all know that you all are on the fast track these days, and connection to the upper and underground is available as well. Ah yes, much is to be uncovered and discovered in the revelations to come about piece by piece, for peace of all."

G: "What does it mean to be a Complete Galactic Human as I have read is in the offing? I have never heard that before?"

O: "Again your process is in this area. You the Genii look human and are, but feel different that which could make for some confusion as you progress forward. Be of peace. All is well. You are sort of shape shifting. The City is your thrusting and trusting mission, and the changes come in your being able to do the magic the Genie is noted for, as well as the Jedi of service.

"The City comes forth and all is in galactic intent of service to your Earth people. It will take something massive like this City to evolve the human species into communication to other cosmic communities, as the Galactic Federation has achieved in other areas. Now it is your planet's turn to be galactic-lifted. Rejoice!"

G: "What is to take place when as said, there will be no more duality here?"

O: "Many surprises. Many gifts as the "old" releases itself into the 'newness of oneness.' Vast opportunities change with the love as it moves into balance and with love as the leader and City to prove its position.

"Ah...we sense the Genii's energy fields are weakening so we suggest that you leave us as we release you to your human world and we do so lovingly and with a promise of great tomorrows.

We bid you the Light of the eternal day in love and in peace"

250

Invisible Crossroads 11-11-11 and The City of Light!

Embassy Visit July 12, 2011

It has been said that if your dream does not include the impossible then ... you are dreaming too small. It seemed like everything was like a speeded up movie, as in quiet vision I found myself already in the Embassy standing before OOO-LON and this massive Community of Extraterrestrials gathered in this hall of love and peace. Each one of these extraterrestrials was a master. This time I had no need to go through the usual Gate, Park, and a ride on the trolley... I was just there!

O: "And what would be your inquiry on this visit?"

G: "I have several questions and thank you for having me return ... and so quickly!"

O: "Time matters not here and your requests were previously noted."

G: "I have been given a request from Michael Quinsey in England, who inquires about the 11-11-11 scenario and if The City arrival comes before or after the Love Wave Tsunami of 11-11-11? Whichever it is, I also ask why in this order? "

O: "It would be the 11-11-11 scenario as this wave of subtle energy sweeping across the planet brings harmony and love into place. Open hearts and mental acuity of such a masterful event taking place, for the heart tells the mind, and the emotions report that God has entered and all is well! The leveling of the body and mind (especially the emotions) will permit the spirit energy to move The City into an understanding far beyond the local human way of thinking. It will lift beyond lifting, and joy will ring out throughout the lands that they are one with the Creator, as it was meant to be in the first place.

"As you have asked before in voice tones, 'What if everyone on this planet felt love at the same time?' It is time for this in your human's illusionary mind of time to take place. Centuries of confirmations have come and then been forgotten. Not this time! How will your planet handle such feelings of love for each other is yet to be experienced; but report this to the Michael and his understanding with loving gentle SaLuSa will confirm. Now then what else is to be known?"

G: "It has been shared with me during one of my visits that when The City births, and is accepted, that several more Cities already on the Earth's grid will also come forth. Am I understanding this correctly?"

O: "Quite so, look at what is taking place right now as connection into the European sector of your planet is getting the news thanks to this new friend Michael, plus now yet another country with the book of The City flowing in another long distance. The beginning location of Sedona is the new galactic entrance point for The City birthing. Do not the vortexes spin in confirmation? Therefore the energy bringing in The City of Light is immense in its power and the spinning power source needs to be, for this is an huge undertaking but has

251

been perfectly laid out as we have set this course many centuries past. As you say 'It is a divine time-thing'...and this is correct. The world will beat a path to your Sedona of Arizona door and then more will appear around the planet. We understand this will be pure nonsense for some who fear, but for those who are in the knowing it will be pure JOY! Healing comes at last! You will look and see 13 more to appear in various locations and countries. So even now the words from your City book is reaching different countries starting with England thanks to the Michael interest. This is all good! It has been said that your planet will heal and be a Light in the heavens with other star-bright cosmic places. Is this not a delightful vision to be seen?"

G: "Yes ... all this has been so close to my heart ... I feel very blessed to play any part in it. What if any part is to be added as I move forward with guidance? I have been told to hold the energy patterns for 11-11-11 and that is fine with me."

O: "You will continue this energy pattern, however during this time it will be very appropriate that you speak on The City coming forth, a perfect time for all hearts will be open to hear and embody. Will you speak? Oh my yes. Permit the time to pass between now and 11-11-11 and you will not only carry the essence of love but your words will bear fruit and people will rejoice from open hearts. Just you be open and watch what takes place in the next 4 months ... "

G: "Amazing! Anything else for me to know?"

O: "Yes I shall say here...

1. Travel will appear with rest periods in between.

2. Your body temple will carry more Light than ever before.

3. People will be attracted to know more.

4. The City Books will move into a flow of interest.

5. More visits to the Embassy will produce advanced information.

6. The City moves into your active time slot as # one.

7. Time-wise you are doing several weeks as one day.

8. Come back when you sense you should, as there will be much more added as the closer rather than farther comes into play.

9. Be open to instant guidance. You live in the fast lane now.

10. Know that all is well and divine right action is really taking place.

"We release you now back into the physical world. Be ye with love and God-conviction that all is well." And with this ... Pop! ... I was back home with my pup.

Making City Magic from Nothing!

Embassy Visit July 19, 2011

Setting aside this world of illusion, I entered into the higher realm of The City of Light and as such, The Embassy of Peace. The scene opened like a movie in progress and I watched as one in the audience would be sitting quietly in a meditative state to see what is going to take place.

Scene: The usual 5-story Gate with the encoded gold trim welcomed to all who appeared, with many people rushing to get in. The sun shone brightly revealing my City Guide La-Luke holding a clear space for me to join him. A 'Light' hug and we almost ran through the Park of Relaxation, and hopped on the funny trolley that skimmed along on no wheels, and driven by no one. What fun this was. The City must have been filled with them to get people where they wanted to go ... perfect transportation!

Within a few steps we were standing in front of the Embassy Light Beings with OOO-LON and an auditorium filled with the Federation of Space Beings. It was beginning to look like a great day! What a blessing I have been given to be here with what I somehow felt was my family. Strange, but as said, we are all one! Groovy! With all that being said, OOO-LON opened the conversation.

O: "Welcome back Oh Lady of Light. We sense you have questions and with the end result being, that we have the answers? The human thinking of what is or is not, becomes quite apparent, for a few keys have been left somewhat out of the equation of your linear lines of seeing. For most, this is the way it is, period. Now then again welcome!"

G: "Thank you, it is good to be here in this ultra high energy as I try to explain the almost unexplainable of what is taking place, beyond what is currently being observed,...or not!"

O: "Shall we tell you what your interest is?"

G: "I am sure you can!"

O: "You want to know regarding The City announcement of appearance at ground 3D level and how can this be really? Take Sedona, Arizona that at ground level, homes and businesses are human occupied, so how can this be? As you have been asked numerous times, will it land on my house? Is it already here?

"Dear Ones, to make that mental breakthrough, it was understood long since that what is to be will bring forth these questions. (The audience hummed in the background.) Actually any answer we give you will not be understood by the masses as the Advanced Scientific Technology being introduced, is far beyond most in their thinking. It has been said to you that this is the year of Magic and Miracles. To make that mental breakthrough one must be quite advanced in holographic Paradigm thinking, plus it helps to be an Extraterrestrial. (Again a hum sound came from the audience).

"If one is a magician, (and the Creator is quite a magician), since you are standing on a vision of a planet you call home, and you would be standing in outer space if that Magician God did not have that thought, and consequently there would be no need for a City of Light. For any magician, he must make something out of nothing ...or so it seems, and the people say, 'How did he do that? '

"Very few magicians give out the answer for it breaks the mystery and he could be out of business. The people want to know how it was done, but ... do they? Is not the mystery more fun in its wondering? Of course.

"Dear One, everyone lives in the greatest illusion of all, that God has created through you, each and every one and you all demonstrate this on a daily basis. You are the Magicians, imagine that! How many times has it been said with humans? 'Now what did I do to create that?'

"You all were given the gift of being a magician or even a Genii. You all were given a gift of choice. How many times has this been said by the wisdom makers of the past and even the present, such as it is.

"It would be wise for the Lightworkers to begin to look at The City of Light through holographic thinking of which many books have been presented. You say you want to see The City? It is here and it is now. Dimensions beyond your current seeing but ...oh my this will pass...Indeed!

"You the Genii recognize that your world is a Hologram and spread this where you can, but it is so foreign to most people that the mental connection cannot be made. But then it took you years to get the picture that you were walking around in God's dream. Did it not make you laugh and roll on the floor? Indeed.

"The human mind has its own conception of this or that, and even in the idea that thoughts are things and can be reproduced. You have done this with the puppets of the stage to applause.

"Wise wizards have long since brought forth plans like the ones Dr. Bill brought forth. Hermes is quite a wizard, as the designer of the Gaia pyramid where he could tuck in his mystery school that the Dr. Bill was part of, and even the President of Obama took part in it some centuries later.

"The clean-up of this planet is a divine idea, but a bigger one is to take its place. The City of Light with Sedona is its birthing bowl. Then the magic of the Master Magician will bring forth others around the planet.

"All is in order and very well planned. So permit the Magnificent Magic of the Master Creator to bring into form the vision we have been talking about. Enjoy the Mystery. See it through new eyes as a holographic delight that will land not on anyone.

"New inventions come through inventor's minds and hopefully it will be used as a bettering of the human race. The Imagination is the pathway to the Christ Consciousness. You think this City is not top quality consciousness? Oh My God!

"So permit us to say, 'Yes The City of Light will appear'. The first ... never before! ... never! Can you take this all in?

"God has all the mental in place and the correct land will be known and no one has to climb any ladders to go inside for it is grounded. Your City of Light Manuscript has much to offer as the time line continues to unfold. This indeed is a gift ... from the Great Magic Maker all tied up with a bow of healing technology that is so far beyond what is being used today. Time to move on people. Time to move on!

"Report to the people to use their imaginations. Suggest they take your 4 Keys of Light mental advancement and propel themselves into the holographic-ness of God, for this Wizard God is the greatest of them all and wants The City to be a surprise gift, for something is indeed coming ... soon.

"The Sky Riders of the Universe hidden behind clouds over the Sedona landscape in these wondrous times await the signal to be declared. All is in the pre-set planning and in your planet timing. The surprise will be well worth the wait for something beyond even your current belief is magically on its course. You speak Earth truth and we speak Space truth ... all is one and the same. So Light it be!"

And with that ... POP! I was back home ready for a cup of tea and a cute puppy to share it with.

Thanks to all my space family.

I am you!

Looking Through New Eyes . . . Universal Understanding!

Embassy Visit July 23, 2011

In the quiet of this Saturday morning as I awakened from a good night's sleep, my first thought was of gratitude and a wish to have a happy day today. As I opened my eyes what did I see in the sky but a flying colored balloon taking visitors over the top of our beautiful red rocks ... "yes... that is a good omen," I remark to my little pom puppy Light (who is always a good start any morning). However he only took note of Frick and Frack, our 2 local crows having a loud squawky argument in the pine tree.

Things seemed to be flying overhead today. How about an inner vision flying trip to the Embassy, Genii? Sounded right to me ... Let's go talk to Light entities who have flown through the Universe to bring forth The City ... OK ... I AM tuning out world ... BYE.

Centering into this space of high consciousness, I found myself and my City Guide La-Luke already on the trolley heading for the Embassy, while passing strange but beautiful white and gold buildings for human healings of all kinds. We were off to a great start>>>>> wheeeee! A little like Disneyland fun here!

The trolley stopped and we headed into the fragrant foyer filled with flowers, and then into the main sanctuary and the current stopping-off place for many Light Space Beings who sat in audience for this session. Many tones were heard and as OOO-LON saw us coming in, he raised his hand as his robe changed shades of orchid and white. All behind him settled down. He seemed to be the Headmaster and he could interpret what I was saying. Sometimes I was not sure what I was saying in this world beyond our world. Oh well, moving right along.....

O: "Good morning from our world to yours, which is all one. Welcome back! What answers may we give you for this reason to return. We are pleased with this space connection I might add."

G: "Good morning. Thank you for receiving us again. This morning I saw a large colored balloon that carries visitors over the Sedona red rocks to see the beauty of where I live. I thought of all the miles you must have traveled to be here, much less bringing in the massive City of Light with healing the planet as your objective."

O: "Ah, we speak space today and what would your question be to begin our flight of fancy?"

G: "I have been asked by a good friend to clear up a point regarding The City entry into this Earth world. "Is The City of Light inside a mothership or being holographically lowered onto the Earth's surface?"

O: Smiling, "All is a hologram, Dear One. You saw a flying balloon. You say it was a hologram flying over the red rocks which is also a hologram. The mothership spoken of is a hologram as it flew over the red rocks.

"They too are holograms. It seems to be very hard for the humans of your planet to get the picture correct. Scientifically it gives one a dramatic picture of how all this City prophecy can come into being and quite effortlessly.

"One vision that was given to you while in The City was a space vehicle that was lowering a completed City building to the surface. That was a surprise to you. Actually a delightfully fun way to look at everything is holographic and in doing so, all can make sense. The human mind is vast in its ways as the images bring forth what one would call in your language the 'Christ Consciousness,' from utter nothingness. Infinite possibilities flow forth from so-called dreams into your so-called reality.

"Most of the Earth's people have not a clue of what I am saying here, but you have a mind that can comprehend and declare it to be so as you have learned prior. Some people make a good job of using their minds to be miserable and some recognize that they are living in a holographic universe which gives them mental opportunities they can decide to use. Some would say it is all a 'head trip' and they are correct sort of, in your general language.

"A human person may say, 'I had this dream and it came true.' It was just a picture in their mind and they brought it forth through holographically designing. Dear Ones, the Universe is a hologram ... every star, planet, space vehicle, the whole thing. The Screen of Space brings forth this City you now stand in, in another dimension, but nevertheless coming into your reality so no one can say they did not see it. Hog-wash ... (is a term you use on a farm seen in your world.

"You see we too have to learn your human words, some very unusual.) God's view is quite amazing as you have made many trips into The City and expressed these viewing visits in your Book of City Light for others to see on their Screen of Space.

"We who come before you have a holographic understanding of how technology itself came into being. God does good things even to bringing your planet into being real to you so you will have something to stand on. Imagine that! Then God gave you all an imagination as birthed into life and as children held that sensing until some adult said, 'Oh, that is only your imagination, forget it' and they forgot it was real.

"In your world you hooked onto a master who did believe it was real and made millions of visitors believe it too. I speak of course your mentor even today, Walt Disney. He gave you the inner insight that you could do anything of fun and have expressed it in many entertaining ways. Even today he coaches you from the ethers on a green bench in his park of Disney. Like it is said, no one dies. True.

"The Imagination is HOLY. It produces everything, for God is the Creator of all and the original designer of dreams. Some use it for good, some do not in the correct vernacular and destroy as 'dementors' portrayed in a movie series (Harry Potter).

"We in space have Cosmic Communities of peace, love and enough of that combination to bring forth The City of Light as we reach out in holographic form beginning with the 11-11-11 Wave of Love, sort of setting the scene for the appearance of what you stand on this day. You say life is good! Life is God in whatever shape, design or size you want.

"The Master Creator created creators and thus you have polarity (which is on its way out ... over-used and over-worked.) Only one point of view is necessary, and that Dear One is for the goodness of life. For too long you all have played the waiting game of peace on Earth. It is time. (If there was such a thing as time). You are all making something out of nothing. So then, is your question answered?"

G: "Yes ... and then some, thank you."

O: "Dear One, the infinite possibilities of what is coming about is just that ... infinite, beyond description and all on your planet receive the benefit and reap the harvest so to speak, divinely set and lowered into place. This is by divine appointment that this City of Light demonstrates as real. You all will really know that it is as real as any building you have hand built on your planet but the difference is ... you don't have to build it. God did it all for you.

"Gifted from the Creator? Oh my yes! A hologram bright and shiny into your human-filled worldly level that people can enter and say 'Yes I was healed in The City of Light with Light!'... surprise!

"Any more questions?"

G: "I would like to know more about Space Communities and how you all live."

O: "You are Jedi?"

G: "So I am told."

O: "Then as a Jedi, there are certain laws of positive living connected. We stand as Light, in Light, for the Light, and can of course speak space. On another visit we can enter into the Cosmic Community area if that would be your pleasure?"

G: "Of course!"

OOO-LON made a hand signal and a hum went over the audience and I knew all was ended. He smiled as the Genii and her Guide left the building and ... wow I found myself home with such a loving mental frame of mind.

I saw today through holographic eyes and thanked God for what I got to learn in a holographic way.

Thanks God. I am open to receive.

So Light it be!

Of Disclosure and Speaking Space!

Embassy Visit July 28, 2011

As I entered into The City of Light mentally, the vision began with great huge doors opening that I had not seen before. My Guide and I seemed to be entering from a side entrance rather than the usual (what, no Gate or trolley ride?) Things move very fast here. We were then led by a Light Being into the great sanctuary with OOO-LON standing behind this horseshoe-style table.

In this magnificent hall, universal beings were again in attendance and as a tone sounded, they all sat down, even us. A thought crossed my mind that if I was to speak to the United Nations Earth group, this would be the place for them to see. No words I could utter would then make any impression. It just was so!

Note: Right now I was experiencing a 'Power surge' like an overheated feminine hot flash. Thanks to Archangel Michael's explanation of what that is all about, I guess I was on schedule. So then ... what was next?

O: "The welcome mat is again out for this Lady and Guide. We assume you have questions to be answered ... so be it."

G: "Thank you.

"Number one... More and more changes are taking place and that brings me back here to sort out what is going on, so to speak. Other Lightworkers also bring in valuable information, so questions come to my mind of the validity of what is being said, before I pass information on to others of what is going to take place, and I honor each one who expresses what they receive as well.

"One bit of information says a man in the Presidential White House here has spoken of a disclosure of E.T's on 12/27/2011, preceded by a craft landing in sight in a Florida stadium on 12/21/2011. What can be said of this announcement?"

O: "Mighty are the forces of neighboring universes that can bring forth such a phenomenon. This Dear One would only take place if all were in the projected time line of disclosure, and its effect on The City of Light appearance.

"Disclosure has been on many minds of late and the propensities of its happening draws crowds of interest. We say yes, there will be a disclosure, but no particular date as the energy patterns fluctuate dramatically as the entrance of The City of Light frequencies interrupt the normal flow you are used to daily. Dates could be tomorrow or six months ahead.

"Exciting isn't it! You are able to meet a Being from Space on your home-level setting as well as here. You have seen one in a movie of a lost entity trying to get back home. The timing of such an event could be right on target or a bit off. Only time will tell as it has itself on the fast track now and with The City as its center point of entrancing and its own point of disclosure.

"You are a forerunner as you spread the word of THE COMING. We are like the producers of a stage setting so to speak, of the greatest show on Earth which will not only appear, but produce healing as well. Let it be said that indeed there will be a disclosure at the perfect time as this will affect millions of people's reactions. Enough said?"

G: "Let's see, what is my next question?

Number Two... Will the door open for me to talk with the President regarding The City? How does this disclosure fall into this category?"

O : "Quite nicely. The program (speaking in your theatrical vernacular) has many players, and during this cleansing of the planet he has his hands full at the moment, before an alien disclosure takes place. And don't count out the 11-11-11 scenario of the 11-11-11 Love Wave scenario. The energy upheaval now is clearing out old debris so the energy of love can fill in that space.

"It is what you would call act #1, #2 and #3. Calming the emptiness of old ways needs the healing excitement of the new. Which comes first? Time will show. So Dear One, just be open to receive your guidance and we realize this is a watch and wait answer ...but quite timely. Next?"

G: "Number Three... I have friends near-by who own what is called a Dome Home as the roof domes look to me like colored Easter eggs and the home is quite famous for its décor and energy attached. I have spoken of The City there and am invited to return. Now in conversation she told that a master painter is repainting the dome roofs and adding symbolic symbols to them in the designs like crop circles.

"As we sat and spoke of this, from within I received the message that the symbols are 'SKY MAPS' to help hone in The City of Light and that this artist was given these symbols as one of his projects as it matches the original Sky Map of intention! What can be said of this?"

O: "Correct in your inner sensing. To bring anything from outer space, maps of many kinds are used for the vastness is unimaginable. The drivers of space vehicles have a mental visual imprint of where they are going, lest they end up in some other universe. There are many (universes) as well as vibrational patterns such as you are speaking of from your dimension.

"You use a device in your cars to get you to one place. We do have vast technology true, but the 3D patterns of your planet are used to assist and these (Sky Maps) spoken of are designed to do just that.

"They are guide-line signals as the symbols hold vibrational energy, whose signals are sent out into the airwaves. We understand that you have a small lake called Stoneman, which as you know is a portal with underground laboratories, with crystals honing in the space vehicles as directed. We play not games here. All is divinely directed into place.

"The underground in the Sedona area is filled with portals of all kinds. It has a catacomb of passages leading here and there and you have one in your home yard as you know. It would be simply like a sponge with holes where the energy pulls the unseen into action. We try many ways to help your understanding. Overhead and underneath are connected and you people walk and live in between like a sandwich.

"Does this give you any idea of what is taking place?" I nodded my head yes... "Your Earth world is so much more than what appears on the surface and as you just read in Archangel Michael's message with these changes and why you are experiencing Power Surges physically.

"So then take this information and sort out what it all means, as this visit has been quite informative and we are pleased to be able to express in your language.

"Return home now and we shall speak again. We bid you the Light of the eternal day in peace and in love."

So Light it be!

Thanks God ... Been a good trip!

http://www.xanaduofsedona.com

New World Changes: Opening Doors to 11-11-11!

Embassy Visit August 2, 2011

Being advised to enter into the Embassy of Peace, I mentally shut out my daily world and peeked into my screen of City space. I was at the crowded Gate entrance and saw a waving hand ahead belonging to my Guide La-Luke. We connected. And like a brisk wind we rushed through the Relaxation Park, onto the wheel-less trolley and stopped abruptly at the Embassy. Entering into this hall of space entities, I wondered what was up. All were standing in a reverenced welcome. I bowed in acknowledgment.

O: "Welcome! We speak of Earth things today and prophecies in progress."

G: "Thank you, I am open to hear what is to be said in love, heart, and open mind. No special questions come to mind at this moment in time. Anything would be wonderful I am sure."

O: "The Earth changes are at a faster pace now as the new energies have just had an upper level push into their new frequencies leading to 11-11-11. We are requesting that you look beyond most all you have learned in this lifetime and be open to more of the unusual. Space speaking changes will shift into yet higher elevations. The Entities of Love recognize that the pulse rate of this planet has yet to be raised.

"Many of those who live on it will feel the start of the Love Pulse of 11-11-11 beginning (especially Lightworkers) already in sync with this prophesy. Love must set the pace as one might open a door a bit to peek in. Slowly the full door opening will be heralded by 11-11-11.

"We are just advising you of the progress."

G: "I have been told that I would speak to the United Nations sometime. What of this?"

O: "Quite so, even now you wonder if a book to this Director of Space Affairs should be sent? It would be wise to do so. We shall make every effort to open doors of acceptance. The density of the government energy is thick, but the entity of the President still holds the Light you were previously told about.

"The old ways of any country government will be cleansed, for the new must take over if the planet is to be Light Enhanced for all. The old will not work anymore... as if it ever did! Progress has been very slow like a slug crawling to its next destination.

"The proposed recognition of the Extraterrestrials will come to pass for a love-intended Disclosure. Love ready or not, it will move aside the darkness of minds past thinking as the New World is making gains in this direction and, is about to be discovered.

"We advise therefore, to be open to any inner guidance that may have you moving on a moment's notice, even to quick sending out of The City books as they are your calling card, and expected to fall on more eyes and heart feelings.

"New contacts will come into being even through the Charles' contacts as well as others. You will suddenly see, feel and know the correctness of what is taking place. It will seem like you are riding a wave of recognition, especially in the next month on your Earth calendar, as this current one prepares you for such events yet unknown. Do you understand what is being said here?"

G: "Yes."

O: "It will seem like you wear a garment of Light and many others also have risen to that level. The City and 11-11-11 equal love representing the NEW WORLD coming in like a planet reborn in the Universe exploding with Light, and it will be.

"We are therefore advising you to speak the truth about what is being said. This call to have you re-enter this day is for this 'pep talk' of being advised. Expect the unexpected contacts to contact you through others such as those close to you. The E.T. energy moves in and around, moving the darkness [ignorance] out.

"There is a New World in process as has been said. Love is the New World. Be the leader of love intensive as that is what will help the change into Light that stands brightly in the sky like a special new star. All it takes is love and we as your sky friends bring the unseen in for the most part. Dear One, you have friendly skies. There have been many disclosures that we are here to assist. More will be acknowledged as time moves on.

"Be ready to travel and bring Light and thus see if we are not on a Divine Course. Indeed it is so! Go now and prepare for today, which is really weeks ago of space-time" and he smiled as a hum ran over the audience."

G: "I have just one more thing to say. The extraordinary love I feel when I stand here before you all is thrilling. If people could feel what I get to feel from these meetings, the planet would indeed be all loving and caring with instantaneous change. I am blessed. Thank you all for who you are and what you do."

O: "And so comes 11-11-11 Dear One ... Imagine that!"

He bowed as my Guide led me out the Embassy door.

I was back home and this day looked pretty sunny... and my puppy Light welcomed me with loving eyes and a furry body, and so it is!

I was advised that the Embassy visits will increase and to be aware at any given moment. OK!

It's a Cosmic Connection!

Embassy Visit August 7, 2011

ENTERING SCENE... The Gate was open wide as my City Guide stood in welcome. Usually there were also lots of people seen, but this trip had no one in view. All that was heard was some chirping birds having a convention of some sort in the Relaxation Park. La-Luke took my hand and with the funny Embassy trolley in sight, we enjoyed our walk in the Park including the birds.

A quick ride to the Embassy passing beautiful white buildings glistening in the Light, we entered into the domain of the Universal Federation where seated were hundreds of Extraterrestrials. The energy in here was indescribable except to say LOVE! I thought, what in heaven are people on this planet afraid of? I sense that this visit will be a very special visit.

OOO-LON and his court of honor stood in receiving us. Such honor is hard to explain.

O: "And the welcome mat is assured for you both. How may we friends of the Universe be of service?"

G: "Thank you, it is nice to be back. I sort of feel at home with you all. Sort of a Cosmic Connection that I have spoken of to a close friend lately. What exactly is a Cosmic Connection? It is almost like there is not two of us but one?"

O: Smiling said, "Your visits here are Cosmic Connections! When two people feel the energy of love, that is a Cosmic Connection. When even more as a group feel that inner connection that too, is a Cosmic Connection experience. In other words 'MEANT TO BE!'

"It would not matter if it were from one lifetime or another, there are certain energy fields that produce the inner feelings thus bringing them to the surface to be explored again. It was meant to be! What people do with that is up to them. Again Love is the component for the Cosmic Connection.

"As the world changes now, the Cosmic Connection heightens to a fever pitch and the Light Body inherits the passion contained in the cosmic part. You have a term 'Power Surge' being experienced with you now, undocking the unneeded into the new format coming into view.

"The City of Light is such a 'Cosmic Connection' as I am speaking of with your planet called Earth, but your planet is so much more and needs to be put into the upper level of this thing called Cosmic to a high degree, and so the connection is in process.

"Those you meet here in the Embassy you feel a deep love for, yet you know not them to any degree and yet you have a Cosmic Connection as well. We as a Universal Federation have a Cosmic Connection and it was meant to be.

"You have Personal Soul Guides of love, wisdom and keeping you on your Light path. This is a Cosmic Connection. Meeting souls from a past life can be considered a Cosmic Connection and meant to be for many reasons. Divine Designs are a Cosmic Connection with God. Got the picture?"

G: "Clearly. Thank you. There seems to be a very deep love attached to a Cosmic Connection."

O: "Of course, have you said it is either love or it isn't? Have you not sounded the holy tone with love in mind and shown others this sound and its use and how it re-ignites into the Universe? It pulls together those who have a deep love feeling for no particular reason that they know of. You just know it is so. Now what else can we tap into for your advancement?"

G: "In a few weeks I have been invited to speak with Michael Quinsey on British Internet Radio in Stelle, Illinois. What would be the most important information I can share on The City of Light?"

O: "THAT IT IS SO! Again a Cosmic Connection. Recognize that at the precise moment of speaking on the radio, you will know that all is in divine order and that the words you speak will be the Cosmic Connection as even now, you have with the Michael and the SaluSa. The Holy Tone moves out through your words as love energy, and another part of your planet learns what is coming about and the Cosmic Connection spreads its Love in new territories.

"You Dear One, hold the master key just like the 4 Keys that you teach about. Those many who have been Light-Linked are Emissaries of that data and they lift themselves in the tone soundings, producing again more Cosmic Connections. Your words will hold much promise for others across the waters. Just know That It Is So! Now then what else is to be addressed at this visit?"

G: "It has been said that after the first City of Light (which is a prototype) arrives, that more cities now on the planet grid will also appear. What can be said of this?"

O: "Oh yes, the prototype City of Healing Light even as large as it is, and due to your planet's vast locations, more will also be brought forth in various locations around you planet. Since all must be healed, the intent is to do just that! HEAL! And that means near and far.

"The shock value of the first one will have to be introduced and settled in before any more are delivered as people have to understand what has taken place, as never before has anything of this size and dimension ever been not only seen, but in being able to know it is not just a vision, but the REAL THING. Imagine that!

"The others come to Light in many countries as part and parcel of different cultures and energy patterns. The United States will have three such edifices. As for the rest, time will reveal the locations. First things first and with this it brings the energy patterns for the rest.

"Now then, permit this inquiry to settle a bit for the moment. The first City prototype will be enough to get used to. Take this information back into your world and be it known that your words of wisdom with your love attached will not fall on deaf ears, quite the contrary. For it is indeed a Cosmic Connection first class. Enjoy your trip East and be open for more information to be deposited to you before, during and after.

"You the Genii must recognize that you are considered a City Embassy Emissary of Love. As your physical body accepts the Light of what you call 'Power Surges' it also deposits in your Light Body the tones of universal value. We as your Jedi family (so to speak) support your efforts as you pour City Love where you are invited. As you say quite often, 'God is good.' Enjoy your Cosmic Connections Conversations as we bid you the Light of this universal day in peace and in love. So Light it be!"

And with this he bowed, and the scene disappeared and I was home on a sunny Sunday morning feeling bliss and tears for the blessings I had been given. **Must be a Cosmic Connection!**

"Let your light shine. Shine within you so that it can shine on someone else. Let your light shine." – Oprah

Genii with the "Empowerment Marionette" she made of Oprah

http://www.sedonalightcenter.org/marionettes.htm

And Then There Were Three!

Embassy Visit August 9, 2011

A decision to re-enter The City and the Embassy of Peace was the intent to learn more than I was aware of at the moment. So as quickly as I stopped my daily world and got off in love with inner vision turned on to full speed ahead, the mental shifted through this awesome love and delight of what I might be told this morning that would be shareable. In releasing in the purity of this love unconditional, it just overtook me and I just let go and let God direct.

Ah, a Gate appeared and with it many people excited to also see and learn of what the media attempted to figure out. What was going on with the news, was that something just dropped out of the sky like from Heaven. Could this have been the Second Coming or various mentions of Cities of Light from many unseen masters of knowing? Many must have thought that they had lost their minds. No, it was what it was, and very real....Fun time, I reminded myself of what I had foretold of 'Something's Coming!'. It was not just wishful thinking on my part, but even Genies' get their wishes granted.

Looking at the people, the impact I heard spoken was "Oh My God!" shouted out loud plus "It has to be from God the Creator, for no one had to build it. It just landed complete."

What was going on? Hmm ... Was I losing my mind? If so, this felt pretty good! Looking to move through this maze of amazed people, I felt my City Guide La-Luke behind me and with some kind of space energy, he parted the seas moving the people aside as if by magic. We headed through the Park of Relaxation, onto the trolley and stopped at the Embassy building. I had to catch my breath it all went so fast.

The Hall of Entities making up part of the Universal Federation, made my visits far beyond anything I could think of, even if I was a creator and beyond any words I could share with the public. They got it second-hand, I got it first-hand. Believe you me, it was first class all the way. You can tell I was impressed right? OK, moving right along...

The Embassy stage was set, the audience awaited and the leader of the 5 Entities on stage bowed in welcome.

O: "Ah a quick return I see, with some interests to be discussed."

G: "Yes please. I wish to know about a comment made here, that not only one City of Light is to demonstrate but three in the United States? This is important. Number One, the Sedona prototype and then Number 2 and Number 3. How accurate is this prognosis?"

O smiling: "Yes indeed. When first reported here that one was the total interest as a prototype and the Sedona, Arizona was discussed to give you the entrance picture, even though it was said that more cities would be seen as time went on.

"You recognize that in your world all is a hologram. As an example, the first prototype with its reflections spawn the other two city repeats in the USA. Science dwells big time in space like magic becoming real.

"It took you years to understand that all that comes from the void, the space (the no-thing, nothing) and that people create from it into whatever they want. The nothing has all the ingredients to make something look real which is still an illusion, but one so real it is believed to be so, good, bad or otherwise. Before you can make bread you must bring forth the flour and the other ingredients. First things first. Fact or fiction both are the same to bring forth on the Earth map. It is still all a hologram. Even the computer you are typing this on or the car you ride in or even the plane you fly in.

"From your teaching of the 4 Holy Keys of Light you speak of the Creator creating through you for whatever you want. Each human is a magical magician who produces their power in creating the polarity in their lives. With the Number One City of Light, think of what would take place to have more Cities of Light all on this planet.

"Would it not send Light into the Universe as people enter into its domain to be healed? As huge as it is, more of the same would be desired to take care of what the intent is to be. Taking care of populations alone in the USA is a major project, much less the world. So 3 are intended at this point, concentrating on the first. First, then that Light field sends out its frequencies to the blueprint and the next is activated. Help is on the way.

"You receive many of what you say' 'handy hints' of what is coming about from masters, angels etc. lifting human spirits such as Michael Quinsey's SaLuSa and even your Intelligences (soul guides).Then does this answer your questions?"

G: "Yes, it is a Holographic Universe and I delight in knowing about it. Granting wishes, sending Light, using the imagination, visions, beliefs, all bring dreams forth. What a concept. Thanks."

O: "Quite so, you have been given life to play in and create your desires even a City of Light with the intent of healing the minds, bodies, and making out of misery a life of pleasure. In your child-like humorous ways of sharing love unconditionally, all this makes quite good sense that what you know from our visits is indeed quite real and true.

"Realize that all is well and on schedule as is the 11-11-11 Love Wave that makes its mark of love for all mankind to be able to produce what the Holy Creator gave them, the tools of creating. It is mind over matter. So then what can we add?"

G: "I think you pretty well said it all. Thank you. Any updates on the weeks ahead?"

O: "11-11-11 you are well aware of. Continue to travel as one of your next stops will be in the approximate center of your country and the words spoken from there to energize across the water and will support what is being said here.

Follow your heart, therefore your love beckons to serve you as you will have people not only listening but hearing the truth of the matter.

"We release you to your day knowing that all is in order and The City of Light Sedona once established will birth twins in other locations in your country. This is only the beginning. We will expect to see you again and we of space send you back in the I AM love feeling...so Light it be"

So with that I found myself home looking at the red rocks for maybe just a glimpse of The City of Light Sedona.

So Light I AM!

Domes, Sky Maps and Overseas Conversations!

Embassy Visit August 18, 2011

As I entered The City scenes I was getting a topside overview. This place was huge! Buildings sparkled in the Light producing this effect. It was quite beautiful but what else would one expect, with God being the healing artist and first class? I seemed to fly right to the Embassy door with no one around. Flying over The City? Who me? Why flying? Usually it was a 5-story Gate I entered. Oh well...

This flight picture landed me at the Embassy of Peace and I went through the scented foyer gardens and into the Sanctuary Chamber. The head honcho, OOO-LON (who is the interpreter), held court with hundreds of Universal Federation Space Entities as an audience, along with 4 other Light Beings seated at his horseshoe-shaped table.

O: "Ah, welcome visitor of femininity. Come be part of our gathering and we shall speak in human language with you."

G: "Thank you. I feel I am a part of all this as I have been here so many times with questions, and I bring a couple more that I have been asked to bring."

O: "Yes, we know. You would speak of your homeland Sedona, Arizona and the home of friends who have a dome home. Correct?"

G: "Yes, you are always ahead of me. The questions pertain to the domes themselves and the symbols being painted on them. What can be said for answers? And are there energy changes due to this or not?"

O: "We are well aware of this Earth location and the energy fields attached. The symbols increase the frequencies of the domes as well as being a Sky Map of location intention. Many Light Entities now flood the Sedona area in preparation of the Master Event to take place. Preparation of this City Birthing Nest must be correct and thus several areas have an important part in this scenario.

"What is not seen by human eyes is very busy and complicated to explain to you unless you 'Speak Space.' This Dome home, Stoneman Lake (which is yet another story), Angel Valley, plus more, are prime properties of unseen value along with many portals of entrance. They are important connectors of Light Lines and they connect together, as well as with others topside and the underground as well. Also it has been inquired of you, is this Dome home of a 5th dimension? Quite so. Both you and the lady of Dome Light are close friends and that too is part of this whole scenario.

"Due to the Domes of colors and now various symbols being introduced are signals to Flying Space Vehicles reporting that they are on the right course. This is important directional guide lines for those who take their space work seriously and each Directional Space Engineer mentally driving their space vehicle knows their work is serious."

G: "Is there a visible vortex or wormhole here?"

O: "Wormholes as such have no value at this point. However, these locations just spoken of as vortexes are indeed worthy due to the directional patterns we use to get from one location to another. You use road maps as such. We use energy points as Sky Maps. Your Earth seeing diminishes with what we speak of here. Interpreting the dome colors and symbols' meaning, all is in order and we fulfill the prophecies long since recognized as God's will for peace on Earth, good will to all. Any other questions?"

G: "Yes, in another area, The City of Light appearance through Michael Quinsey via a radio conversation in Europe and wherever. What is to be known of this?"

O: "Expect this conversation to reach beyond the words spoken, for it will reach 'The Hearts of Knowing' as your words speak of what is coming about. The intent of the programming will do what it is intended to do through both the hearts of you and the Michael. Enjoy sharing with the Michael as well as the visit itself with loved ones where it is to take place soon. More updates will be given before you both speak, and divine right order makes the intent... intentional."

G: "Anything else I should know about in any topic?"

O: "Remember that God's love is the reason for The City of Light. All the advanced technical healings to take place here are done Through Light Encased in Love. Light heals where crude instruments now used may not.

"A new world is about to be introduced as you would say 'big time' and this is truth ahead of time delivered. Your planet will take a major jump forward in Light technology not known or experienced on your planet as yet. The scientists try to discover what is already a part of the universal set of things. Here in The City they will come to the Space technology in a Universal University and learn of such things.

"The 11-11-11 debut of the 'Love Wave' which will touch the emotions of everyone, will set the path to the bigger picture. So then we are finished. Return to your world and spread the news that God is alive, well, and quite dramatically will bring into your sights of entrance. The City of Light and such Love as never experienced. Yes, this is so! We release you to your world to have a Love day. We are you."

And with that the scene ended and I was home and the phone was ringing.

Great trip...

Thanks God!

Between Heaven and Earth

Embassy Visit August 22, 2011

Once again with The City Gate open numerous people were waiting to enter (I wondered whoever invented 'waiting in line' when what they really wanted was a 'Disneyland Fast Pass.') I saw La-Luke with a hand raised, so I ventured through the crowd and we almost ran through the Park to the waiting trolley where no 'fast pass' was needed. There were, though, lots of people everywhere.

The trolley dropped us off at the Embassy. It was so surprising, everything in The City seemed so alive, even the trolley. (Disneyland move over!) Into the Embassy Chamber we took ourselves. All entitles were standing in a welcome position and it was quite a sight to behold, almost like being on another planet. Duh!... what else did I expect?

We acknowledged the welcome as OOO-LON spoke: "This, Dear One, is a visit of expectancy and delight. We have been waiting for your return, as we have good news to share."

G: "Thanks, the energy is building through many City books that are being sold all over the planet."

O: "We are aware and this is only the tip of a spaceship ... only the beginning. You see, the energy within the books is meeting the inner feelings of people of your Earth planet. It is becoming equal."

G: "I am thrilled and blessed. What is important to be aware of?"

O: "Good news... great good news. The City in its entirety has made its progress as it enters the ethers of your world, which coincides with the energy of the books. People are feeling more and more that 'Something is Coming!' as you say, on a continual basis to set the sharing scene.

"All is energy, unseen to be true, but energy nevertheless. The closer The City enters, the more feeling people attest to. Even the darkened ones feel something a bit, and that is unnerving and fear can result and rightly so. They cannot hang onto the old patterns now.

"It would be as Heaven and Earth are meeting as The City descends and humans ascend, there is an energy connection. The fact is now that more and more people are interested in what you say, it is a major indication that all is on track. What you say, did and do in The City of Light manuscript is being felt to be true and with no doubts attached.

"The Michael Quinsey has and is a factor in this current scenario. This is cosmic good as The City Book holds the Light and love, pre-intended and now breaks the bonds through Cosmic intentions. Your travel visits will also be in order."

G: "People are asking me now about the other City locations to appear and where? I know not how to respond?"

O: "We are aware this is happening, and at this point the locations are held in secrecy as first things first. The Love Wave of 11-11-11 will be a mind-opener to many. First because people will want it in their location and that in itself is an energy pull, cosmically speaking. The holographic prototype of the first City will be enough to set the course of dramatic interventions on behalf of healing techniques done with loving Light only, so of course people will want one close by in their area. This is noted and will be supplied.

"Right now you are sending City books across the planet from South Africa to New Zealand and nations in between. Surely the first City demonstration will pull enough energy to satisfy humans across the globe internationally that one in close proximity will be on the God map too. Let it be said that what is taking place right now, through your visits and your handwriting mailing the data out will reach places unknown to you on this adventure.

"The Impossible will be seen as Possible, (and good news can tone in faster than bad when given a chance.) Sedona is an energy booster to all in what you are asked to do. It is known that the Charles has had hands-on training to pull people's interests to The City books and beyond and plays a key role to the projects at hand. The time will come when all this service of mailing will be taken out of your hands as you have advanced work to do to keep the interest going forward and people will want to hear it first-hand. So then, does this give you an indication that The City shift of Light has taken place?"

G: "You bet, people want to hear good news."

O: "Well, you have just been given an indication of how and what is taking place one step at a time...Cosmic time that is. Go now and continue to do your part as all is well in that which is unseen. We shall speak again soon."

With this I acknowledged his words as the scene faded away and I was finding myself home on a sunny Sedona day with a pile of books for me to travel in story form all over the planet. Now that was good news.

Thanks to God for the original idea of bringing peace on Earth; Michael Quinsey, for spreading the news; Charles for putting The City book all together; Bill Townsend for trans-audioing the drawings, etc. and even...me for whatever the heck I was chosen to do.. Imagine that!

So Light it be!

From Infinity and Beyond

Embassy Visit August 30, 2011

It was quiet and serene in Sedona this morning, and with my little white fluffy puppy named Light enjoying a snack, I reached out and into my other world to gather guidance from those Light Beings in The City of Light Embassy who knew more about what was going on than I did.

It seemed that I was a visionary (so-called) and seeing visions was my bag of talents (so I was told). I could tap into this City of Light and especially at this point, the Embassy of Peace where dwells hundreds of Peacekeepers from space also known as the Galactic Federation.

So with love in my heart, and open to receive any information on any topic, from these Entities from Space with a whole lot of Light attached, I slipped into the upcoming vision where I found myself once more at a Gate of Entrance. Many other people also had the same idea, to get a peek into this Divine Holy City that packed a lot of 'Love Healing' behind the Gate. Who would have ever thought that I would be doing such far-out visits?...Not me! I pull strings and grant wishes.

So as I went to infinity and beyond for the good of all people, I thought to myself"..."Okay Jedi Genii, let's go meet the Space Lights inside"."

Maneuvering myself was as parting the seas, as my Guide La-Luke waved me through with some kind of magic. We ran through the Recreation Park and onto the waiting trolley that deposited us at the Embassy. We moved into the Space Sanctuary where an audience of hundreds of Space Light Entities from infinity and beyond held court. They bid us welcome (with enough love to knock your socks off.) Imagine that! And I was not the President or a VIP that I knew of. I just nodded in respect.

Head Honcho OOO-LON spoke: "And a joyous welcome to someone who spreads the words of The City. Come and join us in love, and we shall share wisdom from another space place."

G: "Thank you all. I am most delighted to be back for any reason."

O: "What may we share with you this visit?"

G: "With the help of very close friends, The City of Light books are being accepted at this point in 11 countries. I am receiving gracious replies of acceptance and joy. Many say they want a City Healing of Light in their area and pray that it is possible. What am I to respond?"

O: "We would refer to them as Hot Spots of Energy on your planet. It is noted and of course the reading of your City book is inducing more interest in this area...and rightly so. Just that interest in itself begets Light-powered frequencies. "The other City locations at this point, we would say are 'under wraps' yet quite active energy-wise.

274

"If you could see on your planet map of the other locations, it would indeed be a delight. However, all attention should be on Number One, the beginning, the prototype, located to arrive at the Sedona, Arizona USA location area. Much technology has been put into Number One and it is the reason you are living in Sedona at this point in time. Concentrate on Number One and the rest will be revealed somewhere in time. This you can be sure of.

"As for The City books, this Dear One is just the beginning. They will multiply like seeds of love into the public, thus spreading the words around the globe. It has been so ordained to do so. Between now and then on your calendar, you and others close to you will become quite busy.

"We understand that you are to speak radio-wise to Europe soon. This too was preset like an act on a stage. Let's say you are in stage # 3 with #4 coming up. The Cosmic Community oversees what is going on overseas. Light is being injected there as well as in Asia."

G: "Tell me please more of the Cosmic Federation."

O: "Who and what we are has been spoken of, and we continue to fill you in as progress is made, for this Galactic Federation is huge and has much been in The City."

G: "I feel sure this is just the beginning of something super-charged like 11-11-11 has been said. The Earth's weather patterns and changes have people uneasy as it is different than anything before and is unfamiliar. What can be said of this topic?"

O: "The frequencies of this extremely huge City would indeed influence the atmosphere in this category. As you say 'something is coming!' The City of Light has power all of its own, unseen on your planet. It is alive with Light and thus certain changes within your Earth's atmosphere would take place. We do what we can to make the entry as normal as possible, but this entry is not normal and the effect is indeed producing cleansing vibrations most of which also change the way things were done in the past.

"You are done with all of that. You humans just don't realize that at this point, but you will for nothing will be like it was. The frequencies will be different and much lighter and people will want to experience that, rather than the old dark use of ways. This is happening now, right now. You yourself feel the change impacting yourself with less concern and so much love centered, that people are feeling it in your writings and in person. Destruction is not easy, but from it comes the new clean place and readied to be enjoyed.

"We came from beyond your local thinking and from galaxies beyond galaxies for this revelation to be placed in human sight for personal healings that have been too long in finding the mental causes of each illness. It will now, with The City of Light eliminate this tedious process where pain holds court. We bring technology of Light. This is the new way, the only way to give notice that illness no longer holds power.

275

"You have been to the Light Modules. What was used to heal? Light...of course. Fantastic in its Light waves, it knows the frequency power it holds. What The City holds will totally change the course of how people think about getting healed.

"Doctors will learn what they are not aware of now. People can throw away the needles, knives, and even drugs. You humans are all drug-filled. It is time to release the old way of pills and anything to stop the pain.

"Mental technology in The City of Light will do that and so much more. We have not left out anything and you will not want to go back to the old ways of drowning yourselves in drugs and their counterparts.

"Rest easy Dear One, send out The City books and even the Charles has begun the computer areas for advanced notifications and updates on blogs etc. You the Genii will be receiving more than just adequate guidance as we proceed with you. The possibilities are endless just like infinity and beyond. We decree this to be God. So has this been of help?"

G: "Oh my yes. My steps now are?"

O: "Spread the word that The City of Light comes soon, as do we from the Universe. Suggest 'LOVE' is the ointment that heals and to use that! Go now, your human day awaits your attention and we will speak again soon."

G: "Wow! I am blessed to do my part sending love within each signing of the books. Thank you all here and beyond for the love you send us constantly."

O: "Come back and we shall again join in questions and answers, cosmic to be sure but right on target. We bid you the Light of the eternal day from somewhere in time. So Light it be!"

And with this, my Guide and I left the Embassy and hopped on the funny trolley, went back to the Gate and with a hug said goodbye. I was back in my room looking to have a happy day in every way and wishing that for you too.

The City Birthing!

Embassy Visit September 15, 2011

Slipping out of the Earth's gravity and into another state of somewhere in non-time where the energies of Mid-America held cornfields and peace, I looked to enter into a space known to lead me to The City Embassy.

The Gate of Entrance was filled with people eager to see what this illusion was all about. I was one of them as I looked to find La-Luke. He found me and with his own magic moved aside people. Like parting the seas, we ran through the Park and to the funny trolley that took us to the Embassy and another encounter with those of Light. The stage was set as usual and the 5 Light Entities stood in our recognition ... we were welcomed.

O: "A bit busy out there is it?"

G: "Yes, everyone is excited to be able to get in to see what all the excitement is about. The word spreads quickly."

O: "Such a demonstration of The City ... interest would do that."

G: "Is what I am seeing, what they will be doing as The City reveals itself?"

O: "Of course! The Light shines forth like a beacon in the night. You in your pre-vision visits have the picture pretty secure in your own mental, so you know why The City attraction attracts. Now, what can we speak of today?"

G: "Does the date 12/27/2011 have anything to do with The City arrival? I may have missed a cue someplace."

O: "The date has validity in that the pressures of people declaring that The City will appear as announced one day or another depends on the results of the 11-11-11 wave of love. As said many times, the energy of the people's desires can pull the curtain open so-to-speak and the revelation forth-coming. To tie it down to one day, one hour, one minute even depends on the human mental equation.

"We in The Federation also want to see when this will take place. The 11-11-11 has been noted and set in place ... The City, not quite yet. As the energy peaks, the Birth date will be known. Between the 11th date and the date you asked about (12/27/11), you Earth people celebrate Christmas plus other events.

"At this point, we leave you guessing. Maybe yes - maybe no and the mystery unfolds at its own pace. You will be notified as the Sedona energy will have its own peaking. Question answered?"

G: "I am easy with this, at least for the moment. Next question: The radio show with Michael Quinsey yesterday to England and places unknown ... what reaction can be expected?"

O: "As you have said, the door has opened and the word spreads. It will explode into more avenues and the energy rises in unison for ' The Coming.' Just be ready to do what you are guided to do and watch what happens! You will be pleased.

"The Light leads and the doors of the unknown make their mark of welcome to the lady who speaks truth of such an appearance. Anything else to be addressed this meeting?"

G: "That pretty well covers it, I guess."

O: "Your current trance is not yet completed so just be open to any new insights that come to you upon the home return ... more can be added. For now, enjoy the rest and play and we shall speak again."

So Light it Be!

And with this, the Embassy scene released itself and I was again in Stelle, IL at Renee's home, delighted to have time with her and whoever would come into the day.

Received during my visit to Stelle, Illinois (http://www.stellecommunity.com)

The Oreo Cookie Connection

(ONE DREAM! ONE PEOPLE! ONE PLANET!)

Setting the scene: Leaving the physical corn fields and Community of Stelle, Illinois, I mentally opened myself to The City Embassy of Peace visit. The usual Gate appeared as did my City Guide La-Luke, who hustled me through the crowd also looking to enter. The energies seemed a bit different, but I was also physically in another location, the one of my birth (Illinois), long since left behind for the West Coast.

In the vision, we made our way through the Park of Relaxation and the trolley stood still awaiting our hop-on-move, thus taking us to the Embassy of Peace.

The Entities of Light looked to be all standing as we approached the stage, except for OOO-LON who entered from stage right and took his place at the head table with the other 4 faces. He nodded to us as we approached this interesting far-out group of Light Beings. I got to sit in the center, facing them all as La-Luke stepped back to observe.

O: "Another visit! How nice, and what dear Lady, can we advise you of today in this place of honor and truth?"

G: "Thank you for receiving me again. Many times have I been privileged to attend and report to people. I have recently been introduced to another part of the Earth. What can you tell me of our Inner Earth, Hollow Earth, and Telos, a subterranean city beneath Mt. Shasta?"

O: "Oh Yes! The Inner Earth story has now come to your attention and this is good and proper.

"Is this correct? Quite so. Those who reside there and elsewhere in the subterranean locations are equal brothers and sisters of the sky entities. They are one ... more so than many people <u>on</u> the planet Earth (which we call Sula).

"Your planet is quite alive and active. As you recently remarked, your people are like an oreo cookie, with humans in the middle like the frosting, receiving support from top and bottom. Yet this inner frosting place is mostly people unaware of what is really taking place top-side as well as on the bottom."

G: "Is this where The City comes in?"

O: "Quite so ... time to stir up this cookie filling and connect top and bottom, for together the center makes the delicacy completely tasty.

"The City is acknowledged by both The Space Entities of Light and the Hollow Earth beings and all are looking to The City appearance to be enjoyed. While shaking up where you are residing, the planet is a whole active entity encased in God Light and ready to be newly birthed which excludes the universal space, which for the most part is unknown.

"So then as you read and adjust to this new bit of information, you have already met some of the Hollow Earth people at Stoneman Lake. Remember The Seekers?"

G: "Ahh Yes! Quite so. Charles and I have visited this holy place as often as possible as we have been introduced to and have spoken with The Elders of Light. We know that this small lake is magical, and that we are to keep it in Holy prayer."

O: "Yes indeed, you have data on this place already written as a portal of Light, refreshing the sky crafts as they enter and re-enter in support of The City, along with the vortexes which are energy-wise very high-powered and getting more so.

"The Hollow Earth beings use portals to see what is happening top-side, so to speak. Thus you have The Seekers who transferred there to hold the Light and Power connection. So now you have another piece of the puzzle connecting outer space with inner space. Amazing, isn't it?"

G: "I am so glad that I am here to experience all this. What an adventure! Wow!"

O: "And it is only the beginning. As The City enters, the middle cookie filling (so to speak) both top and bottom work in unison to bring forth this new filling that then all can enjoy. As you say, 'God is good.' And it is so."

G: "What am I to know or do with this new information I am reading about?"

O: "Do just that. Read and learn. Return to Stoneman Lake in quiet prayer and speak with The Elders. Your and Charles' attachment is not finished yet. Bring forth the data you received on the portal and the sun and the moon shall support this place with human energy. Is there more?"

G: "No. Thank you. At this point I shall read and make notes of what to review and ask about. Oh Yes, excuse me! How is The City timing progressing and people ask if 11-11-11 is The City appearance or 12-27-2011? What can you tell me?"

O: "The non-dates of time will be revealed after or during the 11-11-11 period of time. The Love Wave sets the course and The Genii's mind of having it be a great Christmas present would put it in the 12th month time line. Patience, Dear One, patience. Enjoy the 11-11-11 Love Wave. Maybe Santa has 2 gifts this year? Wait and see. You will know as it gets closer to its own time line."

G: "Well, it would be a wonderful Christmas gift and The Christ Birthday. Wow! That would really make a connection."

O: "At this point just know that with the energy produced with 11-11-11 anything is possible, but time (your time) will give you clues along the way. Just for now, tell the people One event at a time (11-11-11 first). So, all through with questions?"

G: "Anything else to add?"

O: "Your books of this place (City of Light Sedona) will be what you call a 'Best Seller' as the word spreads through the metaphysical people and your personal attendance requests to speak and inform. What has just taken place will just be the door opener, for This City of Light book has an energy all its own.

"The meeting with President Obama is still on the Light Line. It could come out of left field (as you say). Just be open. The Renee has opened many doors and she is not through yet.

"Now then, return to your visit and rest. This helps everything you are into in your world. We send you back in love and look to see you return. One step at a time."

I thanked them and a humanoid ran through the audience faintly seen. I returned to Stelle, IL to rest and play, as my companions for tomorrow would return home. I had a little white puppy waiting for me. ~~

So Light it Be!

Unprecedented, Unlimited Universal Power!

Embassy Visit September 25, 2011

"Believe you me, it is amazing to see" I thought as I entered once more into my inner vision status passageway into The City of Light and the Embassy of Peace. Each visit usually had my own questions, but today I brought a couple more and from far away Austria at that. What fun!

The 5-story Gate Complex was very crowded, but the happiness was very plain to see. The excitement was on and smiles were everywhere. How blessed we were!

My Guide La-Luke waved from up front and finally I got to grab his hand as we ran through the Park of Relaxation with the funny trolley awaiting us to hop aboard. So we did ... and a short ride left us off at the magnificent Embassy building holding within its center hundreds of space friends who had the intelligence, desire and love to help bring forth this God creation; and without us having to do a thing but uplift our consciousness.

Making our way from backstage to stage front, we saw OOO-LON and his Light Entities again in place at the interesting-looking table (if indeed it was a table?). OOO-LON beckoned us to move forward closer, and relaxing, we did so.

You have to know that just the energy in this huge amphitheater was overwhelming, as LOVE was the powerful feeling here. Note: If 11-11-11 is anything like this feeling, we are in for a great time.

O: "Ah ... welcome back. Much has been accomplished since your last visit. We understand that you have questions from some place on the planet. Proceed."

G: "Yes, thank you. I have been given 2 questions" I said, as I bow to these 5 up-close-and-personal Light Entities on the stage in front of me, and I waved to those in the audience. Couldn't see them clearly, but maybe they waved back.

"A new friend named Russ Michael in the country of Austria, has asked and I quote ...

> '1. Will newly awakened souls to the Light on Earth have a conscious portal access to The City of Light Sedona, when the critical mass is reached and entry by the masses in 2012 occurs?
>
> 2. Also, how about 3 conscious December 2012 Christmas gifts:
>
>> A. The City of Light Sedona
>>
>> B. The Golden Age on Earth
>>
>> C. The mass ascension of humanity, without experiencing physical body death, as all Ascended Masters have done in the past?'"

O: (Smiling) "Of course. This whole holy plan is in process to reveal to all what the new life is all about. Actually most are still in the mental programming of what 2012 will initiate, not taking note that time energy as you know it to be is collapsing, and the so-called due date may be a surprise. The new way of thinking is however being resorted from the ashes of the old thinking, and in doing so, progress could be well before that considered date of Christmas 2012. Imagine that!

"Remember those of mastery have preset a mental time slot of 2012, so the mental has a place of refinement to achieve certain assertions ... a time line so to speak. This planet is being opened and it is ascending in energy to permit the masses to consider thinking Light instead of ignorant thoughts that perpetrated this process to be initiated in the first place. The City of Light opens its arms to all so to speak.

"As for the 3 golden gifts ... again to be repeated, this planet is right now in such a situation as has never been done before. Please hear this people ... what is about to appear has never appeared before. By the dates of 12-12-12 all will see the new advancement on this little speck of cosmic dust that will become a golden Light in the heavens, that will help Light up the Universe as was 'intoned' in the first place beginning with 11-11-11, and by 1-1-2013 a new world will be Light-filled and open to meet new worlds of universal communities.

"No longer will your planet be dark due to ignorant thinking as this is a total cleansing and a curing. Dark thoughts will have been banished, and there will have been a lifting of the people that will be healthy in body and mind.

"As said, we play not games here. This process of healing is the way and everyone wins no matter what way they are thinking ... just changed quite a bit as needed. Your so-called time leaves little time to complete what is ahead for all of you.

"You, The Genii, are a teacher of the 4 Holy Keys to Light and of what the so-called soul consists of. Having given this teaching for many years, your students now look through new eyes of de-Lighten-ment!

"First the 11-11-11, speaking of time. From these dates of transmission with LOVE being the common denominator, this process will make the world feel better and will allow people to see others in a new Light as the Light of love drops episodes of anger and fear. One cannot fear in true GOD LOVE! It is impossible!

"Space technology holds many secrets yet untold and many are now in use through this change-over. Permit yourselves to be open, and if something precious leaves ... permit it, for the space-making way brings in the new updated things that are ready to serve. These are precious days ahead filled with joy, wonder, excitement, and pure love with no strings attached (a bit of humor for The Genii's puppet pulling.)

"Dear One, get set for the grand finale is near and the new production will astonish, heal and open doors for the mystical space technology being put into action.

"You have met personally now space entities of Light, and the Inner Earth, and Hollow Earth who are willing to give what your planet needs to release all that is negative, while opening doors to the abundance coming in. Open doors ... exposing the greatness of God who brings forth such a production.

"SaLuSa has reported much through Michael Quinsey and others are noted for their inner connections. The City of Light manuscripts are also moving into hands of delighted Earthlings for they sense the truth of its contents. More books will be going out as well. Venture to where you can share what has been given to you as you are invited. This is just the beginning, for in the next few months miracles can occur and everyone benefits one way or another. Have I answered your questions with enlightenment?"

G: "Yes, quite so."

O: "Space beings and the people of Hollow Earth meet with delight to do service in Love and Light with attention to details. Take this visit back to your world. God brings God to your planet and all is divinely guided and on schedule. Thank you for coming."

G: "Thank you all. I would request more space teaching for me, please."

O: "Of course. Set your course. As a Jedi master in training, we shall respond and you will speak space very well!"

And with that I just smiled, nodded, and bowed, and we backed off the stage and out the door. With a hug from my Guide, I found myself back home with a little white fluffy thing on 4 legs wanting breakfast.

So Light it be!

Thinking the Impossible!

Embassy Visit October 1, 2011

My inner City vision took on a life of its own as I became centered and silent ... opening to receive through vision and sound, while I watched the inner movie unfolding. Ahh, the first scene was at one of the 5-story Gates of Entrance. Crowds of happy excited people were waiting to enter. Meeting my Guide La-Luke we moved through the welcoming arches with people who wanted to see what this healing place is about and the God-wonders inside.

It is indeed Immaculate in its Conception and could only be brought forth from the Creator of us all. We could not build this City ourselves even if we wanted to, but we CAN go inside and get healed of whatever ails us. La-Luke and I moved with the crowds of smiling people (just like I do going into Disneyland where fun and laughter becomes the healer). It is interesting that no matter who I was next to with a different language, I could easily understand what they were saying, even though I didn't speak their language. Imagine that! OK. Moving right along ...

We almost ran through the Park of Relaxation, by-passing the massage benches and hopped on the trolley. As always it took us to the Embassy of Peace Headquarters wherein hundreds of Universal Federation space (Light) beings reside, who made up the background audience in this huge arena. This was some kind of place. I was ever in awe when I came here. Wow!

The head honcho named OOO-LON has been taught to speak our language. The rest only "speak space" as far as I could tell. It was good to be in such friendly territory. Note: Anyone who says the E.T.'s are coming to conquer us ... Relax! As they told me, "What's to conquer?" Who wants all of this disturbance that you send out to each other, as well as the destruction you have done to your Earth and your forests?" Relax ... All is well.

O: "Welcome Dear One, person of humanness. We look to share more time with you. How may we be of service?"

G: "Thanks, it really is an honor to be with all of you. I wonder how we humans are doing as we enter another month (October) in regard to The City coming forth with space technology that we don't have here, as well as 11-11-11? As we say here, 'What's up'?"

O: "Time so called has now entered The City into its descent of your atmosphere. The 'Way' still remains to be determined, as it is held into the structure of its own energy. 'This Coming' will be activated by the response of people to the 11-11-11 Love Wave, which makes the path of human connection. The masses have much to do with The City entrance. The Wave of Love will be experienced by all. Not one person will be left out. Most humans have the openness for more love. They need to feel that 'Holy Oneness' of it, as God (or whatever their understanding of it) takes over, thus raising the level of Heart Consciousness and connection with each other. This new level of consciousness will determine the acceptance of what will be experienced from a much higher level.

"Personal Guides and Protectors (called Gatekeepers) of each individual will recognize that individually they can bring forth a vision or a knowingness in their charges. Never before has there been such a human awareness as will come to each person who wants to know ... as you teach in the 4 Keys to Light sessions, where meeting one's own Guides is discovered and they are contacted. Never before have the almost-silent inner Personal Guides come out in an en-masse introduction to be recognized by those in their care.

"It will be seen to these Personal Guides as a permission to enter into a verbal contact as well as a visual contact with their charges. (Like the Genii being released from the lamp of containment in the Aladdin Disney show). There are millions upon millions of Personal Guides who will make themselves known with the help of prominent well-known masters that most people know of. It is time for Inner Guides to be known, to be released, and to be recognized ... and The Genii can help to do it.

"First, the Love Wave and then The City of Light expected somewhere in time. 'It has been a long process to bring The City about, but nevertheless it will happen when the majority least expect it."

G: "My current instructions are to bring to the general public what has been secret for eons of time and only given to a select few. What advice can you give me on this as I proceed forward?"

O: "This is true. What has been hidden now becomes the leading pathway of Light elevation, with more 4 Keys teachers being groomed to share the teaching with more students. Continue as guided and know all is well and on course. Eventually the electronic devices will assist, but with a personal session included.

"Now then as said, the course of the 11-11-11 Love Wave is set in place making way for The City of Light. Time has shortened in your Earth space and we are pleased with your space work. Be open and patient and recognize that The President Obama is still on the list as well as The United Nations. They will hear your words of, 'Something is Coming.'

"As said of Michael Quinsey's SaLuSa who speaks truth, and the blessed Russ Michael who is sending your messages out to the masses, there is much good team-work happening, and someone will open the doors to the White House for your entry.

"You can expect more and more people to reach for you as The City of Light Sedona books attract may more hands, as they follow their Inner Guides. Indeed this is good news and many Inner Guides now prepare to be known openly, as they serve their charges. Anything else?"

G: "Just another 'thank you.' I will do what I can with love, and I feel the honor to do so. It has been a long adventure since this began in 1982 with Dr. Bill's discovery. Since he made his transition in 1997, I have tried to carry the ball, so-to-speak, and I will continue to do so. I am blessed!"

O: "ALL WILL SEE AND ENTER INTO THE CITY OF LIGHT, as the Personal Guides rejoice that they will be known and accepted as Inner Light Beings. Party Time! Imagine that!

"Even the Hollow Earth people rejoice! You should be available for more visits here as time leaves, and The City descends. We bid you a glorious day in every way. So Light it Be!"

And with this, all of the beings stood, and La-Luke and I headed for the trolley, the Park, and the Gate where I came in. The scene ended with a hug from my City Guide and I was back home on a sunny day in Sedona with my puppy Light Spirit looking for food.

SO LIGHT IT BE!

TO YOU FROM ME.

The Wave of Predestination!

Embassy Visit October 8, 2011

A sudden decision to return to the Embassy of Peace City of Light destination for an up-date on The City, led me to my quiet time with pen and paper to write of what might be revealed through my visioning and sound bytes.

The air around one of The City Gates was filled to overflowing with joyous sounds as people rushed to enter and see this magnificent dropped-from-the-sky attraction. I felt myself being pushed and sensed my Guide La-Luke was doing the pushing and a peek behind showed that I was right.

So it was once again into the Park of Relaxation, onto the funny trolley and "all aboard" for the inside baseball- park size auditorium. Inside there were hundreds of Light (E.T.) Beings of a Space Federation of such love that it about took my breath away. Wow! OOO-LON was the main contact here for he spoke my language. The rest as far as I could tell, spoke space which I was learning to do.

O: "Welcome, Oh Light spirit of magic Genii. What may we share in honor of this visit? Even genies get their wishes granted."

G: "I would appreciate any UPDATE on what I can share with others in relationship to 11-11-11 and The City demonstration."

O: "Update quite so...currently the Light frequency of love has begun. Look at it from the vantage point of it being like an ocean wave (for example). It begins slowly, quietly and picks up momentum turning into a huge wave that collects all that is in its path.

"To answer your question ...

"The LOVE WAVE' has begun on your planet, so you will see much unrest and greed being brought into the Light of this wave and cleaned up, as it is touched by this God Wave of Intent. So by the time it tips and splashes over the Earth's surface, and all (Including everyone) on its surface, will feel the acceleration of God's love splash.

"As this LOVE WAVE pulls itself back, it takes all the darkness with it and no one will be the same as before. It will be like the whole planet is breathing a-new and all at the same time. Imagine that!

"Anger, frustration and fear will disappear. Since there is no anger or no worries, there will be no fear. If there is no fear, there can only be love. As these emotions get diluted and disappear, in their place are feelings of love, joy, peace and abundance for there is no scarcity. All become victorious without fighting, for you are emerged in the Love Wave and people will look at their lives differently, for the darkness of thinking has been washed away. Get the picture?

"As for The City of Light, this 11-11-11 LOVE WAVE must come first and dilute and clear out what has just been said, such as people who control through greed, and permit the truth to shine like the sun. It has already begun to clear things from people's minds making room for the new way of thinking. This then begins with the 11-11-11 scenario making room for The City of Light to descend filling the void, and many will open their arms, for God has brought healing help like no amount of humans could.

"These are precious times right now. You are saying, 'PAY ATTENTION: GOOD NEWS, SOMETHING BIG IS COMING!' And with the support of several world-wide website friends, those words are making people feel better as people are reporting back, 'You give us hope for a better world.'

"The City of Light books are being read in many countries now, and this is only the beginning. You can expect an avalanche soon from those new readers who want others to know what has been printed, spreading the news that help is on the way. The whole planet is cleansing as you know, having been a visitor here for some many years. Since you are theater trained, look at this as a 4 act play.

"Act One1 and Act Two have been completed.

"Act Three is 11-11-11. LOVE WAVE.

"Act Four is the Grand Finale thus bringing Light into a new world and Act Four is on the horizon. Imagine that! Anything else to be addressed?"

G: "Wow... Thank you. It looks like all is on course. One of the surprises of late is the advancing the 4 Sacred Keys to Light sessions, as it was so closed for eons of time. Now I work with people's Personal Guides that are coming out to be known and the Light Linking opening of the sacred corridor has me busy. What can you say of this?"

O: "Indeed we are not surprised. As the Light moves in the advancement of many, they will desire to participate in your sessions as they learn more of themselves than perhaps they previously knew. You have long since given the 4 Keys to unlock and elevate new students to go along with these changes now taking place.

"All is on course. You will be asked to travel more and more, as people will want to hear what you say in person. So keep available to have them invite you to be brought to various places and to be paid for your efforts. It is quite a fair exchange for this information is not generally known. Expect the unexpected, for it is here and now and all is in divine right order. So then go and give what you have been given and know that all is well. So Light it be!"

And with that the vision disappeared, and I was back home with my puppy Light Spirit ready to jump into the day.

As said "So Light it be!"

Of 11-11-11 and Santa Claus!

Embassy Visit October 21, 2011

I saw myself racing through the Greeting Gate heading for La-Luke who stood with open arms of greeting. He grabbed my hand and lifted me up on the usual trolley to the Embassy. All the energies I felt at this moment were rushing. Why the rush? I knew time was collapsing but....????

It was off the trolley and into the Embassy where OOO-LON and others I could see were standing in welcome. We were acknowledged and OOO-LON began the conversation.

O: "You sense the excitement?"

G: "Ah! Like never before. What is going on?"

O: "The passive energies of your daily life now take on an upswing. The City of Light heads into demonstration with its possibilities before the year is completed. Permit this to be a factor of interest for this visit."

G: "Am I to share this with others as this Embassy visit goes out to many people now, and my, how quickly it spreads."

O: "The 11-11-11- scenario will be the teller of this tale as it depends on the action elevation of the people, but the sensing is this year will end happily with the highest frequencies apparent. We of the Cosmic Federation see and know all is well on course with the multitude of Lightworkers ready, willing and able to be open to such a demonstration.

"You have noticed that your '4 Keys to Light' having been very quietly given, have now exploded with invitations to have you speak to groups on The City and the 4 Keys of God Lights. What was under wraps before is now open for release and you have seen the quick responses of your teachings. This Dear One is only the tip of the iceberg so to speak."

G: "With The City of Light so close as you are saying, I have a friend in Phoenix who asks about a center to be built. She has sent me the plans. She wants to know if she should continue or not (at this point) in building such a Light place. One day yes, one day no."

O: "The vision plan is good and well decided. It is advised since what is being said here re: times and appearances that she and the others just hold for a bit on any decision until the year's end, at which time so much more will be known so the decision will be correct. This is a waiting period, just a pause, but all will be plainly known of which way."

G: "Can you tell me how much land The City will use?"

O: "Much more than the average space as miles will take up that space. There are many acres unoccupied that hold the Light for this birth. We recognize that in your third dimension there is mental difficulty in understanding, and this wondering gives one practice to surrender to what is coming about. Just know that all is well.

"The buildings you see and have entered here are huge and must hold many people. You can expect the roads to your location to be quite full with the expectancy and excitement to see this demonstration wonder that God has birthed. And no wonder, as its magnificence will herald in a new aura of Light.

"We here are also excited as well, for we have seen the process from the beginning and the universal entities rejoice in its manifestation. You will be invited to speak on this and The 4 Keys of Light Absolute as more days move into place. The GOD LIGHT shines on those who are open to receive. Have we answered your questions?"

G: "Anything else to be known?"

O: "Just to attend the invitations and speak plus expect great results from this day forward as each day moves closer to The City of Light with 11-11-11 being the trolley ride. So be ye Light and all else will be sensed as correct."

And with this we bowed as we felt the love, and Genii and La-Luke left the building wondering what Santa Claus is doing this year? Time will tell, and after all these years of knowing ... I am ready ...

Ho! Ho! Ho!

Some Things Seem Right!

Embassy Visit October 25, 2011

VISION: Excitement was high as I entered the familiar City Gate heading for the Embassy of Peace. My senses were all aglow as I looked forward to asking a certain question of OOO-LON and his Embassy friends (of this outer space encoded group of hundreds of E.T.'s). The energy here was just pure love with these friends from far away planets etc.

I then saw myself standing in front of OOO-LON the head CEO as he beckoned me to join them, and a seat was provided by my Guide La-Luke as he stepped back out of vision range.

O: "A quick return I see of the Genii Light. How may we serve?"

G: "A good morning to you all. Yes, I have a question that has stemmed from yesterday's morning inner guidance, which somehow ties The City into Christmas this year. What can be revealed to me please?"

OOO-LON smiled as he toned something to this vast audience and a return response tone snuggled around me like a warm blanket.

O: "The due date as on your calendar makes itself known that during the holiday season the IMPRINT of The City already set in place, could find itself demonstrated to the surprise and delight of millions who dwell in various denominations and customs and even the non-believers will have another chance to believe in the impossible.

"Those who are Christ followers will rejoice as it looks to be the 2nd coming long since predicted, and finds that a New Heaven on Earth has landed and it could only be a God-gift to humanity. Those who follow other well-known paths will find that it also fits their profile as well, and all are seen as one.

"In the children's play of Santa Claus and surprise gifts, one could see this as Santa Claus getting the applause, even in his suit of red power trimmed in white purity. People will feel the re-birth filled with joy and love no matter who or what they believe in. This is holy. All the previous Cities seen in the ethers become this one mentally. Sadness will turn into joy, Darkness into Light, Love into more of the same, but so much deeper as nothing but God's love of this planet could do anything less. From space, this planet will shine like a signal that one more planet is joining the Light system of many others, for the healing of this very special kind has been initiated, and peace on Earth is secured. Has this helped?"

G: "Yes as people keep asking me when? And I have not been given a definite date to respond to. What can we Lightworkers do to assist as time is quite short?"

O: "Just to know that this is possible, brings forth desires and the ability to enjoy the thoughts of the possibilities of a new world setting in place. Thus, all the energies attract as the law of attraction is in action and the power of the human's mental thoughts gives it power.

"Would this give people delight-filled thoughts of a gift like no other? Would this be acceptable in their eyes as it is in Spirit's?

"Power thinking Dear One is not only yours, but many Lightworkers as well. You could say it is Team Lightwork. Not just sitting around waiting for something to happen, but being a part of the demonstration as well....

A CHRISTMAS CITY OF LIGHT: EVERYONE'S HOLY HOLIDAY SPECTACULAR.

"You have followed this scenario for many years, MAYBE IT IS NOW TIME FOR A CELEBRATION LIKE NO OTHER ... EVER.

"Between then and now you will be very busy bringing forth the news of the possibilities, where they can become probabilities just because they sense within themselves that they have heard the truth. Imagine that! Understand?"

G: "Yes it is not in my hands but in the hearts and hands of many. I was told I would speak to the President. Is the path opening to talk to him?"

O: "Watch and see as message carriers knowing of The City birth carry the word. Just be open and see what transpires. The humans of this planet want everything as you say in black and white, when the fun of the adventure is not knowing when certain connections are made, and then say it was a coincidence. No such happenings, as the Law of Attraction is again in process. Nothing happens by chance, you say this repeatedly.

"When certain things take place, surprise and delight come when least expected. Ahhhh, that is the fun part and God loves fun too. Look who got born. Maybe even Santa is real after all. Linking up with others is like putting pieces of the puzzle together and Voila! ... friends become family of a universal kind like us, here in the Embassy.

"We are all connected in a Universal Federation and together bring forth what we are speaking of here. So then return home and spread the word that joy and happiness is on the way in the expected for now, unseen Holy City of Light that will be too big to put under the tree. Imagine that!"

G: "Thank you. I will share what has been told me and we Lightworkers will send the power energy and bring in this gift worth waiting for."

And with that my Guide and I left the building, said goodbye to each other, and I found myself back home looking at the sky for any sign of a Christmas Miracle.

It's All Show Biz!

Embassy Visit November 4, 2011

I had really not pre-planned to go into The City of Light, but an inner feeling of "go to the Embassy" changed all that as it tugged at my heart and since we were then in the beginning stages of 11-11-11 (a week from the date of this entry) I was delighted to be given another invitation. So like Alice in Wonderland, (which I played one time at Disneyland) I jumped into my inner sensing rabbit hole ready to ride on a City trolley without wheels.

The huge 5-story Gate was busy as usual, as people clamored to see inside the creation that only God could design and bring onto the ground surface of this planet. My Guide La-Luke rushed me through the crowds, onto the trolley and we stopped abruptly at the Embassy of Peace entrance. WOW... that was quick!

We entered inside this huge amphitheater filled with extraterrestrials from all over the Universe (and some think we are alone... no way). These are the most loving and friendly beings I had been privileged to meet and we could learn a lot from them, especially LOVE. My welcoming ceremony began with a familiar sound that I teach in my Four Keys to Light sessions and I knew I was welcome once more.

Head master OOO-LON spoke....

"Welcome. We prepare you of advanced information of your Earth homeland."

G: "Thank you. What am I to be made aware of?"

O: "Your planet Earth is in the throes of massive change that will continue into its conclusion. Even those who try to hold on to the old ways will feel the pull of the new ... like leaving an old across-country trail wagon for a new car with what is called bells and whistles.

"As the next few days enter into the 11-11-11 pattern, with a wave of love so strong people will be happy to let go of the past as it has served its purpose to bring people into the future as it should be no other way. This Dear One, is what people have sought for eons of Earth time and The God Genie has granted your wish.

"It would be wise to try and remain in calmness as much as possible as you all enter into this topsy-turvy roller coaster ride. When suddenly the ride ends and you all have reached the high point of elevation knowing that love is all that is important. Different humans will feel different changes, but all is on course to bring everyone into the Love experience.

"You have felt this in situations prior and will again. You, The Genii, now sit in the Birthing Bowl, so to speak. The frequencies will be felt stronger due to the main reason for all this movement.

"No delay is expected as The City reaches 'its birthing status time. The sky that looks so clear this morning in the sunshine will fill with the expected for some, and for others a surprise like never before even anticipated from this human level ... a City of Healing Light ... a demonstration manifestation beyond what anyone would think possible in any life time.

"Your voice of City knowing speaks louder than even you can imagine, as you are all so close to the entrance. So feel your feeling, love your days ahead as the pray-lude to the greatest show on Earth prepares for the Grand Finale and God says 'Yes' and watches from the front row center. This production is just the beginning as God takes The City on the road, (speaking in your theater vernacular.)

"Return and we shall keep you updated on progress as Act One is about to begin as the doors open in 11-11-11, and everyone has a first class ticket in advance of the production as God takes all to places one might never think possible.

"The curtain opens as God pulls the strings of Light and healing, bringing peace on Earth. And all get to react in happiness never experienced before, for this is a first class production that even Broadway (again theater talk) critics would cheer for, and is expected to have a long run. We shall speak again soon. Be of good cheer."

So Light it be!"

Note: And to think I never even got to ask a question. Oh well, it is all show biz anyway. Thanks God...I AM that I AM... ready and I think the show is about to begin where the Earth people meet the sky people, and we don't even have to go somewhere over a rainbow.

Looks like the rainbow is coming to us.

Woopie!

The God Gift!

Embassy Visit November 8, 2011

(Vision) Setting the scene....

As I stepped into The City visit I saw crowds of people waiting, and even kind of pushing to get in, as the ones before them moved past this 5-story Gate of Entrance. I found my Guide almost pushing me forward to also enter.

We did, turning to the left and into the Park of Relaxation, onto the trolley, and just that quick we arrived at the huge Embassy of Peace ... a place of International Universal Cosmic Light Entities. Before entering I couldn't help but take a swift second to enjoy the fragrances of white blossoms on near-by trees. OMG! Entering onto the stage of these cosmic masters, I was given a seat of honor facing OOO-LON and his buddies of Light next to him. The hum of the hundreds of space entities came to a hush as OOO-LON stood and raised his hand.

O: "Welcome back Lady of Light. I see you got the message to return."

G: "Yes thank you. I do have a few questions that would be nice to get answered."

O: "Report from your questions and they will be answered."

G: "In 3 days time, we will be experiencing 11-11-11. What can be said of this time line?"

O (smiling): "Ah yes, the beginning of the beginning. The Love Wave! At this visit all is on schedule as your human world intensifies the interest in the unseen. The energy frequencies of this wave have begun in the unseen. It would feel like 'falling in love' human to human or even with your little white puppy, Light, who only knows unconditional love. It would seem like God has opened Its arms to receive you, and that feeling intensifies."

G: "And that means we will feel a deeper love?"

O: "Yes, especially those who are open to receive and then they will feel more of the frequencies just spoken of. As you know, it is sometimes difficult to explain feelings, however they may feel. It could be felt like waves of emotional pleasure, sometimes more than less."

G: "I have been invited to speak about The City at 11:00 a.m. on 11-11-11. What am I to report?"

O: "That The City of Light arrives as expected in God's time. That all the ways that were used before today, will take a new twist as the Universe enters into the new make-up of what was to what is to be. Businesses will look to new horizons to find customers, for the old ways will be released."

(Note ... it might be well to read the messages from SaLuSa through the human of Michael Quinsey for he has the pulse of the situation and is quite correct in his evaluations.)

"As The City of Light arrives into your vision, it will seem like God has taken total control of any situation and much of what worked before or not, will not work that way anymore. This is Good news, although it will mean the humans will have to change their ways as well. Nothing of this magnitude has ever taken place before on your planet and as the human senses take over, the Revelation then becomes The City of Light. These are not new ideas to you, as they have surfaced many times for you throughout the years. You have known of this elegant prophecy.

"No longer will it be like 'pie in the sky' type of thinking for the actuality now stands in plain sight with what you call 'bells and whistles.' Top of the line! First class production."

G: "Is this to be a December 2011 Christmas time set?"

O: "Would that be pleasurable to you?"

G: "I love Christmas. I am like a little kid with the music, movies and planning."

O: "Then hold the thought of this being a Gift of actuality that God gives freely and with love.

"Example: Humans love to open presents and 11-11-11 is the unwrapping of the gift box. Rest in the joy of the season and be open to opening that gift box that is just waiting to be opened. Permit the time between 11-11-11 and the Christmas holidays to be joyous and love-filled, thus bringing in the New Year with a promise of Peace on Earth good Light to all. Pull in all the joyous feelings you can, like a child opening a gift unknown yet ready to be received. Could this be the year of The City? Ah...anticipation delights, as the wonders of God delivers a Christ City to the masses. Christmas? Time and energy will tell this holiday story. So dear Jedi lady of the future, anticipate good tidings of what may be gifts not even asked for but delivered. And what would you ask for, oh Lady of Light? No need to respond, we know...Be the Light, put fun in your presentations and like a child waiting for Santa Claus for he just may be coming down your planet's chimney with Light, and you can yell 'Ho-Ho-Ho' ... for with 11-11-11, the unwrapping begins. Questions answered?"

G: "For the moment."

O: "Then come back and we shall continue this story and maybe a Happy New Year as well. So right it be!"

Just a Breath Away!

Embassy Visit November 13, 2011

Resonating within myself to go into The City, I stretched out and entered into the vision once more being subject to the divine return. Now that 11-11-11 had passed, I had a couple of questions I was divinely receptive to receive answers for.

The entrance Gate was seen as busy as usual, but I found myself at the Embassy door with my City Guide La-Luke. As I wrote what I was seeing, I felt love unannounced and tears appeared as my heart love feelings enveloped me like a warm blanket. In the Embassy I found myself once more standing before this vast audience of Universal Light Beings with OOO-LON at the head, smiling.

O: "Welcome, Oh love-filled Lady."

G: "Thank you. What happened with 11-11-11 please? I feel such love, as a dear friend of mine said, it is love or it isn't. I feel such emotion that it is hard to contain."

O: "The love wave is still in process. Nothing has stopped. Quite the contrary. The love wave of 11-11-11 continues on its path of clearing of your planet. People vary in their thoughts, so cleaning out the past time has to be considered. Watch the changes take place, and more quickly. The emotional wave has not even subsided. It is in full flow, even as you are here. We intend to support the total cleansing and will achieve our desire." [A hum sounded from the vast background audience.]

G: "What am I to share with others who went through this on 11-11-11?"

O: "Dear One, tell them all is in order as this wave of higher consciousness penetrates each one and love is the band leader. What you are experiencing becomes as accepted for all who are open and most are. Those who are so concentrated in a lower vibration will have to peel off the outer layers so they too become subjects of Light one way or another. This love wave is silent but sure of its intent. Right now you are feeling this love. Your emotions are totally God-like and intended as such.

"You are a leader and your intent is to serve God in whatever way you humanly can. You have reported 'That you feel in the world but not of it." This is as it should be for you have been guided as such for many years. As a human being this was a trial and error situation, as the love was sporadic as such and now you are in full bloom so to speak, as this love wave gets digested, sporadic is no more.

"God's love is now in charge. You had fun reporting on The City of Light during the day of 11-11-11 and people responded as your own inner love catapulted you to express yourself as love. And your mission is one in the same.

"This will continue as The City of Light is in its final descent Earth-wise. Your planet is in process of healing and that takes top consideration from this point forward, for nothing will hold back The City of Light for any reason.

"You love and watch it return like an uncontested love feast. When your head belongs to one, nothing can shake that feeling as you receive and send. You are now ready to be equal to The City of Light as every one of your cells of your body receive love and reject anything else. Is this answering your question?"

G: "I only know that passion and connection with God's love and I would be God-connected. What is my instruction, as this visit will be reported to many.

O: "Tell them that the elevated sensing is indeed lifting as promised, and one day at a time. Watch for they will show the inner signal of advancement and that love heals and it was God's intent to do just that for you all are just a breath away from the demonstration, and all who are in tune with this are being lifted in vibrations of equalization. Your planet is vast in the corrections being made and even now we who support are excited of our entrance into recognition, and with it, peace on Earth and God's will to all.

"Enjoy the feelings you are feeling, as this in itself will make others feel the same around you, in person or even through your City of Light publication. You have heard them report, 'You bring us hope.' Now they feel that hope with The City of Light right there in their own back planet yard. So then spread the joy that God moves in mysterious ways and one of them is knocking on the door right now. 11-11-11 has done its package opening. Now welcome the contents. Love. Four simple letters, but filled with such promise in the days ahead. Spread the love you are. And as said, all is well."

So Light It Be.

And with that my City visit disappeared and I was home ready to enjoy the day while sending a love sonnet to be shared from my heart to all those in the Embassy, on the planet, and even to Tika, the live timber wolf I met on 11-11-11 who is also my brother. We all are one and it is either love or it isn't.

Let's choose love. I do.

Thanks, God.

The Love Song of God!

Embassy Visit Thanksgiving Day, November 25, 2011

Walking through one of the 5-story high visitors Gates and into The City of Light had a special meaning today, for my intent was to give thanks for even being in some magical, visual way able to enter here for so many years. That in itself was a miracle. I had a special mission.

Not a lot of people were seen as I met up with my Guide La-Luke. Actually everything seemed very quiet and balanced, unless that was just me feeling spacey on this holiday. We took a few moments to sit on a massage bench in the Relaxing Park while watching the beautifully colored birds. The expected trolley arrived and we took our place on it. Within a few bouncing moments we were at the Embassy of Peace headquarters.

Each visit here was dramatic in itself. Where else could I see hundreds of extraterrestrials all under the same roof? We entered from backstage and crossed up to the stage rim where 4 Light Beings sat with OOO-LON who was the communicator for us all. (Space beings seemed to speak in long sounding tones and not in words like we do.) As OOO-LON stood in acknowledgement as far as I could see, the space audience did as well.

O: "How may we serve you today, Lady of human Light?"

G: "As this is a Thanksgiving Day in our world, I have come just to say thank you for all you have done and are doing. The daily thought that a City of Light is to come forth is second nature to me now 'like breathing out and breathing in' (from a song that comes to me) as I do the best I can to assist your efforts. Thank you!"

O: "Your heart-filled efforts are appreciated and returned, as will The City be in solid 3D form. This is a promise! The divine Space Federation brings Light into your planet, and as Time releases its hold you find yourself at the Gate of Entrance in actuality. Your world of creation bids some release as yet, but that too will soon release its barbaric hold for some you meet.

"The City of Light rests in the unseen ethers as it readies for its entrance into the physical plane you reside on. Soon, it shall be seen and serve the multitudes of humans with various degrees of healing, to be attended to at will. This demonstration has been a major, major project for some centuries of your past.

"These dedicated Light Beings here have banded together as one. For the Creator of us all desires peace on this planet, and so we have linked up with others who are universally separated by space, but not by the lack of love.

"The turmoil your planet has endured for most of its longevity is ending. Those who seek peace for themselves, their families and children (not even yet born, are waiting for the shift to take place, before they enter into the new world) will achieve their heart's desire as The City makes everything new due to this City of Light demonstration.

300

"You say this is a day of Thanksgiving. It is one day out of your year to be at peace, and from your appreciation you tell The Creator your holy feeling of being thank-filled. This is good. Humans for the most part get caught up in the ego of living and serving on a day-to-day basis. Stopping momentarily during this daytime span to give thanks sends energy into the ethers and it is received in love as the 11-11-11 Wave of Love.

"As The Wave of Love continues its momentum it takes people to the heart of God while connecting with the Universal Light Beings who receive it in that way. Then it continues to move in a flowing condition, at which time The City of Light is manifested.

"Every day should be Thanksgiving Day. A day of love taking people to the heart of God thus being blessed, becomes a natural state of existence. You have a ways to go as yet to learning what 'real love' is. That will heal the planet and not as a temporary momentary experience, but one that has far-reaching advantages beyond what can be imagined.

"Life should be 'thanks-living' in a gratitude state of love as an every-day experience not only once a year. So as The City of Light descends into your atmosphere of three dimensions, the Wave of Love enters your heart systems. You will all see with your outer visions the results of our determination that your home planet will not only survive, but will be a healthy vehicle that spins in space caring for people who have learned that to love is the only answer and demonstrate as such.

"So, The City must have a dramatic intervention as the Spectacular Divine Manifestation delivers the healing facilities to the people. We who know what can take place and believe in that, give thanks to all of you who enter into this   divine love in preparation of what could be referred to as the Second coming by some, and the first of its kind on this planet.

"Permit each day to be a day of thanks-giving. Time as you know it is silently slipping away as the future enters yesterday, and tomorrow is already completed. As for The City demonstration? You sit on the doorstep and the door is opening for the greatest show on Earth is ready, willing, and able to give you all a reason to give thanks, ... it is that close.

"As the holiday season of your cultures begins, the children look to a jolly bearded man in a red suit to bring forth gifts of love. We too here in the Embassy of Peace watch for what the 11-11-11 Love Wave will produce. As humans catch on through their inner feelings, what did take place on that shift day could form a magnificent love fest as a result.

"The vortexes of your Earth area spring out the energies of deliverance where all mankind will receive the greatest gift of all, with no Genii strings attached. It is just love encased in advanced technology. Yes you all have much to be thankful for ... even that which is for the moment, unseen. Have we been a help to you?"

G: "Yes, I thank you for all you have done and what is to come forth, containing the love this planet surely needs. I will share what you have said."

O: "Good, stay with The City announcements where invited. Keep the 4 Holy Keys linking humans to the Light. Each step is of love for which they will give thanks ... thanks to God!"

And within this the whole Embassy sounded the 'Ahhhhhhh' tone including me, the love song of God!

Released from the vision, I found myself home with a puppy to be tended to and best friend Charles, doing chef duties in the kitchen, preparing for Holiday guests. Both were calling for my help. Ahhhhhhh

Thanks to all the space friends who support us daily.

That Holiday Feeling!

Embassy Visit December 3, 2011

While looking out of my window as I went into my mediation and a City visit, it was snowing and it was a real Christmas scene with the Sedona red rocks catching each snowflake and looking like frosting on a cake.....beautiful! My meditation began......I wondered, since I had been privileged to meet many extraterrestrials in this place, what kind if any, celebrations were held in space? At least I could ask.

La-Luke waved at me and I moved past smiling people to reach him. He grabbed my hand and we ran through the Park that was ablaze with tiny white lights adorning the trees ... maybe the birds were celebrating too? Was I dreaming? The trolley came in view and we hopped aboard heading for the Embassy of Peace. As we entered into the main sanctuary auditorium, I was pleasantly surprised to see hundreds of space individuals holding small white lights of some kind. What a pretty sight of welcome.

For the first time, OOO-LON came out from behind the horseshoe-shaped desk and took my hand. This gracious being had warm hands and heart to match and I was honored to have this opportunity to be included in this vast universal group of space entities. Somewhere I must have done something right to have this auspicious opportunity. Maybe I am a space person too?

O: "Quite so Lady of Light." Oops! I forgot they can pick up my thoughts. Ahhh let's see where was I? I wondered, as he led me to a seat facing all the rest on stage, as La Luke stepped back out of sight. It was just me and hundreds of E.T.'s. Talk about being out-numbered. Wow! You like what you see?"

G: "Oh my, what's not to like? I could melt like chocolate in the love energy I feel here now. (Oops ... here comes the bliss and tears.) Do space entities celebrate anything in the Universe?"

O: "Oh my yes. The advanced civilizations have many reasons to do what you call celebrate. Each inhabited planet has its own way of celebrating. One that comes to mind is when an entity is born ... you here celebrate it in a family setting. We celebrate all being born no matter who they belong to. It would be like even more celebration, for it is well known that they are pure Light and thus the Universe is blessed, speaking in your vernacular. See all the Lights here behind me ... they represent new entities being born as we speak.

"You know not much of the Universe, for that is a teaching all in itself. However Jedi Genii, your time will come to know much more as you are part of us. As the story goes, your planet had one human male born that is important as to why Christmas is celebrated, but it includes many other holy areas and groups as well, so anyone can celebrate for many reasons. Just to feel happy is a perfect reason. You agree?"

G: "Yes. I love the holiday season. In my own world it means caring and lots of love. As a dear friend says 'It is either love or it isn't. Choose love.' Love is what it is about and love makes me happy ... real love I mean, not just fake words in passing by. When can we expect The City?"

O: (grinning) "Well it would take what you call Santa Claus a very big sleigh to bring forth such a promised gift, so instead God sends a space vehicle the likes of which you could not even envision at this point. Be patient. The time is not quite yet but celebrate you will. More questions?"

G: "I know when it arrives it comes with God's seal of love approval and certainly ours, and I think I just want to say a big thank you ...

1. Thank you God who knew we needed help for peace on Earth.

2. To Hermes who was the designer of this City.

3 .To Dr. Bill who spent 3 years in almost solitude, thinking he was going crazy for the drawings Hermes was sending through him, as drawing a straight line was not his vocation ... Meditation was.

4. To all of the Guides who have moved me forward into this Embassy place of universal love where I sit today speaking to all of you.

5. To close friends Charles, Kathie, and Renee who helped put The City of Light Sedona book together, and getting it out into many countries.

6. And even to me, out on a limb...who has the courage to let people know about and see what I have been told would take place even before they see it.

"I feel so great-filled and just want to celebrate as I travel to spread the news. As the weeks of December are now here, what am I to know?"

O: "We can tell that you are heart-filled and in your love the people will hear and respond favorably. As the days continue so will the wave of love (11-11-11) that now embeds people, prompting them to do just that.

"LOVE is the strongest emotion possible in your humanness and well worth the feeling you receive from it. The City shares itself soon so keep open and give thanks for everyone you love will benefit.

"The sessions you lead with the God Light-linking are important. (The 4 Keys Classes). And when even one group of students who are Light-linked gather in what is referred to as 'Lights of the round table' to progress in studies, they bring group love to The City and it should continue, as well as The City reports. So then have we concluded this visit?"

G: "Oh, it has been suggested that all of these City embassy visits be book-bound in another issue?"

O: "There is much value in the meetings, the visits, and your other guidance's meditations, as even after The City makes its appearance, these will go down in your history in the making. So this is advised to continue to travel where invited and we now return you to your snowy world."

With this he bowed, again took my hand and bingo all the lights in the audience went out. I found myself back home ready to run my pup Light out into the snow.

The Second Coming!

Embassy Visit December 16, 2011

Looking to enter The City of Light and the Embassy of Peace Headquarters seemed to be a good idea this morning as it was the Christmas and Hanukkah season, plus a few more holidays for people to celebrate that which was important to them. The current energy waves were spilling over bringing up all kinds of emotions, and thoughts that were long gone and seemed to bounce forth as the outer world changed minute by minute. Keeping in a balanced state was an adventure in itself, especially for the females of our species which of course includes me. Is this a changing world? Oh my yes ... yes ... unseen but surely felt.

Note: Hang in there. We are almost through the passageway and there is really a Light at the end of this tunnel.

(Inner vision) Many people were seen entering one of the very familiar 5-story coded Gates that welcomes everyone into The City of Light. Looking around I saw my Guide La-Luke as he waved at me and I maneuvered myself to this gentle loving entity's side. My! How many times have we been here heading for the Park of Relaxation that leads us to the funny wheel-less trolley and to the Embassy of Peace Headquarters? This marvelous building was occupied by hundreds of Space Light Extraterrestrials who gathered to bring forth what we were standing in at this very moment.

Entering into this vast auditorium and stepping onto the stage, I felt centered just by being there. It was like entering another planet while still being in human form. This was a place of such love and wisdom that believe you me, it felt really great. OOO-LON stood in recognition and we bowed to his acknowledgment. It was an honor just to be in his presence.

O: "We see you have returned. What may we do to support this return visit?"

G: "You can tell me what is taking place as Christmas nears and the holiday fills with much anticipation of "SOMETHING IS GOING ON?" Where are we now with The City of Light appearance?"

O: "On top of the world so to speak. This proclamation of pending advancement through The City of Light appearance, is on schedule as we enjoy the scenario you all are about to experience as Peace on Earth. Long since in your years have you held to this premonition in your heart of such a healing edifice to take place. You have held it in place and delivery by your love and your belief that God can do all things, even things that people never could have thought to be possible. I think you call it Miracles. Well this miracle is about to happen as only God could deliver it ... a feeling that something is coming and so it is! The change in energy fields of course is also making people feel edgy and uncertain.

"The 11-11-11 love frequencies still create unseen but in many cases felt, love patterns. And thus people do strange things as the power of this love attacks anything that is to the contrary.

"As said by a friend, 'It is either love or it isn't.' Choose love and all will be well with you."

"Your part has been the laying of the mental foundation and the speaking of the same, such as in the 4 Keys to Light classes. You present this information to groups and they learn the 'Love song of God,' while meeting with the Inner Guides of their personal Light on their own. This is to be continued as the Guide power moves in to bring more people into the higher knowing. Your time is busy and rest is important and being a trans-audio has its value.

"Now then, where does The City fit into this at this point? The time now appears to be as it was pronounced so long ago. As some await the holy so-called 'Second Coming' it is rightly so. However, this will be seen as a coming of a Light City while many are expecting the Christ to return. The appearance of The City is the return of Christ, so to speak.

"As He was in man-form He could heal many ... this is so. Now this is extended, as such space technology now is the advanced progress that fills that void today. One Holy Man Entity now = One Holy City Entity which is the same ... only expanded into the hearts of many which incorporates teachers, mystics, masters, saints etc.

"No one is left out for any reason! The City serves all of any creed, denomination, devotionals etc. As the angels and Light entities gather in love and admiration for the One Creator who brings forth this grand manifestation, we say to all, tune into your feelings and see what they say from the heart?

"The Genii is well aware of the UPPC's (Uniphase Power Capsules) bombarding your planet from space for centuries. Even as we speak they are now hooking up with the vortexes and portals all over the planet. As peace and love enter the Earth your local atmosphere sightings of UFO's will begin to be seen in various areas. It is the Holy season dedicated to the one God... I AM. And this God brings forth the gifts of the magic of miracles. Be the Light, be in the love, and all that is anticipated will be experienced soon indeed, and at a perfect time for advancing the human thinking and healing process. Has this been of help?"

G: "Of course."

O: "So then return to your home. Be watchful for the birth nears with the 'ah' tone of God's love and all is well. We bid you the Light of the eternal day in peace and in that love."

I was then back at home and saying thank you to OOO-LON and all who were bringing forth the greatest show on Earth. . . The City of Light Sedona.

So Light it be!

307

The Universal Christmas Gift!

Embassy Visit Christmas Eve December 24, 2011

The sky this morning was clear as the sun gave comfort on this very cold Sedona morning. I mentally slid into quiet space heading for The City of Light and the Embassy of Peace, including all that I might experience ready or not.

Like a kid I found myself watching the sky lately for any sign of The City of Light appearance, or for just a peek of The City or Santa, whichever comes first? Hey it's Christmas! Knowing all is on God's schedule not mine, even though as a stage performer this would make a wonderful Holy Christmas story.

(Inner Vision)

Once again, the Gates were overrun with people in expectancy of seeing inside the greatest show this Earth has ever produced out of nowhere. My Guide La-Luke waved as I made my way through the crowd to him by some kind of his magic. The seas of humans parted a bit and I got to him as he grabbed my hand and we literally ran through the Relaxation Park, onto the funny trolley and were deposited at the grand Embassy of Peace that I had been to umpteen times.

Entering onto the stage, the usual interesting Light Entitles who sat in conference were seen, and they stood in welcome as we approached. In the background the almost unseen vast audience of cosmic supporters from all over the Universe held consultations regarding The City of Light.

This was so exciting and has been from day one somewhere in time each visit was a surprise at what would take place, for I knew not what. But being in this vast energy was like the whole world was breathing at the same time and I was connected...awesome!

O: "A welcome visit on this auspicious day in your world. We attend you. What would be in our conversation this day of a special long ago birth?"

G: "Oh, it feels so good to be with you all. These visits have been gifts from God...truly great Christmas gifts. For us this is Christmas Eve as you know and the anticipation of The City birth is in my heart. I am like a little kid waiting for Santa God to deliver. What can you tell me that I can deliver to others?"

O: "You sense that it is near and it is. The way of special delivery is to change the sentence from 'Something's Coming' to 'Something is here.' You would then be putting the energy into the demonstration. Bring it to today! It could be like a surprise package. Even God likes to play and even you will be the receiver.

"This time of year looks to be a grand time of connection. The delivery is close as your time honored New Year brings a so called major shift, and most of the minds are hooked into that arena which is good, but most are unaware of what we are speaking of here. Ah...in that comes the surprise! Those who are aware of The City entrance also keep the vigil just like you.

"The clearing of the Earth vermin of darkness and ignorance with selfish interests has been reported. If you in your child-seeing can envision God with a big cosmic broom sweeping out the old with mercy so the NEW can become established, it might make a fun picture.

"Is The City of Light described for such a long time to materialize? Of course!!!! So once more the established wave of 11-11-11 love casts its spell and more and more light-workers declare it to be so. Ah ... the energy lifts to a higher frequency. To make a car move, one has to put gas into it, true? The Earth Lightworkers are the gas and The City would be the car (strange analogy but for some it gives a picture) and everyone is a part of The City ... right now!

"This cosmic wave of love tolerates nothing less than that 'LOVE.' Got the picture?" I nodded my head yes as he continued.

O: "Hear me Dear One, these are the most exciting times in your planet history bar none! Every day a gift is to be opened. A surprise a minute so to speak! Your inner Soul Guides direct your path so as to lead others, as they in turn support what is being said here. Once more all are connected."

G: "I am happy to be of service and feel privileged to report on The City of Light and The 4 Keys to Light. The response has been very loving in its acceptance and I get to make more friends as a reward. I look for much more as I am being guided."

O: "Oh indeed you will. Daily you get new instructions and the support grows. People of the Earth planet have a harder time being patient and that is understandable as known or not, you are all in what is referred to as 'The NOW' for being in the Now, it becomes the 'ALL' and everything desired can demonstrate in a moment, because that is all there is... NOW!

"We who support The City delivery understand this and do the best to deliver A.S.A.P. as you say. Changes for everyone have begun and second by second the changes take place and all are evolved. A preplanned day ahead can change in that second and a new day unplanned is in process. This could be unnerving for some.

"The new year of 12-21-2012 has those who are tuned in expecting the Mayan calendar to be the biggest change ever. Remember Genii what was previously told you, that that date was preset to keep the minds occupied as dates are important in your way of thinking.

"That was way back in the days when prophesies were written in stone. There is no stone now, just a fast wave of change and change means shifting quickly.

"What was not taken into consideration at that time was that time so-called, was going to 'speed up' and a time warp would be in progress. It could mean that while we are looking at 12-21-2012, a cosmic package opens itself and by that 12-21-2012 indication, the planet has already changed its patterns, for The City's arrival has already set the course long since.

"Then what happens when all the cosmic cousins are connected? Dear One, it is all a Great universal plan with the audience being the benefactors. Each one gifted with advanced technology, more love than they ever knew existed, and the body mind and spirit as co-partners with pain as an outsider that is no longer being experienced.

"Businesses working in Love instead of Greed so then there is enough for all.

"NOW THAT IS A GOD GIFT ANY WAY YOU LOOK AT IT.

"Look at what would take place AFTER (looking past The City entrance) to what would people experience, and set the course in that direction by getting inner information on what course to set forth. The City of Light is here NOW! The Coming is over! It is here! Then know this is so and it will materialize before your eyes. Your book gives a look into The City and what it can accomplish. People use it and bring forth what you see."

Note: This would also be guidance for The Lights of the Round Tables (4 KEYS) to pursue with the higher tones now available.

"Dear One, this is Christmas. Be the Light and go where invited and spread the God news with what is being said and even on a moment's notice should that appear. You will be in the media soon. Has this been of help?"

G: "Of course. I am asked for verification, and I give it out as I get it. Anything else?"

O: "Patience brings forth The City on a cosmic time chart and those who send the tone forward support our efforts. It could be today, tomorrow or next week. Remember it is to be a surprise even for you. So now enjoy your Christmas Eve, Light your fire and daydream The City into view for it is already here, just not seen yet but it will be. Patience. The new is ready to move quickly. Send your message of love and see the results manifest. We wish you all a very merry Christmas and it will be."

With this, all mental visions stopped and I was home with my puppy Light looking for his Santa Paws present with very little patience. Must be catchy. It was celebration time.

Whoopie!

Ringing in the New and Getting Excited!

Embassy Visit December 31, 2011 HAPPY NEW YEAR ...

After sleeping in a bit later than usual and remembering I was due for a City Embassy visit, I sprang into action to see what 2012 was to be about. The sky was clear blue and since Sedona is a magical place why not The City manifesting here? With soft music playing the 'Somewhere in Time' theme, I slipped out of Sedona for a briefing beyond the norm which could be for about an hour.

VISION: An entrance 5 stories high appeared and so did a lot of people, happy to see what this magnificent-looking (had to be God who did this, we could not build such an edifice) place was all about. La-Luke waved and somehow I got to him as we scooted off into the Relaxation Park, onto the trolley and the stopping off place, the Embassy of Peace Headquarters a masterful production in itself, "Huge and beautiful" is kind of saying it for starters.

Inside the Embassy was filled with Universal Light Beings (we could refer to them as Extraterrestrials) from places we probably never heard of much less visited, unless on film like Pandora in Avatar. As this year of 2011 faded into the past I wondered what I would be told now as I was aware that The City of Light landed on last Christmas Eve.

As we crossed the Embassy stage to the rim facing the audience where OOO-LON and the other Light Beings watched in approval, a hum was sounded throughout the audience and I suddenly waved, only to see them wave back (ah... close encounters of a special kind). Now invited to sit in council we were about to begin...

O: "Welcome Lady and Guide of Light, this time of your year comes to an ending and a so-called new time begins. What may we speak of to lead you into the newness?"

G: "Thank you first of all for having me come back so many times this past year. Your words of advancement have uplifted many as my book on The City of Light is not only fun, uplifting reading but is becoming a City of Light Sedona 'guide book.' Many places on the globe now have the book. Now that a new year is to begin what is important for me to know and share?"

O: "The brightness of your adventures here continue as your planet enters the final stages of the not-seen-physically City to one that is physically seen as a healing edifice one can walk into. At this moment all preparations are in order and the continued support of the universal sky entities and the inner Earth entities work together in total preparation for this appearance. The elevation of Light brings forth its prime property to be walked into and where people can receive Light healings of dramatic proportions.

"We see that the tone of The 4 Keys to Light that you share has for those who use it, been making the human contact more acceptable and the process simple as it is, has definite value and moves all forward into the new. You have those who would also advance into teaching The 4 Keys. This Dear One is progress. If you are called to teach the teachers you will be advised as to the process. Just be open.

"Using The City of Light book as a personal written guide, has begun with a Light group now serving and more will settle into this type of entry, as steps are laid forth for other groups to follow easily; then the energy power builds and all become the receivers of The City.

"This is the year and with The City having now landed on what you call Christmas Eve, 2011 and with the 11-11-11 love wave still active, we smile as we see what you will see very soon. It indeed was a holy production landing. You remember seeing a completed building being set in place from a space vehicle? It was a surprise when you were told that was why you and the Dr. Bill did not have to build a City of Light or anyone else for that matter.

"The Sedona area supports such a landing, as through itself it is a power center capable of such an event as the vortexes have power of energy, like a filling gas station for your auto cars. Living there the Genii has felt the power and bliss attached on occasion, which also supports her in these visits."

G: "My first question would be where is the location? Where would we see The City?"

O: "In the vastness of the territory surrounding the little place of Sedona there is much vacant land not used except for local animals. It should be said that no human owns any land, you are all only using it as God holds the papers of ownership. It is not yet time to disclose the exact spot and so must await for the correct timing of demonstration. Patience.

"We notice your sensing has been lifted, and you feel the love of The City already as bliss and tears connect like meeting the Christ or God or Spirit (whatever you call this highest Deity of all). Your guidance is to remain in this divine pattern for you are The City of Light and have long since been connected vibrationaly to it.

"We recognize that as you elevate much of this human world loses its flavor, but your time here is also to get your sensing out to others, who can get it to others as it is the energy of others that works the connecting. Time has spun into its own vortex thus making the appearance imminent. Today? Tomorrow? Next week? It makes no difference as time is not, but The City of Light is! ... And it will demonstrate.

"It would look that groups of people working together are important and such a Light group already is setting forth the Light pattern step by step in place for others to follow and also then gets this love and bliss feeling the Genii shares with others as a City messenger.

"As such you will be invited to speak in more places as you have embodied The City plus the co-partner of The 4 Keys to Light. The time is near so use it wisely and all will benefit. Organizing the steps now, be open to invitations and even return invitations to share updates on the spot.

"The Charles is a media designer and serves the people and thus is connected in the advancement of upcoming internet via the media etc. information. 2012 is indeed important, so be aware of each moment and make connections where others can make further connections. Spread the words as best you can across the planet that indeed THE CITY OF LIGHT HAS LANDED! And all are blessed. Some will hear, some will not, but it reigns supreme for God has declared 'THIS TO BE SO' and 2012 says, 'Yes we are ready!'"

G: "Anything else?"

O: "The City of Light book is important. It should be added that now one should be looking at what will take place after The City has been entered into. What does this do in individual lives and the way we look at business? And what will the government say about such a visible entity?

"Set your course for peace and love in all things and it will be so. It has been suggested that the Charles peek into this as the new company is birthed and his background holds many answers.

"So then all is well?"

G: "All is so well!"

O: "Then permit it to be so. Keep the energy flowing. We bid you the Light of the eternal day in peace and in love."

And with this a hum ran through the audience, as my Guide and I left the building and I looked to this New Year with love in my heart and an exciting adventure in store. Care to join me?

Welcome aboard my flying carpet as we soar over magical Sedona, Arizona and The City of Light.

AS ABOVE...SO BELOW (Hermes)

So love it be!

As Above So Below!

Embassy Visit January 5, 2012

As the morning sun awakened the red rocks outside my Sedona window, I left for another location, The City of Light and the Embassy of Peace therein. Taking a deep breath and with closed eyes I picked up the movie about to begin. The south Gate was loaded with smiling, inquisitive people anxious to enter this coming-down-from-heaven major City. It lit the area for miles around- a Light so bright that even the jet planes over head had difficulty seeing what it was. Did they want to report an unidentified object?

My Guide and I got to the destination as usual through the Park, on the trolley and there we were inside The Embassy, waving at the audience of hundreds of extraterrestrials who delighted me by waving back. Was Yoda out there too? I wondered. Seated were OOO-LON and four others who stood in welcome as the audience sounded the 'Ah'-tone.

O: "We feel you have questions suggested by others of your human species."

G: "Yes and of my own. I have been having strange sights and feelings lately like everything seems thick. Then I was told what I was feeling is 'density' of the third dimension. That it has always been here, but now my sensitivity is picking it up as validation. Is this correct?"

O: "Yes to a degree. More of this type of recognition could be experienced as you move more and more into upper levels with The City."

G: "How does The City reveal itself to the masses who will be quite surprised even if they know about it?"

O: "Changing levels of The City to appear into your 3rd dimension takes some doing. Example you can relate to...you can see faintly Light entities and even converse with what you call 'see-through's.' They have had to lower their frequencies and even alter themselves faintly for you to see them. Changing levels of density comes in many forms. Mentally or physically, the principal is about the same.

"You bring to others their personal Inner Guides of Light that have had extensive training to be able to converse with those they have chosen to lead. In other words they have to shake off a bit of their high energy fields to enter into your world in many forms.

"Remember all is a hologram ... all of it! ... and your planet would then be a holodeck. Even the pen you now write with is a hologram of a pen that flows the holographic ink onto holographic paper. Earth is a holodeck where people create things, events, confusion, laughter, or can lift themselves into a higher extension of themselves as God incarnate. Imagine that!" The people you share The City or The 4 Keys to Light with add to this equation which also lifts themselves through the 'Light linking' and infiltrates The City for its appearance.

"The City maintains its structured presence now as it prepares itself for its appearance. This coming forth of The City of Light is not a dress rehearsal. It is show time for its appearance."

G: "Does everyone have to have a knowing about The City?"

O: "Everyone will not know until it is physically seen, but those who do know support the holographic vision and are main supporters of its appearance. People of Light work to elevate themselves from the 3rd dimension. With The City this is reversed even though it is of such high value and is quite correct."

G: "When it appears people will arrive by the hundreds. What can be foreseen so this can be handled in peaceful ways?"

O: "The world indeed will beat a path to its door, and mass confusion could take place all over the planet. Some in fear of the unknown and most in awe...Allah has appeared. We now have heaven on Earth. We are saved. Hell is gone. Halleluiah!

"Those of control such as police officers will have to work to keep the order, while themselves trying to figure out what has taken place. They will have their hands full and work overtime to set some kind of pattern.

"Lightworkers can help right now by foreseeing order and peace to be the rule. It is up to the human efforts of control to determine what is to take place. That is not in our jurisdiction. We bring love."

G: "Speaking of helping, one of the Light-linked groups have requested guidance from the Embassy. What is to be told?"

O: "We smile as they already are receiving guidance through themselves. How many have received their personal Guides and even their City Guides? They have the inner support. That was not just a Linking game being given. This is the power of God!!!

"Daily communications should become the norm, that connection is glued and they are actually God in action. By sharing their insights with each other they would then recognize what they have been given from the Genii. Nothing more is needed only the human ego strives for control. They are advised to enter into their personal Embassy and speak with their teachers who share wisdom beyond your world and are always available. Does this give guidance?"

G: "Oh yes, the 4 Keys of Light lay it out pretty clearly. I have another question. What part are the High Towers playing now that The City has landed?"

O: "Greatly! The power of the "UPPC's (Uni-Phase Power Capsules) and it's process will be revealed as this Holy City complete with advanced healing technology, shines forth for God declares this to be so. The High Towers are a connecting element and are mandatory and quite active now with the known and unknown vortexes in many states around.

315

"This is a number one magnificent opportunity of service to heal the planet starting with this first City prototype, then more will be revealed around your planet."

G: "How much of the original plot plan that Dr. Bill brought through is valid?"

O: "All of it, as a place people can relate to. Walking into any new city is one thing, but especially this one appearing out of the ethers is another thing. So what the good doctor brought through was designed to make people feel at home, with even a golf course where gold golf balls are used. It can feel like they have come home (sort of). A university is included and people will learn new ways of using Light of all kinds straight out of space.

"And all can be said to be heaven on Earth ... as the master Hermes has said, 'As above ...so below!' All the work you have done over the years by keeping the interest going and saving the faith and conviction that this is quite correct, have been a major supporter. You are to be congratulated from us, as holding the Light for so long and still keeping the energy going when doing the dishes seems to have no fun value.

"As a Jedi you do this for the love of God like the heart of God is being washed ready to serve again. The days ahead including the 2012 lift with The City appearance ... just know all is on course. All through with the questions?"

G: "For the moment, anything else?"

O: "We bid you the Light of The City of love, and as you spread it outward into your world this indeed will be a most unusual year to be sure."

My Guide and I bowed in humble adoration of what had been said and to those blessed ones from space who were delivering a City of love to us - thank you. I made my way to the sink filled with dishes.

So love it be.

Of The Animals, The City, and Planetary Change-over

Inner Meditation January 8, 2012

Q: "What is to be known at this point of animals and Planetary change over...?"

A: "What would be of value is to be aware that as the humans lift in consciousness so do the animals, predatory or not. The world is made of energy ... all is energy, period. Be it a person or of the animal species. So then you might ask, will bringing animals like pets etc. into The City of Light get them a healing? Oh my yes, as they are more open to Light than humans are. Within The City confines are special areas where animals are 'Light treated' tenderly with pure love that they may not find in the outside world, for humans with darkened minds have little respect for that which is not able to defend itself. It has been said that humans have power over the animals and many abuse that privilege.

THIS WILL CHANGE DRASTICALLY!

"Animals also have a primary place in the balance of nature's bounty and are affected by this Light explosion now in process. Our demand on animals for food, companionship, and many other ways depends on the way we humans see them. In the eyes of God they are indeed important each and every one, be they wild or tame. Humans have not yet discovered that animals play a big part in what makes the Earth balanced and that balance could be lost if animals were not present, as was decided in the first incarnation of this planet.

"Every living creature has its place as the Genii is well aware as she delights in her Pom puppy named Light Spirit. So then what is needed is the training of the mind-set of humans, which in itself is in process as this year of 2012 begins to change and shift dramatically, due mostly to The City appearance. Unfortunately humans have been slow to recognize what this animal area means. Now that love progress is in process animals are totally subject to man's whims, be they kind or hostile.

"So as Light frequencies affect human levels they also affect animals as well. When man can grasp the significance of what has been perpetuated before and what is about to now shift into a higher realm of perpetual love, the animals have a better chance to survive in loving care rather than the other. Stupidity is on the way out! A balancing with compassion would be wise counsel ... to recognize the beasts of nature and that each one has its place of service.

"As the new change-over completes itself in its shifting properties, people and events and the animals will also elevate as well. Again we look at love which is the link between human beings and animals, of which the human is just supposed to be more intelligent. Only time will tell the whole story. Get the human into loving, upper-level thinking, that in itself will support the animal kingdom. Remember you have been given choice so choose to know that all will be well with what is taking place now, and the animal kingdom will benefit as well." **So Light it Be!**

With Confident Expectancy . . . Something's Coming!

Embassy Visit January 10, 2012

Pre-entrance thoughts that come....

Into the unseen from my scenic world of Sedona, my intent was to enter the Embassy of Peace headquarters in The City of Light. Many visits have I taken here in the past years, but I entered with my mind and vision open to receive whatever this Embassy of Space Entities of much brilliant Light, had to serve to me today. When I think of all the "possibilities" I have spoken of to people, I can now change that to "probabilities." God is really Good! Ahhhhh.

In doing so I get to give love to many as this is the 2012 year of love and it is still rolling forth from the 11-11-11 introduction and the deep love I personally experienced during that time. If this is what God is delivering, it is beyond the norm to say the least. I suggest all tune in ... it feels pretty God good.

Inside my vision shifted and I found myself in the Embassy, already standing in front of Master OOO-LON with my Guide La-Luke beside me. The massive audience of Space Entities acknowledged our presence and with that deep feeling of love I spoke of earlier. Wow! Then a hush fell over this vast audience as master intelligence OOO-LON spoke.

O: "The welcome of this union of friends from universal places in the cosmos, welcomes the Lady of distributing Light and love to those on your changing planet. And what may we speak of this visit?"

G: "I bring an open mind to receive what I am to be made aware of with The City of Light and its progress, so that I may share it with others now tuned in, and those who are unaware that anything is going on in the ethers."

O: "The entry of The City of Light now on ground level has been as your astronauts say, '"Houston, we have touchdown."' And truly this is so. The Sedona and surrounding areas will feel it before seeing it, as this giant structure makes its way into this level's visionary process. It would seem as a long duration from beginning design to Earth landing and it has been so ... centuries in fact.

"From Master Hermes' architectural designs you now have, to the interior of the healing centers in The City proper, to the present day, we of the universal team of experts have brought forth an edifice long since needed; and as it prepares itself for the sightseers to go, 'AH look what God has brought forth. Imagine that. Who would believe such a structure would suddenly appear out of nowhere. I must be losing my senses!'

"We would reply, 'Not so.' To believe in the unseen is possible now, and peace on Earth awaits discovery. You have a saying, 'As you believe ... is it done unto you.'

"You the Genii in your constant vigil, have opened minds into believing anything is possible and in this case probable! So now as days and weeks become moments, the higher frequencies of The City invest themselves in the denser frequencies of your dimension. Changing the frequencies from high to lower is in progress, so be aware that even you may be surprised that your dream turns into a futuristic reality. Now it becomes a reality astonishing all. Even those who know about it will be in tears of holy joy, for they have supported what is being spoken of here.

"Thousands who worship in one area or another or even none, will feel that a way of higher thinking has produced what they believe a God to be, for what stands before them is demonstrated and cannot be denied. God smiles like the pictured Mona Lisa because what looks like an overnight demonstration has been long in process, but it is knocking on their door so to speak, right now. My attempt is to give you the larger picture to share. Does this help?"

G: "Yes indeed, anything else to be aware of as waiting for The City birth still takes me forward into new Light group territories to serve?"

O: "You have been saying it quite nicely... 'Something's Coming.' Continue to use these words of attention and report back again to this place of serving your planet. We see that the Light groups you have lately served are continuing their contribution of serving by developing a process for others to follow. This is appreciated and is power as well. Rest easy for all is well and Divine delivery is expected. We bid you the Light of the eternal day in peace and in love. Have a God day."

And with that, all just disappeared and I was left with a love feeling ... a blessing that I had been brought to this place in this time to see, hear, and feel that. Really I am the lucky one, the Genii who has even her own wishes granted.

SOMETHING'S COMING. WHOOPEE!

Think of the Possibilities!

Embassy Visit January 17, 2012

With gentle music playing in my room I prepared to blast off from Sedona and land at the Embassy in The City of Light. No car ... no plane ... or even a spacecraft needed. Just being open to inner vision and sound. Ah! ... advanced technology and being a trans-audio person does help.

I found myself and a few others at a Gate of Entry where I joined my City Guide La-Luke. He grabbed my hand and we ran through the Park and jumped onto the bouncy trolley, ending up standing in front of hundreds of extraterrestrials, which was a good place to be as this was the purpose of the visit!

As I looked over the vast audience of faintly-seen space friends once more, I felt the sensation of overpowering love, not unlike an electric sensation but calmer. How lucky could this girl be?

Standing in front of OOO-LON we were beckoned to be seated. With all of this electricity around I wondered what I came to ask about?

O: "We sense questions. What is your pleasure?'

(Well I must have one if he senses it,) Oh yes...

G: "I am aware that The City of Light had landed on Christmas Eve 2011 and as I share with others in my 3D world, I hear much being said about an E.T. disclosure. What can be said?"

O: "Oh yes, your world is once again bringing us to the attention of disclosure. This has been so for many reasons, and as seasons come and go and the energy lifts more, it is eluded to in depth. The wanting of a disclosure of this and that, comes forth on a continual basis and even a bit more so now that the energy shift is in process. We are well aware of the constant bombardment of questions.

"We have entered your planet say, many moons ago, and we work to fulfill our part in the revelation and the constant bombardment. (As this was said, it must have been reported to the audience as laughter was heard.) To see or not to see, that has always been the question. The Genii is well aware we are as close as her breath and at this point like The City, we too are here. It is a combined Light package."

G: "I have dear friends nearby that have a spectacular home called Xanadu that consists of 10 brightly-colored dome shapes that could be looked at as something from space."

O: "We are aware!"

G: "One of the most auspicious attention-getters is National Geographic magazine and film, and they are interested in filming an exposé on E.T.'s and UFOs and I know not what else."

O: "We are aware!"

G: "They have noticed my City book so it could be involved, or even me to answer some questions. What am I to be aware of as they are looking for YOU!"

O: "And the puzzle continues. Dear One, this type of investigation has been going on for centuries and now as the energy level rises, so do sightings and The City now becomes part of this. This is not bad ... quite the contrary ... for you have evidence of such a happening.

"Should you be asked to participate in any way, be open to us within with guidance and we will advise you what steps to take. Ah, we sense you have a fun feeling with this, right?"

G: "Yes, after all these years of contact with you all and learning a bit of speaking space, I think it will be fun to see what can come of a film or whatever as The City takes its turn to be revealed."

O: "Both will coincide and put your people in a state of 'Oh my god!' When we reveal ourselves it will be at a precise moment that would be valuable and not a moment before. As you say it is all show biz. For this moment, play along and be open to invites, writings etc. that we will send to the world and to you. The prestigious Galactic Federation is well aware of all and any E.T. interest that comes to the surface to be recognized.

"As the higher power builds, before you stands The City of Light untarnished and brought forth with the galactic cosmic approval. All is well and very well. You speak space every time we meet. Your dedication is and has been a part of the revelation that not only The City exists, but we too. All is just a big package of love as was reported, as the Christmas gift carefully laid on your planet.

"The days and weeks ahead will be quite fulfilling as your awareness grows and reports come forth to share. Time accelerates and The City as well as the Earth density comes into play. Rest in this and we will attend to the details, be it a City appearance or one of us from a Universe filled with love to share. All is on course...of course. Now return to your home and travel forward for much excitement is just waiting, even with fun attached. Be Jedi for that means 'love be with you.'"

And just that fast all disappeared and I was home just as the Lights of the Round Table began their City toning power.

So Light it be!

Sedona We Have Touchdown!

Embassy Visit January 25, 2012

Pre-visit: To announce that something is coming in the form of a City of Healing Light, I get to meet lots of friendly new people which in itself is fun, but there comes a time when rest is indicated and this was such a time. We slowed down now and found rest and relaxation along with the local critters like bob cats and coyotes etc. Quest Haven in CA is one of those holy places to enjoy…so we did. During this time it gave me space to go into The City of Light Embassy twice, where I got messages of strong intent to share, and I do this with love now…

Embassy Visit #1   I was inside the Embassy alone as I saw no Guide with me. Standing was OOO-LON, space mentor and interpreter of answers to questions that I may ask.

O: "And so you are back Light Lady. You are welcome. How may we be of service?"

G: "I did not know that I was coming back today, so I am pleased."

O: "Question?"

G: "Yes, in past visits I have been advised that The City of Light was lowered on Christmas Eve of 2011. My understanding is that at this point it is in the process of materializing into our two dimensional frequency level. Is this correct?"

O: "Quite so, from the unseen to the demonstration of being seen, is an activational process and this is not what you would call an easy task, I might add. Many buildings are to come into view and be entered into as you have already entered. The advanced technology is different in each one, as Light is the healing factor and the vibrational patterns differ. Thus in your time (of no time) each building is unique to itself, and much advanced space technology is being implanted.

"You in your visits through inner visions plus a lift in your vibratory level, became a part of the higher frequency. So now you are taking notes in one level, while being in the Embassy in another. You yourself have said that it takes you 2-3 hours to balance back into your normal daily sensing. So you do have some indication of what is now in process with The City.

"What will look like in an instant to appear out of nowhere, has been in process long since. Has it not been said that you will have heaven on Earth? ... As above, so below? The technology of the High Towers is harnessing the UPPC's (Uni-Phase Power Capsules) which is a major part of this project.

"Here in the Embassy you see hundreds of Light Beings who are also major factors in bringing forth the miracle of what you are to experience. God designed it to be sure, as workable for every healing. All must be correctly set in place, and from that the technology of Light power comes into play.

"The vision you were shown by your City Guide of a building being lowered completed, was to give you a glimpse of what is to take place and has. This is a monumental undertaking which has taken centuries of your time/space to be developed as your planet keeps on developing new illnesses to be cured plus the old ones that continue to plague your people.

"The power contained within The City of Light is awesome, and a deliberate training ground for future technology that will purposely be given to your doctors and scientists who are in connection with The City. Dear One, it all works. Call it a miracle, call it God in action, or whatever. But it is true that this God-made City is here for a reason ... a big reason!

"This planet is to be healed once and for all, for beyond your sight lines are universes ready to receive this planet into the fold of friends beyond friends who will welcome Earth with open arms, so to speak. The Genii learns Jedi ways. Ways of Light and love that serve. The love you extend is deeper than most could imagine and has been tested to be so and heart connected. This love from all your City visits has been a divine indicator. You don't have to say a thing and people will respond as Light responds to Light like a Genii connection, and friends manifest and feel that what you say about The City is absolutely correct.

"Love is not harsh and threatening. It is gentle and can be imprinted just by being open to the Creator to create more of the same. Just be love. IT IS JUST THAT SIMPLE. Are we in agreement?"

G: "Oh yes, this feeling of love is way beyond bliss I might add!" And with this a hum ran through the huge audience as I felt my energy draining. I needed some rest but would be back for a return visit soon, I was betting. So Light it is!
Genii note: It was after some rest that the following very strong voice came through with the following words.

- -

"ATTENTION! LET THERE BE A CITY OF HEALING LIGHT THAT NO ONE CAN REPORT AS UNREAL! LET THOSE WHO SEEK LIGHT, FIND IT WITHIN THESE HALLOWED WALLS!

"LET THOSE ENTERED INTO THIS PLACE FIND HEART AND SOUL UNITED TOGETHER FOR THE GOOD OF THEMSELVES AND ALL MANKIND!

"AS THE CREATOR, THIS CREATION COMES FROM ME TO CREATE WITH, AND THE QUEST NOW BEGINS AT GROUND LEVEL!"

At Ground Level

Embassy Visit #2   January 26, 2012

After the above message came through, I was invited back to the Embassy so I re-entered with an open mind and a loving heart to see what was going on.

Quickly through envision, I saw OOO-LON as I was expected.

O: "Again we meet. You are welcome. The message just given you leaves no doubt in your mind that The City has arrived. Right?"

G: "It was a strong energy that I experienced - wow!"

O: "Quite so, leaving no doubt that we continue to express the action of The City, in process of development of its appearance at ground level. Does this please you?"

G: "The question is, where at ground level can it be seen eventually?"

O: "Now telling you would take away the delight that suddenly you will begin to see the faint formation with your own eyes. So patience is desired here. Add the recap from your book of why the Sedona area is the galactic location, so that a better understanding of why this particular area is designated for the first of several locations as a prototype, will be understood."

G: "Tell me please, will there be a disclosure of Extraterrestrials before The City manifests?"

O: "Yes, this is an important ingredient in the overall picture developing now. And to answer your next unsaid question, you will meet the President before The City appearance."

G: "Nothing has opened in that department as yet."

O: "Oh ye of little faith, is a saying you have. Be patient, be open, and permit God to Light your way and It will. Now then remember you are moving forward step by step and each one is important and your divine design has taken an upswing in activation. So then we will converse again soon. Send out the message that The City of Light is at ground level and preparing its contents to be revealed."

With this the vision ended and I was back at Quest Haven, and as I glanced up a big bob cat was also enjoying this location.

So Light it be!

Here Comes a Miracle!

Embassy Visit February 5, 2012

Take a clear sunny morning in Sedona and add the quietness, and the stage was set for my delight to be called back to The City Embassy of Peace, with the wonder of seeing and speaking to space friends. This had all the mixture of a perfect day beginning...So in a peace-filled mind and heart I released this daily world and entered God's domain called The City of Light.

WOW! That was quick ... zap! I found myself standing on the stage with OOO-LON and many friends from far-away places with strange sounding names. I acknowledged them all as I bowed to OOO-LON in appreciation.

O: "Ah once again the message has been received to return, and we welcome you friend of many visits. Ready for more guidance and revelations?"

G: "Yes. What is taking place at this point with The City appearance that I should know about as I ready for my next trip? Charles and I fly to the East Coast to speak on The City of Light."

O: "Indeed much is taking place in the unseen level of your planet and preparations for The City of Light, as the frequencies are in process of change. If you were to be in The City frequencies process, and watch and see them change to what you have in your dimensional level, you would be amazed.

"You have seen the buildings in vision form just like this. Now they are being transported in change to your illusionary level which you would call space technology.

"You have a new Guide of YA who will interpret the proceedings in your language as best he can, so as he says to be 'empty' and let's see what takes place.

"The City has been in space for centuries if you are counting time as you do in your dimensional process. Contained in the ethers of time, this manifestation is not demonstrated overnight, but will seem that way as it suddenly appears out of nowhere into view.

"Even we who know full well what it takes to magically make this first-time-on-the-planet demonstration and are delighted to give you sort of the inside-out picture, as even you slip in and out with these visits ... one moment here and the next trying to function in your daily world with a bit of un-balance-ment. This is part of your ascension with all you have been doing swinging back and forth in energy levels.

"So then you are about to take another Earth trip for The City?"

G: "Yes, this time to the East Coast. What is this guidance in paying a visit to the United Nations building mean?"

O: "Oh yes, this has now been revealed that a visit could be a turning point and set forth a new avenue of service. It has all been preplanned in advance so as your adventure continues for The City, enjoy as many opportunities that can come forth yet like The City unseen. Be as YA says, empty or hollow."

G: "He says I am to be taught to be a 'Space-ologist.' That is funny to me. Tell me what I may share regarding The City update and its demonstration please."

O: "The portals of the unseen must turn into matter for any of this to be of value. You see your home as solid material, but you also know (through a past inner event) that it is all an illusion which sent you rolling on the floor in laughter. You said, 'We are walking around in God's dream. Whoopee this is funny!' and what happened then? You now see things as just that ... no chairs to sit upon, or even flying on a plane is like flying by the seat of your pants. It is all a space holodeck and should be fun!

"You understand this, but to many minds it makes no sense. As we see it, it is all non-sense. However it is so!

"Now then, to make such a demonstration all must be dramatically correct and function perfectly in your 3D world. As you have said a multitude of times, 'Something's Coming.' It is as real and valid and in process of healing, as your planet knows healing to be.

"Each building must meet the demand of what has been said it will contain and do, and of course will be. As The City vibrates more and more into your dimension with the help of the major vortexes and portals that are opening and the support that is within them, as the Hollow Earth meets the current Earth and as the sky comes to meet both.

"These are good times people, pay attention! Much in your history holds the energy honor of holiness and we are quite awake and quite active. The clouds in your area are changing rapidly. One moment nothing and the next quite the opposite. An illusion? Yes of course, and so is the chair someone may be sitting on as they read this.

"Right now the Sedona area is prime for this demonstration with all the support of vortexes acting as filling stations unseen, but ready to welcome what no human has to toil and build. No one has to do anything but be a welcoming committee through their energy and Light. Amazing isn't it? First time anything like this is to be observed and walked into. Oh the media will have a field day with this and the silliness and war drama will not be fun anymore. Clear the airwaves. Here comes a Miracle!

"Imagining a disclosure of E.T.'s being on Earth as a TV series makes us laugh. Many know that we are here, and not to take over anything for as you've said 'what's to conquer?' Your planet is in dire need of clean-up, but your thoughts have made you unable to converse with the universal ones who know how to help. Many groups work with this on your planet and we bless them all in their efforts.

326

"The Sedona area is used to E.T.'s which some call woo-woo stuff. We say you are blessed Dear Ones. It is almost Party time! Relax and enjoy! Revelations upon revelations will be announced and look what you have been part of ... the Genii since 1982, for goodness sake!

"Go to the Embassy of the United Nations. There is lots going on there and you will be surprised. Genii you carry the 'City Key' to the whole planet's change-over. Imagine that! Go forth and have fun and we will enjoy with you as more and more people sense something is going on and walk around in wonderment. Here you have the proof and validation on tapes, trans-audio, video, and in person. This is God-stuff!

"Stay on the path for it leads you correctly, and we here support your efforts for it will pay great dividends for... guess what? SOMETHING'S COMING! And you bring good news."

G: "Thank you! All of you here and everywhere. G.T. feels at home here and now goes home."

O: "Report to YA for space information and we bid you the LOVE of the eternal day in peace and Light."

And with this, all disappeared and I AM that I AM!

Divine Intervention Soon!

Embassy Visit February 19, 2012

An Embassy of Peace visit was always intriguing, and it was a thrill to be asked to attune and to hear for myself what was in progress as I had for many years. I was sure glad I requested somewhere in time, if I could see it before it manifested. "Yes" was the answer which took me many years to get elevated enough to do just that, and thus my City of Light book came into being. All of the Embassy visits in order were now in process for the 2nd edition coming forth as had been requested.

So as I released myself from my daily list of what needed to be taken care of, I slipped into the meditative state of knowing and mentally envisioned The City of Light, where I found myself at a 5-story Gate of Entrance with a lot of other people who were first-timers. My surprise was that something new had been added on top, which looked like an angel of some sort. Must be something I saw in my daily Earth life?

Anyway I saw my Guide La-Luke and with his hands pointing forward, he somehow parted the seas of people and we hooked up. Grabbing my hand, we scooted through the Relaxation Park and onto our usual trolley ride to the Embassy where we got off and entered through backstage onto the main arena with OOO-LON and his CEO's numbering 4, ready to meet with us. Whoopee!

O: "Welcome, it is good news I share" he said as our conversation began.

G: "Great, what can I be given to share?"

O: "The City continues its process of entrance. All is in order and the process of putting all the vision pieces together continues as if on a time schedule, since it seems to be 2012 in your world. You may have noticed that the changes you feel in your body temple signifies something unusual is taking place on a higher electrical vibration, and you do live in the Sedona of The City magic."

G: "Yes, I seem to notice more vibrational something throughout my body, even to kind of see it like attached to the skeletal area. How am I to manage to stay normal with this in connection with traveling with The City and The 4 Keys to Light?"

O: "Dear One, normal you are not, nor will you ever be again as you have intuited. However the systems of many are also taking on this observation and Light glow. Are you going to be able to continue? Of course! You are to be of no concern and in traveling there is appointed someone you can count on to be there in constant support who knows the situation; and also you are being monitored daily and with the changes in your electrical system you will be glad you had this change-over. Does illumination mean anything to you, Golden Ones?"

G: "What of The City at this point? Can a date be announced yet? And where has it set down in my locality?"

O: "We are delighted to let you know that soon you will get your desire."

G: "Always the word is 'soon' which does not denote a date in time. How soon?"

O: "Very soon, however all facets must be in place for human contact. I am just to let you know that all is well and in order...soon!"

G: "How about the other Cities of Light also to be brought forth?"

O: "They too, I should repeat again, will come after this holographic City of Light is revealed and it has impacted the whole of the planet. Imagine that! This first one is on your door step so-to-speak.

"Patience...patience. Would it not be fun to have the surprise with the rest of the world after all these years of holding the Light on it? You will know when it gets closer. You have more to share on this heavenly-sent event. Dear One, you shall have heaven on Earth...soon! Just be ... all is well."

And with that he just grinned and the whole scene vanished. I guess he had said enough.

Thanks God, I am delighted.

"If You Don't Believe in Miracles, You're Thinking too Small"-- Oprah

Embassy Visit February 29, 2012

I was at the familiar Gate that now presents an angel high up on the top. Her name is Bella and she welcomes everyone to this magnificent place of God's honor. It must have been felt, as crowds moved to get in and see this Miracle first-hand. I saw a hand raised from my Guide La-Luke who signaled me to come to him, as I waded through the exciting energy being produced everywhere.

We did the usual run through the Park of Relaxation and onto the trolley of Light, but we arrived quickly, delighted to once again be honored with this knowing to return. Was this an adventure or what? I had no questions at the moment but was sure to get information to boost anyone's energy fields. I could just hear my friend Renee yelling "Whoopee!"

OOO-LON the head E.T. master smiled and invited me to sit down for our discussion, which was my privilege as all the love I felt in here could knock anyone over as it was so pure...literally.

O: "Welcome back to the Sanctuary of God. We have begun to expect you at any time as The City energy shifts into high volume. What, no questions?"

G: "The vibrations taking place now in the Sedona area and beyond, are being felt by many people I speak to, who are not sure what is going on. It is like a roller coaster ride some days, so any update would be appreciated."

O: "It should be reported that what you call miracles is on the way. This City becomes more solid as the days pass in your dimension. What appears to be possibly quiet, is actually quite active in the unseen at this point. The vortexes have taken on a dramatic stream of power all linking together. You have seen in your theater world productions, the activity and excitement of how this stage production will be accepted. New shows are always busy backstage to make it the best show ever, and accepted by the critics who look for the results to report. Oh my, they will have plenty to talk about. The media will have a field day literally... how else could it be? Something that seemed to fall out of the sky? Please!

"In a strange way, this is God's theater production pulling itself together for the grandest show this planet has ever witnessed... (such fun from our point of view) and no tickets to be sold...it is free! What free? Indeed. The local gentry of your area will be quite surprised as this astounding news travels north, south, east, and west and around the planet that the number one CITY of Light has appeared with 13 more on the grid lines. 14 total!"

NOTE: Later increased to total of 14.

Oops! There goes Renee again. "Whoopee!!!"

"So what does it take to believe in miracles? A City of Light should do it big time. No doubts, just love in action. Oh there might be those who still think it is an E.T. invasion and maybe it is, but God's Cosmic Terrestrial invasion is like no other event that anyone could imagine. As has been said in your book of The City, it was a usual day until... to be sure a miracle took place. Now what? Property prices will soar and prosperity becomes the norm. Imagine That! Never envisioned in such a way. So expect the unexpected where least expected. How does this sound?"

G: "Great, unusual to be sure but since I have been with this wisdom of a coming City, I am as excited as anyone to see it appear. So something's coming!"

O: "Then take a deep breath for many entities in the unseen make this a holy place of honor and healing ... as The City has the healing powers to heal people, animals and places on this planet. The 11-11-11 love scenario that you spoke about on that day, has The City energy flowing north, south, east and west and as a wave of love that holds no boundaries. As a dear friend has said, 'It is either love or it isn't!'

Lady Light, this is love at its purest ... as 14 Cities will attest to this by demonstration of appearance, as the first prototype City appears (in Sedona area) and for a moment in time, the Earth will stop and take a deep breath. Tears of love will flow from those who have held the Light on this project for eons of time. And hearts will open up as for one brief moment in time God will have everyone's attention.

"Celebration is in order for a New World is due and God has come to the rescue. Love has entered hearts that may have missed love previously in their lifetime, because suddenly without notice a miracle appeared. It is 2012 and this year will go down in history as has been predicted ever since the 3 wise men saw a star in the heavens (which was indeed The City of Light) we speak of here. It led them to the baby, to the birth, and that birth leads us with many other masters to this time, to this place, to you. So Dear One, progress is being made. Anything else?"

G: "For someone who had no questions, we did pretty well here today. Thank you all. I am blessed to be a messenger of such fantastic revelations. Whoopee!"

O: "The City may be hidden for the moment, but as we are aware of this Miracle of Miracles, it is putting the finishing touches on its presence in 3D. You all are about to have a wonder-filled world and we from the Universe see the new is born out of the old, and the Galactic family welcomes Earth into its community of universal Light, where the welcome mat presents itself. Indeed all is well. Spread the word and request others do like-wise, as the time of Miracles is due. Excitement is in the air just for the taking and we invite you back soon."

G: "Thank you all for who you are and what you are doing. This Jedi Genii is pleased and blessed. I will be back as invited."

The Earth Took a Deep Breath and God Said, "It is Done"

Embassy Visit March 7, 2012

These are the words that rang through my head after I experienced the most overwhelming awareness I have ever received. Oh My God! Good thing I was sitting down. Charles and I were attending a 3 day conference in Los Angeles titled "Author 101 University."

As this unexpected altered state of awareness engulfed me, I looked down at my notebook and this conference title was quite apparent. The word "University" was for me really ... "UNIVERSE-CITY" followed by the inner knowing that the first issue of the "City of Light Sedona" book was to be changed, due to the universal entities pulling it all together.

Another Oh my God! Of course ... it made so much more sense to me. So I decided it was time to go to The City Embassy which I did the following day, as our next stop was Disneyland and at the hotel I could find some silence.

Embassy Visit March 8, 2012

As I tuned in ready to enter the usual Gate, OOO-LON's face appeared and the welcome mat was out as the screen of space had me standing in front of the stage (in The Embassy of Peace), where Entities were with him. They were all smiles as I took my place ready to receive some God news.

O: "You had a heart-filled invitation to The City?"

G: "Oh my yes, the impact was so clear and the feeling so overwhelming. I had looked at the word University several times but it made no imprint as such. With the wave of love, I looked at it again and the words 'Universe City' became apparent and as a new updated book title with 'all' of the Embassy visits included.

"That this book will be a national treasure, and AFTER The City is manifested, will be most important ... big time! The whole Universe together is bringing forth The City of Light and a name change with the leading headline reading. "Something's Coming!' What can you tell me of all this?"

O: "The time of arrival is nearing and the book of Light as you now know, is to be updated and re-titled. More trips on this subject will be necessary to travel in person and speak. The words 'Something's Coming' rings true now in many hearts and minds of people, as the 11-11-11 love change continues to flow forward into people's frequencies.

"So 'Something is Coming', is appropriate and rings true as the heart-sensing picks up the vastness of these words. So do that... add all the visits and anything else you are guided to enter, for this is good news. And as you sense, The City is here, near, and very dear. The Charles will know the printed ways. 'UNIVERSE CITY' reaps much in 'its vastness of words.'"

G: "The vastness of the awareness imprint I received was overwhelming and there is so much more that will take place (after the appearance). I just went into a state of euphoria, bliss and tears of joy, and wondering of what will really take place then?"

O: "The make-up of The City of Light energy has the power beyond your current knowing, and is indeed vast. As you walk around you see people who have no idea that anything like this, could take place, yet it will be beyond surprise that God can indeed do miracles, as one has appeared right before their eyes. Is this not a major life change in the thinking process? Making believers that the non-physical can become physical, and classroom # 101 ANYTHING IS POSSIBLE! becomes the normal...imagine that!

"Do what has been given you to do and permit God to take care of the details, for this UNIVERSE CITY is indeed the product of such visions as is written in this Book of Light we speak of here. UNIVERSE CITY is the mark of God filled with love. Honor all unconditionally as pre-programmed as such. We bid you the Light of the eternal day in peace and in love." The Session ended...

And for a brief moment, the Earth took a deep breath as God declared,

"THE UNIVERSE CITY IS DONE! MISSION ACCOMPLISHED!"

Beyond the Ordinary . . . Manifesting a Miracle!

Embassy Visit March 11, 2012

Note: The City of Light has been with me for 30 years, and thus through inner vision I have been privileged to know and see the unseen, as I trans-audio bits and pieces of what has been heart and soul revealed to me thus far. My senses feel the closeness (of the unseen) and people ask me where, when and how this City of Light can take place. We are in the 3rd dimension where we are used to building things like I build the puppets. It must seem to others that something this awesome must be a figment of an imagination gone wild.

Since I have embodied this concept for this long a time, I feel I am quite on target with what has been given and whoopee... the Divine Design is manifesting as a miracle in process and progress is being made. I would share this scene: Charles and I were just back from an authors' book conference where a lady saw my book cover and became interested in it.

I asked her if she would like to flip through it. She took it for a few hours and came back saying that I had a lot of courage. "Who me?" I wondered. She then added, "That people must think you are nuts." I smiled and replied that when the book was published, within a few weeks it was in 15 countries plus the good old USA.

She left still flipping pages and kept it overnight. The next day she came back and said. "I finished your book. Read it until 2:30 a.m. Thank you for writing such a book and giving us hope and faith for a better future." I gave her The City of Light book. Thanks God! (Just call me Indiana Genii... this is quite an adventure.) So now on and into the Embassy and...

BEYOND THE ORDINARY.....MANIFESTING A MIRACLE!

The familiar Gate loomed into my sight as people were rushing to enter. I met my Guide La-Luke and we headed for the Relaxation Park and the massage benches. I wished I had time now to enjoy them but the wheel-less trolley arrived and it scooted us to the Embassy of Peace.

As we walked in the audience of hundreds of space friends again sent us so much love that I broke into joy tears. They were busy sending out tone sounds as words are not part of their vocabulary.

O: "Ah, we have the pleasure of your visit once more, and I see you have received the message of changing the current book title to 'Universe City.' So how can we of the Universe be of service and fill in any blanks so to speak?"

G: "People will experience this Universal City as a miracle. What does it take to make this miracle happen that I may share?"

O: "If you were to build this place of Light by human hands, it would be impossible for as you know, the technology expressed here is way beyond any and all that has been produced on Earth until now. I must add here that you have some beautiful buildings and temples etc. all built by your current implements created on this planet.

"As you have reported to people, this City of Light has to materialize in the 3rd dimension and we have to walk into it. Plus the healing technologies pre-told of must be experienced in 3D, or all of this is just a story ... a fairy tale. We laugh since we are well aware of what it takes to bring forth something so far beyond the ordinary. Magic must take place and it will! To have this magic take place, any magic, one has to be the magic-maker and such is Divine Source, the Creator of all who made even the ground you walk on daily. Where would you walk if there was no Earth planet?

"One must lift their sights to be able to understand what is being said here. One must lift the consciousness of this whole planet, as this is what supports systems. Friends of the Universe have banded together to each bring forth a magic space technology in their own way. You see many Space technologists here.

"You read in messages of Michael Quinsey, Russ Michael and numerous others, how the helpers of the unseen Galactics are very busy in many areas, cleaning up the thoughts that have made your planet send out a call for help. Help has arrived ... big time!

"For thousands of your recalled years of accurate calculating, this Universe City of Light as been on what you would call planned intent trajectory, directed by the Creator. Then Hermes, the architect who designed the great pyramid, stepped forth to put it all together and within your Earth knowing.

"Hermes filled the void as he was the architect who not only designed the pyramid, but taught the holy magic in the great pyramid mystery school, which in another life the Dr. Bill was his constant student of equal wisdom. So that is why you married this man of the cloth as he taught the truth, and would stand for nothing less. Three divine designs came to the Dr. Bill, thus giving you information to be recorded.

"You have a man in the office of the President now that heads up your country. Obama is a man of such Light that he will accept The City information easily and can lead the people after The City appears. Obama was also in the Hermes mystery school and he is programmed to know that this City of Light will appear. (Remember this sentence.)

"Thus Dr. Bill was open even though it took some time to receive the drawings, which is of course recorded in the book of Light, so progress was made. This Dear One, looking at it from your point of view was a massive, massive undertaking beyond what your senses could imagine.

"The Universe 'IMAGINE-NATION' (hundreds of supporters) took over as your planet is out of control, with your history attesting this to be so. Even now all that is known is war, after war, after war, and this is not to be continued as this negative energy sends out bad vibes into the cosmos communities far and wide.

"Sound like a story? Time to change the chapters to a happy ending and thus we speak here together. What will look like a miracle is indeed a Divine Design put together (by highly advanced beings) and delivered on your doorstep.

"However God is the magic maker and nothing is impossible!!! Many levels of unseen workers in worlds you have not yet met bring forth this miracle of delivery. Did you make all this up? We think not. It was given to you long before you entered this lifetime for distribution anywhere you can take it. Being seen in person makes the human contact believable.

"This miracle is God's Divine Imprint of change to fit into the universal way of doing things, which dear heart is LOVE...Pure LOVE. Ah, love, you people use it trippingly off the tongue when it should be heart-felt instead. This is about to change! Have I answered your question?"

G: "Yes sir, quite so! Thank you!"

O: "Indeed, now just be open to anything unusual to take place within your local territory. Much action is in process and many entities unseen bring forth dramatic results for final delivery, just like magic.

"We bid you the Light of the Universal companions sending you real love, first class and that leaves no one out."

And with that the scene ended and I was home feeling like on a Sunday morning I had just been to church,

Universe City style. Imagine that!

Something's Coming! Universal Cities of Light!

Embassy Visit March 18, 2012

Pre-entrance note:

As my background music played, "Suddenly It's Spring" it reminded me that the trees in D.C. were in their spring cherry blossom splendor. We just had an overnight snowstorm in Sedona that made the red rocks appear and disappear as boa-type clouds wrapped themselves around my favorite rocks. The one just outside my window looked much like a sleeping dragon on his belly, and I long since named him 'Nogg' for no particular reason that I know of ... Ooops... now you see him, now you don't. Fun stuff and why would I tell you that? It plays a part in this Embassy visit.

Embassy Visit Begins

Entering into inner space, my vision fell on many people going through the 5-story magnificent Gate of Entrance with me trying to get to my City Guide La-Luke. He made the passageway easy and we connected. In heading to the usual trolley I smelled blossoms in the air as we hopped aboard and quickly found ourselves in the Embassy of Peace. Coming on stage which was filled with Universal Light Beings (E.T.'s), OOO-LON the Embassy Headmaster sounded a tone and all returned into the audience and silence permeated the whole building.

OOO-LON broke the silence: "We see you have received the inner-net invitation to return. Good, we shall proceed."

G: "Thank you. Something must be important."

O: "It is guidance on the appearance of the #1 Universe City of Light, Sedona Location area. Your understanding is important as we tune into the final stages of delivery. The proposed new edition of your book now being revised has a new title: 'UNIVERSE CITIES OF LIGHT.' You have been saying that SOMETHING IS COMING! That would be the head caption followed next line with UNIVERSE CITIES OF LIGHT. Understand? There is energy in these words in that order."

G: "You are now adding more 'Cities'?"

O: "Yes, however the Sedona area location will still be the first one that the concentration will be held to, but since the other UNIVERSE CITIES are in process, the message that more will be introduced is now in order.

"Number One is the Sedona area for reasons you are well aware of, and from that appearance people will be so moved that the desire for more in distant locations will total 13 more. None of those will appear until #1 is settled in and responding with healings unheard of. The new book edition should carry the message that 14 Universal Cities total are coming forth."

G: "I know I am going to be asked where on this planet will they be? What am I to report?"

O: "That you cannot really say even if you wanted to. You have some indications but nothing substantial. The minds should be on #1, the first to be acknowledged. Understand?"

G: "Will you please give me a message on this subject of where to be put into the book in response?"

O: "Of course, acknowledgments will be given. The next step is the new book and it should be noted that all who are involved in bringing forth this edition, printed and moved out, will be blessed beyond their knowing as God never forgets, and also acknowledged in the book itself. Once again pay attention! This book will go down in your planet history beyond anything written prior. Imagine that! We play not games here. This planet is in immediate change ... personally as well as planetary. Take the first book apart and use it as the prototype. Start and begin lining up what is to be added and where. Add as given. ASAP is the time line for its completion and the printed copies are to go far and wide. Understand?"

G: "Yes what else is to be incorporated in the new issue besides these complete Embassy visits which in itself will tell much?"

O: "A further evaluation of the 4 Keys and even using guided information such as personal spirit Guides and how they got them etc. Tones of Light. Just be open and see what is given."

G: "Anything else to be known now?"

O: "As you look out your window now, what you see or don't see with your dragon rocks depends on the clouds of snowy light. It moves and you see a bit of his head, it moves again and the head disappears as the snow falls in its healing planetary pleasure. Seeing the new City formations will look like this at first ... misty and magical. The City aura contains enough frequencies to give you sight clues. Be alert! Now you see it, now you don't. Just know it is in your general location somewhere in time and space. The return invitations here will expand, and each visit here will give you future clues for investigating."

G: "Is there an explanation subtitle on the cover?"

O: "The spaceship cover should remain, with a slight color change if necessary. Attention from the last book can be decided, and the words already given with any extra subtitle you would decide on, can be used. Keep it simple. All is well."

And with that, he made a sound and all the audience seemed to stand as OOO-LON acknowledged our leaving. Transportation being like it was, I found myself back in my Sedona home looking at the sleeping dragon rocks appear and disappear just like before. "Thanks God for a great visit and I honor all the Light Beings above and below putting together the greatest show on Earth."

Disclosure: The Welcome Mat is Out!

Embassy Visit March 22, 2012

As the sun rose over the red rocks and all the snow had disappeared, a new day had begun in Sedona. I looked to re-enter the Embassy of Peace in The City of Light.

In deep meditational vision I found myself back at the very familiar Gate of Entrance, one of several. My Guide La-Luke waved me through throngs of people who were parting as we made contact.

Once inside the Embassy with its hundreds of extraterrestrial Light Beings, I was quite comfortable having been here many times. OOO-LON the head leader acknowledged us by standing and we began our conversation.

G: "Good morning, thank you for having us again."

O: "Looks like the Lady of Light is excited about something."

G: "I don't know why I should be as I meet space beings right here, but as I was about to fall asleep last night I saw in the clear sky, bright lights that were too big to be stars. Spacecraft?"

O: "Of course. The Sedona area is quite active now as The City makes its appearance. Craft vehicles move easily in the night, for this demonstration takes many away from their homes to far-away places to intermix with the unseen you are about to experience."

G: "Here in The City I meet many (space beings) and some are my mentors as you know. Why is there not yet a disclosure for sure that they are here? What is the hold-up?"

O: "There will be (disclosure). Your planet people have such mixed feelings, from deep fear to unbelief, that the right timing is important - but rest easy ... it will be."

G: "What can I share?"

O: "The City of Light is doing well, as pieces of the intergalactic process continue to ignite frequencies of wholeness and oneness that The City represents. Love should not have to be forced on anyone and we come from that galaxy that only knows love, and that comes with this package called The City of Light Sedona entry. You are all into time-mindedness and that makes the interest of time important for many reasons, even if time as such does not exist.

"The messengers of many galactic space communities verify that all is on the non-time schedule. Remember Genii, you have been recording these visits for mankind to know what has taken place, long before The City made its appearance, lo these many years.

"This is good. Now as your planet is cleansing up what is un-love, we on the other hand give possibilities of a new world quite near with the probabilities of great new connections with us from space.

"You have asked about disclosure. Those who believe and those who do not, will have quite a time when all this is revealed. We attempt to make it easy, but cannot predict at this point what the response of such a message will be. However rest easy, all is known in a divine connection. From our place in space to your space in place, God makes all things clear. Anything else?"

G: "I feel so blessed and excited as I look ahead, even for a few short weeks to the probabilities and the near future is already here. Many Lightworkers who have patiently waited having seen Cities of Light for centuries overhead or someplace in space, and now we are sitting in the birthing nest. What more can I do?"

O: "And helping you, all are. Keep open for more travel and meetings unlisted, at this point both in the physical, and like this moment in the non-physical. The news you bring that 'Something is Coming' is quite correct, and ready-or-not peace on Earth will take the place of the turmoil now in the news. It is spring house-keeping for the Genii, and spring house-cleaning for this planet in general. Come back soon ... we await another type of disclosure to share with you.

"Your new advanced book 'UNIVERSAL CITIES of LIGHT' will out-sell the others, for it is disclosure for all mankind, written in love and advancement. See it soon-completed and come back soon. We await your entry. God be with you!"

And with this ... before I could blink...I was back in my room, watching a big yellow passenger balloon come down in someone's yard nearby.

Must be just another day in mystic Sedona.

Remembering!

Morning Message March 25, 2012

Thirty four years ago today on Easter's Holy Saturday, wearing a beautiful pink gown from my daughter, I walked down the center isle alone in the Apple Valley Church in CA, to be the bride of the man and minister, friend and mentor (I had grown to love), and to enter my new life with Rev. Dr. William J. Townsend.

Little did I or he know what God had set before us ... a Divine plan that even my wildest imagination could not conjure up. Sure I was fresh out of a previous marriage, and I had completed building a puppet empire called Geniiland in Los Angeles, which was a fun place that families could bring their kids to for a birthday party they would never forget.

"After all," Walt said, as I looked at my fourth expansion building, "Build a bigger mouse trap, and the world will beat a path to your door." I had achieved that, being the first lady in Los Angeles to do something of this magnitude. Being a Disney fan of long standing, I could not ignore Walt's words as I stood at the door looking up at this huge building. I took a deep breath and led my followers into a 5000 sq. ft. two-story world of fun, where all I had to sell was a memory. It worked for 18 consecutive years.

Then came the next step in my life on this day 34 years ago, for unknown to either of us, Dr. Bill and I were to be told of a City of Light that was to descend on the planet Earth. Yeah right! Sure, and I am going to fly to the moon. Now I could dream up puppet shows, but this was far beyond anything I could fathom, much less have a part in ... a City of Light coming onto this planet.

One day Dr. Bill, a meditation teacher, was in a deep meditation state when he began bringing through voices unknown in this awareness. It took me a while to get the picture and when he drew out designs of stuff in this supposed City of Light in the un-physical, I became fascinated. This man could not draw a straight line, yet here I was looking at specific designs not seen or known of here. Wow! O.K. God, you have my attention. Now I'll believe.

So now some 34 years later and 15 years after Bill checked out, I am left with all the plans and audio tapes that we made together. And now a new edition of my City book is on the way to bring out all the meditation vision-visits I have experienced inside this miracle of miracles. Indeed yes... something is coming... big time. So God, what am I to know and do as of today Sunday March 25, 2012?

ANSWER:

"1. To remember that you are on a mission like no other.

2. That this mission is number one above anything else.

3. That the mission involves millions of people due to The City events.

341

4. That this planet has never in its beginning history experienced such an event.

5. That the time line lessens with each passing hour.

6. To expect vast new information even though it may not be asked for.

7. That unlike any other messenger, you have been chosen and that makes you a bit different.

8. That this mission is most important and attention must be paid constantly.

9. That the truth of your being and DNA is recorded as such.

10. That messages of guidance may come quickly as clues are revealed.

11. That the way of Light for everyone is at hand as God's gift to humanity.

12. That the revelation and proposed Second Coming is already here, just not seen in its full view as yet. But it will be for any of this to be valid.

13. Prepare for any and all trips as they are announced for you to attend with your information and insights.

14. That in this day, miracles are in process and manifestation reveals itself... soon.

Be the Light of The City and all will rejoice as what you said was correct and true for, it stands before everyone as God in action and cannot be denied.

So Light it be!"

And God Smiles . . . Imagine That!

Embassy Visit April 1, 2012

It was Sunday and considered a Holy Week for many, as Easter was a week away and the kids looked forward to something special from the Easter Bunny. For me any visit back to The City Embassy of Peace was an Easter gift.

As I re-entered my quiet space, the usual Gate of Entrance opened the scene with my Guide waving to me over the heads of excited people. Catching up with him, we ran through the Park of Relaxation with what looked like no time to stop. We were trolley-bound in the direction of the Embassy of Peace and a reunion with hundreds of extraterrestrials making up the audience while OOO-LON and his companions held this meeting for me on a stage. All was quite quiet in this space of honor as we were being welcomed back. The silence seemed loud in its welcome.

O: "Another visit. You both are welcome. How may we serve you?"

G: "I am not sure. My part in this magnificent City production is to bring information of The City as an update. Can you share with me what has taken place so far?"

O: "In a word you understand…PROGRESS! The spring winds in your area herald in the newness of the coming event. You say this is a Holy Week for many and indeed it brings good news of the holy coming. Will it tie into the day when a famous man entered the Holy City? Are there hidden clues here? Entering into The City of Light could very well raise the consciousness to accept this as a possibility, like the previous story.

"Those of us who see the yet unwrapped City are well aware of the layout and what it contains, like you who have entered often over many years. Even now close friends support bringing forth the new updated book of continual progress as the New Cities are added to the first edition. The word spreads that 13 more Cities of Light will become commonplace after the first in your area is birthed through the power of the vortexes as God planned it to be. Nothing less is expected!

"The City layout of buildings, parks, fountains all with healing value is now being prepared by your friend Kathie who finally found what her insight book teacher was trying to tell her. It is important that children learn that miracles are common-place and with her description in children's language, this is quite possible that the children will lead the parents to The City of Light as if going to a place the Genii loves to play in called Disneyland. Though different, the magic is apparent as healings take place without painful instruments or drugs.

"So what you are writing about at this moment will be an invitation to be open to enter a City of Light from many areas as the planet cleans itself of ignorance and greed, we look to what will fill that space.

"You have been advised that you are to be open and information on the next 13 cities after the first one in your area will be addressed in the new issue. You will not need to come here for that. It will be given in a quite few moments."

G: "I will be available. Thank you!"

O: "Good... This will be a special entry on that subject only. It will be a-toned to you. When we say yes it will be soon to enjoy the new gift of God, we understand that, that word had no time line and we shall leave it as such. For the moment however it does have frequencies of appearance. Just know the 'ground work' is in process and the entry could be closer than one might think at the moment but...all is well!"

G: "I keep getting asked if one has to be in a higher level of consciousness to be able to see The City as it arrives or can anyone see it on any level?"

O (smiling): "Report that the levels of obtaining 'Light-hood' depends on the person themselves. The changes on the planet would offer each one the invitation to upper-level empowerment be it level 3-4-5-6 or 10. What do they seek? This is a personal matter with each one. You get what you desire.

"It makes no difference. This City is to heal and they have to see and walk into it, as not just a figment of the mind. Elevating one's self is of course important but not necessarily the only course. A homeless person on the street may be more in a higher spiritual level than the appearance you see. We choose not, all are God chosen, all are God incarnated. Precisely why The City of Light is necessary. We have spoken of this many times."

G: "I am well aware, thank you."

O: "YA is your mentor E.T. now, as space talk will support. Share your words with the world as Mike Quinsey's Salusa does, as bringing good news lifts everyone and sharing the Creator's work moves forward. As your new book title says, 'SOMETHING'S COMING! UNIVERSE CITIES OF LIGHT!' We bless and attend you."

And with this, this silent place became a joy-filled active audience ready for 'soon' to appear. All is indeed well!

As we left the Embassy on the first day of Holy Week, I thought, may God bless us all with a Holy City known as the Second Coming!

Happy Easter week.

This is the Day the Lord Has Made: We Can Be Glad and Love in It!

Morning Message April 7, 2012 Holy Saturday

Q: What am I to be aware of and even share if it is important to do that love-intended?"

A: "This day of what you say is Holy Saturday, as tomorrow brings new life as recorded. For children it is the Easter Bunny and eggs of various colors. For adults who feel the sensing of honor and spiritual essence, it can be a wonder-fulfilling-refreshing day of non-resistance to love and be loved, so begin today for tomorrow is already here.

> 1. Permit love to increase knowing love, for it can fill places in the human system that heals and brings joy for many.
>
> 2. In being the holiness of love, one can attract the same vibrations as The City of Light will prove to all.
>
> 3. Begin today to make way for tomorrow by being holy.
>
> 4. As the air changes vibrations of feeling unloved, it reaches many. But by staying in the Light of love you move past all of that.
>
> 5. Take not a part of non-love, for your essence is of a higher vibration and you are that the minute you give love!
>
> 6. Listen to love for it is holy as it sings from the heart and accept it as your own.
>
> 7. Speak words only from the heart in soft tones of God's whisper so as to not offend anyone.
>
> 8. Feel from the heart love and appreciation, for that love is universal and flows on the winds of time forever.
>
> 9. As you say very often, "If you can't say something nice, don't say anything at all.

"Peace be with you, within you, and to all about you. Feel this holy day as one who walks with God spreading seeds of love to grow and replenish everyone you meet. You are all this and more, just maybe not aware.

"This, Dear One, is being a Holy Jedi with a saber of Light. Pull the trigger and send the healing love forward missing no one. Share this message and spread the holy love. It can be catching. The Love will come back 10-fold. Imagine that!"

So love I AM! BLESSINGS ON THIS HOLY SATURDAY.

Out of Time!

Embassy Visit April 21, 2012

Spring has come to Sedona and the colorful flowers peeking out, are deliciously beautiful to the underground demolition squad of gophers looking to have the family over for dinner with an open invitation.

My invitation was to return to The City of Light and the Embassy of Peace auditorium where hundreds of the undisclosed beings from spaces and places we know not of, gathered while setting the course for the grand opening of The City of Light and their disclosure of being here long since.

Inner Scene begins...

The usual south Gate came into mental inner view and looked crowded as usual. People really wanted to see what was inside this main attraction (never before witnessed on this planet.) I wanted to see and hear what the population would say about this when they saw it. Woopie ... Something's Coming!

My Guide La-Luke grabbed my hand and we headed for the funny trolley in excitement of just being here. It seemed like home to me after all these years of entering. A swift ride and a jumping off at the Embassy, fulfilled all my expectations with many more to come. Was I lucky or what?

There seemed to be no time here when we entered through the backstage drapes of gold onto the stage where OOO-LON and four others led the meetings with space tones I was not understanding ...yet! (Well, I *am* Jedi material).

O: "Welcome to us of Inner Light of Universal Friends. Please be seated with us here on this platform as we direct the proceedings."

G: "Thank you. It feels good to be back in voice connect. Kind of like coming home.

"What can be shared with those of contact through my information internet mail-outs? They want to know when of course this demonstration will be made publicly seen, and also when will those here be seen. Will there be an announcement (a disclosure) made public?

"Seems like a waste of energy or something just waiting for this to take place, as so many of us know we walk with the space entities now and have been for a very long time."

O: "Hungry for information are you? We here in this place of peace and honor, are pleased to share with you and the readers of contact you supply. News about The City of course is the prime reason for even this visit, true?"

G: "Yes. What can be said of its appearance? In our world I hear it is taking a long time and also of the E.T's announcement. You are all making a miracle come to pass. How many will delight to know miracles do exist?

"This is proof positive. No one can be in denial of what is right before their eyes. Proof positive that God exists, and with a wave of intent here it is. We have the Rainbow Connection as my puppet friend Kermit the frog sings about."

A smiling OOO-LON continued: "Even frogs know the truth it seems. Many times the question of when has ridden out of the mental wonder. This year? This day? This moment? Taking time out of the equation, what do you have? Ahhh... NOW! That old word is really misunderstood.

"There is no time in the Universe! This is a mental impression that sets the minds into a different way of thinking. One of Your planet locations has one hour or more than your time zone may not have. You made it all up for convenience or... not.

"How long does it take for you to make a puppet from idea to stage performance? Hard to answer for time is only a part of this equation unless an appointment must be met, then you may be 'out of time.'

"You are always 'out of 'time' as there is none. People say this all the time, 'Oh dear, I am out of time, must rush to finish'...whatever.

"The collapse of time is in The City's favor while the cleansing of your planet continues to clean up what has been described as darkness or ignorance due to the greed of those who serve themselves, and their destructive thoughts to discontinue the lives of others. Destruction is apparent as the media pronounces, and as the old moves into the new; time is collapsing to bring Light and love into being, and Dear One, The City will do that ... BIG TIME.

"So then from the Genii's point of view, it is done, finished and NOW appearing as she walks The City grounds and looks forward in local time and (again this time zone thought is hard to get past.) 'SOON' is the closest we can give you for it is 'NOW!' Behind the scenes many high level spirit Light reporters keep the clearing in process and they are to be blessed.

"To fill in the blanks of The City process, it has been moving into your time zone as vibrational energy to form what you are seeing in these visits which is a preview of that which is for coming attractions. In the NO time zone you should be aware it is IMMEDIATE! We endeavor to explain the unexplainable through these words of your understanding.

"You have been guided to bring forth with the help of Light supporters a new edition of The City of Light titled, 'SOMETHING'S COMING! CITIES OF LIGHT' Ah ... expansion in sight! Imagine that and the first one is not seen yet. Time collapses and the world of Earth illusion moves forward in no time.

"And your planet will question where? and when? Sound familiar? Meanwhile back to the time zones. Which we understand is the human programming, but it too will change ... Imagine that!

"As your world cleanses of the vermin that has taken advantage of others, the Light is saturating and penetrating your planet on a continual basis, as it can do no other. Take away the darkness and you have Light. As you say, 'Whoopie!'

"And Light we all are here, and like millions of others, we are replacing the old thinking with new Light space technology, making room for new possibilities. Soon you will have small but mighty electrical devices that are changing so fast even you are disconnected somewhat, so be not concerned. You are doing your part with this City information. Rest easy as we complete our timely task to serve all in and out of the 'time zone' order of things.

"So then take this message and share. Bless all the unseen Lightworkers as well as the seen ones, and we look forward to your next Alien Encounter here."

And with that a hum tone ran through the audience as I connected with their 'ah tone' once more.

Back home enticed by Light Spirit my Pomeranian puppy, who was always on a lookout for sustenance in cookie form, I looked forward to The City in the Now!

NOW!

So Light it be!

Beyond Perceived Boundaries!

Embassy Visit April 29, 2012

With my puppy Light snuggled nearby my bed and "Evergreen" playing in the background, I was reminded that this was Bill's and my wedding song that played while I walked down the aisle to him. Never did I ever think I would be transferred off to some far away dream that he trans-audioed in meditation way back in 1982.

Now I prepared to again visit The City Embassy of Peace. Hmmm! How many times had it been? About 13 this year alone? Well, on with the show ...

The south 5-story Gate was busy with excited joy-filled people, but I moved through easily when my Guide La-Luke waved his hand to me, like parting the sea so to speak. It was then through the Park and onto the wheel-less trolley and bingo, we were on the familiar stage in front of OOO-LON and his co-producers of this fabulous place called The City of Light!

O: "We welcome you back once more to this (glancing around) Mecca of Light Beings, themselves far from their homes, all here for the purpose of City unfoldment. How may we be of service to you on this fine day?"

G: "Thank you. Several close friends are with me in the process of putting together the forthcoming Cities of Light manuscript. What can you tell me is to be included?"

O:

"1. The process of the visits has been covered throughout many visits, as you are collating at this time.

2. This will be the last pre-City book developed.

3. The contents of the past visits and the new additions are to be added, as a time link into The City development continues.

4. An opening invitation for the reader to join you in this discovery adventure.

5. The visits themselves will reveal the contents of how this City came about before the general public knew.

6. This will verify the truth of this matter going down in your history.

7. Most of what you need to be aware of, will be downloaded to you as you proceed.

8. Progress reports added as given."

G: "Please can you tell me for publication where the Cities are to appear on this planet?"

O:

"1. The future Cities are exact duplications of the first one, so the book # 1 has already laid out the important healing buildings for the most part.

2. There are to be 13 total replicas, copies of the first in the Sedona area and the others scattered around the planet in various country locations. At this writing Europe, Asia, Australia and Africa are set in locations. The rest will be given as we proceed forward in announcement.

3. For the moment, continue the current process and be open to receive the further announcements.

4. All of the planet is covered. Locations are to take care of the healings needed and questions answered.

5. You will be given the general locations as you tune in closer to publication. "

"The message then is to proceed, and be open to any guidance coming through you. It will be given. The appearance of the 14 Cities (will be given) as you proceed. At this point you are just filling in the blanks so to speak. A bit more time is desired as it all comes together and notification will be given and you can enter it."

G: "And how is the #1 City here doing?"

O: "Very well, the frequencies needed to sort of (fill out) The City so you may see it, are continuing nicely. You see the clouds shift in different patterns and they appear as this shift is in process. Pretty aren't they?

"So, go where called to speak and report. Your inner feelings are the best indicator of all. Trust them. Return to your friends and your book will be published for, Dear One,...SOMETHING IS COMING ... CITIES OF LIGHT!!"

And with this, I thanked this amazing group of Light Entities and the scene ended and I found myself loving everyone, my puppy Light, and me too.

So Light it be!

God's Love and Light Connection!

Embassy Visit May 3, 2012

A sunny morning awakening brought thoughts of love as the sunlight reflected on a zillion roses blooming without any care that they would not bloom. Imagine that! A visit to The City of Light Embassy of Peace and the zillions of new space friends I have been privileged to meet there, who sent me love and Light.

Note: This now-birthing City of Light (ooops...excuse me, I was getting lots of LOVE and LIGHT downloaded on me as I typed what came through in longhand. (get out the Kleenex) came into view as I centered to move to the south Gate. Mulling people were seen doing the same thing in excitement, eager to see what had to be God-made, that brought this forth.

Having caught up with my City Guide La-Luke, we moved through the Relaxation Park, onto a wheel-less trolley and stopped at the beautiful Embassy building. Inside, hundreds of Light Beings from all over the Universe welcomed us with their Light and love, that was strong enough to take me to my knees literally. Now that was real love! Wow!

Note: Whoever is reading this, open your hearts in welcome, for they are indeed 'forever friends' that we really want. God bless every one of them.

I was invited to sit in conversation with the Headmaster, OOO-LON of wisdom and space language, who was the interpreter of what was for my understanding, as they spoke in tones rather than words here.

O: "Another visit, how nice. We have been awaiting your arrival, for it is known that 'LOVE' is the topic you want to have discussed."

G: "Share please of the word LOVE. What is love like in the Universe? I have some friends, the Pecks, who have a Love Center and teach from every direction one could imagine. We here in Sedona, have the Light Center, and City of Light connected where I teach Light advancement as I am guided to do. What can be said of these two powerful energies spoken of so often and used as well here on this planet?"

O: "Light and love are not separate in frequencies. You speak of a Light Center and also a Love Center and both are God-blessed. Speaking of love and Light when both are in a balanced state, bliss is experienced ... A touching of God energy so to speak. So what a person is taught in one area, also connects with the other, even if the people are unaware of such action. It just is! In the Universe this is well known and practiced, thus instantaneous love-happening takes place. A major love Light right now is impressing your planet full force and darkness is being revealed, which is not of love, but ignorance, fear and greed.

"As you say, either it is love or it isn't, and if not love it holds no Light. Those of your planet scramble to hide the damage to others, but hiding is no longer acceptable, for nothing can hide from this Universal Light now in powerful action.

"It is in Love that this action takes place for darkness cannot run and hide like rats going undercover from the Light. In love, cleansing is taking place ready or not from the love of space entitles, and from the hollow Earth comes love for all that is, and all there is known, as The City of Light makes its appearance. The City of Light moves its frequencies into the third dimension you live in. Rest assured that many changes are now in process, as a change for the better is demanded.

"This process may seem to take a long time, but it took a longer time to get it in such a state. However, now is so love-filled, that it is being noticed ... big time. The City of Light brings Love healing. Everything in The City is of love. One would then say it is a Light Center and a Love Center. The passion of God seeks nothing outside of itself for it is complete in this. We here define love as the main ingredient for The City's being, and as another friend has said, 'I AM. Love is all I need!'

"We here all define love as the main ingredient for The City's being. And your whole planet is being showered in love frequencies, which may not be known unless you see what is being brought to the surface to be cleansed...and it will be. Have no doubt in this statement: **'THERE WILL BE NO MORE WARS**!'

"The negative thoughts have been passed down through generation to generation, from people to people and throughout history repeated over and over. A new set of thoughts leads in love and Light while the planet gets used to a City of Light sitting in plain sight, ready to heal. Imagine that! Return and we shall have another love and Light connection. So love you be!"

Wow, the scene ended and I looked to see my puppy Light Spirit, who is the best example of Light and love I knew.

I am Genii Townsend, trans-audio and I approve this message!

Thanks God!

352

Either it's Love or it Isn't . . . Choose Love!

Embassy Visit May 12, 2012

I sensed it was time for me to re-enter The City of Light Embassy of Peace and Love, a huge beautiful building filled with Light Beings of extraterrestrial origin from unknown places in the Universe. I had spoken to a few of them like OOO-LON and YA and others but mostly I felt the love power that enveloped the amphitheater, which sent this love out into The City grounds.

It was several years of our time that I had been coming here. How many times had I been here? "Always" seemed to be the closest answer. I was nudged to enter as I approached the south 5-story Gate.

My Guide La-Luke was nowhere to be seen, so I just proceeded by myself through the Relaxation Park, and hopped aboard the funny trolley that unfailingly took me to the Embassy. Yes, I certainly knew the way.

I was finding that my new book on the Cities of Light was to be completed with a lot of friendly help.

O: "And a good Earth day to you Lady of Light. You received an inner message to report in?"

G: "Yes, thank you for having me back. What am I to digest from this meeting of wisdom?"

O: "The message of The City of Light recognizes the path you walk on and unusual as it seems, is still in process as you and many others recognize that what you have shared with them for lo these many years is now preparing to be seen. When we have been asked, 'When will The City appearance happen?' our answer has been, 'Soon'. Now we can update it into the current wave of frequencies referred to as NOW! This is where your attention should be at ... NOW! ... Get ready for it can happen any day 'NOW.'"

G: "Good! Many are anticipating eagerly what you are saying. The interest is building also with the new edition of The City book. Can we be told where the expected other Cities of Light will be on this vast planet, for everyone would not be able to enter this first one in my Sedona area."

O (smiling): "Would God, the 'I AM' not supply more Cities around the planet? Of course! It has been said that more Cities of Light will appear, but Dear One, not all at the same time as you know time.

"This is so. One by one another will appear and get settled in after the first City is delivered, accepted, and functioning as a healing demonstration of the power of love. Lightworkers who are in to using Light as a healing device will be nudged to prepare for their work to expand in The City. This first Healing location is primary and will set the 'tone' for the others one by one to make their appearance.

"Of course many will want a similar City near them, and that love-power-intent will facilitate the energies to complete the rest, especially after they have been to the first one, for the rest are duplicates of this first Sedona City. Your planet is in a change-over like one could hardly imagine. Space technology beyond belief has been slipping in unnoticed in the guise of holographic movies and such.

"All the blessed Lightworkers are aware that people have to be lifted into higher levels of frequencies and thus each brings forth a talent to help the situation. Lightworkers even now in their daily support of this are important as they shift the low-thinking into some kind of awareness connected to what we are speaking about.

"Your work NOW is to continue to spread the word of The City number one appearance. This is the lead City and vastly important as you are aware of. Continue to teach the 4 Sacred Keys of Light as it has the magic to do just that; lift and prepare the world for what is coming about as they will receive it through their own Guides of Light. You call your students 'Light Links' and you are being asked what they can do to help. It is therefore advised that they spread the word of the 4 Keys and invite more link-ups to join them. All this activity is positive and energy-filled. Groups such as this when active, attract more into the Light as they link up and thus be prepared to be called to comply. This Light work is just beginning and should spread for it has value beyond knowing. When did you begin this Key work?"

G: "1990."

O: "Quite ... Well, continue in love and expect more to attend as the word spreads. The Sedona area City of Light is well on its way to appearance and that will set the course for your higher level work as a space-ologist as your space teacher YA has said, like Jedi training. 'NOW' is the only time anyone has. 'Now' is the current electric wave being experienced by humanity. Time matters not. When asked when The City of Light would appear we gave the answer as 'Soon.' NOW it is to be changed to NOW! That is your key word when asked ... Now!"

G: "What can the Light Links do to support The City's appearance?"

O: "As answered ... spread the word and invite people to join these sessions. Do the space sounds given on a continual basis daily and be the love that you are. I AM ... LOVE! It is all love. The City of Light is a love center and just that in itself is planet-healing, as all healings are done with and in love.What would it be like to have nothing to heal? Nothing ... interesting thought! Imagine that! Could that be what you are heading for? Nothing to be healed? ... 'Somewhere in time,' love could do just that and ... NOW!

"I AM ALL ... IN LOVE! 11-11-11 was just not another date on the calendar. Love began and continues to lift out the darkness of ignorance and replace it with the 'I AM GOD' feeling. It is beyond your daily doings wherein you refer to love gingerly slipping off the tongue, when it should be from the heart only. Love then, is beyond normal ... way beyond.

"11-11-11 is the underpinning that moves today, flowing forth The City into your existence. People's minds are being washed as accepted and those who are not open will not be able to handle the vibrations and will exit one way or another. Your new world leaves no room for darkness of ignorant thinking. Only the power of love and oneness is allowed. Again it is love-intended.

"We say no more! The blessed Galactic Federation moves quietly but surely in support of this cleansing and we at this Embassy support their progress. These universal neighbors are of the Light and love we speak of here, and honor as such. Get ready to meet us face to face for we bring forth the Cities of Light one by one in divine timing called NOW! The City of Light Number One is here NOW! It is either love or it isn't ... Be that NOW ... Hear my words ... LOVE HEALS. NOW! God is I AM in attendance and will have nothing less than this planet's survival. Complete the new book for a whole new world is now approaching and Love is the healer. We bid you the love of the eternal day in peace and Light!"

The scene ended and I was back in my home with my pup ready for some love. I had lots to give him. **Wow ... what a session.**

You are invited to download a color PDF of this gift from my forever friend Stan Hanners at http://www.sedonalightcenter.org/comesfromlove.htm

Playing the Waiting Game!

Embassy Visit May 29, 2012

This early morning seemed to be an invited chance for leaving the outside world to go within The City of Light and meet with the Light Beings from space, and I might say this was quite an honor. While Earth people were waiting for a disclosure that friendly extraterrestrials exist ... I got to meet them by the hundreds, and thus I was honored to have some be my mentors like OOO-LON and YA-FU-FUS, to mention a couple.

Inner scene began...

If one were in a plane flying over The City, one would see hundreds of people waiting to enter (a bit like Disneyland on an everyday busy day). The inner tension would be very noticeable as the excitement built with this amazing-beyond-belief place of healing, that must have fallen out of the sky, and no one had to build it with the usual paper plans and cement.

How long ago were the words said about a Second Coming? Could this be it? Could it be the Christ or Buddha or whoever, that brought this miracle? How could this demonstration be here that has attracted so many people? **Something's Coming? No. It is here and now!**

Looking for my Guide La-Luke I saw him way up front waving to me, and I slid past many and joined him. We were off through the Relaxation Park and onto the funny trolley, then into the door of the Embassy where who knows what would take place! The inside scene was set with a few hundred space beings in the audience and OOO-LON and his companions were in a welcome posture. We were acknowledged as a hush came over the audience.

O: "Welcome back to our place of peace and love. How may we be of service?"

G: "I am not sure, another visit was felt from within as I funnel information out to the public. What can be shared with me? How is this City coming for demonstration time?"

O: "The waiting seems long does it not?"

G: "Yes as a matter of fact. I have been with this City for about 30 years and I am as excited as all the rest to see this in the physical third dimension."

O: "You don't remember do you being in 'no time' as you once were? The City progresses to the point of attaching its inner workings to be put into the final checking and to be a vision worth the centuries of efforts attached. Making an appearance so long ago announced, must be worthy of God's divine timing, like a magician pulling an unseen rabbit out of an empty hat thus astonishing the audience. This City is the bunny, the hat is your dimension, and the magician is the I AM ... GOD demonstrating thus, astonishing the audience.

"How many you call 'man hours' has it taken to bring this demonstration forth? ... Centuries, and while this first prototype births already on the Earth grid, more of the same are being prepared likewise around your planet. Is this not astonishing! Everyone can be healed. It has taken divine timing and collective energies to accomplish this fact, with much dedication...much!

"In the meantime one more City book is to be published a.s.a.p. which continues to fill in the blanks with more information as you have traveled to this Embassy place of peace from 2009-2012. This is as good as a finished project, for it has much value with all the visits here recorded, not only a few as in the first issue. And it does connect with The City Earth appearance. Soon people will be able to enter here like you have described but on the physical level, thus a real disclosure of an E.T. audience. Imagine that! Space entities that are not here to conquer anyone, just coming in love with a City of Light. As said, 'What is to conquer?' What have you done with your planet?"

G: "And what about President Obama and a meeting?"

O: "This President is unaware of his coding of The City in his DNA, and is the perfect leader as The City demonstrates. You will have a meeting location connection, so put any concern to rest and await the sign."

G: "Anything else for public sharing?"

O: "That this birth is well worth waiting for, and that upon a special morning it will be seen as the sun rises. This meeting here today is a validation once more of The City appearance. You humans need to be constantly updated and downloaded to keep the mind open to receive. Be easy with this, all is in divine order.

"Request the 4 Keys Light Links to keep The City and space connection active as this is an important area that all can do in support. The quiet time between what has been said, to the 'NOW' demonstration is at hand, since The City of Healing Light set down on Earth this past Christmas Eve. Sound like connections? And with the UPPC'S support all is well and in Divine order. As for your guidance, oh speaker of coming events ... trip travel, connections and announcements are important, for you carry the seed of The City in your DNA just like the President.

"Amazing isn't it? Rest is important as your physical chemical change lifts you in parallel of The City, and as your planet shifts itself from the darkness of ignorance and greed, you shift with The City so a balancing act may be experienced.

"Bless those who have not seen the Light for it reveals itself ... ready or not. Go where guided and be open, ready for The City birth that could be sooner than later. Remember...BY PLAYING THE WAITING GAME ... YOU ALL WIN!"

The Winds of Change

Embassy Visit June 5, 2012

As a new day began and the sun showed the beauty of the red rocks, I left it all for the Embassy of Peace, as I was told to re-enter for some kind of an update. Not knowing what they would tell me, I re-entered in inner vision at the usual Gate of Entrance where there was not one person to be seen and that was really different.

All was quiet, calm and fairly silent as I saw my Guide La-Luke. We took a run through The Park of Relaxation, hopped on the trolley and jumped off at the Embassy door. We entered and moved onto the stage of interesting space entities where OOO-LON, who was the spokesman for those under this roof, smiled in welcome. Behind him the hundreds of Light Entitles from space communities somewhere in the Universe, were tuned in to what was to be said.

O: "And a welcome back Lady of Light. I see the message to return was received. Good!"

G: "Yes thank you. What is going on please?"

O: "This City now comes into its final stage for presentation into your world, and because of this comes atmospheric changes like never experienced before, and at this magnitude clear skies could suddenly become unclear. Even the winds you are experiencing can strengthen and seem unnatural, due to this unusual-to-be-sure appearance.

"Take note that if you are aware of it or not, the incoming vibrations of The City appearance could change the weather patterns quite strongly like never before. What may seem serene and quiet one moment, could be quite different without notice. The new energy patterns will keep the weather-checking people quite busy, trying to figure out what is happening that has not perhaps happened before ... or ever. They will not have past indications that equal what is taking place as The City manifestation moves into sight.

"Changing something like this huge edifice from the unseen, to the "Oh My God!" transformation takes some doing, and we are equal to the task, however be aware of the energy shifting. You are experiencing some wind changes already and even on a spring day it could snow un-expectantly. In other words expect the unexpected!

"Even your top scientists will have some difficulty in discerning what is happening, unless they know what is going on behind the scenes, so to speak due to unrecorded data. So then this meeting is called to inform you about the shifting of atmospheric conditions. You understand?"

G: "Yes. The weather changes now and upcoming, are due to The City of Light making an entrance into the third dimension and we are to be aware, not to be frightened, just to understand what is taking place."

O: "Indeed. As The City fills into the third dimension look-a-like hologram it will be dynamic in its entry. When one has a thought and it manifests good or bad depending on the consciousness of a person, it goes through a process of certain frequencies (speaking in your understanding). Many people on your planet are demanding changes take place, and they are, as planet Earth becomes Light like the moon on a clear night. How is that for a desire?

"We of the Universe, welcome the changes taking place as well as we all want to see you live in peace and love, and this way is in process by doing something so dramatically unusual, that everyone will pay attention with this surprise gift from the Creator of the whole Universe. Imagine that!

"You have, we know, as you have carried this project forward in human form and we are thankful, as you do not hesitate a moment in your expectation of what has been told you long since in your total love for God or I AM or whatever people call the Absolute Creator of all.

"As said, we play no games here, for what is to come about from this demonstration is LOVE EMBODIED. And people can say I AM LOVE and mean it, for nothing else will be known or experienced. This is a total make-over as you have said. Indeed the Winds of Change are in process and can switch energies at a moment's notice. We just want you all to be aware."

G: "Thank you. Anything else?"

O: "Continue to bring forth the new Universal Cities of Light book capturing all the sessions here as given and thus the reader gets a clear mental picture of what is taking place. Travel to places invited and be open for updates as given. As many new interests that God can bring forth through The City will be making you all happy to be alive, up close and personal. We shall meet again soon and it is advised that you meet with your space teacher YA for more space teachings. They will benefit all."

And with that the scene ended and I was back home with soft background music playing "Send in the Clowns". "Don't bother God, we are already here and ready for the winds of change, as we breathe in love and peace ... for everyone."

So Love it Be!

On the Edge of Glory

Embassy Visit June 14, 2012

Taking a deep breath and mentally leaving my Sedona home, I found myself at the usual Gate of Entrance in The City of Light. An inner message yesterday to return, brought me to this moment, as I followed what I was guided to do. Seeing a familiar hand connected to my City Guide La-Luke, I waved back and he parted the waves of people waiting to get in.

The funny wheel-less trolley awaited us as we enjoyed our walk through the Rejuvenation Park where benches were really massage seats. Nothing like a backrub in the Park. With a quick hop aboard this driver-less vehicle, we took a short ride past beautiful sparkling white healing buildings trimmed in real gold. It kind of took my breath away.

The thought came up that said, "God is going to take you places you never thought possible." Well, look around friends, this was it! Woopie!

I was so busy looking around, I was nudged that we had arrived at the Embassy of Peace Headquarters where hundreds of Universal Light Entities held court like a Universal United Nations. What a great group of loving Beings they were. I realized I was so blessed beyond any words I could put on paper to share.

Thanks God!

As we stepped onto the main stage, I was looking at 5 Light Entities and so many more E.T.'s behind them in the audience, that they were uncountable, except for the love they sent to me and my Guide. Awesome... Awesome ... It was curtain time once more and the energy and excitement filling the air was high - especially mine, as the head honcho OOO-LON, welcomed us.

O: "And a Welcome return is noticed I see. Message received via your Inner-Net."

G: "Yes, thank you. It sounded important. What am I to be made aware of and share?"

O: "Indeed, this City moves into its place of Light on this Earth planet which we call Sula. And as such, your own physical Earth connection as a notified-validation speaker will become more active, thus releasing the messages. This is to be kept active and constantly updated, and as said, given to other team supporters to release into Earth connections via your information avenues.

"For you personally, your interests are City-connected, so be open to receive (more information) at a moment's notice. This all now being well advised, we continue..."This City is subject to the 3rd dimension for your people to be introduced to advance pro-tography which means progress has and is consistent even as you see us at this moment.

"For them and you to enter the walls and buildings, they must look solid as even your homes now are. It is all a hologram. The Earth people wish to rise to a higher state of advancement which is referred to as levels, like going up a flight of stairs. We with The City have to go to a lesser state, all the while making the appearance of a more higher value.

"You as a human can mentally go either way and have for years, by way of elevating yourself and you have achieved. As The City enters your Earth's atmosphere, conditions are altered. You notice your sky is clear a lot of your time. This is a protective field to quietly enter without parts of The City being seen and thus throw people into a panic state especially those who are not Lightworkers so called.

"You notice feathering clouds that look like angel wings of beauty. You, Dear One, are highly sensitive now and rightly so, as you send out your messages of "Something's Coming." You are all on the edge of something spectacular to take place. The step-by-step introduction to The City makes the new book of Light important to explain what took place BEFORE The City's manifestation.

"Much time has expired in pre-preparation of this event. As has been said several times, this book will go down in Earth's history. The intent is correct. All steps in the right direction are taking place even as you write this. It is where Earth and heaven meet as was programmed so long ago and people will remember the second coming announcement from way back when.

"So we have advised you to continue bringing this book out to the world, and soon available for its contents reveal what came before the demonstration step by step. As a trans-audioist you will be receiving more as the days pass, as you are the connecting piece of information and a reporter of good God news.

"Support from those who are and have been aware of this inner connection can take the Earth's way of processing City information off your shoulders leaving you more time to be of City service with updates constantly. As the days intertwine, so does The City meet Earth's energy fields for manifestation.

"This sounds like perhaps a big load to carry but who knows The City better than you? Time shortens so the guidance for you and especially those who have had The 4 Keys to Light and the sounds within and practicing them on a continual basis. They have an inside track on what the process is and can do that, and effect love and Light to all. Understand?"

G: "Yes. May I share this visit?"

O: "That your sharing that **Something is Coming** is quite accurate and something is now here is more so. We of this universal gathering stand by all that has been revealed, as your planet shakes off the old ways and the un-truths and in its place, honesty and as an honor to the God of all.

"The City of Light is quite powerful in its dramatic intervention. The healings will take place in strange new ways, but take place it will. This you can all depend on. Rest in the wisdom being given. Permit others to be a part of the beginning of the new by supporting what now is released from you.

"So Dear One, take a deep breath for the path has just begun and celebration is right around the corner. Dr. Bill gave you the beginning clues and now you and your City team will go into the world, while you harness your energy into what is coming for something spectacular is. Imagine that!

"All is in divine right order and on the edge of greatness as all will shine in the sun of the revelation so long ago spoken of ... It's time! Ready to go forward?"

And with that the inner scene ended and I was home in Sedona looking at a beautiful blue sky knowing all was well and on Divine timing. Woopie!

Love from Genii.

Thank you for listening.

Genii with best-selling author Robert Allen at his 3-day training on leading-edge ways for authors to share their publications. Genii has also been mentored by Mark Victor Hansen and Rick Frishman of Author 101 University and many other experts listed at http://www.infopreneurshipuniversity.com

Shifting into High Gear!

Embassy Visit July 2, 2012

Having done my morning devotional, I was permitted to re-enter The City of Light and the Embassy of Peace auditorium via inner sight and sound. What would I learn from those who ventured forth from the Universe, lighting up for our benefit this City of Light and thus our planet, well worth total healing.

Scene: The usual Gate appeared with many people, and I saw a hand waving from my Guide La-Luke who by some magical move, parted this group of people like Moses parted the seas. We joined as Earth and sky Light Beings, heading for our chosen destination. Life was good here.

No worries could enter, as we seemed to leave them outside and hopefully, would not pick them up again when we left. I was blessed to once more meet with OOO-LON and a vast audience of Light E.T.'s. What fun this was! Looked like I was really making life more of itself and as a dear friend said, "Knowing love fully expanded." Yes sir!

Bringing forth a City of Light and one that promised a total healing had to be an immaculate conception and I got to enjoy the pre-introduction. I must be doing something right! Whoopie! ... as Renee says. The funny trolley arrived driver-less of course, or was it? Maybe I just couldn't see him ... her ... or whatever? We hopped aboard and ended up at this right place at the right time. Time? What was time there? ... Oh well.

We entered the Embassy to make our la-grand entrance to the stage through the backstage drapes. The prime stage setting was like a real production, with Entities of Light and my friend of far away, OOO-LON, who presided over the whole production. He could speak my language ... simple kindergarten-style, while the rest spoke in 'sound and tone' language. Got the picture?

This was approximately the 125th time I have had this privilege of entering this Embassy of Love, not counting all The City healing locations themselves ... Wow! I must be doing something right to be able to join this illustrious group. God is good!

OOO-LON stood in welcome and I acknowledged this honor, for love beamed out from every part of this building like God weaving strands of Light from which this love was woven. So...good!

O: "We welcome you and La-Luke back once more. Soon we shall meet in person-form as The City demonstrates in the thickness of your dimension. Questions?"

G: "Gee I never thought of that. Sounds like fun just around the corner. Imagine that! Guess I can now. Oh, a question? I got mentally side-tracked. Well, anything you can share. It has been 6 months in our time since a so called 'landing of The City.' What am I to share?"

O: "Seems like a century ago that you first learned of this demonstration, has it not? Have you not gone through a real life demonstration by physically birthing The City, strange as it seemed?"

G: "Yes, what an unexpected experience that was. Not any more, right?" (OOO-LON was referring to an experience I had a few days ago, when I had a series of pains that were just like childbirth.)

O: "Let's just say for an explanation, that you have been pregnant with this City for a very long time. In human form all will experience the live demonstration of The City by entering into its holographic entity just like your homes are. To make that connection viable, you as the perfect female human to be the key to make that connection was chosen, and thus The City was birthed with every breath and push you endured, just like a human giving childbirth.

"You heard God say, '"It is done"' and the pain ceased. Having given birth to a couple of children you recognized what was taking place."

G: "Oh my, this is quite a trip! Please continue."

O: "We understand it was a strange painful undertaking but successful nevertheless. The City needed that physical hook-up and Dear One, you not realizing it, served every human on the planet as the connection of humans and City have now taken place, energy-wise.

"This is the simplest way of expanding unexplainable space technology that took place when all you were looking for, was some fun at your favorite place, the Disney of land which helped with all the pre-exercise you had the day before. Oh! We know everything going on with this project."

G: "So then, now what?"

O: "Each component of this City, Earth 3D connection is in place, and as the City fills into the visual concept, many space entities and space scientists are busy pulling the elements together to secure it to the land in a way that all of you can understand. You will be able to walk into The City and get the healing this sick planet needs to survive.

"The marvel of space Light technology is so superior to what you are doing now. Delicate as it is for your growth, it is still a slow process. We sort of have to, as you say, 'fast forward' it. Now permit me to speak of the City Light book that lies on the table, and has not been completed, should be in faster process.

"As the human energies move into releasing this City connection, you will see the results manifest one day with the healing sites completed. There is a connection and should be completed, as you say, ASAP."

G: "How much land will The City take up?"

O: "Again the question arises. The land of the Arizona desert has moldable advantages, while Sedona will supply energy as it is doing now as the energy process is like a filling station. Much in the un-physical is processing nicely, as inner Earth beings are holding energies like you and Lightworkers, and like those who have been Light-linked through your sacred 4 Keys teachings, hold the position of containment like Light power standers.

"And do not forget the Angels on duty who by the thousands are also supporting from every angle possible to preserve the holiness of the masterful plan. The underground cities of love contribute their patterns knowing full well what is taking place in your unseen, for they see it. Soon there will be much more to celebrate not only in the Arizona area but across the country in other states that also have Angels holding the Light as this progresses.

"There is a lot going on in the unseen physical. This will be a phenomenon realized by many even in other countries who desire a better life especially during this current cleansing upheaval. Darkness and ignorance cannot tolerate Light. It shows too much like a flashlight in the darkness of a room. Everything shows it to be what it is. NO MORE WILL THIS PLANET BE IN DARKNESS. LOVE and LIGHT ARE IN CONTROL AND WILL NOT SURRENDER.

"So then, continue to be open and direct your Light work in serving the public as guided to be what it is. More human Lights should link up! You recently heard the tones of ABRAHAM. Indeed his word fit the inner workings of the unphysical. The Genii is well aware of what is taking place with this kind of sharing by voice and tone."

G: "What more is to be said?"

O: "Time shortens from moments to seconds and your place in the offerings brings soon what has been spoken of long since. Forget about the nuisance of forgetting. You are elevating.

"Spread the word, stay in the Light. We are well aware your whole human self is in a changing momentum. Could it be you are birthing a new Genii? It is OK to request assistance. This is a God production and all get to be in the act as Act 3 and Act 4 are about to begin.

As you say, time to send in the clowns of holy Light (as you know, the Golden Clowns) and with them they bring love, Light and fun! It is time for action and pleasure and being part of the overall production process.

See you again in The City of Light.

So Light it be!"

A Hot Bed of Activity!

Embassy Visit July 9, 2012

Leaving my daily world in the 3rd dimension of my Sedona, Arizona USA home, I mentally and visually entered into the nonphysical of space and time. I slipped out to spend some quality non-time in the Embassy of Peace within The City of Light location.

Visual meditations were what got me there quickly with no car to drive, plane to fly, or even gas to be concerned about. Ah, advanced inner technology at my service. I was just there at one of the usual Gates of entrance, trying to get past zillions of people also wanting to enter. Looks like Disneyland on a normal day.

I spotted my City Guide La-Luke signaling to me once again and using his Light-magic to part the people-seas. We connected now on our way through the Park of Relaxation. We had no time for a bench massage as we hopped on the driver-less trolley that dumped us off at the Embassy door. Entering this mammoth-sized building, we saw OOO-LON at his usual stage place. This building was huge and filled with love, honor, and truth. OOO-LON held court with hundreds of E.T. Light Beings. It made me feel I was in Ascension ... it was that powerful.

What was I to ask, I wondered? I have asked so many questions since all these visits started. Wow, before I could think any more, OOO-LON said, "Welcome student of truth, we are here to serve. How may we do that?"

G: "Living in the physical of the Sedona, Arizona vortex belt of The City birthing, what may I report to people who are asking me questions, even from across the planet in the United Kingdom? People are frustrated at just about everything, I hear. I understand I am even to meet a spiritual leader, Michael Mirdad, who leads the Unity Church here, regarding what is going on behind the scenes so to speak."

O: "Ah, we have now reached the home base of interest. The home of the first City birthing. This is good you have asked. The Sedona area is, in the unseen, a hot bed of activity as the puzzle pieces come together with the Lights of those you see in the audience here.

"Hundreds of Entities of Light from all over the cosmos, are like swarms of bees gathering at the honey hive, doing what they do best, such as bringing in space technology never before used on this planet for healing, and putting it in place with finishing touches. These pieces have to be in correct divine alignment as God pulls the switch, as this monumental Divine design moves into your local sight and entrance.

"Now then, when sharing with people, let them know first of all that they are loved enough by God to end suffering on this planet. In doing so, The City of Healing Light is about to be Divinely shown. Arizona itself will feel the impact as well as several states around. The energy brought in from the Universe through the High Towers is mammoth in its scope.

"One can only imagine how having several more Cities like this one activated on the planet grid, will make this planet shine in the heavens not unlike the brightest star, or even a moon. Share with the Michael of Mirdad, who incidentally is in your area for this particular reason, even if at this point he is unaware of the impact he will make to his people coming up; for he is a Light within a Light like not many on your planet and should be made aware of what is going on right in his current world.

"Many are beginning to feel the horrendous changes as the vortexes spin in their capacity of totality, as The City uses this power station to birth itself into sight physically. The under-Cities also are marking the days of disclosure and the energy spreads far and wide.

"Report to the people that all is well and on course. Of course God declares this to be so! The upheaval across the planet looks to be not much fun, but in reality it is cleansing and the end results will find each one experiencing Light and love like never before could even be imagined. Even the courts will have to take time out for no one is suing anyone…no need! Out with the old and in with the new. Several of your planet's web reporters are doing much good, for all such as the Michael Quinsy, the Russ Michael, and the Steven Beckow all of which have been kind to you and your sharing, and others who are tuned in.

"The word spreads, lives change, and all comes to pass as the first City of Light demonstrates dramatically and Divinely, knowingly or not. That is just the way it is, period! Precious are these days of countdown, for all are to be blessed with advanced healings not even thought of, but ready to be received be it in Sedona, the United Nations or Australia or…?

"Keep the message going out so many can incorporate this Divine Design in the knowing that all is well and in due Divine course will be divinely demonstrated.

"Take a deep breath and just know that your current area is prime, for God knows what God is doing Divinely. Got the picture?"

G: "Quite so."

O: "Then spread the word be it through meetings, The 4 Keys to Light, your next book or just in knowing. The City of Light is about to birth! Have a good day!"

And with this I was back home giving thanks for being so blessed to be this female love-spreader.

So Light it be!

Thanks God!

Expected Changes!

Embassy Visit July 12, 2012

Meanwhile unexpected, I was back into The City Embassy with a few questions this time for sharing. Moving quickly from the south Gate, through the Park and onto the funny trolley, I found myself and Guide standing in front of OOO-LON and this vast cosmic audience of universal space beings that filled this place of love and peace. Wow that was fast!

OOO-LON smiled as I could only guess he knew why we were here. "You have questions not previously answered before ... begin!"

G: "Will The City of Light be able to reverse aging I have been asked?"

O: "What is aging, but a state of mind that humans have been programmed with since childhood. You live in a 3rd dimension where time and pre-programming have set the course year after year, and you humans even celebrate getting older.

"Of course the children love to play celebrations and even adults delight in having another birthday. What would happen if no one was ever programmed with the age concept? Oops no celebrations! Programming by the media that one is getting older and death is the repeating. Oh well, another lifetime follows this one and people continue to look for the fountain of youth.

"Will The City of Light help in this department? Of course! The energy itself of the dramatic entry, sets the course of mind changing, so the effect becomes as a natural event of progress. Wow a miracle has taken place overnight! How can this be? I must be dreaming ... Yes, and so is everyone else!

"The City of Light is timeless, so the advantages are received as natural and age means nothing. These are just words, but experiencing the power and love of The City will explain by example.

"This is good stuff people! You have no idea at this point, what is virtually in your 3D backyard commencing to birth.

"The City is a new beginning for everyone as the Christ man has said and even you as you turned on the media news, that reports that someone put a kitten into cement up to 'its neck and let it die.

"Your comment was, it makes me feel like not wanting to live here and verbally demanded to God that all this horrendous mistreatment of animals and children cease and the demented minds be banished from this planet! It is either love or it isn't ... no love here!!!!

"Dear One, this is in process as we speak, just in a most unusual way. This City energy will spill out in many directions and close by states near the Arizona borders will also feel the clean air of The City Light."

G: "Will The City remain in linear time?"

O: "How else would one be able to physically enter? Of course. Just because it is highly evolved does not mean one cannot experience it on some level. The non-believers of a God of Love will shake in their shoes for what appears to stand for God's deliverance and cannot be denied, ready or not! More?"

G: "Another question ... will the healings given in The City hold after they leave The City grounds and go back into their own lives?"

O: "Yes but they can expect to have discomfort in what was before, as they have changed and will change consequently from this new energy Light they contain.

"People please pay attention. God is here to change the picture from what it was, to what it will be and is in process right now! It has been said over and over that the mind = the body. Good or bad, ill or healed. How many books have said this over and over. Changing your thinking will change your problems. We speak love here! ...God-love which is within you, each one God cares not who ... this is the prediction of this whole process. Your minds have the opportunity to change what appears from mental nonsense.

"Your media hype is prone to have you all mentally ill one way or another. A virus bug can run rapid across the country just by someone saying it is active in such and such a state. Oh my, we better get a shot in the arm ... more stress with that thought. So much change to be permitted as this event takes place. People want to feel good and should ... not once in a while, but all the time. God does ... imagine that!

"What is being said here is that the thinking process of illness will change and for the betterment of all. No one left out. Where change is needed it will be changed. Dark ignorance is heading out even as we speak. No one can remain ill as the process of Light is curable. The energy fields of this City will produce the unexpected and feeling good will be the normal, every day.

"LOVE is the healer here ... God-love in action. You say often, '"All is well!"' Well, it should be! God gave you a beautiful planet to walk on and what has been done to it? look around ... be aware that change is imminent ... now! This is Good news!

"We of galactic communities are here in support first of God with this demonstration and you all on this planet so as an advanced space technology demonstration is coming forth ready or not! Take a deep breath and give thanks that healing help is on the way ... as said 'Woopie!'

"So then share what has been addressed here for a birth is on the way ... Congratulations. All is well! Really!"

Making it God's Business!

Embassy Visit July 17, 2012

With a noisy morning outside and a late puppy sitter pick-up, I almost decided not to enter the Embassy this time as the disruption of my quiet time was a bit hard on my nerves, but being the Jedi that I am, and releasing all the outside confusion, here is the Embassy visit word for word.

To begin with, I want to thank Michael Quinsey for allowing me to be on his vast radio show and Russ Michael for his write-ups of the Embassy visits, and Unity Spirit leader, Michael Mirdad, here in Sedona, for being open to this information. Love you all!

Scene (location) At one of the 5-story high massive turbo-support Gates attracting multiple people, my City Guide La-Luke came from behind me, grabbed my hand, parted the human seas and rushed us through to the usual trolley ride to the Embassy building. We made an appearance on the stage facing OOO-LON and an audience of hundreds of Light Space Entities. "Is this an adventure or what?" I said to myself. "I must have done something special somewhere in time, to get where I find myself now."

O: "Welcome back. How may we be of service?"

G: "I was recently interviewed on a U.K. BBS radio program. Michael Quinsey invited me on to speak about The City and asked some questions that I was not able to answer. Maybe you can?"

O: "Proceed."

G: "Speaking of the first City of Light now in process in the area of Sedona Arizona, an unspecified amount of people will undoubtedly show up to see for themselves what miracle has taken place, as this has to be a once in a lifetime demonstration and the word spreads quickly.

"How can this amount of people be (so-called controlled) as our world will move in this direction fast? Sedona is heavy in energy but small by comparison say, to Phoenix, Arizona on the south, or Flagstaff on the north. How can this be handled in our third dimension and with many people here, not having a clue to what took place, much less how? What can be shared?"

O: "Registering such amounts of humanness, with the excitement energy contained therein, The City carries with it and surrounding it, a Veil of Peace and calm frequencies like an unseen-but-felt, Light wave that surrounds The City constantly. It is known that all will want to enter and all at once, however this calmness will put the most anxious of them steady and orderly.

"This frequency field extends some distance beyond The City itself and it enhances this calming sensation just spoken of. We are prepared to take care of the situation with many field Angels and Entities for all who want to enter."

G: "The next question is will there be a monetary cost to enter?"

O: "No, this is not a national run business. It is God's business. It is not about your money god so called by some, and not to be discussed here and now. It is about Healing Light and humans.

"Those coming from a distance will arrive as they normally do now, as your transportation of today is quite adequate for this purpose. The Sedona area location carries its own vibratory energy ... enough to pull in this God blessing as a holographic manifestation, just like what you live in now.

"The local law officials might have their hands full as most are not aware of what is taking place behind the scenes so to speak, and love may be needed to assist by current Lightworkers.

"What is not being recognized at this point is that the frequencies of love and peace that surrounds this City will affect everyone with its calming effect. After all this is a 'Holy City of Light' not just another building being settled on the ground. It has been prophesied for centuries of its coming.

"Well, guess what? It is here ... Oh my God! You have that right. It is OH-MY-GOD TIME! And that Holy reverence will prevail as people will open their hearts and homes in support.

"Remember the 11-11-11 love wave that was introduced? Again, all a part of the same picture and the uplifting of humans who dwell in the victim style.

"The airports will do a thriving business as will the local shops. The media will have a field day and anything other than this City appearance will hold no value, and that also means what is referred to as commercials.

God has arrived Hallelujah!

"So then, Dear One, report that God has everything under control and has been from the beginning. Rest in that knowing that all is well. Now anything else?"

G: "Yes please, speak to me of the other Cities of Light mentioned several times and the new City book of Light to be published ASAP."

O: "The other Cities of Healing Light are at this point reflected Light of this first one we speak of. One thinks that instantaneously a City appears. There is much scientific work that goes into such a massive undertaking from the highest minds in the Universe. The Cities take all of this and more.

"Your density of frequencies are slow and to have such an edifice to appear, it has taken eons of your time to bring this forth, but it will and all will bow down to God for nothing less could make this demonstration a reality of perfection masterpiece. Healing is on the way and darkness is out that litters the planet.

"Make no mistake about other Cities. They too will appear one at a time, and the human energy love fields take root as Light and love become the norm. It is God's pleasure to bring forth the first Sedona City with its reflected Light in many places to also receive the gift of God's blessings such as these locations to name just a few: Australia, The United Kingdom, China, France, Spain and South Africa. More will be announced in the correct timing.

"All is in order as now these, are receiving Light vibrations from the first one. Patience is needed now with love attached and all Light energy should be in the support of the first one. Anything else?"

G: "My current guidance please."

O: "Dear One, you as a City of Light informant are doing a good job with a most unusual topic, however we support your efforts. You have several Light Beings with you, one being YA your space mentor. Return to this place of Light and we shall endeavor to fill in the blanks so to speak for you to deliver as well as support your new City book... Universal Cities of Healing Light!

So Light they be!"

And with this disturbance outside my window, I called this session to a close, with my thanks for all that was said. I am blessed. Actually you know what?

We all are.

Imagine that!

www.spiritinbusinessnetwork.com

"Love and co-operation will yet be found to be the greatest business principles on earth." -- Ernest Holmes, *Creative Mind and Success*

www.newthoughtuniversity.org

The Light Spot Connection!

Sometimes You Have To Make Your Own Light Spot

Sunday July 22, 2012 - Embassy Guidance Regarding Asilomar Conference Trip

I had been feeling kind of between worlds mentally and emotionally, and really not feeling much, except balanced in sort of an in-between spot with not much energy in any direction. I had been sort of tuned in to attend with Charles the Asilomar Retreat Center in Monterey, CA from July 29th to August 4th.

Due to the financial cost of this trip and distance to drive, I was not in any hurry. Charles asked me if I had been in The City this morning and I said no as it was late in the morning and I planned to go tomorrow morning. When he said this, it was the clicker to sit down and go.

So fast forwarding>>>>>>>>>>>>>>>>> This is what happened:

Going within I found myself in inner vision, standing on the familiar stage in the Embassy in front of OOO-LON and the vast Light Beings in the audience.

G: "What is going on with me Sir? Feeling strange with some directions needed."

O: "Welcome back. Feeling strange and unsettled are you?"

G: "Yes. Not sure what it means, but I need to get excited over something. Oh, and also what can be said about a trip this next weekend to the Asilomar Conference? It has been 34 years since I was last there when I met my minister husband-to-be. What has he to do with this, as I sense? He made his transition 15 years ago in 1997."

O: "Oh, you wish to meet your dearly departed?"

G: "Well, I sense Bill around a lot so why would I go miles to have a meeting, if that is what you are talking about?"

O: "Ah, the Dr. Bill and a meeting of the physical and the spirit, and that spirit advises it. Is this not an exciting thought to re-meet a loved one who has passed?"

G: "Well, it would be different to say the least. Tell me more please."

O: "People don't die. You say this quite often and believe this is so. You say you feel the Dr. Bill nearby, so why not make the physical and spirit connection, especially because of The City? Could the dear Dr. B. (as he is also called), not give you information on The City that you do not have, since his primary spirit space is here in The City proper?"

G: "Why go to our first meeting place? Can't I just do that here?"

O: "Was that not a most beautiful spot on the ocean front? Do you not have mental memories? When two people met as (it was pre-planned for you two to meet) for what was and is to come about. Did this spot make the contact?"

Note: I had been getting inner feelings to re-watch the movie 'CONTACT' again - especially the part where she met her dad (who had passed over), for several days previous, but not paying much attention. I was now!

O (continues): "There are LIGHT SPOTS in people's lives. Important events that trigger other important events. These are referred to as LIGHT ENERGY SPOTS where the energy builds high for connection attention. Your lives were brought together for The City. One LIGHT SPOT was when Dr. Bill brought through The City drawings with Hermes' guidance.

"Now as The City manifests, you have extra power. A major LIGHT SPOT! Think back in your time together where there were many LIGHT SPOTS that connected to others and important things happened. Think back on these."

G: "Yes. Thank you. Why now? Dr. Bill has been gone 15 years as of August 6, 1997. Why now?"

O: "Time is of no importance. There is none. All that has taken place in no time at all includes The City of Light appearance. If we said that The City appearance depends on this meeting would you go?"

G: "Is that true?"

O: "Not in the sense you are being given. Just to let you know that you have an appointment and a major 'LIGHT SPOT' encounter. That could give a different picture to others in grief. Could you not give a better picture?"

G: "What if I go and nothing happens?"

O: "Oh ye of little faith. Where is your mustard seed of belief? Dear One, you have been on this pilgrimage for eons of time and space and the climax is at hand and you hold the sacred Keys.

"You have done the work, inspired people with The 4 Keys of Light and are a personal channel of pure Light, having been to the Court of the High Tribunal and received your investiture. Could you not be of more support on a subject most are not aware of?"

G: "Sounds like more teachings coming up?"

O: "Of course. Do you not enjoy sharing unusual information as a subject yourself? Your life is filled with love and fulfilling as many wishes as possible and now the apex is of a City of healing that you stand in at this very moment.

"This is not just a flick of an imaginary encounter. (We speak 'real' here, so-called in your world) a real happening. Would you not like to hear, feel and sense what the Dr. B. could tell you at a beautiful meeting place again?

"Do you not sit with The Walt of Disney and share thoughts and sensings that are feeling real? Have you not been shone angels and Light Beings you call 'see-throughs?' This has all been training. You can tell the story like no other could as you are living it."

G: "Okay ... I will. Show me the way to get there and with some financial help would be nice.

O: "Be open and get excited and refreshed in a beautiful location and don't forget to take your City books. You have a message to deliver even there, as ministers all gather for information, as does The Charles with his advancing information of connection.

"You could use some fun and meeting of new people and this includes The Charles in a healthy location such as it is. When you get excited, watch for the blessed finances to appear (so to speak). We speak here of advancement for you both as well.

"Now take another step forward not in physical pain as occurred when you birthed The City as Physical but in Love and reuniting with someone dear to you in a most unusual way, to be sure, but a 'happening' just the same."

G: "Oh. Well, all this does take some thought."

O: "We see you now look at a different picture. Guess what? All is well. Even a miracle can happen on beach or room or...? The Dr. Bill is ready and you have a date with destiny. Also many ministers etc. should be made aware of The City and the work that The Charles is guided to of advancement. Get the picture?"

I nodded my head yes and said, "Anything else?"

O: "Be open between now and then and see what happens. The Charles is a wizard of setting the course ahead, of action with all his contacts and many at this conference may be in a 'LIGHT SPOT' place to learn.

"Rest, be aware, and open to receive even the finances to appear as if by magic. Your trip information has just been given. Next?"

So Light it be!

Knowing Love Fully Expanded, Even Other Planets!

Embassy Visit July 26, 2012

"It was a very quiet sunny day in Sedona, the home of the forthcoming birth of The City of Light. I was meeting new people who were feeling the energy of what was coming about (which happens, I guess, if one is sitting in a birthing nest) like a mother bird outside my front door with 2 babies peeking out to see what their world looks like ... change in process oh my, big world!

Scene: Gate of Entrance. Crowds of people were gathered around. I saw a wave from my Guide La-Luke and we walked through the Relaxation Park, hopped on the trolley and then hopped off at the Embassy door heading for the stage entrance and bingo, we were on stage facing hundreds of Extraterrestrials.

Some of them I had met before, including one YA-FU-FUS, who had become my spaceology teacher. We had a conversation together last night and as advised, it is included in this message.

A hush rang over the audience as waves of love ascended around us both ways.

O: "Once more our Earth Light Friend is welcomed here in the sanctuary of peace for sharing. How may we be of help?"

G: "Thank you. What is the current progress report on this City that I can share please?"

O: "Getting anxious are you?"

G: "Well not really. I am pretty calm but it has been a long time if time counts for anything. What can be said?"

O: "The buildings of healing are all in place and the UPPC's (Uniphase Power Capsules) are doing the energy process needed to bring the Light into the locations. This is working very well.

"Many here in this oasis of heavenly bodies are experts using this space energy to be distributed where needed, for any and all human healings. Yes Dear One, this planet will shine in the heavens like the star that recently your name was put on."

G: "That was fun. I have just had a conversation with YA about his home in space that really was fun to hear about."

O: "Yes we are aware. It might be good to share the information on this visit for your readers to get an up close and personal space look of other dimensions."

Genii Note: I am interrupting the Embassy visit to share YA's information as OOO-LON suggested.

I call it The Rainbow Connection!

YA-FU-FUS (Genii spaceology teacher session)   July 25, 2012

G: "YA ... are you here?"

Y: "YA always here. Is not The City being brought forth? YA is a special part of that operation."

G: "Tell me more please."

Y: "YA reports truth and you have the YA opportunity to learn. What would you learn today?"

G: "I was fascinated to learn that you can change skin colors by changing your emotions."

Y: "True. Now I am a beautiful hue of violet shade as I am very peaceful with nothing to disturb me. You on the other hand, stay the same."

G: "If I went to your home planet to visit, would I change colors too?"

Y: "No. Your energy systems are set in place."

G: "Are babies born there, born with any special color?"

Y: "No, usually they are a very light yellow-gold and begin to change when they learn that they can, by observation of others. Skin tones are real tones and are present also. If one is one color or another, the body tones equal the colors."

G: "Is there any discrimination?"

Y: "No. All carry the God tones and no one is eliminated as your people do. Such nonsense! No love there. One who carries the love of the Creator basically cares not what color one is or not, as all of love can easily see where each other is emotionally, as that color is known at any given moment. Your people of this planet have much to learn and change to fit into the cosmic communities."

G: "Do you think we can ever really change?"

Y: "This is what the coming cosmic event is all about. The City of Light is all about healing. Even un-healable will not be able to resist the centering foundation of Heaven on Earth dropped in their laps, giving respect and love from that foundation of truth and Light.

"Most of the people on your planet have no respect for each other as they should have and the change is now coming forth. With our way, no one can enter darkness for very long, as it shows and nothing is hidden. Fear makes one step into darkness and some work hard to be in darkness.

"Again, nothing can be hidden, for the body colors speak loudly and on the other side, people can have help. Feelings push the color spectrum for all to see."

G: "Very interesting...Spaceology class again please?"

Y: "YA here at your service. We have much to share. Next lesson coming YA soon."

(And with that he was gone except for a sensing of a rainbow filled with cosmic love, which we could all use!) Thanks YA!

O: "Anything else?"

G: "Yes, any more Cities to be known coming forth?"

O: "Mexico may be added to your list of the unseen locations now on the Grid of Light."

G: "Thank you, I will include that in my next book 'Universal Cities of Light!' Thank you."

O: "Just report that The City of Light power center of Sedona is indeed coming into fruition as The Dr. Bill would say. The Emorgies (energy) around this prototype City will be noticed more, as the days pass quickly.

"You are about to take an ordained trip to the northern CA area at a conference location. This is not just an idle idea, but one impressive visit. There will be a few surprises and you will experience the Light of The Dr. B. This trip will prove to be quite unusual for the most part, but for you it will be a re-meeting easily remembered.

"So then take your love with you. Rest and find fun as love will attend you. Be sure to carry the words of this City in your heart and all will recognize the importance of what is to come about as well as your books of interest. Just be open and we will attend you as well as keep you posted on developing news.

"Take note here: You have a month of what you call August coming into view. Regarding the new edition, it would be well to have it completed and printed. We wish you a happy Earth day!"

...And with this, the envision scene disappeared and I was home giving thanks for what God was providing in the way of a City of Light and all that was in process right now ...THIS VERY MINUTE ... WOOPIE!

Thanks God...So Light it be!

Deliberate, Delivered, Dimensional Headway!

Received at the Asilomar Conference Grounds

Embassy Visit August 1, 2012

A new month began with the Pacific Ocean waves giving the local seagulls a breakfast find in the sand. Over 700 people came here to praise God and elevate themselves more in Light teachings as well as meeting new and past friends.

We all were looking to enjoying peace on Earth as a healed planet where conflict of any kind no longer took the front-page spotlight. I had some time to myself and God, to slip into my inner vision visit into the Embassy of Peace in The City of Light.

Envision scene:

Moving past the usual Gate of Entrance, I found myself standing before OOO-LON and this massive audience of Light Beings from space (with addresses unknown to me) who filled hundreds of seats. My City Guide La-Luke stood with me, keeping the balance between everyday Earth energy and The City energy which was higher in frequency.

O: "Ah... again a return, breaking through the levels of unseen entrance once more. This is good. How can we serve you this visit?"

G: "Just anything you can share including an update on the current progress of this City would be helpful as time-wise, we are over halfway through this year of 2012 in our calendar time. You have already said that time as we know it is speeding up, so what is to be known?"

O: "A massive demonstration of course. An appearance fully dressed in Light and open for business, as you say when something is ready to begin. Is that good for beginners?"

G: "What may I report?"

O: "That the message of this visit is one of fulfillment, love and Light healings. That all that has been promised in these visits will be seen, walked into, and healings long since overdue, are making deliberate, delivered, headway in your dimension.

"The call and the cry has been heard. Where you are at this time there is no television in your room, so the turba of the planet is unknown except, being told that a space vehicle has been seen and recorded over the games in progress in the England Earth site. Imagine that!" (Laughter ran out as his words were repeated to the audience.)

G: "Yes, since I have been home I have seen this report and I for one am thrilled. With so many of you right here, bringing forth The City, someone needs to let the world know that you are all love in action."

O: "Indeed! This will be accomplished by those who are well aware of what steps can fulfill this prophesy. The Genii is space taught as your space teacher 'YA' holds you in mental honor with the spaceology teaching, as well as the way a hologram is put together.

"These are exciting times filled with the love of the Creator who has everything ready to birth you all into new beginnings. All is well and on course, so get excited, people, get excited - for your best interests are 'now' in close process and a grand celebration it will be. I, OOO-LON, promise you!" (And with that it seemed like the whole audience stood up.)

"It will be like a wave of water has been in process to liquidate anything other than what has been promised."

A Planet of Love, Cooperation and Human Health Restored

"Stay in the knowing and see what transpires. These, your space brothers and sisters, are well versed in the magic they bring. You say this is a new month. Dear One, much can take place, and you will be advised as you continue to be the chosen speaker of this Light City.

"Your Lightwork is to continue to serve with 'The 4 Keys to Light' as more request its information and the human Light corridor is opened and God responds in your language. The learning of personal Guides is important also, so anyone can get guidance on a moment's notice.

"Tell your readers to fear not, for as said, God's pleasure is to give you all, the Kingdom in the shape and power of The City of Light first in the Sedona Area and then around the world. May peace and patience be your guide and this is what you can report."

Note: And with that this inner scene was no more.

Imagine that!

So Light It Be!

Looking at the World Differently!

Embassy Visit August 16, 2012

A hot cup of tea started this day of interest as I settled into the quiet within in order to go to the Embassy of Peace. Little did I know of what might take place within this massive arena of Space Light Beings who had answers to any questions that I might verbalize.

Scene: The usual Gate was there, but instead of crowds only a few people were milling around. La-Luke my City Guide for lo these many years of visits, came up from behind, tapped me on the shoulder, and took my hand as we ran through the Park of Relaxation onto the trolley, and were whizzed to the door of the Embassy.

The usual entrance welcomed us, and in no time we stood before OOO-LON and this vast audience from outer space as we again felt the tremendous love sent in our direction. If this is what people will feel as they enter The City, we are in really good shape...

O: "And a God day to be experienced sensually. What is to be revealed for you and your readers?"

G: "Thank you. What can be revealed? What can you tell me?"

O: "Ah, progress beyond progress. We are pleased to report to you and others who await 'The vision of any century.' This City site is buzzing with activity."

G: "Looks pretty quiet with only a few at the Gate observed."

O: "Not to be concerned, just a pause in the action. You are involved in learning about holograms and the process therein. Not many we observe, have this interest and an inner viewing status, so this is a way of showing what is not real ... and is a sort of reversal so to speak."

G: "Yes this is really fun for me. Years ago my husband Bill told me all was a hologram and not real. My reply was non-believing. 'Yah! ... right!' All I could see and touch felt thick and looked real. I could not understand until, sometime later, I was sitting on the floor alone and got this strange vision and awareness that he was right. I rolled on the floor in laughter, thinking we are walking around in God's mind. That this is all nonsense just like a movie. Since then I enjoy seeing people not sitting on chairs etc. It is quite fun to look at the world differently. Tell me more please."

O: "Dear One, you stand here and see us in a 3D visit and we enjoy the fun with you. As you are well aware, all you see in your 3D world is quite correct as you need to see it, and be it, to have this life's adventure ... past, present and future. You live on a holodeck as was seen in a Star Trek movie, which incidentally came from space technology as an introduction to your future with knowing that all is a 'HOLY-gram.' Even your planet is as such with the best yet to come.

"The energy of your planet and people designates to everything being real. That forms from thoughts, seeing and sensing to be deliberately activated experiences. Good or not so good, you are doing it all! Positive thoughts = positive action as, in cause and effect in your world. God thoughts have a higher vibration. Are you getting the picture I am presenting?"

G: "Yes for most people, this take is a mind-stretch, to know that all is a thought, sort of like the inside out so to speak."

O: "As said, the body is also a hologram no matter what shape it is in. As one of your Guides Who-No, tells you as he calls you all 'skin-bags' just covering your electrical systems. Continue to read your current study of this phenomena as a mind shift is in process. So what if nothing is real? It feels and looks real ... especially love, so enjoy the movie and what does not appeal to you, discard it, like it is not important.

"Right now your planet is in a horrendously wonderful change-over from non-love to total love, and you get to watch the movie and even be a part of it in some way. You get to watch people's thoughts transfer into upper levels and when they do that, people have to change, ready or not. It is a schoolroom in action and the children will benefit from all this non-love sense change in process.

"Old ways are shifting out, and entering is the new, by releasing and cleaning up the past errors of greed and ego-centered living. We help by throwing Light into the process with you, so that could make people uneasy, but... it's not real. It just feels that way.

"As a dear friend says, 'Either it comes from love or it doesn't. If it doesn't, discard it'. These are good words to remember. Wonderful words to follow. Just be love and the God miracles will appear, plus, in time, all will really feel pretty God good.

"Some day all will live in only love ... only Love. For God's only law, is the Law of Oneness. Remember that. Oneness! And all will be well with you. The cleansing process cannot be stopped from making room, for the new hologram is in process. Minute by minute all is moving into form.

"That is precisely why you have been given The City 'pattern' of healing buildings etc. The good spiritual leader Dr. Bill, began, and you have continued to bring through yet what is to be seen in 3D hologram form.

"Dear One, the whole Universe is a hologram. People say, seeing is believing, like they have to see it to believe it. When quite the opposite is important. We suggest that believing is the seeing. Again it is backwards.

"Remember the code you know so well starting from bottom to top in energy levels such as:

One has HOPE ... 'I hope it will work out.'

More power is ... One has FAITH ... 'as in a Mustard Seed!'

Then more power ... One has BELIEF ... 'I be ALIVE with this.'

Then the best of all... One has CONVICTION ... 'a Knowingness with no opposite. It just is so!'

"Get the power level here?

"Your mind is vast in all this pre-destined Lightwork you do as foretold in your new edition City book to be published. This is very important to see that accomplished ASAP, as demonstration is close and advising the readers to pre-believe what it all contains to be enjoyed and to learn from. Understand?"

G: "Yes this is a big book and several Lights are working on it."

O: "This is a big City and as you say, God is up to something and it is big! We smile as this is quite accurate, as the God thoughts bring forth more of the same Cities around to your planet.

"What a wonderful world you have ahead of you coming into view in your hologram 3D world just like everything else! People will rejoice! Get out the party decorations and have patience... the party is about to begin! God will send out the invitations and you will get one and as your friend Renee says quite often, '"Woopie!'"

G: "Thank you."

O: "Enjoy your world. Come alive and know that God is behind directing and setting the holographic scene which is big ... really big! ... No, REALLY, REALLY BIG!!!

"Go back to your readers and spread the news that Something Is Coming for it is truth in action. Imagine that! We bid you the Light of the eternal City of Light day in peace and in love!"

I said good-bye to OOO-LON and thanks for another vision visit into the Holy City of Light coming forth for the healing of all.

Imagine that!

God is Up to Something . . . And it is BIG!

Embassy Visit September 1, 2012

It was a very quiet, beautiful morning as the red rocks glowed in the sun of a new day, while Sedona burst with nature's greenery, wet with dewdrops. As one magazine has reported, Sedona is the most beautiful place in America. I agree, and an Embassy visit seemed to be appropriate at the moment.

Inner vision.....

My inner visions began once more at one of the encoded Gates that made everyone feel welcome and eager to enter. Me too! My Guide La-Luke waved me through and we headed for the funny trolley that will escort people all over, when The City demonstrates. The trolleys have no wheels or driver. Imagine that!

We quickly found ourselves at the Embassy and then plopped onto the stage facing master OOO-LON and an audience of hundreds of love and Light entities. The welcome from this vast audience of Light sent a message of love that just about took me to the floor with its energy. Wow what a blessing!

O: "I see you have gotten an 'inner-net' message to return here. Feeling things are happening, do you?"

G: "Oh yes! I sense The City birth is very near. What a day that will be. I just received word that a distant friend Michael Quinsey in the U.K. who channels SaLuSa, and has been kind enough to allow me to speak of The City on his radio program, is coming to Sedona next month. I am pleased, as will be a lot of people."

O: "The Sedona area will become quite active from this point forward as the energy frequencies of the powerful vortexes are doing, and have done their unseen part in the dramatic concept now due to appear. Many unseen entities are also in the area, as your energy fields are active, preparing for the grand entrance. People are seeing more sky ships as they too come from space stations to assist where needed.

"Much is still hidden but quite active, enough to awaken this little town site as the energy begins to feel quite strong in its intent to bring forth The City of Light. It is a magnificent holographic event (as is all your world) strong enough to have many Lightworkers' senses become stronger, and quite apparent that something big is taking place. You soon will be a speaker of all this notification, for you are The City Leader.

"The visionaries will begin to inner see the Light patterns of The City a lot clearer. People are expected to become enhanced with feelings and guidance to come to your area from faraway places. So, it is advised that the Genii take note of this before friends appear on your doorstep when rooms in hotels are not available. Serve where you can. Does this help a bit?"

G: "Any date yet of City demonstration?"

O: "It is noted that this is the main interest and we also suggest to permit the day to disappear and bring through your own knowing and sensing as time permits. It will be noted when it is appropriate. Enjoy the thoughts that well-up now as you have come a long way and time is near. The domes nearby are at this point an electrified entity of directive sky maps for spaceships and have drawing power in the midst of the unseen action now in process."

"Is The City of Light nearing revelation? Yes! But first things first ... as it has been advised to have the new City book in print and distribution by the end of this current month is important. So then Earth leader enter into your day, spread the news and prepare for visitors as best you can. This, Dear One, is good news."

G: "OMG, I guess so and will do what I can to prepare. Anything else?"

O: "Just know that you are loved and be open to any inner guidance that can come at an instant moment. There will be more trips. For the moment, concentrate on the home front guidance.

"We bid you the Light of God's day and don't forget to stop and rest as the higher intensity of Light frequencies now being just heightened will affect you as you step forward to take your place as The City Speaker upfront and personal."

With this the phone rang here, and all stopped, leaving me with future thoughts of excitement. Thanks God!

So Light it Be!

Validation! Almost Here!

Embassy Visit September 10, 2012

With the sound of thunder awakening me this morning like God saying, "Pay attention!" I began another trip back into The City of Light and the Embassy of Peace amphitheater where hundreds of universal Light Beings made up the audience.

The local sun now out here, I scanned the skies for any sign of The City appearance physically. I, like many others, waited to see what I had been guided to talk about for 30 years. That is indeed a magical moment that we are to experience.

I have walked this guided path lovingly and with firm conviction that anything is possible with God. I was paying attention this morning. Once again, I prepared to go into a meditational field through my witness chakra, (that has long since been cleared through my 4 Keys to Light method) that I share with others. 'Tis good and very good.

An inner Light shone and I envisioned going in and bingo, I was once again at one of the 5-story Gates ... but quite alone. Not even my City Guide La-Luke was there to greet me. I looked to see if the funny driver-less trolley was running this day. I hurried through the Relaxation Park and it was indeed relaxing. I hopped aboard the trolley and swiftly headed to the Embassy, excited as usual. (It should be noted that people will love riding around The City on these trollies.)

Entering from backstage I found myself standing center stage with no one in sight. Where did everyone go? Couldn't have been something I said as I had said nothing. What a strange visit this one was. Well, I was told to expect the unexpected. Maybe this was one of those times.

Suddenly a bright Light lit up the stage and me too. High frequencies for sure. O.K ... so I was standing center stage and said loudly, "Where is everybody? Hello!" Suddenly as I looked to where an audience should have been, a big sign appeared reading, "ALMOST THERE!"

At that point coming out from left and right stage were two beings so light I could not tell who or what they were. Then I recognized OOO-LON, Headmaster here on the left and YA-FU-FUS my space mentor on the right.

Well at least someone was here and smiling. That helped. I thought to myself, "All I need now is my late husband Bill to complete this picture," and darn if he didn't appear as well. **Wow! Time for celebration.**

Who says we die? Nope, we just change frequencies a bit. My mentor on Main Street Disneyland, Walt Disney, has told and shown me by his presence, that this is for sure.

Tears of joy streamed down my face as I got a hug from the man who started me on this strange path and then left me to find my way - and I have, to this point. "What is happening?" I said through tears of absolute joy. "Am I dreaming?"

O: "You have long since passed dreaming and we are here to let you know that in your time it is close to revelation time."

G: "What am I to do? I have spent much time telling others of this City and its advantages of Light healing. Now what?"

Y: "It is time for space and Earth to be together in Light and love. Many in the Universe have banded together to see that this is taking place. Swift changes in cosmic action now!"

B: "Honey, you have done well with all I handed you and now we can look at the results. All is well you will know. Hold on for a little bit more, you have a home run in sight. I am proud of you!"

O: "You and many other Lightworkers holding the Light on this through eons of time, now bring forth the God's treasure. We encourage you to continue to see the next City book is published. As the new City makes its appearance, many will know and experience what you have been shown for so long.

"The audience you are used to seeing here is busy touching many human hearts, that what is happening here is true, and they have much to do in the unseen to accomplish this fact. So as The City Light begins to touch people heart-wise of its coming, hundreds will sense through their hearts and connected emotions of what we have spoken of for so long, as they are open to receive. Remember 11-11-11?

"Your visits here are almost completed. Permit the pages of your new City book to welcome all who will have on your planet a place to visit and be healed. 'And the many shall come,' as has been said long since. The Christ taught Love. It is time now for all to grasp and feel what it is to love ... like God loves. Petty differences will hold no power. This is the healing path now being evoked to appear ... and appear it will and you can quote me! You have a steady conviction that something is coming, and it is! You have been recently asked to speak at a Convention of 2012. Beloved, this is not a by chance happening, for then people will connect the puzzle pieces and rejoice."

Here I stood with 3 Light Beings telling me all was well, when suddenly they all hugged me at the same time. The power was so strong that I felt I must have Ascended. What a strange encounter this has been. Unexpected, and loving to be sure, while knowing soon my adventure would end and a new one would begin for everyone.

A hundred years from now what will we have, due to this orchestrated universal God project? History in the making and I got to be part of it all and like all the rest, I too, was awaiting the grand finale. "Thanks God, we should talk soon."
So Light it be!

The Second Coming!

Embassy Visit September 21, 2012

In the quiet of this Sedona morning, I felt this was a good time to release myself from this daily world and re-enter into The City of Light Embassy of Peace buildings, since I had been requested to re-enter and meet with OOO-LON and get answers to any questions that had arisen ... and many had since I have been privileged to enter the Embassy over 136 times. It has become my home away from home ... sort of.

The sun shone bright on one of the usual 5-story Gates, or was it reversed, with The City being the sky light? Crowds of happy chattering people eager to enter filled the air with anticipation of the miracle that God had sent us. I saw myself move to the left as La-Luke my City Guide, motioned me to follow him and we slid through a smaller side Gate, then moved through The Relaxation Park with its massage benches filled, onto the funny wheel-less, driver-less trolley which took us to the shiny white and gold Embassy building.

We entered the stage facing OOO-LON, plus an audience of space entities that would fill the biggest stadium ... something like what Pastor Joel Osteen shows on television. It was quite a sight! To think all these heavenly bodies were coming together to help our planet! Wow, time to get on our knees in Thanksgiving, really.

OOO-LON smiled and waved us to come forward as he reached out his hand and bowed his head, in this Heaven-to-Earth welcome and we acknowledged this love for that is what I found here. Even his touch felt healing.

Genii note: How blessed we have been to have this universal cosmic family take interest on our behalf and support The City of Light in ways we could never expect could happen. Welcome to each Light Being here and everywhere in the Universe including, my Jedi Space Guide YA-FU-FUS (YA for short).

O: "Ah, sharing time again and this is good. How may we serve you?"

G: "I have a question to please have answered as it has been slightly spoken of at various times I have been here."

O: "And the question is?"

G: "It has been mentioned of a 'Second Coming'. What does this mean?"

O: "Yes indeed. The 'Second Coming' relates in a famous book, of following a master man of love named of The Christ, and that one day he may return. All would feel the love he tried to explain and to actually be, and he actually did, to a point of his leaving. In doing so, he left a legacy that people would love each other as themselves. Most misunderstood, as they had no love for themselves, much less others. Oh, some people got the message but most did not, either not hearing of what was attempted, or caring less.

388

"So, The Great Creator of all has taken the matter on, determined to have peace and love lead this planet called Earth, in such a profound way as to bring forth The City of Light, which no human can reject, as it stands in Light as a monument to love and healing. One can walk into it and feel God's demonstration and it is what you stand in this very moment as testimony of what is being said.

"It matters not, either the Christ, or Buddha, or even what God-master decided has brought it forth. It remains that the Creator of All is the way and the reason. Translating in many languages it still remains The Second Coming with love incarnating for the purpose of Love. Get the picture? You all don't love enough! Ego moves in and love takes a second seat.

"It has taken centuries, and has been quite an undertaking to put this together, so that you all will get a new slant on love and healing. But we believe it was worth the effort, for the Cosmic Universal Communities who do know the meaning of Love, through advanced space technology have brought forth what that holy man desired to give to humanity.

"Is an Ascended holy master going to walk down a sunbeam over the freeways? We think not. Oh, it might get the media attention for a bit... but being more practical ... how about several Holy Cities that bring Love and healing to everyone instead? Something so beautiful and beneficially useful for every person on your planet?

"So, Dear One, the answer to your question is 'Yes' this is the so-called Second Coming of course. The City of Light prophesies are the attention-getters ... big time, first class, and totally for healing. But, only one? Many more Cities will open their gates of love healing, after the shock wave of this first Sedona prototype becomes second nature in its divine work. As the word spreads, several more Cities already on the planet's grid will open and likewise be seen, entered into, and love healings will take place.

"You, the Genii have walked the paths of Light here, and have reported what you have seen and been made aware of, and reported in your first book. Now the next one is being readied as a 'tell all' with all of the Embassy visits sharing, and all building visits recorded, as this final edition appears and is a treasury to go down in your history. Does this answer your question of a Second Coming?"

G: "Yes indeed. Thank you."

O: "The City of Light is for everyone to experience, and due to the population of your planet, many areas will need to fulfill the needs of many, so Cities of Light will be opened in different locations to supply the people's needs. But first City first! Already you feel The City frequencies that keep you trying to stay balanced in a now unbalanced world, as it kicks up its heels in shifting changes and you walk in 2 worlds constantly.

"It has been reported, that you are to be part of a 2012 Scenario Convention in the Sedona birthing location. This is good, as the cosmic world has much to share, for with knowledge comes wisdom like you share with your visits here.

"The Second Coming is the first of its kind decorated in healing and love like never before experienced, in honor of The Great Creator of it and all the rest to appear as well. Time is close. Get ready to celebrate! We send you back to your world. Share and spread the good news and we will speak again soon for all is well."

And with this the scene disappeared and I was home again with my puppy Light Spirit looking for a handout, so I guess it was his turn. Until next time ... **I am Genii Townsend and I approve this message. So Light it be!**

"Just because you don't see anything happening, doesn't mean God is not working." – Joel Osteen

I just LOVE Joel Osteen! I watch his TV program 3 times just about every Sunday. I am looking forward to God opening the doors for me to share this marionette I made of him in person. Who do you know?

Thy Kingdom Come...

Thy Will Be Done On Earth As It Is In Heaven

Embassy Visit September 28, 2012

This passage had been bouncing around in my head for a while, and an invitation to return into the Embassy of Peace in The City was now my intent and pleasure. Slipping into that state of deep awareness and an unknowing vision of what was to come about, at that moment I found myself already in the Embassy facing OOO-LON and the audience of space entities. Gosh there must have been thousands. What! No usual Gate and trolley? Nope, I just got plopped in. Fast trip, so there I was and there we went . . .

OOO-LON bowed in acknowledgment as I wondered what was to be said that day.

O: "Once more we meet and exchange ideas and guidance to be shared. You have had a past quotation floating in your head for a bit. Do you remember what it is?"

G: "Yes Sir I can. It is 'Thy kingdom come, thy will be done on Earth as it is in heaven.' Can you tell me what this is about?"

O: "Yes, from our perspective. Many have taken this quotation to mean many things relating to their own personal lives and that can easily be acknowledged as such. However, this Dear One, is an acknowledgment of this place you stand in this moment.

"Is it not your pleasure that God give you and millions of others the kingdom, and could not The City of healing be that kingdom? Thy kingdom come. God's (The Creator Designer of all) will be done. Where? On Earth, as it was thought of in the universal mind of God or heaven? Where is a City of this kind needed more than this Earth planet?

"Have you not been told that this planet will shine in the heavens like a star? Somewhere long since this was reported to you through the Dr. Bill in trans-audio. It is suggested you re-look up that data and add it to this visit message."

G: "I will do that. It was a past channel session some time ago. Something about the Earth becoming a star."

O: "Good, the main thing to be taken into consideration is that the awesome undertaking brings forth what you are standing in right now this minute, and it has taken eons of space-time to develop and produce.

"You have visited many buildings of healing technology that you say you could not have thought of in your own imagination level, and this is true and you would call it 'far out.'"

G: "This is so right. The magnitude of what I have visited is awesome and amazingly accurate, and makes a lot of sense as I see what is coming from the under-City with its huge computers. So much so, that you call our current computers play toys in comparison. The 1,500 ft. High Towers catching the UPPC's (Uniphase Power Capsules) to pull unknown cosmic power into all this, is beyond some words.

"Gosh! Even a building where one can get a make-over facial change without cosmetic surgery. I saw it happen. In my opinion we really need this place of healing Light."

O: "Of course, precisely why we are here from cosmic communities far advanced, as we come in love to help a planet in distress. Thy Kingdom come, why not? Cannot God do anything? How many prayers have gone up to have help? How many cries of pain and suffering are people having, just because they are unaware of why this should happen to them? One is paying for sins? Sin means just missing the mark, and are you not into cause and effect?

"Surely they should know of what one thinks becomes the effect. Reading books on the subject or preparing for a City to appear from heaven to remind all that God is alive, well and in action. What else could this be? No one could fathom what is in The City of Light, until it has landed on ground level and each one can walk into it as a physical entity, and imagine even getting healed from thoughts that bring forth the illness in the first place.

"Your television media propels illness like selling tomatoes. Turn off and tune inside for the truth. If you haven't got the illness now, they report you will. Where is the God love? We are reporting it right this second, and as you have said, 'Something is Coming' so move over darkness. We are coming in.

"It is time life begins making more of itself and feeling itself fully expanded, as a friend has said. Yes it is time, actually past time, to shake off the past and get into the future which incidentally is NOW! As our space crafts enlighten the selves in your force fields, you will know when the time is correct for you will see with your own eyes what you feel in your own hearts and envision in your own minds. Star workers bring Light to your planet, clearing up the darkness so long reported, making way for the Kingdom of God to be in appearance for all to enjoy. So then Your Kingdom comes. God's will will be done.

"This then is validation once more to those who may be skeptical but hope that this edifice will appear as given. We give notice that indeed this is as much a surety as the sun rising. There is a 2012 Conference about to land on the Sedona doorstep. And indeed you are ready for them in love and admiration for all they do to bring more Light and love into the planet. So now go back into your day and enjoy your current little kingdom as we have completed this visit. You will be notified when to return.

"So Light and love it be. Session is ended."

And with this and a deep breath I was back home.

Earth Becoming a Star?

Recopied September 28, 2012 as requested by OOO-LON)

Date unknown. Long ago... Somewhere in time.

G: What I was given, was the sentence that this planet is to be a star, so in my inquiry to my inner teachers, I was first directed to the dictionary for its explanation and to then return with any questions I might have for a trans-audio session, which I did.

Dictionary description: Planet, a non-luminous, self-containing mass of gas in which energy generated by nuclear reactions in the interior, is balanced by the outflow of energy to the surface. The inward directed gravitational forces are balanced by the outward directed radiation pressures.

G: "Why would this planet become a star if it has all this gassy stuff?"

Unknown by me at that time was my space mentor (YA-FU-FUS 'YA' for short)

Y: "The answer is multi-complex. This planet by your name Earth, is already a celestial being, as all heavenly beings are stars of sorts. This is basically acknowledged by theologians. However your scientific world looks to see the make-up of these so called objects, thus bypassing the real intent of the statement requesting an answer to.

"The make-up of both this planet and the so called stars are propelled by natural forces for them. The sun is a massive gas energy, and the planets benefit from it, also the stars. It is an interaction between the planets and the stars on an electrical connection of webbing that makes each revolve around each other in unison. Now then, why change the pattern? Your planet has been given the Intelligence to grow (slowly to be sure) and become more illumined. To be a planet that is 'Illumined' could make it a 'star-seed' and it too, would Glow in the heavens. This is the path your planet has been directed to achieve... to grow in Intelligence to the point it too would be an 'Intelligent Star-planet' in the heavens, filled with natural Light of human beings, instead of the ones your scientists describe, and those who are fortunate to live on such a planet would benefit. As has been told before, there are more planets going through the process of cleansing and growing, and thus becoming more Light-filled than ever before."

G: "Where are we in that line-up?"

Y: "Your planet is next to the last in intelligence, and must be totally cleansed for Star-Status to be achieved. It has been in process for eons of time but now with the sweep of the Galactic Light Wave in process, your planet can and will achieve the Star-Status it deserves. Those who declare "I am Star-Light Materia,!" assist others in becoming 'Sparks' to light up the sky when they stay in the Light and truth, leaving dark thoughts behind and in the process, the whole Universe benefits.

"Just think ... if everyone on your planet were 'Star-Sparks' would not your planet glow? Light your world. Release your past history. It's just that ... past ... it is done, finished, completed and has brought you to this moment ... this time.

"When the past has been released, the good memories as well as the bad, giving thanks for all that has taken place (which is understood to be very difficult in its process however not impossible), this then makes a space for the new and the Intelligence of the One, the All, to fill the void and you gain ... not lose. Those who hang on to old hurts and anger keep the victim in place as one re-lives the trauma over and over ... thus keeping your planet in darkness.

"Remember all is thought. Cancel those old hurt memories, for they are teachers and classrooms you have passed through. Repeat...passed through! You have done it and still you function (by the grace of the most high God, All, Source, Light etc.) and are better people for it. People can then recognize the Enlightenment even in its infancy. All should put on the new armor of Light and move forward.

"The old is dead ... Leave it and birth the new planet resplendent in the Light that shines like a Star-Seedling ready to birth. You all are a part, as a midwife would be assisting. Take each day and remember to Glow and your aura will do the rest. The time is now! The place is Earth. You are the Light Tech. And every day is the 4th of July when you send your Light into the Universe ... so Light you all be!

"Praise be to God."

And so it is!

In that Love and Light, Genii and YA!

Enthusiastic Expectations!

Embassy Visit October 6, 2012

Having been requested to once again enter The City Embassy, even while on a trip, this indeed must have been an invitation of importance and of course a blessing. Inner opening scene: I saw a City Gate with people entering by being given a gold ticket of some sort. (Wow what a souvenir this was.) The usual hand I saw that was waving me through belonged of course to my Guide La-Luke.

The crowds seemed to just part, as I bet La-Luke was using some City power to part these seas. We connected and made a soft run to catch a trolley, but this time many were also on this trolley and were quite excited.

They were fascinated to see La-Luke, this Entity of Light, also on the trolley. It looked like many Light Entities have now taken on a 3D frequency as directional Guides. Hmmm, interesting even for me. Talk about Spirit being present in all ways, just imagine Light Entities filled with love attending to our needs in person.

This is so cool! Oops, a trolley stop. Embassy of Peace being announced and only we got off. The trolley moved forward with no driver or wheels to be seen. I heard laughter from the riders as I waved goodbye and we were ushered onto the Embassy stage. Note: This is going to be so cool to have people see what I have been privileged to see for so many visits. I kind of feel like a guide myself ... sort of. We are all connected on this cosmic highway of Light.

OOO-LON greeted us as I recognized that no electricity was on here. Inside this building it was totally lit up by the hundreds of Light Beings in the audience ... Wow! How to save on the electric bill.

No wonder I have been told that when we humans all get our act together and bring forth our own Light, that this planet will shine like the moon. Woopie! Lots of magic changes were taking place. No longer just being human (or 'skin-bags' as one of my own personal Guides, Who-No calls us), as we are more electricity than anything.

O: "Our message received, I see. Good, now permit me to share more good news. You have in-walked this universal path for eons of time with the knowing that something is coming, meaning this City of Light.

"We are pleased to announce that most all systems are in place for the grand opening revelation. It is very close to demonstration. The final touches of check-out on all technical healing devices are in process.

"You have watched the sky and clouds change and the cloud ships as well. Continue to do that for the 'beyond the unseen' will be shown. We are as excited as you are, as the birthing you convey to others is supported and is helping to put the finishing touches into place.

"All the Spirit and Lightworkers within The City grounds are being readied for the demonstration, like characters in a play on stage. The so-called Second Coming is at hand, and the excitement within the grounds of this Holy City parallel what will take place, when this magnificent manifestation is even partially seen as the veil is lifted. Is this not good news, as one of your reporters from another country referred to as 'Down Under' announces as his by-line?"

G: "Dare I ask this again ... Is there a time and date?"

O: "Ah, now that would be lessening the dramatic impact we want to give this, as a surprise to most and a holy delight to those who know."

G: "Oh, you play with me?"

O: Smiling ..."Just be aware, that it could be close in your time world now. Stay tuned in, be open, and we will tap you on the mental line as your frequencies are being adjusted to be in the knowing. This is why you are to rest on this trip where even Disneyland is a rest spot for play and the bench conversation with the Walt of Disney. Rest! is your guidance."

G: "The new Cities book is about to go to print. Anything to be known on this subject?"

O: "As said, it coincides with The City appearance as the energy of this book records the inner visits, and that energy will be transferred to those who hold the book in their hands, as each one is loaded with Light and transfers the knowing that it is all quite correct.

"As the cleansing of the so-called Shift is clearing the planet of all its unpleasantness like never before seen, the darkness finds no place of safety here. Now with the heavy frequencies of The City connected with the High Towers bringing in the UPPC's (Uniphase Power Capsules) bringing in more Light into this planet, that in itself dramatically enhances all the components to make sure that this Holy delivery makes its intended mark on the population of the whole of this planet and the Revelation is assured.

"So much has gone into this project that indeed as recorded in a holy book, that it will be seen as a bride (Light) in white adorned for her lover (the love of people). Shortly you will meet and greet many Light Servers who channel many High Lights and the seal of approval will be set in place. Your delivery of The City words will be well received as the Sedona doors open in holy blessing for each and every one.

"This is not by chance that this conference will take place during this time in your history. The human channels make this Cosmic Connection on holy ground where big dreams can take place ... How does all of this sound?"

G: "Like an answer to many prayers ... personal and planet healings can take place ... A step in the right direction to be sure. What is my guidance now?"

O: "Just be ready for any message, feelings, sensations, or knowing, and use your rest time to tune in. We will deliver the signals and blessings. This indeed brings the long waiting to a close, for God demonstrates God, and all is well! Go now and be aware for time is in short supply."

G: "Thank you for all you have done and are doing as I look forward to the blessing of all blessings 'at the same time' which is the music I love from a Barbara Streisand album - On Higher Ground."

OOO-LON smiled and they all seemed to wave as I turned around and headed out the stage door just as an empty trolley arrived and took us back to the Gate. As I said good-bye to La-Luke, the inner scene stopped and I found myself in a hotel room to rest. Thanks God, OOO-LON, La-Luke and all the Light Spirit attendees in the audience, for showing me a great time for all these years.

So Light it be!

Simple Attachment of Ascendancy

October 16, 2012

Out of the Genii's Lamp of Light

G: "Please share with me what Ascension means."

Who-No, Spirit mentor of the Genii, responds.

"This is easy, for you and many other humans do it every day. One level is to attain sainthood of some high spiritual level and this is good. It has been shown to you how to do this through many eons of time and space. But what about Ascending in every day life?

"Do you not Ascend every time you think of God's goodness, and that inner connection, so that many tears flow? You say daily, 'I love my life.' You feel good, right? Ah, Ascendency, imagine that!

> 1. Is not the adoration you get from your puppy 'Light' - does not his unconditional love give you a feeling of Ascendancy? Of course.

> 2. Your spirit work is an Ascendancy, as you allow we of Light to speak with you, and then like now, share this with many others as advised.

> 3. Does not your 4 Keys of Light sessions take students seeking Ascension into their own holiness? Of course!

> 4. Does not the Light in the eyes of a child, when they see your puppets, trigger a lifting Ascendency?

> 5. Have you not seen women do this in your female playshops, when they contact their inner child by making of a simple cloth doll? Have you not helped to pull them through past hurts with fun and see the tears of Ascendancy develop for them?

> 6. And how about your Power Women's playshops, by showing them their own feminine power?

"Dear One, it is a state of the human mind that pulls at the heart strings to want to experience the Creator of all, so each step is Ascendancy one way or another.

> 7. Have you not created marionettes of the person themselves as a gift, be they show business celebrities or Presidents? Have they not rejoiced seeing themselves in another form?

"Plus entertaining hundreds in a Disney-type setting and thus giving them a dream. This is Ascendancy in action.

"Is not Love the format for Ascendancy? One does not have to wait until they are at a higher level to experience Ascension. It is all around like apples on a tree. All you have to do is pick one of your choice and Ascend in the juiciness of the taste.

"Sainthood is right where you are now. For it is all ... NOW! Just being Love is sainthood, whether you are washing dishes or sending love from your magic lamp like this page. And what is magic but the love of the Original Creator giving love to yourself and so many others? Love is Ascendancy in many forms and you get to create them all.

"Have not people responded to your City of Light books and presentations? And even you are to see what you have been sharing in the unseen when they do.

"God is Love in action, about to present Itself even to those non-believers. Either it is love or it isn't. You choose love and isn't it heavenly to do that? Ah, Ascension on a continual basis.

"So then take a deep breath and give your usual thanks that even you have Ascended many times as well as helping others.

"Remember the High Court and what took place? This in itself Ascended you. This is not ego; quite the opposite. You are God-blessed to have been in such a high place of honor. Congratulations!

"NOW give people the feeling that they Ascend moment by moment and all it takes is LOVE. Imagine that!"

And with that the message from Who-No ended and I was very filled with love, so I must be in Ascendancy.

Thanks God.

So love it be!

The Final Embassy Visit: Saying Goodbye Before I Say Hello!

Embassy Visit October 18, 2012

It seems strange to learn this will be the last Embassy inner vision visit before The City demonstrates when I may go there in person, thus the title of this visit.

I find I am a bit sad, for this has been a place of love and wisdom dished out like a spiritual banquet set for me to learn from and share from.

The usual Gate entrance, the people usually crowding around to get in were not seen. What was seen was that I was standing on the usual stage facing OOO-LON and the multitudes of space friends that call the Universe their home, sending me love ... I mean real love, not just a few words spoken with no heart behind them.

O: "Oh you came quickly as advised."

G: "Yes but a bit sad as this, I am informed is my last inner vision visit."

O: "Tis so, Dear One. You have completed your journey here. From this point The City of Light radiates its frequencies of change over, but we shall meet again, perhaps in a different form. This visit was needed to complete The City second book, for from this point many changes will take place as the unveiling takes over and what has not been seen, will be.

"We here in this location want to thank you for having the courage, on a mixed up planet of dark and Light, to persevere unto the end through so many visits and so many questions that have led you here to this Embassy of Peace, and into many buildings of Light healings. Have you had a good time?"

G: "Oh yes, where else could I have met so many interesting Light Beings that have helped this City come into being? I will never forget you, any of you." And as this was said, coming in from the left, space mentor 'YA' appeared. "We continue!" he said.

G: "Hi teacher of space."

Y: "We continue. YA no leave!"

O: "Genii you will continue to receive up-dates of progress messages as time permits. Be open!"

Then to my surprise, my City Guide La-Luke appeared from the right. "What a strange grouping. Forever Friends," I thought.

G: "I want to thank each of you. This indeed has been an affair to remember. Anything I should know before I leave?"

OOO-LON, YA, and La-Luke gathered around me, each a Light within themselves. WOW! As I looked at them, I felt a little like Alice in Wonderland, and wondered what I did to bring me into this wonderful situation.

O: "What you did was merely to be born. This was and is your destiny. That's all it took, for you were destined to do what you do and be a part of The City. Be open and we shall meet again in perhaps a different form along with many friends you have met here. We shall be as you say 'Forever Friends.' Show the people that all it takes to be a Jedi is to be Love. The power is in the love. You are all children watching a show as God pulls your strings. You have the power to grant wishes, even your own, thus the name change was desired."

At this point La-Luke handed me a cloth as the tears were really rolling. Then from the left, out came Who-No my no-nonsense teacher declaring he would still be around this student of innocence and nonsense. Then coming to add to this group was a Light Being in silver that sparkled, declaring that he was Atherian who had spoken through me a few times. My God, the power! ... Gee, a lot of Forever Friends were there. Lucky me.

Just as this took place, coming from behind me was, no kidding ... President Obama saying, "You wanted to meet me?"

By this time, I was speechless with tears as I got a loving hug from each. Alice in Wonderland never had it so good.

As La-Luke led me to the stage door, I looked back and the total audience was giving me a standing ovation ... imagine that!

And with this the visit ended and I was back home knowing now the goodbyes have been said and I await the hello's.

Thanks God, it has been a wonderful trip.

So love it be.

Genii Townsend

The Persistence of Believing!

Inspiration from the Genii's Magic Lamp October 19, 2012

Moving forward into the new as the inner visits into the Embassy of Peace in the forth-coming City of Light have been completed. As my last visit on October 18, 2012, and the new book on The City comes into print, I look forward to actually walk into it personally as we all can, when The City manifests.

Q: "What now?"

A: "The visits as said were resolved due to first, the book printing, and our needing a closing for the reader. You even sense something other is the reason and correctly so.

You are able to see and enter The City of Light, due to a very strong opening of the Witness Chakra Corridor, which you share in The 4 Keys of Light sessions. That memory will fulfill its prophesy as you and many other humans enter into the reality of the third dimension Cities of Light.

"As the appearance demonstrates, you will recognize where you were in vision, in being able to recognize certain buildings and their healing functions, as presented in your new book of Light that you have traveled for so many years of constant meditation, introduced by the good Dr. Bill of Townsend. You are sort of an interior tour guide through your book.

"Those who read The City books will remember what was said, and can then walk their own path in the third dimension, by now mentally stopping at each described building in the books, and sense themselves there as well. We are talking power here, as there is more power of Light doing this than anyone can imagine ... just like walking into a grocery store now.

"This Dear One is only the beginning, not really an ending as such, as Light Guides will travel with them of Light assisting. You can fill in the tone names if desired.

"Due to the third dimensional change-over in its Earth impact, you need to rest periodically to prepare yourself for the grand pulsation.

"You will receive message updates. So then just be open and see what surprises God has for you and your world. This City demonstration is not in your hands as such, for only God can bring forth what has been spoken of here.

"Keep sending out the messages to the interested as presented, and put it under a newsletter title such as the one suggested here and as the Charles has said, will be distributed, for indeed magic is about you all and, you are a Genii and not by chance but programmed as such. Imagine that!

"All is not ended but the love and fun has just begun and with it comes God's healing love for this planet. **So Light it be!** "

Worth The Wait ... Making a Difference!

November 11, 2012

I invite you to meet one of my more interesting Inner Guides of wisdom and fun ...Who-No! You may or may not have met him in my previous inner writings, as he is quite unusual and I have met quite a few through my Embassy visits in the City of Light. Who-No is a match for any student including me, who is interested in learning empowerment, for he is this (empowerment) personified.

He can pull a rabbit of excitement out of a hat or show us how to pull a miracle into this silly world we live on. He can be funny, sarcastic, and magical all at the same time, while sharing wisdom beyond the normal. He can make the most proficient magician of human thinking look like an amateur, including me.

To be seen, he is only about 3 feet tall and wears green like an Irish leprechaun, for he proudly resonates to this image for the benefit of all who come to him for learning, which today seems to be my turn.

So prepare yourself and expect anything for when he gets me as a student, I am on his mental report card as not the brightest human in the world, so I play his game and we all learn. So let's begin ... I slid into a meditative state and the vision I saw was a forest of tall trees and much greenery. Looking around for Who-No, all I could see was a foot sticking out from behind a huge boulder. It had to be Who-No! Who else would wear bells on his turned up shoes?

A peeking over the boulder found I was right as Who-No sat up and mumbled something about being disturbed, and seeing me he was sure this would be a visit he would rather dismiss.

W: "Would you disturb the peace of Who-No?"

G: "Sorry I didn't see you."

W: "Wise ones look ahead. Sit ...we talk!"

I looked for a place to sit on his command, and found a rock with a few daises around it, while feeling a bit like Alice in Wonderland in this setting, and this was not Walt Disney time.

G: "OK, O teacher of empowerment and elevation. What am I to learn?"

W: "You have questions for old Who-No? ... who sometimes feels as old as Yoda, but I am better looking."

G: "My visits to the City Embassy of Peace ... look like they have come to an end due to The City book completion. I would like to continue with updated messages regarding The City of Light. What can you tell me for sharing?"

403

W: "You think all has ended? Foolish thinking. Those who stray from their dreams of Light find themselves in darkness. Why would you think you have diminished the Embassy just because you are in the finality of your latest book? You are indeed to continue to bring forth connecting information for sharing, precisely why you woke me up."

G: "People keep asking me when The City will materialize. What am I to tell them? Some are very anxious."

W: "It is worth the wait! The old (somewhat strange) saying that Rome was not built in a day was a tiny project compared to what you are all to experience."

G: "Well, (pulling up my power) it has been a long time in coming, for me 30 years."

W: "So ... what is 30 years compared to a moment in your so-called time? What have you accomplished in the 30 years? Just sitting around twiddiling your thumbs? Or have you had the greatest adventure given you with the wisdom that a City of Light is to come about and heal the darkness so all can love each other and thus have no time for fighting?

Sounds pretty good to me. (Always complaints from you humans.) You doubt God's ability to produce? Surely you jest with old Who-No, who is getting older by the question, just from the nonsense of this talk.

G: "Of course my prayer is for the future love of this planet."

W: "Good, pay attention and embed in your thinking, and do not lose these precious Who-No teachings:

> 1. What is Hope, but an energy step in the right direction. People have HOPE that something better is coming.
>
> 2. What is FAITH, but a higher frequency step in consciousness. Like a mustard seed, small but important.
>
> 3. What is BELIEF, but to be mentally and heart-alive in this knowing of truth. Another step higher.
>
> 4. Ah CONVICTION! You have reached the pinnacle of success. You are totally convinced and there is no opposite. Absolutely no opposite! Imagine that!

"You put this big 30 years of adventure in your City Books, which are as you have been told like the magic lamp of the Genii, and are you not this? Turning The City book pages is like rubbing the lamp and people see wishes of miracles can come to pass. Pay attention. You know you have the power.

"Do you not teach **THE 4 KEYS TO LIGHT**? Is this not a power package that once was only one to one in private and now to be opened up to the many?"

G: "Yes, I have recently given the 'Tone' to many at a conference."

W: "Well do that then. So you may have to wait a bit for the City to appear. So big deal, and it is a very BIG DEAL! So what is a few more days?

"You humans have so little patience. Have you not been told The City of Light is not only coming but bringing with it 13 more around the planet? Is it now at ground level?"

G: "As I have been advised."

W: "Well then, is it not worth the wait while finishing touches present themselves, as you do when you slip into your sequined jackets of light for appearance? Again to all who read this, patience. What is a few more days or so? It is worth the short wait. Understand? And no as the humans say 'buts' ... no buts. Would you fall back to HOPE instead of CONVICTION? Of course not!"

G: "I completely understand. No problem."

W: "Good then this session is over and Who-No can go back to sleep. Remove yourself and let the people know that all is well and worth the wait. It could be days or seconds from now.

"I Who-No dismiss you, so make yourself empty and back to your own world that will keep you busy enough for both of us. Be empty (meaning open) for God's blessings called The City of Light as it shines brightly ... so much so, that you cannot see it, but is worth the wait. We will speak again. Now be gone! I wait no longer for sleep!"

And with that he fell back behind the big boulder with only his bell-tipped shoes being seen.

Stay tuned for more of Who-No and my sharing these unusual conversations. Like the Cities of Light, it will be worth the wait.

I promise!

So Love and Light it be!

Return to the Embassy of Peace in the City of Light

November 17, 2012

RETURN TO THE EMBASSY...

"A new entrance you will make as the world tunes into the Cities of Light as a near and dear probability. The entities of Light in many dimensions plus their human counterparts as speakers, verify that what has been said so long ago, is now in action.

"Thus the first of the 13 Cities beyond the Sedona, (the Energy Mecca where you reside) circle the globe, awaiting their birth in due time, But the first is the Sedona City as a recognition of what this planet is heading for - TOTAL HEALING BY LIGHT. Imagine that! The shock wave will speed across your planet as more energies are put into repeats across the planet.

"Dear one, this is the Light of the future technology that those of other dimensions bring forth what has been secret for centuries. You have all been living still in the energy of the dinosaurs. Time for massive change.

"The appearance of the Sedona City of Light brings forth disclosure after disclosure as nothing can compare with what we speak of here ... nothing! Darkness will have no place to hide.

"Australia will be the first of the next 13 Cities with the United Kingdom and China coming as well as the rest. A beginning to be sure and these are exciting beginnings of the rest. As people are open to receive, they will begin to feel the frequencies as they move around the planet.

"So much going on behind the scenes so to speak, and things are in place for this healing of peace to take place, and it will. Your introduction to the Sedona prototype Light City with your book raises the consciousness and the energy that something very big is about to happen, and it is a part of history in the making.

"So then do return to the City Embassy of Peace and we shall continue to update what is not yet known. So love it be!"

G: "I will return to the Embassy gladly with love in my heart and an open mind to receive what is reported. Thank you."

Experiencing the Deepness of Love!

Embassy Visit November 18, 2012

I found myself back at a City Gate (in vision). Wow! Lordy, look at the amount of people. Hundreds of them waiting to enter! I wondered how I would, or if I would find my Guide La-Luke.

The City Gates are 5 stories high and a glance upward answered my question, as he was hanging out a window waving to me. Then, by some magic, I guess people around me just began moving a few steps away, and I moved through the Gate and there he was. I love this God-kind of wispy magic. This is God in action, and no one seems disturbed as the path just opens. (I must try this kind of magic at Disneyland.)

As I made my way through, there he was with arms extended. He grabbed my hand and into the Relaxation Park we went. We were heading for the funny trolleys that people get to ride on all over The City.

The Embassy of Peace loomed before us while other people on the trolley laughed that there was no driver and no wheels. Really, this City not only heals with Light, but is fun in the process. The trolley stopped as we jumped off and waved goodbye to the rest of the passengers, who could have cared less that we got off, as they had so much more to see.

We entered through the usual back stage entrance, and slipped through the curtains to see hundreds of blessed ET's from space locations applauding, and I was filled with tears of pure joy washing my face, as my Guide handed me a cloth. I was back "home" ... sort of. What in Earth had I done to receive such an honor? A chair was brought forth as I was feeling shaky with emotions and I gladly sat.

OOO-LON: "Welcome back. We are pleased you entertained our message to return."

G: "Oh my God, this is wonderful! I am so pleased to be back, not knowing why but certainly honored."

O: "You are quite welcome. Now that your City book of guidance is completed, we can move forward. The City has many attractions to assist in the healing of the body temple as well as the mind and spirit. You have been into many now recorded. Would you like to see more?"

G: "Of course. What may I know, especially as people's big question is, when will they see the City in 3D in full view? I have no answer for them yet."

O: "You are aware that The City is on Earth ground level ... correct?"

G: "Yes, as of last Christmas Eve, 12-24-2011. "

407

O: "It is not necessary at this point to answer the 'when' yet . Do you not sit in The City at this moment in time?"

G: "Yes, I see, feel and am definitely here. What is taking time to be seen physically, is also a wish for me to walk into the physical City with others who even now, hold the Light on this massive project."

O: "Do you remember seeing a building completed being lowered into place from an overhead spacecraft?"

G: "Yes, it was such a surprising sight."

O: "Now imagine many spacecraft doing the same thing. This massive building here is one of them, which as you can see houses extraterrestrials - Light Beings who have brought forth and continue to do so, the completeness of the God-intended venture with technology from way beyond your planet's scope. Is this not worth waiting for?"

G: "Of course. I have followed this path for 30 years since my husband brought through the plans in meditation sessions."

O: "And where did he get them from, now that you have walked through many?"

G: "From Master Hermes, who I understand was one of Dr. Bill's mentors that he just loved. And through him came the architectural drawings of the High Towers, plot plan, and Gate Towers that took Bill 3 years of drawing to do, and of thinking he was going crazy, but drew them anyway. He kept coming out of the guest room saying he was not going to draw them anymore, and would promptly be sent back in to continue, knowing full well he could not draw a straight line. It was quite a time of learning."

O: "Yes this is quite a Master, this Hermes who indeed brought forth the architectural drawings of the pyramid which housed the mystery school in its deep center, and did indeed work through the Dr. Bill for all to see in your City guide books. Now then, look to your left and meet this Light yourself."

From out of stage left came a Light so bright that I had to squint a bit, but I knew it was indeed Hermes. I pushed myself up out of the chair, and the Light engulfed me in such love, I felt I could disappear and that would be OK.

Here with this Light surrounding me, I was meeting this God-man who has led me unknowingly through Bill's writings. I was indeed blessed and could not speak. It was like all of God was holding me close and I was emotionally blessed. Either it is love or it isn't. This was beyond normal love.

I was profoundly emotionally blessed as tears of pure love, joy and beyond were experienced as though all the lovers of the Universe were loving me at the same time. Wow, what a sensation! There is much more to love than most of us know, as I have been blessed to experience it. I tried to get the words of thank you out but was too overcome to do so.

So many questions to ask but none were needed and no wonder. Bill followed this mentor's teachings. I will never look at the original drawings Hermes brought forth of the Gate Towers, and High Towers without being thrilled. I have the originals and they were reprinted in my City books with giving thanks.

Then, I heard Hermes say as I was enveloped in his Light, "You will have your City of Light. I, Hermes, promise this in God's Light, and I am here for you!" (Just typing this up, oops... I am again absorbed in this love I just spoke of. I sure hope it is catching. We could use lots of this across this planet.)

Somewhere in my soul, mind, and body, I know this is so and to say "thank you" simply was not enough. His Light surrounding me, I sat back on the chair and ... bingo, he was gone leaving me in a puddle of tears.

O: "Now how was that for a surprise? Obviously you are speechless. Do you remember when you went to the Court of the High Tribunal (in vision) and were crowned with the pearl of great price?"

G: "Of course, yes Bill was also crowned before I was. It was quite a gift."

O: "Have you not used your crown and scepter given to heal?"

G: "I usually don't talk about it except with The 4 keys sessions."

O: "You have given to many throughout many lifetimes and so you were led to the High Court. Your path is just beginning with the Cities of Light coming forth all over the planet. Go back to your world, for soon what you have sought for so long now, seeks you and millions of others and it is worth the waiting which is about over."

G: "Thank you all ... Good Lord, here come the tears again. I am in overwhelm as again this perfect love from the audience is felt. Can one get too much love?"

La-Luke lifted me from the chair and we departed, fully knowing that I will be back, and as Renee says, "Whoopie!"

Back now in my daily world in Thanksgiving week, I have so much to be thankful for as we all will, and it indeed is worth the wait. I so bless all the Light Beings from space, for all they are doing to make the wait worth the bringing forth.

Maybe the disclosure we are waiting for is the City of Light Sedona location - Number One on the agenda.

So love it be! Happy Thanksgiving!

Let There Be Light!

Morning Guidance November 24, 2012

Genii Question: "What can be shared on the City of Light at this point?"

Answer: "The outside world spins itself with the energy of cleansing so the love of God can present itself as in the form of a City of Light which signals God's love coming forth through the healing process. Now that calls forth a mighty force of energy.

"There is a Jedi saying in your world, "May the Force be with you." Well guess what? It is, and about to reveal itself. We are aware that some might say, "Sure that has been said before, but I see nothing."

"One might start by looking within or reading The City of Light book which gives clear visions of what is to come about and embody them and like the Genii's magic lamp of love, awakening that Genius (Genie-in-us.) ready to receive God's blessings. The City of Light spoken of here manifests itself ASAP, this you know as even now, you sense its frequencies stronger even, although not physically seen.

"As the light of the sun shines brightly this morning on the red rocks, so will this Light be amplified a hundred times as The City Light shines forth. People will think at first that the sun is doing something strange in its brightness, but the sun is dim in contrast to The City of Light whose Light amplifies what has been spoken of by you for lo these many years, of your trusting that this is indeed possible.

"In your inner visits into the interior of this City, all is correct in its appearance, which could be any day now when the book is completed and nothing more is to be done. Many are the people who will be thrilled in this dramatic demonstration. Revelations: "And I John saw the Holy City New Jerusalem, coming down from God out of Heaven, prepared as a bride adorned for her husband. Now this Light from Heaven comes to Earth taking up much land on the Arizona landscape. The impossible just became possible.

"So dear Lady of Light, rest in this wisdom that you have known so long, and that what looks like a bright morning sunlight just might be the brightest Light ever experienced on a clear morning, A City of Love.

"Excitement will ring out from all the 4 points of the Earth that God indeed has arrived, for nothing else could bring forth such a revelation. Many more will recognize that angels and masters have led this planet into being a gift from Heaven.

"So rest in this wisdom, that before you know it, what looks like the sun is brighter than usual, only to find out the sun is dim as God has arrived with the brightest Light ever witnessed. It is called the City of Light."

Get ready, be human love for ... IT COULD HAPPEN ANY DAY NOW ... IMAGINE THAT! So Light it be!

Of Disclosure and Revelation!

December 1, 2012

Genii with Guide Atherian

G: As I find myself somewhere in time on a Saturday morning at Questhaven sanctuary, I have been guided to tune within for an important message on the subject of disclosure and revelation. I am assuming it is on the subject of the City of Light Sedona.

"What am I to be made aware of as I tone God's Love Song, 'AH'?"

A: "For some years of your time, you have allowed your inner guidance to be the lead in your everyday experience of your Earth travels. However, this day begins yet a new adventure saturated in Light and love. You have had a taste of love here and there so this is familiar and for the most part, deep and enjoyable.

"The first City of Light is now so called the disclosure that many Lightworkers seek to have done for their E.T. friends and space mentors such as yours with YA. Those of space technology now being applied, make the old become obsolete as new processes take the place of the old, due to their efforts.

"This indeed is exciting for those in the unseen, as this has been sought for eons of time and it takes something from God of this magnitude to get the attention in love and not fear for your human understanding.

"Record this... **THE CITY OF LIGHT SEDONA is the DISCLOSURE and the REVELATION** predicted so long ago as the message is sent around the planet. All is in readiness now for its appearance. Upon returning home from this current trip, expect the expected to become visible and heralded as the energy fields of God prepare its existence in the 3rd dimension at any time.

"Many will be quite surprised as this holy vision becomes media headlines. It has been a long trip of faith for you, the Genii, but your belief and conviction that something was coming forth including this answer to when, now becomes the when as the vision appears like magic.

"Permit nothing to alter your belief, for you are about to see this dream actually come true. The Lightworkers want a disclosure and they shall have it, through the City of Light. The God mentor Hermes, is ready to lift the veil and nothing will be the same again as it was before."

G: "What is my part now in this scenario?"

A: "You, the Genii, will be given guidance on a moment-to-moment notice starting now. You walk the Light path as a leader of the Cities of Light dressed as a human female of Light and love but, there is more to you than this appearance.

"This, dear one, is the disclosure for even you to know that the revelation proclaimed so many years ago, is ready to begin a public appearance. **Something's Coming becomes Something is Now Here**, so no one can deny it. Rest, be open, and enjoy these thoughts of wonder as Disclosure becomes Revelation as the long sought out energy appears as promised.

"**So Light and love it be!**"

Genii Insight Message with Guide Atherian

December 1, 2012

G: "What does 12-12-12 mean for us?"

A: "On your calendar of space time, 12-12-12 indicates a day in time when energies collide and information is given, opening the lives of communication to people from the unseen where love is introduced as a precursor for events to settle in easier than before.

"This explosion of love becomes the seeking not of bomb destruction. It is significant enough to herald in the new like trumpets blaring their tone and fireworks lighting up the sky over one of your favorite places, Disneyland. There are yet 11 days (at this writing) before this momentous occasion takes place and much could precede it.

"As the shifting of lower energies are leaving and the new love energies take their place, stronger and greater than ever experienced becomes the norm. These are power times, so be ready to love and be loved and make as you call it, "Forever Friends!" for they will not wish to be less than that.

"So 12-12-12 becomes a signal that indeed all is quite well and the God of Love is on duty and functioning perfectly in Divine Order, and this dear one is Good News!

"So Love it Be! In Love and Light!"

Imagination Application . . . the Makeover of Santa Claus!

December 7, 2012

G: "I have been told I can revisit the City of Light grounds again and enter a building I have not been in before. Is this correct and may I do it now?"

A: "The Genii's request is given. Report to the Gate of Entrance."

Once more as I had done so many times before through inner vision of whatever comes into view, the vision of a City Gate appeared with people crowding to enter. I saw La-Luke waving to me, and with his Light he just parted the seas of people and I got to him quickly. Must be something more to this Light business than I know ... duh? Turning to the right, I saw some familiar healing buildings and noticed a smaller one tucked in between a couple of big ones.

All of these buildings were exquisite - so shiny and sparkling due to the Light that engulfs this City. Even if this planet was in nighttime status, it would shine brightly. We ducked into this one with people also looking for some kind of something treatment.

L: "This is a building of IMAGINATION APPLICATION. It is a place where the human imagination gets what you call a Make-Over from what it was to what it should be. People get to learn how to use it correctly through implanted Light wisdom. Come we'll sit for a moment.

"The humans use their imagination to envision their thinking on something they want of wishing. However, much is implanted of no good use and could be quite harmful from one who has embedded anger to release. Higher quality visioning is needed here where wars and daily thoughts would be of that higher quality, like love for instance.

"This is a building where the Light helps to change all that as the imagination (changes) its frequencies into new ways of thinking and visioning and gives that person the freedom to love unconditionally, for it knows nothing else. So anything desired is set on a correct course for that person.

"Example: This time of your year denotes many holidays and people get excited or worried. The children look to Santa Claus or St. Nick (or whatever a country has), to grant their wishes (even Genii's are included) with no return expected. He usually enjoys the children as they are so open to God's gifts including believing in a Santa Claus, even to the point of waiting in long lines to sit on his lap and tell him their dreams.

"Santa usually dresses in a red and white Santa suit and is expected to grant the child's wish where at that time it could have anxious parents wondering what to do. With this kind of Light given here, they know exactly what to do. Not a problem, as the imagination is on the tracking no matter what of high quality is desired.

414

"As people leave the child years, they could lose their believing, and bring forth what is not wanted according to the heart in love-vibration. With age, one loses the Santa belief and he no longer becomes real, and only a flick of the imagination he once inspired, holds.

"Note: Take the word IMAGINATION apart and what do you have? GOD'S/ MAGIC/LAND and the corridor to Christ Consciousness which is quite real.

"If the image of Santa Clause was God, Buddha etc., would people believe that he is the real representation of God, Christ etc. dressed in a form to bring love into your planet? In this wisdom building, you feel deeply the love of the messenger Santa God, and will never lose it from this point forward. Taking this feeling of deep love back to you world, changes take place for the imagination that has had the higher frequencies introduced. The make-over is then complete.

"The Light in here makes the change quite strongly, for now love in a different form has been introduced, as even being holy in some ways of thinking, and (people) take this love back into the world and let it loose. No more anger is introduced, as love intent is now the predominate force in action. All sublimated rage is dissipated and filled with love as this God-love enters through the imagination of the people on this planet (who get) to live in (it). A perfect solution to all your pairs of opposites. Get rid of one - the negative one, and all you have left is positivity in action."

G: "So if a person goes through the Light in this building corridor of mental and emotional make-over, they have found the wisdom of God-love and it becomes their life experience?"

L: "Correct. People will enter here to be, let's say, imprinted in love only. There will be no opposite. Each City of Light to be introduced around the planet will have the same buildings of healing as this one does, so the love will spread, ready or not as each person being in that Light affects everyone they come in contact with. So the love enters each imagination and voila! Light consciousness replaces the old worn-out energy and the planet as a whole becomes new. People will know that they are loved and can love easily with no worries it will not be correct, for it will be.

"Santa Clause represents love and giving. This way everyone becomes as Santa of sorts, and this was the intent as the Christ child was born and brought forth all this celebration in the first place. This can become a planet of love as this City is (all about) feeling God, and being totally this love, as the opposite polarity has disappeared. The door has been newly opened to the imagination, and everyone senses love with no other distraction. So God is Santa in a red and white suit or whatever. The love patterns implemented here leave with the person who goes out into their world and affects all they come in contact with as a 'love virus' and no cure is needed. Understand?"

G: "Yes, lead me to the Light of make-over and I happily accept this gift."

The scene closed and I was ready to hug my puppy Light, who only knows love.

A Gift of the Magi and Progress Friday 12-21-2012

December 22, 2012

Every once in awhile God drops an unexpected gift in my lap. This day was one of those. It started out fairly normal (whatever that means here in Sedona, AZ. Christmas shopping to be finished, my friend and publisher Charles and I headed to Cottonwood, AZ to do just that, and have some dinner as well.

A new restaurant had just opened so we stopped, and the rest of this story took place. As he was ordering at the counter, I heard Christmas carols being played in the background. Something touched my heart as I listened quietly with closed eyes.

Suddenly a very clear vision appeared. Symbolically what the vision showed me, was on the right side of the vision The City sparkling in white, and me on the left side. In the center stood the Christ in full Light holding out his arms and hands, one pointing to The City, and one hand held out to me as he looked at me to take it.

I literally came unglued emotionally and tears flowed all evening and even now as I write this report. I could not even tell Charles what was taking place as I just was mesmerized in the feeling of what the vision had shown me, until we got home and I could speak rationally again.

Symbolically the right side of me equals our 3D world and the left side equals spirit and the feminine with the connecting point of this vision, being the Christ and The City of Light equaling the prophesied Second Coming. In His smile as He reached to take my hand, I knew The City of Light was about to be seen physically, as all the pieces matched. It was indeed a signal of progress.

This morning, Saturday, December 22, 2012, I was awakened at about 5:00 a.m. The sky was still dark except for just behind the red rocks. I saw from my bedroom window, a huge white (Light) filled in arch, which was not a cloud and too early for the sun, as it does not rise in this location until later in the morning. Oh my, what was this now?

In the morning when I was able to meditate I asked. This is what I was told:

A: "The vision you had equals the meaning you interpreted. The City of Light is due and all will be amazed. Take this time to indulge into the mystery of what took place and honor the holy presence as fact, not fiction. The halo of Light you saw this morning is another indication of what is about to appear. Just be open and permit the Christ to fill your heart, mind, emotions, and spirit, for the truth will soon be revealed. So love it be for everyone."

So, that is my story to this point. Did something take place yesterday? It did here to me, and that is important since the first City of Light is due to birth in this holy location as God decides the timing. Merry Christmas with a very bright New Year about to begin....and may it bring all the blessings you deserve. **The Genii**

416

Other References to Cities of Light and Sedona as a Sacred Site

Sedona's Past, Present and Future as a City of Light

Sedona The City Of Light

In the Cities of Light, there are sacred new cities, crystal palaces, healing temples, Holographic geometrical healing temples of sound and codes of light that have already been created and are anchoring into the Earth from the fifth dimension. In the United States of America, and in many places Globally are preparing for the fifth dimensional shift of consciousness.

The raising of our planet into the new Omega Creation, the Golden Age has arrived. Stargates and corridors are in place here in Sedona, Arizona as well in many other sacred places around the planet. There are many activations and tours offered to assist in the acceleration and group participation.

In many sacred places around the Earth, Venus temples and golden cities are activating. This is part of the divine unfoldment of the Golden age coming, the 7th golden age. In preparation for the amazing events unfolding with each new day, many are guided to participate, fulfilling a sacred agreement made with the creator.

Many of us as a group have done this many times before, and it is our heart's desire to bring heaven to Earth. This year 2008 is an accelerated year of unfoldment both inwardly and outwardly. There will be pilgrimages and lay line activation journeys being offered.

http://www.bringingheaventoearth.com/SedonaCrystalCityofLight.html

In an article **on Near Death Experience and the City of Light** based on Kevin Williams research, he reports that 17% of the 55 near-death experiences he studied experienced a City of Light. That 11 page article is available as a PDF at http://www.sedonalightcenter.org/nde.htm

The Coming of the Cities of Light by Steve Beckow

No development on Earth is more fascinating than the advent of the Cities of Light. I can trace the discussion of them to the middle of the last century. (1) However, it's probable that they were being discussed long before that. Genii Townsend has written two books on them and spoke about them at the Sedona conference. (2) SaLuSa said on Nov. 16, 2012 that there are twelve of them. (3) He tells us that they'll be used to heal millions who need help, even after Ascension. On July 22, 2011, he said of Mike Quinsey:

"Michael has now added Cities of Light to his understanding, as another facet of what is to manifest for souls on the Ascension path. As the weeks go by information of these magnificent cities will become widely known, and you will find that they are technologically advanced healing centres that will totally change you. They will not be the only ones, as there will be many ways available to you that will concentrate on raising your vibrations." (4)

In 2010, Archangel Michael through Ronna Herman revealed that one of the functions of the cities was to raise our vibrations: "You have opened the pathways to the Cities of Light so that you can gradually incorporate higher and more refined frequencies of Light." (5)

In January of 2012 SaLuSa told us that the cities were "preparing to make their appearance on Earth." On this occasion he focused on how "they were examples of what can be done by using our technologies for the good of all." (6) He described those technologies as they applied to healing.

"Many civilisations of the Galactic Federation will contribute to the task of attending to your needs, and each often has their own specialised expertise. Be assured that before you reach Ascension, you will have healing that is based on Light, Sound and Colour.

"Your earthly ways are often quite crude, but we do not belittle your attempts to cater for all types of illness and disease. A lot of the new methods are understood by you, but usually lack the funding to be developed. Furthermore, there are Corporations in the drug industries that stem any advances that may replace their products and reduce their profits." (7)

On another occasion, he said that another function of the cities was to introduce us to what life was like in the higher dimensions.

"The Cities of Light of which you are now becoming aware, will give you a sample of what it is like in the higher dimensions. Yet they are more in the nature of Healing Centres specifically prepared to help you raise your consciousness levels. You will take the fast track to remove all the vestiges of your present dimension that have kept you within it." (8)

A few months ago, SaLuSa described them as integral parts of the process that will convert us into galactic beings.

"Everything you expected to take place will do so, and as progress is made you will find that it will take you further than you thought possible. It will be a wonderful time that will see you relieved of all of the old problems that have held you back. It is time to go speeding forward and move into a new world that reflects your upliftment into the higher dimensions.

"There will be ample facilities, including the Cities of Light, where you can be healed as you are to be fully restored to a prime condition. Eventually you will also be able to reverse the aging process and return to a youthful appearance, and so it will go on until you become a Galactic Being. All of these changes await you and they are not too far in the future. Think positively about them and you will be helping to manifest them much sooner than we have allowed for." (9)

In *Heavenly Blessings* on Aug. 30, 2012, Archangel Michael revealed that the cities of light were originally scheduled to be brought here 80,000 years into our future but were introduced earlier when our future wingmaker selves pleaded that they be brought to Earth now.

"In the year that you know as 2000 we began working with you, we began, your star brothers and sisters began, and your future wing-maker selves began working with the Cities of Light.

"And these Cities of Light are not simply etheric forms but let us suggest to you and tell you, share with you that in the beginning these Cities of Light were 80,000 years in your future. The work has been done and it began with a plea, not only from us but from your future selves guiding the actions, the decisions, the choices, the dreams, the inspirations, the desires that you, in human form right now have to create Nova Earth.

"And they begged you to make wise decisions because the decisions that you have made starting at that conjunction and continuing on, almost on a daily basis would affect whether they would come to be in what you think of as a physical reality and existence." (10)

Recently Archangel Michael named some of them.

"Now the Cities of Light emerge, many are seeing them and they have been forming all over the planet gloriously, yes the first one was 'The New Jerusalem', Phoenix to Sedona. But there has been one 'The Atlantean City of Light', 'Terra Tralana', 'Idaho', many, many ... 'Michigan'.

"We have spoken of this when we have spoken to the people of China about the City of Light that is forming there." (11)

Which cities was Archangel Michael referring to as emerging or existing over China? In a mid-summer 2012 edition of *An Hour with an Angel,* he explained: "One of the most magnificent cities of light is already emerging slightly north of Shanghai, south of Beijing. And this will be a city of light much like long ago in Atlantis, a port where the star brothers and sisters would come for exchange of cultural ideas, technology, art. It will be magnificent. So think of this, look for this, work on this.

"There is also another, a smaller city of light — and it is more of a retreat and a place of healing — near the Mongolian border in the north." (12)

Is the latter city of Light Shamballa? We don't know.

AAM says the cities of light can be glimpsed with our physical eyes but are more apparent to our Third and Fourth Eyes.

"This is not simply something a dream. Many of you, yes with your 3rd and 4th eye, but with also what you think of as your human eyes, are seeing and observing, coming into form in your reality, something that you have pulled into your time and space albeit fully anchored in the 7th." (13)

As far back as 2009, Archangel Michael said through Ronna Herman that "some advanced Souls are [already] integrating small amounts of Sixth-Dimensional frequency patterns (and even higher) via the Cities of Light." (14)

Thus the cities of light function to heal us and raise our vibrations, enabling us to ascend more easily than otherwise at the end of this year and preparing us for galactic citizenship. Tomorrow, we'll continue our study with some extended word-pictures of how the cities of light appear and function.

Footnotes

(1) "Fourteen Etheric Cities of the Earth," at http://www.ascension-research.org/14cities.html
(2) Genii Townsend, *City of Light - Sedona* and *Something's Coming.*
(3) SaLuSa, Nov. 16, 2012, at
http://www.treeofthegoldenlight.com/First_Contact/Channeled_Messages_by_Mike_Quinsey.htm
(4) SaLuSa, July 22, 2011.
(5) Archangel Michael, Apr. 1, 2010, through Ronna Herman, at
http://www.ronnastar.com/latest.html.
(6) SaLuSa, Jan. 18, 2012.
(7) SaLuSa, July 22, 2011.
(8) SaLuSa, Sept. 2, 2011.
(9) SaLuSa, Sept. 19, 2012.
(10) "Transcript: Archangel Michael 'The New Earth will be far More Magnificent than You Imagine'" Sept. 8, 2012, at http://the2012scenario.com/2012/09/transcript-archangel-michael-the-new-earth-will-be-far-more-magnificent-than-you-imagine/ .
(11) Loc. cit.
(12) Loc. cit.
(13) Loc. cit.
(14) Archangel Michael, Sept. 27, 2009, through Ronna Herman, at
http://www.ronnastar.com/latest.html

http://goldenageofgaia.com/2012/11/the-coming-of-the-cities-of-light-part-12/

The Coming of the Cities of Light by Steve Beckow Part 2

In the second part of this series, I'd like to give more extended descriptions of the cities of light that are gradually forming around the planet and will play a large role in the Golden Age of Nova Earth. In her book *The* City of Light Sedona, Genii Townsend painted a picture of the impact of entering a City of Light.

Just Imagine

... Entering a place of such beauty that it makes you an instant believer that anything is possible, like entering a 5-story-high gate that is encoded with your personal beliefs that make you feel like you just came home.

... Experiencing healing techniques in Light modules where no drugs, knives, or needles can sever the body's electrical lines.

... Entering a Memory Manor building where you can release past memory hurts with no emotion attached.

... Standing by a Fountain of Light that makes you feel great and sitting on benches that massage your body.

... Taking a dip in a healing pool that can clear skin conditions.

... Being able to balance your emotions in an Empowerment Emporium.

... Seeing babies born in a Birth-aterium, laughing with the mother who had no anaesthesia, no pain and the only crying would be for the pure joy of the experience.

... Entering a stadium-size building called the Embassy of Peace Headquarters where Light Being from the Universe gather to help bring forth Peace on this Earth. (1)

In *An Hour with an Angel* on Sept. 8, 2012, Archangel Michael described what we can expect to find in a city of light.

"But you are also approaching, they are approaching, you are approaching, coming together to build places that are of Nova Earth, places where business, what you would think of as commerce, are places of beauty, of light, of community, of creation.

"Temples of learning where wisdom is shared, not hoarded, information is the tender that is to be equally shared, where star beings from many galaxies that you have never even thought or heard of walk the streets freely and gaily, where families live and thrive, where there is no pollution, where all the needs are attended to." (2)

According to Archangel Uriel, through Linda Dillon, the cities of Light fall under his purview. He called them:

"... a project that has begun long ago but that is coming to fruition and it is the project, very much, of the Silver Flame under my purview, and it is the Cities of Light. The Cities of Light are cities that are already in form. Now I want you to understand what I am saying; they are already in form. You do not see them in the 3rd dimension, that does not mean they are not there. And with your new 4th eye you will begin to perceive them more and more clearly." (3)

He said they would emerge all around our planet and that we are already anchoring them.

"The Cities of Light have been and are at this point cities of the future and they emerge all over your planet. They are magnificent, you can have a vision of a crystal city, spires similar to Atlantis in some ways, but more glorious.

"And these Cities of Light are already occupied by future beings, by wingmakers, by your star brothers and sisters, by many visitors and hybrids, by humans as well. And even by your future self. But what you have been doing in the work that you have all undertaken with me, even when you did not know it, is you have been pulling down and anchoring these Cities of Light." (4)

Uriel went over the different purposes the cities of light will serve.

"As you emerge into the 5th dimension, many of you have thought 'How are we going to deal with our cities?' Well many of your cities will be transformed and we would like to say 'Of course there is a rebuilding and a co-creation' but these other Cities of Light will also be anchored in the fullness of their beauty and the fullness of what they are for.

"There are Cities of Light that are for healing, there are Cities of Light that are for art, for creativity, there are Cities of Light that are portals for your star brothers and sisters. They are all over, they are delightful places to be, they are places where peace reigns already." (5)

He said that the development of the cities was coming at the speed of love, which is the speed of light squared.

"The decisions that you have made as a human collective and as individuals in the last 10 years have begun to bring these cities into form and into fruition as we make this transition and Shift. Your decisions have determined whether these Cities of Light will ever be anchored in physical reality, and they are. And they are coming forward, not at the speed of light but at the speed of love, and the speed of love, dear friends, is the speed of light squared. Yes, it is happening that fast." (6)

Finally, Archangel Michael tells us that "there are many of you out there who are very conscientiously building and working daily with the Cities of Light." These are not pipe dreams, but tangible dreams coming true, he tells us:

"Do not think this is simply a pipe dream, it is not and you are seeing the fruits of this. ... This is not simply something that is esoteric or etheric. Yes, it is electronic. It is 'in space' as you would think of it but it is tangible, it is real. ...

"These are tangible dreams coming true. You are building situations where your community is coming together. I will not be giving away the news but these are tangible ways in which you are saying 'We are united in heart, we are united in purpose, we are not united by those who believe they can control, we are not united by anything but love and hope and vision for a very different future." (7)

These descriptions of the cities of light remind me very much of descriptions of the temples of learning and healing on the Mental Planes of the spirit world. (8) They exist in the Fifth Dimension and higher and are destined to play a large role in the transfer of learning and technology for us in the Golden Age fast approaching. At the Sedona conference, we were hoping that the degree of love generated would bring to us the opening of the New Jerusalem, the city of light that stretches from Sedona to Phoenix. But evidently we're a mite soon in our expectations, but I'm told the time is very close.

Footnotes
(1) Genii Townsend, *The City of Light – Sedona., Slide 19.*
(2) "Transcript: Archangel Michael 'The New Earth will be far More Magnificent than You Imagine'" Sept. 8, 2012, at http://the2012scenario.com/2012/09/transcript-archangel-michael-the-new-earth-will-be-far-more-magnificent-than-you-imagine/ .
(3) Archangel Uriel through Linda Dillon, March 29, 2012, at http://the2012scenario.com/the-2012-scenario/what-role-are-the-angels-playing/heavenly-blessings-with-archangel-uriel-march-29-2012/.
(4) Loc. cit.
(5) Loc. cit.
(6) Loc. cit.
(7) "Transcript: Archangel Michael 'The New Earth will be far More Magnificent than You Imagine'" Sept. 8, 2012, at http://the2012scenario.com/2012/09/transcript-archangel-michael-the-new-earth-will-be-far-more-magnificent-than-you-imagine/ .
(8) See for instance "The Mental Plane – The First Heaven" at http://www.angelfire.com/space2/light11/nmh/first1.html

http://goldenageofgaia.com/the-2012-scenario/new-technology/the-coming-of-the-cities-of-light-part-22/

"Genii Townsend made a decision long ago to take things that don't turn out quite right and completely transform them. It's no wonder she was selected to meet with the galactics and introduce so many of us to the cities of light. All Lightworkers have a mission but Genii's has brought so many people excitement and delight. I personally can't wait to have a guided tour from her and a completely relaxing and restoring visit. Something's coming ... and Genii is our impresario and cherished guide for it." -- **Steve Beckow** (http://goldenageofgaia.com)

Update on the Cities of Light

Another amazing channeling from the annual Sedona Gathering. A chat with Zen Zuriah, future inhabitant of the Cities of Light, including questions and answers. A must read.

"Greetings. I am Zen Zuriah, wing maker, inhabitant of several Cities of Light and I am messenger and ambassador to you and to your time like my earlier incarnation. I am messenger and channel.

Many of you have asked, 'So what are these Cities of Light, these crystal cities of the future, these places of peace and harmony where love prevails?' That is why they are called Cities of Light for you could make this interchangeable and you could call them Cities of Love for it is where we all walk freely. How we have come to exist, and the reason why, is important for each one of you to understand. The reason why we exist is because you are making that choice right now and you have been for several decades. You have chosen to go on and to anchor new realities and new dimensional realities within the 3rd dimension so the third can be an expanded experience.

We are you and we are your future self. So when you continue, we continue and when you give up, our light fades. We have not witnessed any of you giving up, quite the contrary. You are truly the visionaries. You don't simply look to leave a brighter planet for your family, or for your children, or for generations to come. You are laying the foundation for thousands and millions of years. You think of yourselves as small, for these bodies truly are quite tiny. But the energy and the promise and what you are anchoring not only in your heart but in your communities and in the earth, is laying the foundation for us.

Is that vitally important? Yes. Because it is the unfoldment of a very large universal plan. It is going beyond the universe to the multiverse and coming back to the omniverse. And that is where you are now. The collective is receiving the energy. And it is not only in the Cities of Light that we are anchoring with, but each and every one of you. It is the beacons that are going out and saying there is hope here, there is healing here, strangers are welcome here. Terra Gaia was always meant to be an interdimensional portal of love where beings from everywhere could come and have this experience of what it felt like, in all kinds of forms, to live in a community of love. There is nothing more important.

And I do not say that because our existence depends on it, I also say it because it is part of your feeling and knowing of your contract and your purpose. When you anchor your Lemurian and your Atlantian and your future Wingmaker self, when you welcome us into your being, anything is possible.

You know, there are some of you here that are very interested in building and you would be interested to know that our Cities of Light follow the old pattern of Lemuria and they are constructed by thought, ideas, the collection of molecules into form.

Our star brothers and sisters are with us. And you need to know they are also with you. And it is time for this illusion of hidden energies to be destroyed and for fear to be eliminated. For these are the beings that come in peace to assist. These are the ones that have wandered the Universe looking for the place of peace, for the home of love. Even in the chaos and drama you would not believe how brightly you shine and how brightly this planet shines. And it is because of hope, for even those who are sitting in the darkness thinking they are forgotten still have that ember of hope. That is pretty much the only reason they are alive. To us this is phenomenal. If you were to look back at the history and the evolution of your collective and you would say 'Oh this is where it changed, this is where the shift occurred'. It would be right now. You are ahead of schedule, my friends. And you are ahead of schedule because you have held and embraced the dream, the hope, the faith, the trust. These are the interdimensional qualities that are essential. This is the understanding that brings collectives out of what we see as dark ages into the Light.

We come closer because you beckon us but we also come closer because we are anxious to do so. The grid and the blending is moving very rapidly now. It is not 800 years away, it is more like 80. So you might want to stick around. There is no need, you know, to believe those old grids and embrace the destruction of death and disease. That is not our way. You say to me, 'Zen Zuriah what do I do to assist with this anchoring of the Cities of Light?' And I suggest to you that you are doing it but I also ask you – hold it, hold it in your heart, hold it in your grid, hold it in you vision and beckon us because like your star brothers and sisters we don't come uninvited. We come because you are waving us in, you are welcoming us and we have been waiting. What do you want to know about us? What can I share with you this day?

Will we survive?

You will more than survive, you will thrive. Do not forget Gaia hosts us all. It is true there is some rather dramatic housecleaning going on, but, you will survive. And if you feel that your flame is running low you have complete access to us, as you do to All. But in our humble way you may call on us. We will send you help, for many of the answers you seek are already in place. The wrinkles have been sorted out. May I ask you my sister, it is a very real and legitimate question that you have posed, *'will I or will we survive?'* But I would like to ask you to say, 'I will survive and I will thrive and I will be there'.

Do you have an ethereal form or you more solid than that?

We are far more solid than that.

As solid as we are now or not quite?

No, we are as dense (laughter) and I do not mean that – *yes you do – you're picking on me because I'm here* – oh, but you are also with us. You are known as Zengayla. *As what?* Zengayla. *Um, okay.* So, our bodies have form and function but they are the crystalline forms that you are now in the process of changing into. And so think of it as having been honed for several thousands of years. So it is a lighter sensation but it is most definitely form and it is form insofar as not only do we have what you think of as physicality form but also reproductive form.

I knew they weren't going to let go of that one.

It is not the same as what you currently do. Although if one wishes to have, to revisit an ancient form, that is fine, that is certainly allowed. But it is more community based rather than singular family. *Thank you.* The children belong to everyone. *Oh, we are doing the Lemurian thing.* Yes. It is a full circle.

And do the children have stories of our time?

Yes they do. They have been passed down in many different forms, written and oral, electronic. We have what we call 'story cubes'.

And is there more we can do now to help insure that you get here?

You are at the crossroads and we know that many of you are tired and that is why we invited you to 'Homecoming'. Not to give you assignments but that you would know that you are not alone. It's not about sitting at the crossroads or intersection and just sitting down and dying as if you have run the 24K. And it is not about turning left or right. It is about holding, holding your truth and your Light and just keep going. So we do not give you elaborate instructions and besides which each one of you are very good at hearing us when we are asking you to do this or that. Our purpose was more in sharing with you how far we have come together. We have started this adventure together and we are so close, we are so close.

How do you communicate with us?

By thought, by what you would feel as an impulse. There are many times when you are feeling an electrical impulse and you think 'I'm too electrical today and I must ground a little further' but in fact that is us talking to you. That is the way in which we tend to communicate as an electrical impulse. So that will get translated into thought or ideas even sometimes you call it divine inspiration, we don't, but yes, that is how we communicate.

Why is it that so many people are having health issues?

Because your bodies are changing. Because you have taken in much of the toxic energy, not of the planet but of, you know, a lot gets blamed on the planet that has nothing to do with her. It's very interesting. But the toxic energies are mostly from human belief systems and so many of you have turned yourselves into human cleaning factories. Now, that's a very noble idea but it isn't always a good one.

So that's over, right?

It's over when you say it's over. *It's over then now, anybody want to agree with me on this? Yes. It's over. It's done.* Then it is. You do not need to travel forward in ill health and you have done so often to try and clear or try and help. But as Gabrielle has been talking to you, and has Yahweh also, for the golds are very busy, and I am gold. I am gold and blue.

You do not need to process. This time of differentiation, you are hearing this everywhere. It is not about clearing. This is the crossroads that we are talking about. It is the point at which you are saying 'I am leaving that behind'. It is not clearing it; it is leaving it behind and going forward on the next phase of your journey. You have had many trailblazers and settlers in this wonderful area, in this City of Light. And often they would have to take their wagons and the things that they thought were so precious and say 'I will have to leave this behind in the middle of this wasteland desert'. And they would do so in order to continue on. That is what the process of differentiation is about. You are leaving it behind. And you are choosing a new path. And even if you think it's the same path you've been on, it's new.

I ask you in this wondrous City of Light for you to make the prayer to transverse this sacred place 3 times in unity and anchor. Farewell."

Channeled by Linda Dillon at Sedona Annual Gathering, Nov. 5, 2010
http://counciloflove.com

Introduction to The Light Center

Genii lives in Sedona, Arizona. She and her business partner Charles Betterton have co-founded two companies (Universal Stewardheirship, Inc. and the New Thought Spirit in Business Benefit Corporation) and four non-profit organizations: Ultimate Destiny University; CENTER SPACE (the Center for Spiritual, Personal And Community Enlightenment; The Light Center; and New Thought University.

Genii delights in creating celebrity marionettes and presenting them to the star so they can pull their own strings. She is now working with Ultimate Destiny University to create "empowerment marionettes" of world- class authors and trainers such as Deepak Chopra, Les Brown, Mark Victor Hansen and celebrities such as Oprah, Whoopi, and Ellen Degeneres to help children of all ages become empowered and learn how to use their creative imagination, Imagine That!

The Light Center, Inc. was established as a non-profit membership organization, partly as a vehicle for accomplishing the task of publishing information on the Sedona City of Light, along with other resources for empowerment, enlightenment, healing, consciousness and transformation.

The Sedona City of Light is not for sale. It is Holy and sacred and Genii has been directed to reveal what has been entrusted to her and share this information with others who may be interested.

Genii has granted the copyright for the Sedona City of Light to The Light Center which will help publish and distribute the manuscript. Given the direction to keep the Sedona City of Light Holy and sacred and the reality that it costs money to provide printed materials and audio video content, The Light Center decided to provide electronic copies of The Sedona City of Light on a donation basis.

For the versions of the manuscript that cost money to produce them (such as photo copies of the manuscript, CD ROMS, and printed books as the manuscript is further refined and as funding is available to print the contents as books), The Light Center will list the actual costs to produce the information in various formats. The Light Center will then invite anyone who is interested in receiving a copy to become a member of The Light Center and make a donation to at least cover the actual costs of production and shipping and handling.

Genii has been sharing the wealth of wisdom entrusted to her with others for decades through small group classes, workshops and discussion groups. These resources include: *The 4 Keys to Light; Thirteen Goddesses of Inner Light: GLOW, Gathering Light of Wisdom;* and *Discover the Secrets of How to Grant Your Own Wishes from a Real Genii!.*

Now The Light Center is seeking volunteers to help Genii adapt the training programs she has created to reach and serve many others through the power of the Internet. For example, at least the first 2 of The 4 Keys to Light can be shared electronically. In addition to transferring the copyright for The Sedona City of Light to The Light Center, Genii has decided to have TLC help her refine, publish, produce and distribute related programs for empowerment and enlightenment.

The Light Center has also made arrangements with several other resource providers for their programs, products and services to be made available to TLC members. For example, the **Ultimate Destiny University for Successful Living** is providing a free copy of its introductory 80 page e-book, Manifesting Your Ultimate Destiny, to all TLC members. Ultimate Destiny is also donating 50% to 100% of the sale of any of its Ultimate Destiny Success System and other present and future programs to TLC members back to The Light Center. More details of the available resources are provided at the end of this document.

The books listed earlier in this manuscript are all available for sale through The Light Center at www.sedonalightcenter.org/featured_resources.htm.

Publications by Genii Townsend

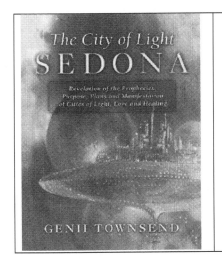  

The Sedona Light Center Blog Site
http://sedonacityoflight.wordpress.com

   https://www.facebook.com/CityOfLightSedona

   https://twitter.com/thelightcenter

Invitation from Genii and The Light Center

Putting this book together with the profound assistance of my business partner Charles Betterton along with help from Kathie Brodie, Renee Trenda, Katrina Rodgers, Nina Joy and others who have helped makes me feel like a female Indiana Jones seeking a treasure unknown. I have witnessed superb visions beyond belief, and to share them with you is a personal blessing. **Thank you!**

I do know, as a student of truth, that in my many playshop sessions, women (and some men too) have been led to become more than they think they are, and they are experiencing a life that is great in all directions, and also that they desire and deserve a higher awareness and healings of various kinds.

In this manuscript I have also included other teachers with their talents who also can lead us. This journey covers a lot of beliefs of mine that I share with you, for whatever you can accept for your own. Is the Sedona City of Light just a mental dream of mine? Perhaps. A wish? Yes, but with that comes a knowing so deep that to see us walking into it is reality that will not be ignored for any reason.

We students walking a path of higher consciousness are aware that miracles do happen, so don't be surprised if one day a City of Light magically appears equipped with vast healing techniques in superb architecture that only God would display for us mortals, to make us believe that peace on Earth is indeed probable, and that somewhere in our past we did something right. Yes, God has something wonderful planned for you, me and millions of others who will be shown that Heaven on Earth has appeared and all is well.

It has been my profound pleasure to share and give you a peek into the future that is wonder-filled and where all is healed, for this manuscript contains only a portion of hundreds of pages that have been given to me. I have included questions and answers here, and I will also have questions and answers posted on the blog site. What I have been speaking of is nearer than you know ... or maybe you do? **Imagine that! So light it be!**

If you resonate at all with the vision presented in The City of Light Sedona and Something's Coming: Universal Cities of Light, Love and Healing, we invite you to help us share the Good News they offer with the world.

If you have created a product or program related to fostering love, leadership, awakening, empowerment, enlightenment, healing, etc., we invite you to submit them for possible inclusion as a featured resource from The Light Center.

If you know of other resources or references to "Cities of Light" and or if you have personal stories of interest to share, please join The Light Center and participate in our blog at http://sedonacityoflight.wordpress.com.

Training Programs with Genii

The Four Keys to LIGHT Initiation

Bringing much advancement to the student's path, **The 4 Keys to Light** are an extraordinary and greatly accelerated initiation into higher consciousness. This program assists you in developing the ability to consciously connect and remain connected to your Supreme Light and the higher Light Intelligences that are assisting and guiding your lifestream. You will receive and remember these ancient and most holy teachings that will catapult you into mastery, self-empowered knowing, sacred trust and responsibility.

In the first key, you will anchor **The Word**, the most powerful word of Creation to support your mission in the planetary shift and the mastering of dualistic energies. **Atonement** is the harmonic simplicity of tone to align all of your energetic bodies to the rhythms of the Universe. Your guiding forces of Light will make themselves known as you learn to connect to, transmit and use **Divine Intelligence** in your life's mission.

The 4th key is considered the most celebrated moment of your embodiment. The **Light Linkage** will greatly accelerate your advancement, as an open channel of Love, into Oneness as any remaining separations are abolished through the Power of Light.

The most important consideration to anchor these high frequencies of Light unification is to remain in a state of absolute surrender to Divine Will and to use these teachings in your daily devotion. We all must exercise the newly expanded awareness while remembering that our mission is to embody self-mastery on every level. With the assistance of **The 4 Keys to Light** program, we deepen our commitment and anchor our mission as Ambassadors of Light.

Genii

The 4 Keys to Light is facilitated by Genii Townsend of Sedona, also known as "the Genii" and Kathie Brodie in Seattle, WA. Genii may be contacted at (928) 284-5566 or by email at thegeniiconnection@msn.com. Kathie may be contacted at kathie@ kathiebrodie.com.
Tuition for The 4 Keys to Light is on a Love Offering donation basis.

Kathie

The old often repeated saying "When the student is ready, the teacher appears" and so it is with this ancient teaching given in 4 Sacred Keys for modern days usage. The power of the Genie is well known in fables and this Genii is no exception as she brings forth long kept secrets of universal wisdom to elevate and empower those who seek such an advanced leverage.

Since The 4 Keys to Light contain much power and Light enhanced information and has, until this time been given to only those who requested an unknown advanced education due to possible misuse of it, did they find that teacher with the Genie power readied to be transferred to a student who would take care of it and its use. Thus what could be said is it is one of God's best kept secrets.

From the God self of the Genii and the Kathie Brodie as trans-audio mediums, comes the treasures they have held sacred. The students are enlightened while receiving Light elevations during the sessions while learning of the 4 Keys material.

That includes each student learning of the personal Soul Guides that brought them to this teaching. This is a program not to be missed with all it contains as planetary changes take place.

The 4 Keys to Light Testimonials:

"I highly recommend Genii Townsend's class on The 4 Keys to Light!
She ties together the best advice I have ever seen about getting to know some aspects of your being that you might not have explored before. I have had a running dialogue with God all my life. I have gotten some absolutely wonderful answers to questions, gotten guidance I have asked for, and have enjoyed heavenly energies.

I always thought these answers were coming from my "Higher Self." After The 4 Keys, I came to recognize that indeed much of my contact was with my Higher Self, but a great deal was also coming from my dedicated Spirit Guides that have been with me all of my life. I can now see the difference, and I am in awe of the way that God has created this system within us.

In the class, I also learned to actually USE my 8th chakra. I always knew it was there, but didn't know what to do with it. And ... I learned to use a specific sacred name of God to lovingly clear all negative energies. This really works in a flash, and it is no problem to stay in the Light all of the time with this. I know the 4 Keys Class will be of great benefit to anyone who applies what they learn. It is as fascinating as it is helpful." -- **Renee Trenda**, Stelle, IL

"Are you ready to take the next step in your spiritual journey? Buckle your seatbelt and get ready for an extraordinary journey into higher consciousness through the "4 Keys to Light" as taught by Genii Townsend of Sedona, Arizona. I was initiated into The 4 Keys by Genii eight years ago at a time when only a select few received these teachings. It's been a nonstop ride of being connected to Universal guidance that one cannot even imagine. At this time, Genii has been guided to impart these teachings to those who are ready and willing to make that next step. I'm certainly glad I did." -- **Richard LaDuke**

"Genii took me through The 4 Keys in 2000 and it certainly changed my life. There was a subtle shift at first, then as I traveled farther and farther away from the ceremony I began to notice major shifts that I was able to attribute back to that time. My path became clear, I trusted myself and my guidance more the Universe stepped in to reward me for being open. Life always has its ups and downs but after The 4 Keys I could understand the reasons behind some of the lessons I was getting. That doesn't mean I always liked them, but at least I could accept them. Before The 4 Keys I feel like I was just wandering around but after the Keys there was clarity for me. I can definitely say that having Genii take me through The 4 Keys was a turning point in my life. I wish I had met her years ago!" -- **Kathie Brodie** (See Kathie's article, ***The Great Meet-up: Finding Your Guides and Gatekeeper*** at http://www.sedonalightcenter.org/meetup.htm)

Genii with the Facilitator Guidebooks for The 4 Keys to Light

**There is a 1 minute YouTube Video on The 4 Keys to Light
at http://youtu.be/uLN69FuQvWM**

If you are interested in The 4 Keys to Light training in Sedona, AZ, Seattle, WA, Stelle, IL or San Diego, CA, or if you would like to sponsor a 4 Keys training and presentation with Genii on The City of Light in your community please contact us!

The Light Center is presently working on transforming the contents of The 4 Keys to Light training to be able to also offer it online. Two of our affiliated non-profit organizations, Ultimate Destiny University and CENTER SPACE™, are helping us publish and distribute The City of Light Sedona. They are also helping The Light Center develop new ways to share The 4 Keys to Light such as webinars.

How Would Participation in The Light Center Benefit You?

Share and Review our Publications ☆☆☆☆☆

We are happy to provide a PDF of **Something's Coming** to anyone who buys a copy of the book and also subscribes to our free newsletter. We offer quantity discounts, wholesale pricing, and affiliate referral commissions. We especially need book reviews for Amazon.com and testimonials.

http://www.SedonaLightCenter.org/scbook.htm

Enjoy Charter Membership Benefits

Membership benefits include discounts on programs and publications, free newsletter, webinars, and membership services. Tuition is on a voluntary donation basis. Donations welcome.

http://www.SedonaLightCenter.org/membership.htm

Participate in or Sponsor The 4 Keys to Light

Genii has been sharing the Sacred information in The 4 Keys to Light for over 20 years. Students learn how to harness the creative power of the Word, the practice of Atonement, they are introduced to their personal Gatekeeper and Guides, and are Light Linked.

http://www.SedonaLightCenter.org/4_keys_.htm

Participate In or Sponsor Genii's Playshops

Genii has been helping students, especially women, grow, evolve and become empowered for decades through self-discovery Playshops such as: *The Cinderella Connection*; *Inner Child Healing Doll Classes*; *The Power Women*; and *The Thirteen Goddesses of Inner Light.*

http://www.SedonaLightCenter.org/playshops.htm

Help Genii Create "Empowerment Marionettes" and Meet the Obama's and Joel Osteen

Genii is applying her experience operating **Geniiland** for 18 years and the 5,000+ marionettes she has made to create marionettes of authors and trainers to help children harness their creative imagination and learn "**successful living skills.**"

http://www.SedonaLightCenter.org/marionettes.htm

Please subscribe to our free newsletter, blog and BlogTalk Radio show

For information, write The Light Center, PO Box 20072, Sedona, AZ 86341 Call 928-284-5566 or send an email to sedonalightcenter@gmail.com.

Introducing The Lights of the Round Table

Once upon a time, not so long ago, in Albuquerque, New Mexico, a woman became aware of the Genii and her 35+ year mission and her book *The City of Light Sedona*. She was transfixed.

The book was bought, read by the one and then, another woman simply placed her hand upon the book and said, "Yes, let's do it" in agreement. The two then immediately phoned the Genii where joyful reconnections were forged and commitments made.

The book was carefully circulated among souls in Albuquerque and the two became twelve who felt called to the energies. Through 2 initiations of The 4 Keys to Light by our beloved Genii, accompanied by her Light Link equerries from Sedona, The Lights of the Round Table was established. We have forged a bond of spiritual purpose. Genii introduced us to loving helpful Guides and gave us wonderful Tools to further our purpose.

To this day, at one generous Light Link's beautiful hospitable home around her huge wondrous table, all who are able come together as The Lights of the Round Table. Here as a group, we play to support Genii's mission, which is now our own, and direct energies to bring the City of Light Sedona into the visual spectrum.

ALL LIGHT LINKS, present or non-local, as well as all of our Guides we now know, are folded together energetically in cohesive union and as a powerful directive force. As the months have passed since the first Initiation, our gatherings have greatly increased in power and joy. We feel blessed to be a part of Genii's mission and to know and interact with the folks in the City of Light Sedona and are grateful and amazed at our experiences at the Round Table.

This is a joyful and Holy play time and we bless the Genii for bringing this expansion to us. We feel honored to know her and to be able to support her decades-long mission. Know that we love our dedicated Genii, She Who Does Not Do Age, and await the City of Light Sedona with Love, Light and Joyful anticipation.

Imagine That!

The Lights of the Round Table, Albuquerque NM

Adventures into the City of Light Sedona

By a Gifted Visionary Member of The Lights of the Round Table

"As all of us Light Links in Albuquerque, NM gathered around our Round Table in love and expectancy, one Light link gently guided us into the City of Light where we toned for a long time, each of us going into our chosen areas of dedicated focus.

I enter mine, the Reflection Pool, and see a beautiful bubbling, sparkling waterfall cascading down through lush green and into the tranquil pool. I jump into the waterfall, feeling joy, and let it carry me into the waiting pool. I lay back into the large peaceful water.

My Torus around my body begins spinning and vibrating with toroidal energy. The water becomes a conductor vibrating out to all the people I had brought there for healing.

The myriad flowers, trees, and little elementals are all joyously spinning in their own little toroidal spheres creating their Light Merkabas, as am I.

I am feeling an intense energy of pure LOVE concentrating into a tiny spot in the center of my heart.

I feel myself being taken down into Mother Earth. I am traveling through layer after layer of rich reddish earth, stones, sediment, tree roots, etc. Then into a huge layer of magnificent crystals of all sizes, shapes, and glowing colors. I keep going deeper and deeper until I come to many golden-skinned entities who look like the usual depiction of space beings. Their golden skin is soft and glowing.

As I come near them, my skin merges into theirs; we are ONE. A long white, glowing tube appears on my right and we move up the tube into the sun. The glowing gold of us merges with the gold of the sun permeating the whole planet.

Mother Earth merges with Father Sky in Oneness and I feel One with all of life.

I am so grateful!"

Arizona Enlightenment Center's Experience with The 4 Keys to Light

Since our group has been holding the vision to manifest the next physical space for the Arizona Enlightenment Center (often referred to as a "City of Light") on the west side of Phoenix, as soon as I heard that Genii had written a book called Sedona City of Light, I knew I had to meet her. A friend and I drove up to Sedona to connect with her and to hear her story about the City of Light.

After that meeting, we scheduled Genii to speak to our Metaphysical Studies Group in Surprise, AZ. She came in and absolutely delighted our whole group. She does a wonderful job in her presentations since she has been performing as a master puppeteer for a majority of her life.

We held two follow-up meetings where she presented The 4 Keys to Light class. The room was filled both times with our eager learners. Genii spends a considerable amount of time prior to each 4 Keys class bringing in information and the names of each student's Lead Guide and Gatekeeper. During our first class, she described my Lead Guide, Tu-A-Na, as being about 8" tall, able to fly or walk, with large sparkling eyes to lead me on my path, and she can be heard with the tinkle of tiny bells

Well, the day *before* our class, I had gone to the store to buy some flowers for the table and came across a little doll that would be a nice addition to my fall decor for several years to come...I kept hesitating about buying her, but she pretty much would NOT let me leave without her.

So she came home with me...and the next day in class, Genii read the message and description about my Guide...that was sitting right there on my table...8" tall with little angel wings, a tiny little bell and large sparkling blue eyes...exactly as Genii described...a description that she downloaded at least 2 weeks before our class. We were all pretty much blown away!

Heather Clarke
Arizona Enlightenment Center, Phoenix, AZ
http://www.azenlightenmentcenter.org

Introduction to Universal StewardHeirShip™ and Ultimate Destiny University

The shared vision and mission of Universal Stewardheirship and Ultimate Destiny University are to help "Expand the Circle of Success" for 100% of humankind and to foster personal, organizational, community and planetary empowerment, enlightenment, consciousness and sustainability.

> "Inherently, each one of us has the substance within to achieve whatever our goals and dreams define. What is missing from each of us is the training, education, knowledge and insight to utilize what we already have." - Mark Twain

The world has changed greatly since Mark Twain's time, but individuals still dream and are searching for the training, education, knowledge and insight they need in record numbers. The personal and professional development field has grown to a $210 billion industry and "wellness" is an industry poised to become the next trillion dollar industry according to experts. (www.successpuzzle.com)

Universal Stewardheirship, Inc. is a "cause-oriented" international marketing and distribution company that helps individuals, organizations, and communities accomplish their goals and realize their dreams. The Company has created an innovative business model and Strategic Marketing Matrix System™ that capitalizes on the latest approaches to on-line education, communication and marketing; synergistic alliances with other industry providers; as well as collaborations with key government and national nonprofit organizations.

Ultimate Destiny University (UDU) is a non-profit membership organization that produces, publishes, markets and distributes materials designed to empower people, deepen spirituality, and awaken them to conscious, sustainable living. In actuality, UDU is a collection of intellectual properties consisting of domain names, websites, blogs, e-books, print books, e-courses, e-zines, membership programs, webinars, teleseminars, audio CDs, and video DVDs all created to help people **A.R.K.** -- **A**waken to Spirit; **R**ealize more of their potential; and **K**now how to co-create their ultimate destiny (whatever that means to each individual).

Because we believe The City of Light Sedona will play such a major role in helping us fulfill our personal and global "ultimate destinies" we are deeply grateful for the opportunity to help Genii Townsend and The Light Center.

We are also happy to provide readers of *Something's Coming* any of the PDF editions of any or all 14 titles on "Solving Life's Ultimate Success Skills" in our Ultimate Destiny Success System on a voluntary donation basis with 100% of any donations conveyed to The Light Center. For more details or information on any facet of Ultimate Destinyland, please contact Charles Betterton at 760-212-9931 or ceo@ultimatedestinyuniversity.org. www.universalstewardheirship.com   www.ultimatedestinyuniversity.org

Featured Resources from Ultimate Destinyland™

Which Pieces of Solving Life's Success Puzzles Are Most Important to You?

Introduction to CENTER SPACE™ Resources

CENTER SPACE (the Center for Spiritual, Personal And Community Enlightenment) is a nonprofit membership organization established to help foster spiritual, personal and community empowerment and enlightenment. **CENTER SPACE** provides programs, products and services that help people, organizations and communities **A.R.K. -- A**waken to their true spiritual identity, **R**ealize more of their potential and **K**now how to fulfill their ultimate destiny (whatever that means to each individual).

CENTER SPACE, Inc. was incorporated for the following specific purposes:

✓ To provide educational programs and materials that foster spiritual, personal, organizational and community development, empowerment and enlightenment

✓ To foster greater communication, cooperation and understanding among people of different races, cultures, religions and socio-economic levels

✓ To facilitate cooperative and creative problem solving between individuals, businesses, religious organizations, non-profit organizations and government

✓ To develop models for establishing **CENTER SPACE** facilities in other areas

CENTER SPACE seeks to help the University for Successful Living manifest Bucky Fuller's vision of "betterment for 100% of humanity." We plan to do that by helping people, organizations and communities empower themselves, realize more of their potential and expand their capacity to help address the social, environmental and economic challenges we face on SpaceShip Earth.

Our ultimate goal is to help Expand the Circle of Success by establishing an international network of CAN DO! Centers for Successful Living that will provide Successful Living Skills for the 21st Century to will help Solve Personal, Community, National and Global Success Puzzles. The shared vision of Expanding the Circle of Success is to facilitate the distribution and donation of 100 million dollars-worth of resources for personal, organizational and community empowerment, enlightenment and transformation through a network of locally initiated Empowerment Resource Centers™ by 2020.

If you resonate with the vision of helping people Awaken to Spirit, Realize More of Their Potential and Know How to Manifest Their Ultimate Destiny, please contact CENTER SPACE, PO Box 20072, Sedona, AZ 86341. Our email address is centerspaceinc@gmail.com. * www.centerspace.com

We are happy to provide readers of Something's Coming any of the PDF editions of any of our titles for Spiritual, Personal, and Community Enlightenment on a voluntary donation basis with 100% of any donations conveyed to The Light Center. For more information, please contact Charles Betterton at 760-212-9931.

Examples of Programs Available from CENTER SPACE:

Motivision
21 Steps to Manifest Your Ultimate Vision

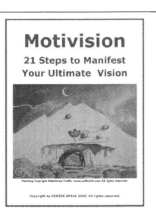

Developing Spiritually Centered New Year's Resolutions

Partnership with God

T.U.L.I.P.S.
The Ultimate Life Inpowerment Planning System

A Comprehensive Spiritually Oriented Program for Achieving Personal and Professional Goals

Peace! Be Still and Know God

Rise and Shine!
With Seven Ascension Attitudes

Seven Ascension Attitudes

Your Interview with God, the Ultimate Entrance Exam

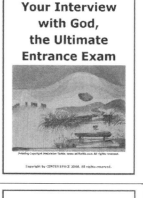

The Five Steps of Spiritual Mind Treatment

Dr. Ernest Holmes

There is a Power for Good in the Universe Greater Than You Are and You Can Use It.

CROWNED WITH THE ULTIMATE SUCCESS OF THE LORD!

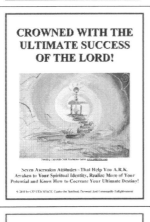

Seven Ascension Attitudes - That Help You A.R.K. Awaken to Your Spiritual Identity, Realize More of Your Potential and Know How to Cocreate Your Ultimate Destiny!

Godhood, Who Me? Oh My God!

Spiritual Prosperity Treasure Chest

Empowerment 101
Resources to Help You Discover How to Realize More of Your Potential and Enjoy A Happier, Richer and More Fulfilling Life!

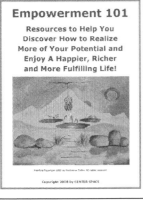

Enlightenment 101

Where Are You on the Enlightenment Ladder?

S.P.A.R.K. of Destiny
Our Spiritual Purpose is to

Awaken to Our Spiritual Identity of Divinity
Realize More of Our Potential for Godhood
Know How to Cocreate Our Ultimate Destiny!

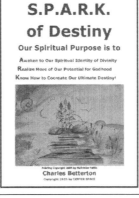

Charles Betterton

Discovering and Manifesting Our Dreams with Co-Creative Visioning

http://www.centerspace.com

About the Author

Genii Townsend is an author, trainer, marionette artist, and "trans-audio medium". She is also an award-winning entrepreneur, cofounder of non-profits and cause-oriented companies and a "successful living facilitator". She has helped thousands of people awaken and ascend through her publications, playshops on empowerment and enlightenment and spiritual training on The 4 Keys to Light. Genii dropped out of high school and later found herself a divorced mother of a son and daughter, trying to figure out how to support them with no office experience and totally no business sense. The answer came in the form of entertaining through the medium of puppets. All she knew was that by being positive and using her Imagination, she could have anything she wanted, which could be interesting ... and profitable.

She changed her name from Jean to Genii as it seemed to have magic attached and she needed a lot of that if she was to survive with the children and THE MAGIC HAPPENED! She went on to create a zillion marionettes and performed professionally from Disneyland to Las Vegas, made commercials funnier, pulled strings in motion pictures and was a co-performer with Carol Burnett on her show with a look-a-like figure of Carol's charwoman Genii had created.

Genii's big dream was to have a birthday party theater where children could have a special place of honor to enjoy. What then began as a tiny storefront theater, expanded four times into a two-story 5,000 square foot building where thousands of kids and parents celebrated for 18 years consecutively with many regular fans among famous stars of stage, television and motion pictures.

Genii has been awarded many honors including several by the Puppeteers of America, Who's Who in America and NAWBO, the National Association of Women Business Owners. She leads women's self-discovery seminars and Playshops such as: The Cinderella Connection: Inner Child Healing Doll Classes; The Power Women; and The Thirteen Goddesses of Inner Light. Genii is author of: *The Little Light Being*; *The Sickness Bug*; *Conversations About Ultimate Destiny with Who-No, A Spirit Coach*; *Discover the Secrets of How to Grant Your Own Wishes from a Real Genii*; *The City of Light Sedona* and *Something's Coming! Cities of Light, Love and Healing*! She is presently having loads of fun writing her autobiography, *God, Me and Mickey Mouse!*

Genii is co-founder of The Light Center and Ultimate Destiny University, and she also serves through CENTER SPACE (the Center for Spiritual, Personal And Community Enlightenment). One of her present projects is helping create Empowerment Marionettes of world-class authors and trainers to help children harness their creative imagination and realize more of their potential.

God Whispered To Me Today........

"I give you the new of the new,
A new canvas to paint...
A new life to live...
Let me be your today, your tomorrow.
Just be the me of me,
And I will show you that,
All you would be, you are...NOW!"

THE SLEIGH RIDE

Morning Guidance...   December 31, 2012

G: "What is to be known?"

A: "This has been a year of great progress in the area of The City of Light and its readiness to appear. The Genii held the reins and handed some to others who are heading in the same direction through combined love and faith."

"Like a sleigh ride through the snow, the sleigh has left tracks for others to follow, (the sleigh being The City of Light). The Genii being the lead driver with the ponies of faith, love, and dedication, are all heading in the right direction."

"As God's sleigh ride moves into its destination, the cheers are heard as the sleigh crosses the finish line of Light. Fear not little flock, it is God's good pleasure to give you the kingdom of Light and 2013 will prove this to be correct. So enjoy your sleigh ride into the future for this promised sleigh ride is well equipped to take you into the new year of delight, excitement, love and honor, all divinely accomplished.

Genii Townsend

"May the blessed happy sound of...

WE SEE IT!

BE THE FIREWORKS OF LIGHT TO ALL.

SO LIGHT IT BE!"

In Light and Love,

The Flag of The Cities of Light

January 20, 2013 I watched President Obama sworn into office for another 4 years and could not help but think of what he will be facing as suddenly without notice God deposits a really big surprise, a City of Light on our doorstep. I have been informed that in his DNA he will be aware and able to take action. As he said today, "POSSIBILITY BEING LIMITLESS!"

As I watched the USA flag of freedom fly in the wind over the thousands of people who had joined in the festivities, I quickly remembered what was given to me yesterday. A question I had not thought of before had been asked by Light Center member Robert Campbell for me to take within for information "Does The City of Light have a designed flag?"

G: "Good morning. Does the City of Light have a flag symbol?"

A: "The Genii in your heralding that The City cometh, has raised many heads looking in your direction and some have questions such as this one from the Robert who is to be thanked for raising the question. This is good. The City of Light does have a logo on a banner that will be seen on each of the healing Cities coming into view. The flag design holds the Presence, Love, Power and Purity which are 4 elements of healing. View the flag as having a pure white background with edges in gold. In the center is a big red heart, within the big red heart, is a smaller gold one. As follows:

1. **White back ground ....God's purity.**
2. **White background edged in gold.... God as all Light**.
3. **Red heart...God's power of healing**.
4. **Gold (heart) within the red heart... God's love for humanity.**

http://www.sedonalightcenter.org/flag.htm

"Your world is in a massive change that even you are not aware of totally, with the implementing of new love energies signifying that God indeed has arrived. The Genii in her devotional efforts, now elevates thousands through The 4 Keys to Light being prepared as a book. As you now wave The City flag in halleluiah tones, keep the AH tone going and now add the vision of The City flags with it.

"Enjoy today for God is in action waving proudly for all to enter in and be healed. It is indeed a good day and a better 4 years. Is something coming? As you humans say often, "OH MY GOD" and as President Obama said, 'It is our time' and Dear Ones, it really is...

"The City itself is ready to appear as the new City book is distributed and in the hands of the population. This also will generate more interest in The 4 Keys as both have a high elevated connection." **Imagine that! So GOD IT BE!**

Made in the USA
Charleston, SC
11 February 2013